Covenant and Causality
in Medieval Thought

Professor William J. Courtenay

William J. Courtenay

Covenant and Causality in Medieval Thought

Studies in Philosophy, Theology and Economic Practice

VARIORUM REPRINTS
London 1984

British Library CIP data   Courtenay, William J.
                                Covenant and causality in medieval thought.
                                —(Collected studies series; CS206)
                                1. Philosophy, Medieval
                                I. Title
                                190′.9′02   B721
                                ISBN 0-86078-154-2

Copyright © 1984   Variorum Reprints

Published in Great Britain by   Variorum Reprints
                                  20 Pembridge Mews London W11 3EQ

Printed in Great Britain by   Paradigm Print
                                  Gateshead, Tyne and Wear

                                  VARIORUM REPRINT CS206

CONTENTS

> This volume contains a total of 350 pages.

PUBLISHER'S NOTE

The articles in this volume, as in all others in the Collected Studies Series, have not been given a new, continuous pagination. In order to avoid confusion, and to facilitate their use where these same studies have been referred to elsewhere, the original pagination has been maintained wherever possible.

Each article has been given a Roman number in order of appearance, as listed in the Contents. This number is repeated on each page and quoted in the index entries.

PREFACE

Two interrelated themes are explored in these essays. One is the theme of divine omnipotence and causality, especially the scholastic distinction of absolute and ordained power created to handle the potentially conflicting notions of divine freedom and the reliability of the laws of nature and grace. The second theme is the idea of ascribed value: that some things in this world (both objects and human actions) need not be causally effective on the basis of some inherent "nature" but could operate instead through value ascribed to them in a convenantal or contractual system.

Both ideas drew upon the social, legal, and economic validity of contractual agreements and credit instruments, as they were developed in the twelfth and thirteenth centuries. But the theological and philosophical version of these ideas depended less on the legal enforcement of contracts and more on the voluntary, self-binding nature of the relationship of God and man, of God and creation. Initially the ideas that contributed to the conception of covenantal causality were worked out by theologians from widely different traditions: Benedictines, Cistercians, Austin Canons, secular priests, and Dominicans. The conceptual framework thus created, however, eventually came to be the special property of Franciscans and authors associated with late medieval nominalism.

In origin the essays grew out of an interest in the meaning and wider implications of a theory of sacramental causality based on ascribed value, which in turn led me into monetary theory, social welfare, political thought and a comparative history of the central themes, East and West. All but three were written between the spring of 1969 and the spring of 1972. Much of that time was spent in the classroom at Madison with students whose interest and questions stimulated some of the ideas and approaches presented here. But the research and writing were facilitated at the beginning and end by grants from The National Endowment for the Humanities (1968-69) and from The Institute for Research in the Humanities at the University of Wisconsin (1971-72), to whom I am especially grateful.

The arrangement of essays in this volume is chronological and thematic, but it may be useful to know the order in which they were conceived and written (something the publication date does not always reveal). The paper on Pierre d'Ailly was first (1969); followed by "The King and the Leaden Coin" (1969) for the American Historical Association meeting in New York; "Token Coinage" (1970) for the Renaissance Society meeting in San Francisco; "Nature and the Natural" (1970) at the request of the Medieval Studies Program at Rochester; the Anselm paper (1970) for the Anselm Congress at Bad Wimpfen, Germany; and the essay on the Mutakallimun and Nominalism (1970) for the American Historical Association meeting in Boston. Those findings were then applied to the broader problem of divine omnipotence and volition, already touched on in the Anselm paper. That resulted in the articles on Mirecourt and Rimini (1971), Bernard of Clairvaux (1972), and initiated the research on the dialectic of divine omnipotence that was eventually written as a paper for the conference on omnipotence and future contingents at Ohio State in 1982. The version that is printed here as article IV is a slightly altered and expanded version of the text that will appear in the volume of conference papers to be published by Reidel in Dordrecht, Holland. It is included here because its content provides an important part of one of the central themes of the book. Finally, in the winter of 1971-72, I was requested to prepare articles on the broader but related theme of Nominalism for *Theological Studies* and for the Ann Arbor conference on late medieval and Renaissance religion, organized by Charles Trinkaus.

Now, more than a decade later, these essays are joined into one sequence spanning the eleventh to sixteenth centuries. I am indebted to the original publishers and to Variorum for the opportunity to have them assembled here as one collection. Despite occasional overlap and repetition of information originally needed to make each piece independent and self-sufficient, the combined effect reveals a picture considerably different from traditional accounts. The essays clarify the background and meaning of concepts closely associated with late medieval nominalism, concepts which still today are subject to misunderstanding. Perhaps more importantly, they reveal the "antiquity", the early background of these ideas, the broad range of writers who contributed to their development (particularly Dominicans in the second quarter of the thirteenth century), and the social and economic influence of one of the most fascinating conceptual innovations of the high and late Middle Ages. For a period that many historians have described in terms of closing frontiers, hardening class lines, and shrinking intellectual horizons, the wide-spread adoption of convenantal causality in the fourteenth and fifteenth centuries points to the ability of men of that age to live secure in a world open to divine power, a world of future expectation based on concepts of credit and assigned value.

WILLIAM J. COURTENAY

Madison, Wisconsin
March, 1984

I

NECESSITY AND FREEDOM IN ANSELM'S CONCEPTION OF GOD

In the sixth chapter of book one of *Cur deus homo*[1], Boso, presenting the critique of the unbeliever against the Christian doctrine of atonement, raises a serious objection to Anselm's initial argumentation. To say that the particular form of the atonement, namely the incarnation and crucifixion of Christ, was the only way that man could have been redeemed is to place an intolerable limitation on the omnipotence of God.

Boso's objection, in a sense, covers any of the then current explanations of atonement, including Anselm's. The earlier, dramatic view of atonement, where God rescues man from the power of the devil, suggests to the unbeliever that God is not fully omnipotent, for if he were, why did he go to such great lengths and bizarre ploys in order to exercise his power? In the Anselmian view, where man is saved from the wrath of God rather than the power of the devil, one is seemingly left with a God almost powerless in the face of his own conflicting motivations, wishing to save man and yet wishing to exact punishment for the indignities done to his honor, a God who in the end chooses a method that is as punishing to himself as to man, bringing about what to those outside the faith might appear as an even greater indignity, namely the suffering and crucifixion of God. Does not the whole concept of the *necessity* of atonement and incarnation, asks Boso, make a mockery of the omnipotence of God? If the situation needed rectifying and God chose to do so, why did he not correct it by a simple command, for surely everything depends on the will of God, his will to punish and his will to save? If God forgives and does not wish to punish, then he automatically, by that very decision, wills to save man and has removed all barriers to rectitude. Injustice or the lack of righteousness exists not because man's behavior in Adam was absolutely wrong but only because God chooses to view it in that way, only because God feels that his dignity has been compromised through the breaking of his commandment. If God decides to forgive and to consider man good, just, and righteous, then man is so, and no further cause need be sought beyond the will of God. Supposing redemption to be necessary, the simplest and most direct means open to God would have been through a change in or a command of his will alone, *cum sola voluntate potuit*[2]. You Christians, says Boso, summarizing the

---

1) S. ANSELMI *Opera Omnia*, ed. F. S. Schmitt (Edinburgh: Nelson, 1946–1961), II, 53–55.
2) *Ibid.*, II, 54: "Quapropter si humanum genus salvare noluit, nisi quo modo dicitis, cum sola voluntate potuit: ut mitius dicam, videte quomodo eius sapientiae repugnatis."

position of the unbeliever, contradict yourselves by making God powerless. Does not the omnipotence of God reign everywhere [3]?

The question is more than a passing, rhetorical query that provides Anselm with the proper mood or context for his next statement. One might well view *Cur deus homo* in its entirety as an attempt to explain how the incarnation and atonement can be considered proper, even necessary, without unduly compromising or undermining the omnipotence of God, an attempt to develop an explanation for the atonement that would see the divine action as being at once necessary and free. Moreover, the problem is not unique to *Cur deus homo*. Anselm touched on the question of the necessity and freedom of divine action much earlier, in *De libertate arbitrii* [4], and considered the problem of limitations on divine omnipotence as early as *Proslogion* [5].

The recurrence of this issue in the thought of Anselm across a period of twenty years or more demonstrates the importance of the question for Anselm, an importance which has been generally ignored in past scholarship in favor of a concentration on the ontological argument, the Anselmian theological method, and the particular concepts of justice and rectitude. Anselm's understanding of divine omnipotence, however, is neither simple nor self-evident, and its implications for other areas of Anselm's thought as well as for the subsequent development of the question of necessity and freedom in God have gone largely unnoticed. Three problem areas in regard to Anselm's view of the omnipotence of God stand out. Most basic is the question of how Anselm resolves the seemingly conflicting notions of necessity and freedom in regard to God's actions? Is God so free that no necessity determines the choices of his will or is he bound in some way to act according to certain norms of justice, goodness, and truth? The second problem area concerns those factors that shaped Anselm's solution. Did Anselm, as has recently been suggested [6], treat the problem of divine omnipotence against the background of Boethius' discussion [7], and was his solution essentially one of logic, or was Anselm responding to or attacking contemporary notions of divine omnipotence, and was his solution essentially theological? If, as is becoming increasingly apparent, the dialogue with Judaism and Islam forms the apologetic focus of *Cur deus homo* [8], was it a particular Jewish or Islamic stress on the

---

3) *Ibid.*, II, 55: "Nonne dei omnipotentia regnat ubique?"

4) *Ibid.*, I, 207–212, 214–217, 220–223.

5) *Ibid.*, I, 105–111.

6) D. P. HENRY, *The Scope of the Logic of Saint Anselm: L'Homme et son destin d'après les penseurs du moyen âge* (*Actes du premier congrès international de philosophie médiévale*, Louvain-Bruxelles, 1958; Louvain: Nauwelaerts, 1960), pp. 377–383; D. P. HENRY, *Remarks on Saint Anselm's Treatment of Possibility: Spicilegium Beccense I* (*Congrès international du IXe centenaire de l'arrivée d'Anselme au Bec*; Paris: J. Vrin, 1959), pp. 19–22.

7) BOETHIUS, *The Consolation of Philosophy*, Books IV and V.

8) For the Jewish *Sitz im Leben* of *Cur deus homo* see: P. G. VAN DER PLASS, *Des hl.Anselm Cur Deus Homo auf dem Boden der jüdisch-christlichen Polemik des Mittelalters: Divus Thomas* (Freiburg i.d.Schw.) 7 (1929) 446–467; 8 (1930), 18–32; B. BLUMENKRANZ et J. CHATILLON, *De la polémique antijuive à la cathéchèse* (sic) *chrétienne. L'objet, le contenu et les sources d'une anonyme Altercatio Synagogae et Ecclesiae du XIIe siècle: Recherches de théologie ancienne et médiévale* 23 (1956) 40–60; F. S. SCHMITT, *Die wissenschaftliche Methode in Anselms CDH: Spicilegium Beccense I*, 355, n.6. For the Islamic background see: René ROQUES, *Les Pagani dans le Cur deus homo de Saint Anselme: Die Metaphysik im Mittelalter* (*Vortrage des II. internationalen Kongresses für mittelalterliche Philosophie*, Köln,

Necessity and freedom in Anselm's conception of God

omnipotence of God to which Anselm was responding and, if so, was he responding to it as early as *Proslogion*? The third problem area concerns the influence, if
any, of Anselm's formulation of divine omnipotence on later discussions of the
problem. In particular, does the later device for expounding and defending divine
omnipotence without, supposedly, endangering the necessity or predictability of
the established, ordained order — namely the distinction between the absolute
and ordained powers of God — have any place in the thought of Anselm, writing
more than a century before this distinction supposedly developed[9]?

The method of inquiry will be to examine, in turn, each of the works of
Anselm that treats the question of divine omnipotence and, on the basis of that
exposition, to formulate a precise picture of Anselm's teaching, its sources and
purpose, and its implications for later thought.

Anselm's Early Formulation: *Proslogion* (1077—78)

Anselm does not define the omnipotence of God as the power or capacity to
do anything whatsoever. There are certain things that God cannot do, even if, for
purposes of discussion, one were to imagine that he desired to do them. The three
examples Anselm gives are (1) that God cannot be corrupted, (2) that God cannot
lie, and (3) that God cannot make false what is true, for example, that God
cannot change the past. To be capable of such things is not a form of power but
of impotence[10].

It is not immediately clear, on the basis of Anselm's treatment, exactly why
God cannot do these things. Several possible interpretations initially suggest
themselves, and these interpretations, in turn, can be grouped around two different approaches. One approach, rather attractive in light of the recent emphasis
on Anselm as a logician of high quality[11], believes that Anselm limits divine
omnipotence only in those activities that involve a contradiction of some variety.
The second approach, more traditional in Anselm scholarship, considers Anselm's
limitations on divine omnipotence the result of a conviction that God acts accord-

1961; Berlin: Walter de Gruyter, 1963) 192—206; Julia GAUSS, *Anselm von Canterbury und
die Islamfrage: Theologische Zeitschrift* (Basel), 19 (1963) 250—272.

9) The dialectic of the two powers, *potentia dei absoluta et potentia dei ordinata*, is usually
associated with late medieval thought and, in particular, the Nominalists. The distinction,
however, was known and used in the thirteenth century (Cf. THOMAS AQUINAS, *Quaestiones
disputatae de potentia dei*, q.1, a.5), and its origins have been traced back to HUGH OF ST.
VICTOR, without, however, being totally convincing. Cf. M. GRABMANN, *Die Geschichte der
katholischen Theologie seit dem Ausgang der Väterzeit* (Freiburg, 1933), p.288; R. P.
DESHARNAIS, C.S.C., *The History of the Distinction between God's Absolute and Ordained
Powers and Its Influence on Martin Luther* (diss. Catholic University of America, Phil. Sutd.,
No. 211; Washington, D.C., 1967), pp. 47—50.

10) S. ANSELMI *Opera Omnia*, I, 105: "Sed et omnipotens quomodo es, si omnia non
potes? Aut si non potes corrumpi nec mentiri nec facere verum esse falsum, ut quod factum est
non esse factum, et plura similiter: quomodo potes omnia? An haec posse non est potentia, sed
impotentia? Nam qui haec potest, quod sibi non expedit et quod non debet potest. Quae
quanto magis potest, tanto magis adversitas et perversitas possunt in illum, et ipse minus contra
illas. Qui ergo sic potest, non potentia potest, sed impotentia."

11) D. P. HENRY, l. c.

ing to some norm. Since Anselm frequently mentions these specific limitations on God's power and his meaning and intention have been evaluated differently, it may be useful to include here more interpretations than seem warranted at first glance.

The first approach covers several possible interpretations. One interpretation of Anselm's argument might consider that each of these examples of things God cannot do contains a logical contradiction and therefore is impossible even for God. All three examples would fall within the same order of logical incompatibility as would theorizing about whether God could draw a square circle or whether God could solve an anagram incorrectly[12]. Similar in nature, although not strictly self-contradictory, would be the problem of whether God could create a stone larger than he could lift. Although Anselm's examples might be conceived of as entailing a contradiction, they do not appear to be of the same variety of self-evident, logical contradiction as the example of the square circle.

A second interpretation might also see in Anselm's examples an inherent contradiction, although not exactly self-evident. Once one understands what is meant by the term "God" as expressed earlier in *Proslogion* in Anselm's famous ontological argument, namely a being, than which nothing greater can be conceived, it is a contradiction to say that God could be corrupted or that God might not exist. Since all creation, all being, depends on God, who is the only necessary being, it is impossible to conceive that God could be corrupted, for such would be a contradiction in terms. In the same way, God, being the sole source of truth, because he is Truth, cannot lie; whatever God says or establishes is by definition true, and therefore, to say that God could lie would be to posit a contradiction. Likewise, for God, who exists on the level of eternity, to make what is false true, would be to make the same thing true and false at the same time, which is again a contradiction. Viewed in more strictly logical terms, such phrases as "God cannot lie" or "God cannot be corrupted" can be reduced to tautologies or analytic statements. If God is initially defined as "He who cannot lie" or "He who cannot be corrupted," then these statements would mean: "He-who-cannot-lie cannot lie" or "He-who-cannot-be-corrupted cannot be corrupted," or "God is God"[13].

The last two Anselmian examples of things God cannot do have a certain similarity in this second interpretation. God cannot lie because whatever God says would be true because it is God who says it. If, for example, God were to say that Socrates never existed, then Socrates would never have existed, because God, who

12) Cf. G. RYLE, *The Concept of Mind* (London, 1949), p. 131; D. P. HENRY: *Spicilegium Beccense*, 21–22.

13) It is interesting along this line that ANSELM's propositions about God, which depend on an equality or identity between the predicate and the definition of the subject, were used in medieval discussions on whether identity statements were always logically true, a discussion that precedes and sometimes parallels a much debated issue in modern logic. Until the fourteenth century the answer was affirmative; see, for example, BONAVENTURE, *Quaest. disp. de myst. trin.*, I, 1, 29, in *Opera Omnia* (Quaracchi, 1882–1902), V, 45. On the negative side stand OCKHAM, *Sent.* I, Prol., q.2, a.3, in *Scriptum in librum primum sententiarum ordinatio* (St. Bonaventure, N.Y., 1967), pp. 111–113; *Summa logicae*, II, 14 (St. Bonaventure, N.Y., 1962), pp. 258–260; and ROBERT HOLCOT, in J. T. MUCKLE, *Utrum Theologia Sit Scientia: A Quodlibet Question of Robert Holcot O.P.: Mediaeval Studies* 20 (1958) 127–153. I owe this information to the generous assistance of the late Julius WEINBERG of the Philosophy Department at Wisconsin.

Necessity and freedom in Anselm's conception of God

is Truth, by saying this statement, would make it true. In other words, the term "lying" when applied to God has no standard of reference apart from God and, consequently, no judicatory function or meaning. It is not a term or category with a specific, fixed content to which God must subscribe; rather what God says and does is true and whatever he does not say or do or allow to happen is automatically not true. Any change in the will of God would automatically result in a change in the physical, moral, or historical order of creation.

A third interpretation, also developing out of Anselm's definition of the nature of God, is based on more practical or methodological considerations. God cannot do certain things not because they involve, in themselves, a direct contradiction but because by doing them God would contradict other aspects of his nature as expressed by the Anselmian definition of God. It is methodologically invalid to describe any one characteristic of God, for example his omnipotence, so that it lessens, alters, or confuses the understanding of any other divine attribute, such as God's goodness, truthfulness, or justice. One should not understand God's goodness and mercy in such a way that his justice is denied, or understand God's omnipotence in such a way that his goodness is denied. Viewed properly, God's omnipotence, or man's description of God's omnipotence, is limited only by the fact that God cannot be said to do those things which are not good or which are unjust and still remain God. Such formulations entail a contradiction only because of the nature of God provided or described by Anselm's definition. We should not attribute to God or intensify our description of his omnipotence by viewing him capable of those activities that would contradict some other part of his nature as provided by the definition of God.

Apart from the problem of whether Anselm intends to limit God's omnipotence or only our understanding or description of God's omnipotence (a problem already anticipated in this last interpretation and one which will be dealt with later), the belief that God's omnipotence is limited by the demands of the other aspects of his nature brings us around to the second approach, namely that God's actions respond or conform to some norm and are not the result of arbitrary will restricted only by the law of contradiction. It should perhaps be remarked here that these two approaches are not necessarily exclusive of each other but rather indicate where one is to place the emphasis in interpreting Anselm's thought on the question of divine omnipotence. To say that God's actions are limited by the principle of contradiction is essentially a negative statement. It explains why God cannot do certain things. To say that God's actions must conform to some norm, regardless of what that norm may be or what may create that norm, is a positive statement. It explains what God cannot do only in terms of what he does do or must do. Theoretically, the same action could be negatively limited by the principle of contradiction and positively required by conformity to a norm. The question is one of emphasis.

Among the interpretations stressing a norm and yet most closely approximating the preceding view would be one that sees the nature of God as the only limit in Anselm to divine omnipotence. The emphasis in this fourth interpretation is on the unity and consistency of the nature of God expressed in Anselm's definition rather than on the methodological requirements of the definition itself, as in the third view. To put it another way, this fourth interpretation speaks about limitations on divine omnipotence, not limitations on our understanding or description of divine omnipotence. God cannot do certain things not because they

I

entail a logical or inherent contradiction nor because the only necessary definition of God prohibits ascribing such activity to the deity, but rather because God's nature is one and consistent, a nature to which his actions will always conform. Viewed in this way, Anselm's definition of God is valid because of the consistency of God's nature and actions, a consistency revealed in the Scriptures and in the life of the Church, and reflected in Anselm's definition of God. Whereas the third interpretation would say that we know the nature of God automatically when we hear the term "God," and we know that the divine actions will be in accord with that nature because of the Anselmian categories or the Anselmian definition of God, in the fourth view, we know the nature of God through Scripture and the life of the Church, and thus we know or trust that God will always act in conformity with that nature.

To provide an example, God cannot lie because it is his nature not to lie. If he were to do so, he would not be acting according to his true nature and thus no longer be God (as we understand him). Here "lying" has a specific meaning and content apart from what God gives to it by speaking its opposite and therefore making it a lie. Socrates, for example, existed, and to say that Socrates did not exist at one time would be a lie, even if God said it.

A fifth interpretation moves a little further toward establishing a norm to which God's actions must conform, a norm that limits the divine omnipotence. God cannot do those things which would contradict the order he has already established (regardless of whether these actions would also involve a contradiction, violate the definition of God, or reveal a conflict in God's nature). God cannot (or at least it is his nature or habit not to), having once established the physical laws of the universe or the moral laws governing human behavior, change those laws. Again, the consistency of God's actions is a necessary corollary of the divine nature, but the consistency here is not necessarily a direct expression of God's true nature but rather a result of the fact that it is part of his nature to act consistently. God cannot, for instance, reverse the pattern of the sun's motion or make murder and adultery just and meritorious, having once established the physical and moral laws of the universe.

It is important to stress that there is, in this fifth interpretation, no necessary link between the nature of God and the ordained order, as there was in the fourth interpretation. God could have established an entirely different order, both physically and morally. One cannot, therefore, argue from the nature of the revealed order to the nature of God, but only from the nature of the revealed order to the inscrutable but presumably benevolent will of God. Similarly, one also cannot argue from the nature of God to the necessity of the revealed order. One can never know for certain the reasons for God's choices; one affirms that they are reasonable and good because they are experienced as such and because one respects the divine choices and has trust in God. Presumably, the theologian, on the basis of his belief that God always acts wisely, may present probable reasons why the order ordained by God is the best possible order. However, he would never limit the omnipotence of God by calling that order the only possible order. To call it the best is saying nothing more than that God chose to act in a certain way, and that it is part of the definition of God that he would not choose what was not, in *his* view, the best way for *man*. So, because of the definition of God, the theologian considers that the way chosen by God was the best way, or rather it is best because God chose to create that way and thus made it so.

Necessity and freedom in Anselm's conception of God

Because of the human understanding of God, it is believed that God is consistent and trustworthy, and that he will not in the future change his mind or will and alter the physical and moral universe in which man lives.

Finally, a sixth interpretation of Anselm's meaning might conceive that God is tied to some external norm of right and truth, a norm not of divine or human creation but one consistent with the natural, human view of justice and truth. For instance, justice, in this view, is a term with specific content, a content innately known by every man, so that philosophically the meaning of the term can be explored and applied, and so that theologically or morally every man may be held accountable for his actions. It would seem, on the surface, that to state that God, by definition, cannot do unGodlike things (which is what Anselm seems to be doing) is to confine God within the limitations of the term "justice" or "good" as these are known and understood by man. According to the simplest version of this interpretation, Anselm would limit God's omnipotence and even his nature according to human views of justice, morality, and acceptable, divine behavior, and would force God to subscribe to some objective, absolute standard of right and wrong, good and evil, truth and falsehood.

A closer examination of the seventh chapter of *Proslogion* and of those chapters that follow immediately upon it make some of these interpretations less likely than others. Having suggested that the ability to do those things that God cannot do is a form of impotence rather than power, Anselm proceeds to reinforce his argument through a linguistic or grammatical explanation. In common usage we often state something in a positive way that has only a negative meaning. To agree with someone that a mythical creature does not exist may have a positive ring to it, "it is as you say," but the meaning is negative. To say that someone sits or rests means that they are *not* doing anything. Summarizing his linguistic argument, Anselm states that for God *to have the power of doing or experiencing what is not for his good, or what he ought not to do, impotence is understood by the word 'power'*[14].

D. P. Henry, in calling our attention to the interests and ability Anselm possessed in the field of modal logic, concludes certain things about Anselm's argument and, consequently, about the meaning of the seventh chapter of *Proslogion*[15]. As Henry notes, Anselm distinguishes here and elsewhere between two senses of 'can' *(posse)*, one which implies a power or ability, as in the statement "I can spell," and one which, although stated positively, expresses a liability rather than a power, as in the statement "I can misspell"[16]. Moreover, according to Henry,

14) S. ANSELMI *Opera Omnia*, I, 105: "Non enim ideo dicitur posse, quia ipse possit, sed quia sua impotentia facit aliud in se posse; sive aliquo alio genere loquendi, sicut multa improprie dicuntur. Ut cum ponimus 'esse' pro 'non esse', et 'facere' pro eo quod est 'non facere', aut pro 'nihil facere'. Nam saepe dicimus ei qui rem aliquam esse negat: sic est quemadmodum dicis esse, cum magis proprie videatur dici: sic non est quemadmodum dicis non esse. Item dicimus: iste sedet sicut ille facit, aut: iste quiescit sicut ille facit, cum 'sedere' sit quiddam non facere et 'quiescere' sit nihil facere."

15) D. P. HENRY, l. c.

16) Although RYLE (*Concept of Mind*, p. 131) uses these two statements and similar performance expressions that contrast success and failure as examples of capacity and liability, "I can misspell" is not strictly liability as opposed to competence because it is not equivalent to the statement "I cannot spell." "I can misspell" usually means that I can occasionally (or sometimes intentionally) make mistakes in spelling; in no instance does it mean that I cannot spell at all.

I

Anselm was undoubtedly familiar with Boethius' discussion of ability in the fourth book of *The Consolation of Philosophy* and, in *Proslogion* and elsewhere, utilized Boethius' distinction between antecedent and concomitant capacity. Anselm supposedly altered the Boethian table of modalities or modal expressions in regard to *facere* and *posse* and differentiated within antecedent or undeployed capacity between those expressions that describe an actual ability or power and those imprecise expressions that attribute to something or someone a capacity or liability actually possessed or potentially exercized only by another. In particular, Anselm rejected the assumption that a non-existent has any real capacity, in and of itself, to exist before it exists. Such capacity lies in its potential cause or creator rather than in the thing itself.

According to Henry's interpretation of *Proslogion* 7, Anselm is saying two things. First, the proposition "God can lie" is a loose, imprecise use of the term *posse*, and the proposition "God can make what is true, false" is a loose, imprecise use of the term *facere*; in neither case does this describe a true ability or capacity possessed by the subject of the proposition. Second, the power or capacity in this instance lies with another, which Anselm darkly terms the forces of adversity and perversity. Thus to say that "God is able to be corrupted" is roughly equivalent to saying "a book is able to be written;" the power in both cases lies not with the subject of the proposition but with another [17].

When one looks back on *Proslogion* from the vantage point of Anselm's later works, especially *De casu diaboli,* it would appear that such is indeed Anselm's meaning and intention. This grammatical argument is Anselm's way of saying that certain expressions that seem to express capacity, such as "God can lie" or "God can be corrupted" do not have the meaning they appear to have. They do not describe a power possessed by God and therefore are meaningless when applied to him. Moreover, to exclude the improper uses of the terms *posse* and *facere* when applied to God is not to limit his omnipotence but to reinforce it.

There are, however, some problems with this approach, problems that make Anselm's argument less than successful and suggest the idea that there may be, beneath Anselm's linguistic argument or attached to the end, some theological or metaphysical presuppositions that more truly reflect his position. To say that "God can lie" is not equivalent to saying that "a book can be written by me." The second statement is a passive way of stating that "I can write a book." No such grammatical reconstruction can be made in the case of the first statement. The reason why the book lacks power in and of itself to be written is because it is an inanimate object. The reason why God lacks the power to lie is because the Anselmian understanding of the nature of God excludes that characteristic. These statements, therefore, are not equivalent. Moreover, it is not clear how lying is something that can be done to God or can happen to him. Someone may possess the ability to write a book; how can anything possess the power to make God a liar?

Anselm's grammatical argument, regardless of its importance for the development of modal logic and the problem of future contingents, does not seem to meet directly the question of the limitations on God's power. If such phrases as

17) The statement "a book is able to be written" as an example of power possessed by another was used by ANSELM in *De casu diaboli* and will be examined further in connection with that work.

Necessity and freedom in Anselm's conception of God

"God cannot lie" or "God cannot be corrupted" are loose, imprecise statements which really mean that "God always speaks the truth" or "conditions could never be such that anything could have power over God," does one consequently know whether, for Anselm, the terms "truth" or "lying" have specific content apart from that determined by divine action, or does one know why God cannot do these things?

There are two phrases in Anselm's discussion that make his meaning somewhat clearer and thus narrow down the field of possible interpretations. The phrase *adversitas et perversitas*, which dominates the conclusion of Anselm's linguistic analysis about the meaning of propositions about divine omnipotence, is not a logical explanation of the limitations on God's power. It reveals Anselm's belief that if such actions were possible for God (and Anselm does not differentiate here between capacity and activity or between capacity to act and desire to act), then God would be willing himself impotent and would thereby be giving potency to the powers of adversity and perversity. The fact that this is impossible stems from an inherent contradiction, not one of logic, however, but one that grows out of Neoplatonic metaphysics[18]. In short, if the linguistic argument indicates that such statements as "God can lie" or "God could be corrupted," far from being meaningless, refer to power possessed by another agency, then that agency seems to be the power of adversity and perversity, that which is farthest removed from God in the Neoplatonic hierarchy.

The second significant phrase is *quod sibi non expedit et quod non debet*, a phrase which, like *adversitas et perversitas*, is repeated as part of the concluding argument at the end of the chapter[19]. That which is not advantageous or that

18) To the best of knowledge the dual phrase, "adversitas et perversitas" or forms thereof, occurs in ANSELM only in the seventh chapter of *Proslogion* and in the twelfth chapter of *De casu diaboli*. The term "adversitas" seems to have a stronger, more positive force than representing, in Neoplatonic terms, a turning away from God or describing that which is not-God. For the period in which ANSELM was writing, the term "adversitas" implied hostile opposition of a most positive kind. Cf. *Mittellateinisches Wörterbuch* (München, 1967), I, col. 252–253. Cf. O. LOTTIN, *Psychologie et morale aux XIIᵉ et XIIIᵉ siècles*, Vol. I (Louvain, 1942), pp. 530–531.

"Perversitas" occurs more frequently in ANSELM, especially in *Cur deus homo*, where it is opposed to the beauty and order of God's universe. Referring to the systems that require satisfaction or administer punishment, ANSELM remarks, *Cur deus homo* I, 15 (Opera Omnia, II, 73–74): "Ita quamvis homo vel malus angelus divinae voluntati et ordinationi subiacere nolit, non tamen eam fugere valet, quia si vult fugere de sub voluntate iubente, currit sub voluntatem punientem; et si quaeris qua transit: non nisi sub voluntate permittente; et hoc ipsum quod perverse vult aut agit, in universitatis praefatae ordinem et pulchritudinem summa sapientia convertit. Ipsa namque perversitatis spontanea satisfactio vel a non satisfaciente poenae exactio – excepto hoc quia deus de malis multis modis bona facit – in eadem universitate suum tenent locum et ordinis pulchritudinem. Quas si divina sapientia, ubi perversitas rectum ordinem perturbare nititur, non adderet, fieret in ipsa universitate quam deus debet ordinare, quaedam ex violata ordinis pulchritudine deformitas, et deus in sua dispositione videretur deficere. Quae duo quoniam sicut sunt inconvenientia, ita sunt impossibilia . . ." Cf. *Oratio 14 (Opera Omnia* III, 58–59) and *Meditatio 2 (Opera Omnia*, III, 81).

19) S. ANSELMI *Opera Omnia*, I, 105: "Nam qui haec potest, quod sibi non expedit et quod non debet potest. Quae quanto magis potest, tanto magis adversitas et perversitas possunt in illum, et ipse minus contra illas." "Sic itaque cum quis dicitur habere potentiam faciendi aut patiendi quod sibi non expedit aut quod non debet, impotentia intelligitur per potentiam; quia

which one ought not to do covers not only the three examples Anselm gives but all the things that God "cannot" do. It may well be that recourse to such phrases as "ought not to do" or "power of adversity and perversity" are Anselm's way of expressing or dramatizing the fact that such actions, when attributed to God, do not express any real meaning or power. The only meaning they could have would be that other forces would have power over God, which is impossible by definition, since God is omnipotent. But even granting the Neoplatonic viewpoint, such phrases as "ought not to do" suggest that, regardless of origin, the nature of moral truth is such that it stands over and above both God and man, defining permissible or improper behavior. Therefore, in spite of the linguistic nature of the argument as a whole, Anselm does not seem to have been thinking in terms of logical or methodological contradiction but rather in terms of a theoretical discrepancy between what God might be said to be able to do and our conception of what God, being God, *ought* to do. God cannot be viewed capable of certain things not because they are meaningless or inherently impossible but because they would upset the established order and would undermine his omnipotence. For God to stop doing or being the kind of things we think of when we think of God, that is our conception of God's nature and divine action, would mean that God would not only be doing unGodlike things but would be allowing the powers of adversity and perversity to dominate him. God would have left a power vacuum into which the forces of evil would step. The situation would be similar to one in which a king might cease to exercise his royal prerogatives and allow others to exercise them. Then he would no longer be king, and far from having any power, others would have power over him.

On the basis of the total Anselmian discussion in chapter seven, it would seem that logical contradiction is not the essential factor limiting the omnipotence of God. Most of the examples and the form of the argument suggest that Anselm has in mind those actions which are not in conformity with the nature of God as Anselm understands it, i.e., those things which would contradict his nature. This even seems to include reversing the physical or moral order, which would somehow lead to a contradiction of the nature of God as it exists or at least as we know it. For God to lie or to say that some past event never happened would not be an impossible act but an act not in conformity with the divine nature. Otherwise Anselm would not need to stress God's theoretical ability to do "what he ought not to do," and he would not stress the loss of power by God and the consequent increase in the powers of adversity and perversity.

On the basis of this passage one can say that Anselm, at least as of 1078, did not wish to describe or intensify the omnipotence of God by making a distinction between what God theoretically has the power to do, in spite of his revealed nature and his past actions, and what God has in fact done and has promised to do. To use later terminology, it would seem that Anselm strongly rejects the distinction between the absolute and ordained powers of God and equates *potentia absoluta* with *impotentia*. In short, to intensify or expand the conception of divine omnipotence by attributing to God possibilities not in conformity with his nature and will *as revealed* or as known a priori is for Anselm an improper and unfruitful avenue of theological discussion.

quo plus habet hanc potentiam, eo adversitas et perversitas in illum sunt potentiores, et ille contra eas impotentior."

Necessity and freedom in Anselm's conception of God

While it seems clear that a proper interpretation of Anselm would fall within the second approach, as described earlier, it is not clear which of the three interpretations found there is correct. What establishes the norm for divine action and is there always direct continuity between God's nature, God's actions, and our human conceptions of justice and truth by which we evaluate God's actions and nature? Part of the solution to that question lies in the chapters of *Proslogion* which follow immediately upon chapter seven. In these chapters Anselm examines the appropriateness or the meaning of the term "just" when applied to God in light of the fact that certain divine actions seem to contradict our human sense of justice. Anselm continually seeks a solution along the lines of differentiating between the human view of God's actions and God's view or rather God's true nature. God is compassionate only in terms of human experience, that is, we experience God as compassionate when in fact no change has taken place in God or no such emotion is present in God[20].

Throughout this section in *Proslogion* certain basic assumptions are present and shape both the method and the conclusions of Anselm. First of all, Anselm works *from* the nature of God, who is all good, powerful, and just, *to* the actual divine actions as revealed in Scripture in the form of past action or promise, *to* the content of the various terms that apply to God. Behind that methodology lies a more basic proposition that excludes one of our earlier interpretations of Anselm's understanding of necessity and freedom in God, namely the sixth that holds that God conforms to some norm of goodness and truth not of his own choosing. The term "just" ultimately has no meaning apart from God whose actions give the term content[21]. Similarly, only God's actions give content to the terms "good" and "true" and, conversely, to the terms "evil" and "false." "Good" and "just" are automatically whatever God decides to do.

But what, if anything, determines God's choice? The question is difficult to answer. Anselm seems to believe that the inner nature of God is the source of his goodness and justice, but that his nature is hidden from man and ultimately unknowable[22]. We are seemingly forced, therefore, to apply contentless categories to God (e.g., God is good or just inasmuch as whatever God does will determine what is good or just), and we can only attempt to understand and explain God's actions as revealed in Scripture and the life of the Church, to apply a consistency to those actions in order to give content to those categories that apply primarily to God.

It should not, however, be inferred from this that Anselm is open to the charge of voluntarism. Whether it is a result of God's desire to act consistently or a result of the fact that God's nature is one and is consistent with his actions, there is a consistency in God's actions based on the identity or interrelation of his will and his nature. If God's actions seem contradictory to us – for example how God can,

---

20) *Proslogion*, ch. 8 (*Opera Omnia*, I, 106).

21) *Proslogion*, ch. 11 (*Opera Omnia*, I, 109): "Nam id solum iustum est quod vis, et non iustum quod non vis."

22) *Proslogion*, ch. 9 (*Opera Omnia*, I, 107): "An quia bonitas tua est incomprehensibilis, latet hoc in luce inaccessibili quam inhabitas? Vere in altissimo et secretissimo bonitatis tuae latet fons, unde manat fluvius misericordiae tuae." "Cernitur unde flumen manat, et non perspicitur fons unde nascatur. Nam et de plenitudine bonitatis est quia peccatoribus tuis pius es, et in altitudine bonitatis latet qua ratione hoc es."

out of all those who are wicked, decide to save some and not others, and yet remain eternally and completely just — it is because we can never fully understand the nature and actions of God. But in God there can be no contradiction[23].

Believing in the consistency of God's nature and actions, it is impossible to conceive that God might change his mind or contradict himself or lie. Therefore, while God is the source for the meaning of all these terms or categories, the consistency of God's nature and will gives to these categories or terms only one meaning which is known, in part, through revelation and the moral judgment of our inherent reason. God is bound to be consistent with the content of those terms, it is impossible for him to act otherwise, not out of any external necessity but only because it is his nature to choose to do so; but that has binding force, and it is true to say that God could not act otherwise. Such a limitation or inability to act in a way that contradicts God's nature and past actions does not, for Anselm, diminish the freedom and omnipotence of God.

Among the interpretations of Anselm's conception of divine omnipotence presented earlier, it would seem that the fourth and fifth interpretations come closest to describing his meaning in *Proslogion.* They form a middle ground that explains what otherwise might seem conflicting tendencies in Anselm's discussion. They make it possible to see why Anselm can say in chapter seven that there are certain things which God cannot do because these things have specific content and to do them would be inconsistent with the nature of God as we understand it, and then, in the next few chapters, seemingly reverse that position and claim that only God gives content to these terms or categories. But does Anselm believe that God gives these categories meaning and content by his actions *initially* (from our time-bound point of view) and is consequently bound to act accordingly because it is his nature to be consistent, or does the content of these categories develop out of, depend upon, and adequately reflect the intrinsic nature of God?

It is with this central question in mind that we now turn to Anselm's treatment of the question of necessity and freedom in God as seen in his later works. Does Anselm define his position with greater clarity or perhaps alter it? What is the continuity, if any, between God's true nature and his revealed will, and what disposes or forces God to act as he does?

The Middle Period: *De libertate arbitrii* and *De casu diaboli* (1080—1090)

One of the most striking features of Anselm's treatise on the free will[24] is his rejection of the Augustinian definition of free will as the power to sin or not to sin[25]. He seems to do this for two reasons. First of all, Anselm believes that it is

---

23) *Proslogion*, ch. 9 (*Opera Omnia*, I, 108): "Nam etsi difficile sit intelligere, quomodo misericordia tua non absit a tua iustitia, necessarium tamen est credere, quia nequaquam adversatur iustitiae quod exundat ex bonitate, quae nulla est sine iustitia, immo vere concordat iustitiae." *Proslogion*, ch. 11 (*Opera Omnia*, I, 109—110): "Sed si utcumque capi potest, cur malos potes velle salvare: illud certe nulla ratione comprehendi potest, cur de similibus malis hos magis salves quam illos per summam bonitatem, et illos magis damnes quam istos per summam iustitiam. Sic ergo vere es sensibilis, omnipotens, misericors et impassibilis, quemadmodum vivens, sapiens, bonus, beatus, aeternus, et quidquid melius esse quam non esse."
24) *De libertate arbitrii*, (*Opera Omnia*, I, 207—226).
25) *Ibid.*, 207—209.

Necessity and freedom in Anselm's conception of God

necessary to have a definition of free will that will be applicable to God as well as man. If God, who possesses free will, does not have the ability to sin (a point the reader of the seventh chapter of *Proslogion* supposedly is willing to grant), then the ability to sin cannot be part of the true definition of free will. Secondly (again in light of the seventh chapter of *Proslogion*), for Anselm freedom equals power or ability, and if the ability to sin is not ability in the strict sense of the term, but rather liability, then freedom to sin is not freedom in the strict sense of the term. The power to sin is not the same kind of capacity as the ability not to sin or to act in conformity with rectitude or justice. Anselm restricts the definition of freedom to the capacity or power to conform to rectitude which, in the case of God, is the divine nature and, in the case of man, is justice or righteousness.

Twice, in chapters five and nine of *De libertate arbitrii*[26], Anselm raises the question regarding human moral behavior of whether one could or should lie in order to save one's own life. The passages suggest that there exists a given, moral order, restricted and grounded in God's approval of truth uttered for its own sake, but there is no speculation on the source of that moral order or how the moral order applies to God. The implication is that doing what is not right, for man or for God, is not a form of freedom or power but a form of bondage and impotence.

In chapter eight, Anselm indicates a further limitation on the power of God[27]. Once having created man, God cannot remove from the rational soul either the freedom of choice or the rectitude of the will. God could destroy his creation, if he so chose, but he cannot, according to Anselm, alter the terms of that creation as it presently exists. In particular, God could destroy man, but he could not simply remove from man the freedom of choice, the freedom or power to achieve and sustain rectitude, the uprightness of the will, for such an action would involve a contradiction. It would mean that God willed against his own will, because God's present decision would go against his past decision. Inasmuch as rectitude means conformity to the revealed will of God, to the revealed moral order, God would, by removing the freedom or ability of man to conform to the will of God, be contradicting his original revealed intention[28].

The case that Anselm describes here would seem to be an illustration or an application of the rules laid down by Anselm in the seventh chapter of *Proslogion*. To remove the human freedom of choice or the rectitude of the will would be an instance either of God's lying or of making what is true, false, that is, changing the past. As Henry has correctly noted, for Anselm, God's eternal present has more in common with the temporal past than with the temporal present[29]. What is past, in Anselm's view, can never be changed or become "not past."

Moreover, as Henry has already seen, there is in the discussions of ability and power a similarity between the seventh chapter of *Proslogion* and the whole of *De*

---

26) *Ibid.*, 214—217, 221.
27) *Ibid.*, 220—221.
28) But if God reduced man or creation to nothing, that is, if he withdrew his sustaining, creative power and thus reduced creation to its original nothingness, would he not also be denying his original intent? On the basis of this objection, it would seem that ANSELM is concerned about a conflict within the moral order. With the annihilation of man or the created order, the moral question would no longer apply. Rather ANSELM is concerned about the man who would know the revealed will of God and yet not be able to conform with that will.
29) D. P. HENRY in *L'Homme et son destin*, 380.

libertate arbitrii, especially chapter two. There Anselm again states that power improperly called is power actually held or exercised by another, as when a rich man puts himself under the power of a poor man, and then one says that the poor man is exercising power. As Anselm expresses it, *Even if a free rich man were able to make himself the servant of a poor man, he is properly described as free and the poor man is not said to be able to be his master as long as he does not do this* (i.e., act against his own best interests or, more strictly, do what is not advantageous for him or what he ought not to do)[30]. *Or if it is said* (that the poor man can master the rich man), *it is said improperly, because this is not in his power but in that of the other*[31].

Several aspects of Anselm's analogy are of interest. Henry sees it as an example of modal expression, the tendency in common usage to say things which are not really meant or intended[32]. Such negative expressions as "A cannot be conquered by B" mean that "B cannot conquer A". Beyond that, however, Anselm seems to be describing two different kinds of impotence. The first is something of a logical contradiction. For a rich, free man to give away his money and to place himself under the authority of a poor man might be theoretically possible, but the man, in his new state, would no longer be termed rich or free. If God gave up his power and authority, he would no longer be God, which is impossible. The second kind of impotence grows out of Anselm's linguistic analysis. When one says that the poor man can possibly in the future have power over the rich man, the power mentioned is a power possessed by the rich man, not the poor man. Power is inappropriately ascribed to the poor man.

In light of this analogy, there may be two reasons in Anselm's thought for the limitations on divine omnipotence. Not only would certain actions not be a form of power but would rather place God under the power of other forces, for God to cease to exercise his proper powers or to do the things associated with the name "God" would simply mean that the being who did such things was not what we mean by God, not the being, than which nothing greater can be conceived. If both aspects of the analogy of the free man apply to Anselm's understanding of God, then *De libertate arbitrii* has further clarified Anselm's discussion of the limits on divine omnipotence.

By contrast, the terminology of *De casu diaboli* covers ground that is already familiar. In chapter twelve Anselm reintroduces his qualification on antecedent capacity, namely the loose and strict senses in which a thing can be said to have power. The passage forms a significant parallel to the seventh chapter of *Proslogion*.

> *On account of this impropriety of speaking, it happens that frequently we say 'a thing can' not because it can, but because something else can; and* (we say that) *a thing which can, cannot, because some other thing cannot, just as if I say: 'a book is able to be written by me,' when a book can do nothing,*

---

30) The parallel with the limitations on God's omnipotence is obvious. It is questionable, although tempting, to conjecture whether this passage affords some insight into ANSELM's attitude toward noble and ignoble service.

31) *De libertate arbitrii*, 2 (*Opera Omnia*, I, 210): "Nam et si dives liber possit se facere servum pauperis: quamdiu hoc non facit, nec ille nomen amittit libertatis, nec pauper illi dicitur posse dominari; aut si dicitur, improprie dicitur, quia hoc non in eius sed in alterius est potestate."

32) D. P. HENRY, in *Spicilegium Beccense*, 21.

Necessity and freedom in Anselm's conception of God

although I can write a book. And when we say: 'this man cannot be conquered by that man' we understand nothing other than: 'that man cannot conquer this man.'

Hence we say that God is not able to do anything contrary to himself or perverse (sibi adversum aut perversum), since he is so powerful in beatitude and justice (nay rather since beatitude and justice are not in him separate things but rather one good, so that he is omnipotent in the simplest good), that nothing is able to harm the highest good. Therefore he is not able to be corrupted nor to lie.[33]

In this passage the consistency and unity of God's nature are reaffirmed, yet the discussion does not really answer the questions raised by the passage in *Proslogion.* Is the freedom of God restricted by a norm, either in a negative or positive sense, and if so, what determines that norm and gives it content? This question became increasingly important for Anselm as he was drawn into the controversy over the incarnation. How can the appropriateness and necessity of the incarnation be affirmed without endangering the affirmation of the freedom and omnipotence of God?

Anselm's Final Solution: *Cur deus homo* (1095–1098)

The central problem of *Cur deus homo*, the problem of establishing the reasonableness of divine action, leads Anselm to alter or further refine his understanding of freedom and necessity in God. The theological method used in this work does not differ dramatically from that used in *Proslogion.* Anselm gives to the categories that apply primarily to God, such as 'good', 'just', 'righteous', a content derived from a study of God's past actions. But the incarnation raises problems not so much for the justice of God as for his omnipotence and reasonableness.

In a sense, the attack on God's omnipotence which *Cur deus homo* tries to meet comes from a different quarter. In the earlier works, Anselm tried to answer the objection that God was not completely free and omnipotent if he did not possess the power to contradict his nature or at least his past decisions. The discussion there was consequently of a theoretical nature. In *Cur deus homo* Anselm tries to answer the objection that the Christian doctrine of atonement limits the omnipotence of God by not permitting him to act in the simplest, most direct way, namely by an exercise of his will alone. Consequently, while in the earlier works Anselm was preoccupied with the various senses of the term *posse* and the question of whether the things God does not or cannot do limit his

---

33) *De casu diaboli*, 12 (*Opera Omnia*, I, 253): "Ex qua improprietate loquendi fit ut saepissime dicamus rem posse, non quod illa possit, sed quoniam alia res potest; et rem quae potest non posse, quoniam alia res non potest. Ut si dico: liber potest scribi a me: utique liber nihil potest, sed ego possum scribere librum. Et cum dicimus, iste non potest vinci ab illo, non aliud intelligimus quam: ille non potest vincere istum.

"Hinc est quod dicimus deum non posse aliquid sibi adversum aut perversum, quoniam sic est potens in beatitudine et iustitia, immo quoniam beatitudo et iustitia non sunt in illo diversa sed unum bonum, sic est omnipotens in simplici bono, ut nulla res possit quod noceat summo bono. Ideo namque non potest corrumpi nec mentiri."

I

power, in *Cur deus homo* Anselm seems more preoccupied with the various senses of *necesse* and the question of whether the things God does do or did do limit his power.

Throughout *Cur deus homo* Anselm maintains the position that no necessity, within or outside God, forces him to act in any particular way. His actions are totally and always free. In particular, the desire to redeem fallen man was a free act of God, and no outside force or necessity drove him to act in this way. At times Anselm seems to imply that the method of redemption was necessary; no other *way* of redeeming man was open to God[34]. But the choice of whether to redeem man or not was a free choice on the part of God that was in no way necessitated by another agency.

In order to protect the freedom of God's choice to act (although not, seemingly, the freedom of choice over the *method* of action), Anselm applies three distinctions. The first is a distinction between an action necessitated by some outside force or compulsion and an action necessitated by an inward and free decision. In stating this, Anselm elaborates or perfects a distinction found in Augustine but one which now in *Cur deus homo* receives its classic formulation from whence it was to play a dynamic role in Western thought for the next five hundred years: the concept of a necessity or causality based on promise and covenant. When a person, of his own free will, makes a binding promise to act in a particular way, we can say that his fulfillment of that promise constitutes a necessary action on his part, although it is done freely and under no compulsion. The same action, when finally performed, can justly be termed both free and necessary. Anselm's description of this type of necessity is so basic for later developments that we should look at the passage in its entirety.

> *For this is not to be called necessity, but grace, since he undertook it and holds fast to it freely, and under compulsion from no one. It is true that if you promise today of your own free will to give something tomorrow, and give it tomorrow by the same free will, you have to do the latter, if you can, just as you promised, unless you are to be a liar. And yet the person to whom you give it does not owe you any less for the costly favor than he would if you had made no promise, since you did not hesitate to make yourself a debtor to him before the time of the actual giving. It is just the same when someone freely takes a vow to live in the religious state. Once the vow is made, of course, he is necessarily bound to keep it, if he is not to incur the condemnation of an apostate; indeed, he can be compelled to keep it if he is unwilling to do so. Nevertheless, if he keeps his vow with a ready will, he is not less but more pleasing to God than he would be if he had not made the vow. For he has renounced, for God's sake, not only ordinary life but even his freedom to live it, and we must say that he lives this holy life, not by necessity, but rather by the same freedom by which he made the vow.*
>
> *Much more, then, if God performs for man the good work which he has begun, we should ascribe the whole to grace, even though it does not befit him to fail in a good undertaking, because he undertook it all for our sake, and not for his own, since he is in need of nothing. For what man was going to do was not concealed from him when he made him, but despite this, in creating man of his*

---

34) *Cur deus homo*, I, 10 (*Opera Omnia*, II, 66): "... sed quoniam — sicut dictum est — mundum erat aliter impossibile salvari."

Necessity and freedom in Anselm's conception of God

own goodness, he freely bound himself, as it were, to complete the good work once begun. In short, God does nothing of necessity, since nothing whatever can coerce or restrain him in his actions. And when we say that God does something by necessity, as it were, of avoiding dishonor — which, in any case, he need not fear — it is better to interpret this as meaning that he does it from the necessity of preserving his honor. Now this necessity is nothing but his own changeless honor, which he has from himself and not from another, and on that account it is improper to call it necessity. Nevertheless, let us say that it is necessary, on account of his own changelessness, for God's goodness to complete what he undertook for man, even though the whole good that he does is of grace [35].

In spite of Anselm's obvious displeasure or uneasiness in applying the term "necessity" to God's actions or in viewing them as motivated by a desire to avoid "dishonor", his meaning and intention in this passage are clear[36]. The only thing that binds or forces God to act in a particular way, the only kind of necessity that determines divine action, is the necessity that results from God's promise to act, a promise enforced by the consistency of God's nature and will, his integrity and sense of honor owing to himself, first of all, but also owed to those to whom the promise is made. Contained in this statement of Anselm are all the elements of God's ordained power and the reason for and reliability of its operation, and one does not find a better nor really a different description of *potentia ordinata* in Ockham, d'Ailly, or Biel. God freely binds himself to act in a particular way, he

---

35) *Cur deus homo*, II, 5 (*Opera Omnia*, II, 100): "Non enim haec est dicenda necessitas, sed gratia, quia nullo cogente illam suscepit aut servat, sed gratis. Nam si quod hodie sponte promittis cras te daturum, eadem cras voluntate das, quamvis necesse sit te cras reddere promissum, si potes, aut mentiri: non tamen minus tibi debet ille pro impenso beneficio cui das, quam si non promisisses, quoniam te debitorem ante tempus dationis illi facere non es cunctatus. Tale est, cum quis sanctae conversationis sponte vovet propositum. Quamvis namque servare illud ex necessitate post votum debeat, ne apostatae damnationem incurrat, et licet cogi possit servare, si nolit: si tamen non invitus servat quod vovit, non minus sed magis gratus est deo, quam si non vovisset; quoniam non solum communem vitam, sed etiam eius licentiam sibi propter deum abnegavit, nec sancte vivere dicendus est necessitate, sed eadem qua vovit libertate.

"Quare multo magis, si deus facit bonum homini quod incepit, licet non deceat eum a bono incepto deficere, totum gratiae debemus imputare, quia hoc propter nos, non propter se nullius egens incepit. Non enim illum latuit quid homo facturus erat, cum illum fecit, et tamen bonitate sua illum creando sponte se ut perficeret inceptum bonum quasi obligavit. Denique deus nihil facit necessitate, quia nullo modo cogitur aut prohibetur facere aliquid; et cum dicimus deum aliquid facere quasi necessitate vitandi inhonestatum, quam utique non timet, potius intelligendum est quia hoc facit necessitate servandae honestatis. Quae scilicet necessitas non est aliud quam immutabilitas honestatis eius, quam a se ipso et non ab alio habet, et idcirco improprie dicitur necessitas. Dicamus tamen quia necesse est, ut bonitas dei propter immutabilitatem suam perficiat de homine quod incepit, quamvis totum sit gratia bonum quod facit." The translations of *Cur deus homo* used here are by E. R. FAIRWEATHER, *A Scholastic Miscellany: Anselm to Ockham* (Philadelphia, 1956), pp. 100–183.

36) To take God out of the realm of eternity in which his nature and will are changeless and, for purposes of discussion, theorize about the time before God chooses or the motivations for choice is always awkward and leads one to state things that could not apply to God, properly considered. Yet ANSELM, in order to solve the problem of necessity and freedom in God, adopts this procedure more readily in *Cur deus homo* than in *Proslogion*.

makes himself a debtor to man, on the basis of a promise freely made and freely kept[37].

The second distinction made by Anselm in order to solve the problem of necessity and freedom in God is the distinction between ability *(posse)* and will *(velle)*[38]. While in earlier works Anselm frequently stated that there were certain things God could not do, he qualifies such statements by indicating that *posse* presupposes *velle*, so that power to act without the will to act never results in action. Consequently God may have the power or ability to do many things which he does not will to do. It is therefore inappropriate to state that there is anything that God does not have the power to do, and when it is said that God cannot lie, it is meant that God does not — can never, if you will — will to lie, although he might possess the theoretical power to do so.

This distinction between ability and will provides a new solution to the questions raised concerning the omnipotence of God in Anselm's earlier works. God may possess the theoretical power to do these things, but he does not possess the will or desire to do them and consequently will never — in a sense, could never — do them. It should be noted here that Anselm is not stating positively that God *could* do certain things that he does not do, such as lie; rather he is stating negatively that it is inappropriate to restrict the omnipotence or power of God by stating that there are things that God *cannot* do because he does not have the ability to do them. In reality, Anselm is talking about two kinds of power or ability: the ability to act and the ability to will to act. He is not talking about the desire to act or 'the desire to will (which are synonymous)[39]. At times, Anselm seems to be talking about a desire to act or to will to act, and such is the obvious inference from the analogy of promise and the monastic vow. If God's will to will or will to act is all that causes him to act, then his actions are free and no necessity is attributable to God, except in the loose sense of fulfilling a promise made to himself and man. If God, however, lacks the *ability* to will certain things, then his power is more limited and Anselm is closer to the position he adopted in *Proslogion* and *De casu diaboli.*

This is indeed the direction taken by Anselm when one compares the fifth chapter of book two (the passage on promise, where the freedom of God has no

---

37) An interesting parallel to the divine covenant is the idea of a contract with the devil. ANSELM considers and rejects this idea, and in doing so reveals his familiarity with commercial contracts. Cf. *Cur deus homo*, I, 7 (*Opera Omnia*, II, 58).

38) *Cur deus homo*, II, 10 (*Opera Omnia*, II, 107): "Omnis potestas sequitur voluntatem. Cum enim dico quia possum loqui vel ambulare, subauditur: si volo. Si enim non subintelligitur voluntas, non est potestas sed necessitas. Nam cum dico quia nolens possum trahi aut vinci, non est haec mea potestas, sed necessitas et potestas alterius. Quippe non est aliud: possum trahi vel vinci, quam: alius me trahere vel vincere potest. Possumus itaque dicere de Christo quia potuit mentiri, si subauditur: si vellet. Et quoniam mentiri non potuit nolens nec potuit velle mentiri, non minus dici potest nequivisse mentiri. Sic itaque potuit et non potuit mentiri." Cf. also chs. 16 (II, 120—121) and 17 (II, 122—126).

39) The inability to act would mean, for example, that I do not have the physical strength necessary to lift some large stone. The inability to will would mean that I do not have the ability to want to lift that stone; although I am strong enough, I lack the power of volition, perhaps because it is against my nature so to act. The lack of a desire to will would mean that I could lift the stone if I so chose, and I have the power so to choose, but I do not desire to do so, which is the same thing as saying that I do not desire to act.

Necessity and freedom in Anselm's conception of God

restriction beyond his desire to honor his agreements and promises) with the tenth chapter (the passage on ability and will, where God or God in Christ lacks the power to will certain things – not just the desire to will them – although God in Christ has the theoretical ability or power to lie[40].

The difference between the desire to will and the ability to will does not seem to have been apparent to Anselm, or, better stated, Anselm does not really intend any difference here. He feels that for God to preserve the power to do or not to do something is a sufficient safeguard for the freedom of God. If God's will is consistent, he can never will more than one thing. While he might retain the power to do the opposite, he can never retain the will to do the opposite. Therefore, to say that God or Christ cannot lie against his will means that God or Christ cannot will to lie.

It might appear at first glance that if Anselm views the actions of God as dependent on nothing beyond his own desire to act in a particular way and his faithfulness to his promises (the basic concept of *potentia ordinata*), does he not also, through his distinction between ability and will, maintain a dialectic between the absolute and ordained powers of God, a dialectic between what God theoretically could do – what God always retains the power and ability to do – and what he in fact does and will do according to his revealed promises? So it would seem, although again Anselm does not appear to have had this in mind. While a fuller evaluation of Anselm's understanding of the absolute power of God will be attempted in a moment, it is sufficient to remark here that the dialectic between the absolute and ordained powers of God rests on the distinction between the ability to will and the desire to will; Anselm's distinction, as has been stated, is between the ability to will and the ability to act.

The third distincton utilized by Anselm to solve the problem of necessity and freedom in God is the distinction between antecedent and consequent necessity, or the type of necessity that precedes and determines a particular effect as opposed to the type of necessity that simply describes an action as it happens or a necessity that results from a particular action[41]. This distinction is very close to

40) *Cur deus homo* II, 17 (*Opera Omnia*, II, 124): "Quapropter cum dicimus quia homo ille, qui secundum unitatem personae, sicut supra dictum est, idem ipse est qui filius dei, deus, non potuit non mori, aut velle non mori, postquam de virgine natus est: non significatur in illo ulla impotentia servandi aut volendi servare vitam suam immortalem, sed immutabilitas voluntatis eius, qua se sponte fecit ad hoc hominem, ut in eadem voluntate perseverans moreretur, et quia nulla res potuit illam voluntatem mutare. Plus enim esset impotentia quam potentia, si posset velle mentiri aut fallere aut mutare voluntatem, quam prius immutabilem esse voluit. Et si, quemadmodum supra dixi, cum aliquis sponte se proponit facturum bonum aliquod et eadem voluntate postea perficit quod proposuit, quamvis cogi possit, si nolit promissum solvere, non tamen est dicendus necessitate facere quod facit, sed ea qua proposuit libera voluntate – non enim necessitate aut impotentia fieri vel non fieri dici debet aliquid, ubi neque necessitas neque impotentia quicquam operantur sed voluntas – ; si, inquam, ita est in homine, multo magis necessitas aut impotentia nequaquam nominandae sunt in deo, qui nihil nisi quod vult facit, et cuius voluntatem nulla vis cogere aut prohibere valet." A similar point is stressed in *Meditatio* 3 (*Opera Omnia*, III, 86).

41) *Ibid.* (*Opera Omnia*, II, 125): "Est namque necessitas praecedens, quae causa est ut sit res; et est necessitas sequens, quam res facit. Praecedens et efficiens necessitas est, cum dicitur caelum volvi, quia necesse est ut volvatur; sequens vero et quae nihil efficit sed fit, est cum dico te ex necessitate loqui, quia loqueris. Cum enim hoc dico, significo nihil facere posse, ut dum loqueris non loquaris, non quod aliquid te cogat ad loquendum. Nam violentia naturalis condi-

the first distinction and would differ from it only in that consequent necessity can describe present action while necessity based on promise is not the result but the cause of the later action. The motion of the heavens is a result of antecedent necessity, for according to Anselm it is forced to follow that pattern and could not do otherwise. But it is also clear that Anselm intends by the term "consequent necessity" to cover the example of divine promise [42].

Through these three distinctions Anselm has been able, to his own satisfaction, to affirm in the strongest language the freedom and omnipotence of God without, seemingly, endangering either the reliability or predictability of the present order or the appropriateness and "necessity" of God's actions, once accomplished. Anselm seems to go rather far in basing everything on the will of God.

> . . . it is improper to say that God cannot do something, or that he does it by necessity. Rather, every necessity and impossibility is subject to his will, while his will is subject to no necessity or impossibility. For nothing is necessary or impossible save because he himself so wills it, but it is altogether untrue to say that he wills or does not will something because of its necessity or impossibility. Therefore, since he does all that he wills and only what he wills, no necessity or impossibility is prior to his acting or not acting, any more than to his willing or not willing, . . . [43]

This emphasis on the will of God is offset by several things. Most importantly, the will of God is a direct outgrowth of or is rather synonymous with the nature of God, and thus God can only will that which is in conformity with his nature. Consequently, God can never will conflicting things, and, moreover, he can never will things not in conformity with his nature, which can also never be composed of conflicting elements.

The second factor that offsets the seemingly exclusive stress on the will of God is the concept of eternity. Whatever God wills is willed for all eternity. Not only, therefore, is the idea of conflicting wills absurd (for two contradictory things would be true at the same time, which is impossible) but the idea of a change in God's will is likewise absurd.

Therefore Anselm continues:

> When God does anything, once it is done it is impossible for it not to have been done, but it is always true that it has been done; and yet it is not right to say that it is impossible for God to make what is past not to be past (which would seem to be a direct contradiction to Anselm's position in *Proslogion*, until one remembers his distinction between the ability to act and the ability to will). For there the necessity of not doing something or the impossibility of doing it has no effect, but only the will of God, who, since he himself is truth,

tionis cogit caelum volvi, te vero nulla necessitas facit loqui. Sed ubicumque est praecedens necessitas, est et sequens; non autem ubi sequens, ibi statim et praecedens."

42) *Ibid.* (*Opera Omnia*, II, 124).

43) *Ibid.* (*Opera Omnia*, II, 122−123): "Iam diximus quia deus improprie dicitur aliquid non posse aut necessitate facere. Omnis quippe necessitas et impossibilitas eius subiacet voluntati; illius autem voluntas nulli subditur necessitati aut impossibilitati. Nihil enim est necessarium aut impossibile, nisi quia ipse ita vult; ipsum vero aut velle aut nolle aliquid propter necessitatem aut impossibilitatem alienum est a veritate. Quare quoniam omnia quae vult, et non nisi quae vult facit: sicut nulla necessitas sive impossibilitas praecedit eius velle aut nolle, ita nec eius facere aut non facere, quamvis multa velit immutabiliter et faciat."

Necessity and freedom in Anselm's conception of God

wills that the truth should be always unchangeable, as it is. Similarly, if he unalterably decides to do something, although it is necessarily true, even before it is done, that it is going to be done, still he is subject to no necessity of doing it or impossibility of not doing it, since his will alone works in him. For whenever it is said that God cannot do something, there is no denial of his power, but rather an indication of his unconquerable might and strength. For this way of speaking simply means that no circumstance can make him do what it is said that he cannot do[44].

In this way Anselm arrives back at his earlier solution to the problem of freedom and necessity in God. To attribute to God the *power* to act in any way, at any time, without restriction is a sufficient defense of the belief in the omnipotence of God. The further ability to will that which goes against the divine nature or against previous manifestations of the divine will is not a form of power but rather impotence. As in *De casu diaboli* and elsewhere, Anselm returns to his linguistic argument about the meaning of the term *posse* in different contexts. He even repeats his example that the phrase "A cannot be conquered by B" does not describe a power possessed by 'A' but rather a lack of power possessed by 'B', and consequently means that "B cannot conquer A"[45]. Analogously, necessity inappropriately applied to God is really a necessity possessed by other things as a result of the fact that God is not bound by necessity.

Nor do we say that God does something by necessity, as if there were any necessity in him, but because there is necessity in something else – as I remarked concerning lack of power, with reference to the statement that he (God) cannot do something. For every necessity is either compulsion or prevention, and these two necessities are mutually exclusive, like necessity and impossibility . . . But when we say that something is or is not necessary in God, we do not suppose that there is any necessity in him, either by way of compulsion or by way of restraint; rather, we mean that in all other things there is a necessity that prevents them from doing, and compels them not to do, anything contrary to what is said about God. For example, when we say that it is necessary for God always to speak the truth, and necessary for him never to lie, we are simply saying that in him there is such great consistency in maintaining truth, that of necessity nothing can have the power to make him either not speak the truth or lie[46].

44) *Ibid.* *(Opera Omnia*, II, 123): "Et sicut cum deus facit aliquid, postquam factum est, iam non potest non esse factum, sed semper verum est factum esse; nec tamen recte dicitur impossibile deo esse, ut faciat quod praeteritum est non esse praeteritum – nihil enim ibi operatur necessitas non faciendi aut impossibilitas faciendi, sed dei sola voluntas, qui veritatem semper, quoniam ipse veritas est, immutabilem, sicuti est, vult esse –: ita si proponit se aliquid immutabiliter facturum, quamvis quod proponit, antequam fiat, non possit non esse futurum, non tamen ulla est in eo faciendi necessitas aut non faciendi impossibilitas, quoniam sola in eo operatur voluntas. Quotiens namque dicitur deus non posse, nulla negatur in illo potestas, sed insuperabilis significatur potentia et fortitudo. Non enim aliud intelligitur, nisi quia nulla res potest efficere, ut ille agat quod negatur posse."

45) *Ibid.*

46) *Ibid.* (*Opera Omnia*, II, 123–124): "Nec dicimus deum necessitate facere aliquid, eo quod in illo sit ulla necessitas, sed quoniam est in alio, sicut dixi de impotentia, quando dicitur non posse. Omnis quippe necessitas est aut coactio aut prohibitio; quae duae necessitates convertuntur invicem contrarie, sicut necesse et impossibile. Quidquid namque cogitur esse prohibetur non esse, et quod cogitur non esse prohibetur esse; quemadmodum quod necesse est esse

I

It seems clear on the basis of this last passage, in light of the foregoing, that Anselm believes that the actions of God conform to some norm, a norm however which is not the creation of some outside agency or even the result of his desire to abide by his past actions, but a norm consistent with and produced by the nature of God[47]. It is God's nature which sets the standards for truth and justice, a nature that is revealed by his will through action. The reliability of God's will and of God's promises is grounded not so much in the consistency of God's actions but rather in the fact that his consistency is a function of the unity of his nature and the identity of his nature and will. *The will of God is never irrational*[48].

The Implications of Anselm's Concept of Divine Omnipotence

We are now in a position to return to the remaining questions raised at the beginning of this paper. First, did Anselm establish the foundation for the dialectic between the absolute and ordained powers of God, was he antagonistic to that distinction, or was he totally unaware of that type of thought? Second, was Anselm's understanding of divine omnipotence shaped, either positively or negatively, by contemporary influences, especially those of Judaism or Islam?

The seeds for the distinction between the absolute and ordained powers of God can be found in Anselm's treatment of divine omnipotence, but these ideas do not function in Anselm as they were later to function in the thought of Ockham, d'Ailly, or Biel. Among those elements which would seem to make a direct contribution to the development of the dialectic of God's two powers are (1) Anselm's clear presentation of *potentia ordinata* and the idea of covenant and promise so crucial to later theologians, especially the Nominalists; (2) the strong stress on the will of God which is bound by no necessity and which determines what is good or just; and (3) the distinction between ability and will which allows Anselm to stress that God's ability or power to do anything whatsoever can never be limited.

The similarities between Anselm's view and that later maintained by the Nominalists are, however, only superficial. The differences are so much greater that Anselm and the Nominalists might better be seen as opposite points of view. The idea of covenant or agreement, the idea of a necessity based on promise rather than direct force, does not in Anselm fuse with the idea of the unrestricted, absolute power of God. Even Anselm's concept of covenant concerns only the *obligation* on God to fulfill his promises; it does not concern the actual *operation*

impossibile est non esse, et quod necesse est non esse impossibile est esse, et conversim. Cum autem dicimus aliquid necesse esse aut non esse in deo, non intelligitur quod sit in illo necessitas aut cogens aut prohibens, sed significatur quia in omnibus aliis rebus est necessita prohibens eas facere et cogens non facere contra hoc quod de deo dicitur. Nam cum dicimus quia necesse est deum semper verum dicere, et necesse est eum numquam mentiri, non dicitur aliud nisi quia tanta est in illo constantia servandi veritatem, ut necesse sit nullam rem facere posse, ut verum non dicat aut ut mentiatur."
47) This same point is made later in *De concordia praescientiae et praedestinationis et gratiae dei cum libero arbitrio*, I, 5 (*Opera Omnia*, II, 253–255).
48) *Cur deus homo*, I, 8 (*Opera Omnia*, II, 59) "Sufficere nobis debet ad rationem voluntas dei cum aliquid facit, licet non videamus cur velit. Voluntas namque dei numquam est irrationabilis."

Necessity and freedom in Anselm's conception of God

or the way in which the specific terms of the covenant or promise are fulfilled, an idea directly related to the problem of causality and essential for the later understanding of covenant, but one which does not seem to have made its appearance before the middle of the thirteenth century[49]. For Anselm, the concept of covenant or promise has nothing to do with the problem of causality, even theological; it concerns the question of the necessity for action, not the cause of action or the means of action.

Likewise, the ideas of the will and the absolute power of God do not function in Anselm as they would later in Nominalist thought. Although the Nominalists always affirmed a close relationship between the will and nature of God on the level of *potentia ordinata*, that relationship was, for methodological reasons, ignored when one was engaged upon a theoretical discussion, *de potentia absoluta*[50]. For Anselm, the will of God was inseparable from his nature in all types of speculation. Consequently, the idea of God's altering his will or changing his mind, even for purposes of a theoretical discussion, is never envisaged by Anselm. The farthest Anselm is willing to go along such lines is to imagine the situation of God's *not* having acted in the way he did[51]; Anselm refuses, however, to discuss the positive side of the same formulation, namely what God *might* have done instead or might have considered doing, the major function of *potentia absoluta* argumentation in Nominalism.

There is a good reason why Anselm does not do this, and it was certainly not for lack of opportunity or imagination. For purposes of analysis, Anselm is willing, with Boso's help, to go as far as conceiving the time before God chose or acted, the time when what is past had not yet happened. At such a time a human observer, supposing there was one, would not know in what way God was to act (although reason might give him a rather good idea) and therefore would not know the content of the terms "true" and "just"; he would be waiting until God acted and gave these categories meaning. But these categories, in God's mind, already have meaning and conform to the nature of God. While God reveals their meaning by his actions, that meaning results from his will and ultimately his nature. Therefore, while we may not know what is right until God's actions or words reveal it, there is only one "right," and God knows and acts accordingly. In

---

49) Cf. W. J. COURTENAY, *The King and the Leaden Coin: The Economic Background of Sine Qua Non Causality. Traditio* 28 (1972) 185–209.

50) The same holds true for THOMAS AQUINAS, *Quaestiones disputatae de potentia dei*, q.1, a.5 (*Opera Omnia*, Vol. VIII. Parma: Fiaccadori 1856), p. 10: "Sicut enim manifestatur divina bonitas per has res quae nunc sunt et per hunc rerum ordinem; ita potest manifestari per alias creaturas et alio modo ordinatas: et ideo divina voluntas absque praejudicio bonitatis, justitiae et sapientiae, potest se extendere in alia quam quae facit. Et in hoc fuerunt decepti errantes (those who assert that God could only act in one way): aestimaverunt enim ordinem creaturarum esse quasi commensuratum divinae bonitatis quasi absque eo esse non posset. Patet ergo quod absolute Deus potest facere alia quam quae fecit." *Ibid.*, p.11: "Absolutum et regulatum non attribuuntur divinae potentiae nisi ex nostra consideratione (thus also for OCKHAM, PIERRE D'AILLY, and BIEL): quae potentiae Dei in se consideratae, quae absoluta dicitur, aliquid attribuit quod non attribuit ei secundum quod ad sapientiam comparatur, prout dicitur ordinata."

51) *Cur deus homo*, I, 10 (*Opera Omnia*, II, 67): "Ponamus ergo dei incarnationem et quae de illo dicimus homine numquam fuisse . . ."

retrospect, returning to the present, no other course of action was ever possible or was ever open, even to God.

The key difference, in a sense, is that for the Nominalists, God retains the ability (although not the desire) to will many things apart from and even contrary to what he has willed (and will uphold); for Anselm, God does not have the ability to will that which he has not willed or that which is contrary to his nature. For Anselm only *one* way was ever really correct or possible, for God's will has to express God's nature, and God's nature, in turn, can never have been subject to multiple possibilities, since in such a case God's nature would have no consistent meaning. Anselm's entire theological method depends on the fact that there is one best way of doing things – the way God did them, consistent with his mature and wisdom – *therefore,* one should be able to establish that the way God did act was the only valid way, otherwise God would not have done it that way. The theologian may never be fully successful in explaining divine action, in justifying God's ways to man, but a solution is possible and can be partially achieved even in this life[52]. The very reluctance of Anselm to engage in what have been termed *"potentia absoluta* discussions" follows from his refusal to differentiate divine nature and will or to differentiate between revealed will and the possibilities open to God before he acted. The refusal to make that distinction explains the absence in Anselm of a distinction between the ability to will and the desire to will; the distinction is meaningless if you are dealing in all cases with an identity of nature and will[53]. Therefore, although important aspects of the later scholastic formulation of the freedom and necessity of God can be found in Anselm, most of his thought is opposed to the direction and implications of the Nominalist position.

Does this last fact mean that Anselm unwittingly developed the terminology and conceptions for certain aspects of the later system or, on the other hand, does it mean that Anselm was already aware of an early formulation of that thesis and, while accepting certain parts of it, sharply rejected the approach and the conclusions? The question cannot be adequately answered on the basis of our present knowledge of the background to Anselm's thought. One can note, however, that although the dialectic of the powers of God and its incorporation within a system of covenant and promise had not yet been worked out, the concept of the theoretically unlimited power of God was already present in Anselm's day and possibly familiar to him in some form[54]. Certain passages in the Old Testament

52) This is the meaning of ANSELM's statement that "there is some other way (of human redemption) than the one we have spoken of." ANSELM does not mean that God could have redeemed man in some other way; rather other explanations for the reasonableness of the way God did act are possible.

53) It also explains the difficulty encountered initially in deciding whether the fourth or fifth interpretation correctly applies to ANSELM.

54) Certain similarities in the thought of the Mutakallimun and Nominalism, especially the thought of AL-GHAZZALI and OCKHAM, have long been noted, although neither the details of the relationship nor an adequate comparison of their views has yet been undertaken. The similarities may be grounded in little beyond the fact that "because the God of the Old Testament was common to Christianity and to Islam, a similar tendency will sometimes affirm itself in the history of Christian philosophy" (E. GILSON, *History of Christian Philosophy in the Middle Ages* (New York, 1955), 185). For further discussion see M. FAKHRY, *Islamic Occasionalism and its Critique by Averroës and Aquinas* (London, 1958), and a contrary evaluation in my *The Critique on Natural Causality in the Mutakallimun and Nominalism: Harvard Theological Review* 66 (1973) 77–94.

Necessity and freedom in Anselm's conception of God

suggest a God whose actions cannot only not be understood or questioned, but whose will seems subject to periodic changes. This particular view of the omnipotence of God tended to be preserved and strengthened within Islam, especially in the Mutakallimun tradition, which considered the moral and natural system ordained by God the result of an arbitrary and to some degree a chance decision on the part of God. He could as easily have chosen another norm for truth and justice. There is, therefore, no necessary connection between the character of the revealed order and the nature of God. God probably will not alter his commandments and decisions, but if he did his new choices, no matter how much they might contradict the old, would now determine what was true and just[55].

René Roques has already pointed out some ways in which Islamic thought, especially the traditions represented by Al-Ghazzali, shaped the structure and approach of *Cur deus homo*[56]. The influence, it would seem, goes deeper and affects the content of the work, both in problems raised and conclusions given. One of these problems is divine omnipotence, and it is surely not accidental that the major Islamic figure chosen by Roques, Al-Ghazzali, was the author of the *Tahafut al-Falasifah* and one of the most gifted representatives of the Mutakallimun tradition. This explains, in part, why the position of the *pagani*, as expressed by Boso, places so much stress on the absolute freedom of God and argues for a divine activity that has no other motivation behind it nor uses any means or secondary causes to effect its decisions except the sheer will of God. Such a position was not typical of Islamic theology or philosophy as a whole but rather descriptive of the position of the Mutakallimun.

Viewed from this perspective, the stress Anselm places on the will of God may be not only an expression of an idea found within traditional Christian theology but may also be an attempt at establishing a common basis for the Christian dialogue with Islam. In general, however, Anselm interprets the concepts of the will of God and divine omnipotence in a way that, although it tries to convince the unbeliever, is ultimately opposed to the Mutakallimun formulation[57].

The conception of God often attributed to the Mutakallimun tradition tends to consider divine will and actions more from the category of time than eternity and to permit God all the freedom to change his mind, to act willfully and arbitrarily without being questioned, as would be permitted a petty despot. If God is to be considered free and omnipotent, should he not be allowed at least as much freedom as an earthly king? According to this view, true omnipotence

---

55) The attitude toward natural causality within the Mutakallimun has received more attention, and it is in that regard that scholars have attributed to the Mutakallimun the idea that the world is always open to the periodic interventions of God's absolute power which can alter any of his past decisions. Cf. GILSON, 182–185.

56) René ROQUES, in *Die Metaphysik im Mittelalter*, 192–206.

57) It is inviting (though somewhat misleading) to see in ANSELM a parallel to the Mutazilite school in Islam. Anselm employs arguments based on reason and necessity. He is concerned with establishing the absolute unity of God and the justice of the divine will. Although he fights against it, he seems "to submit the will of God to an intrinsic law of justice" and therefore "to admit the existence of an objective good and an objective evil which reason is able to discover and to which men have to conform their acts" (GILSON, p. 182). Perhaps ANSELM was not only aware of Islamic thought but also aware of different traditions and was attempting to utilize those differences.

always includes the power to do evil as defined by those who suffer the consequences of a capricious will.

Regardless of how the stress on the will of God in the Mutakallimun tradition was viewed by Islamic theologians, Western Christian theology, including Anselm, was suspicious of a power dependent exclusively on the will of God and unchecked by any other attribute or agency, such as God's wisdom, benevolence, or faithfulness. Without pursuing the question of whether and to what degree the Mutakallimun conception of God was modelled on certain forms of human kingship, it may be that Western theologians shaped some aspects of their idea of God on the basis of their experience with the misuse of power. Europe was all too familiar with the power of a local lord that went unchecked by any sense of justice and who could not be relied upon to keep his word. Power without responsibility, without conformity to accepted standards of justice and truth, was a clear invitation to evil and perversity.

One reaction to the Islamic view was to temper the will of God through conformity to some norm, be it either God's nature as revealed or some external norm of justice and truth, or to confine God's activity for all practical purposes within the boundaries of the laws and institutions to which he voluntarily committed himself. Both of these devices occur in Anselm, but he generally supports the first. In the generations after Anselm these two approaches toward limiting the power of God tended to separate into two different approaches toward theology that came into open conflict toward the end of the thirteenth century and were to influence theological discussion well into the sixteenth century[58]. The effect on later theologians of Anselm's treatment of divine omnipotence, especially its effect on the development of the concept of the two powers of God, would seem, therefore, to be an advantageous area for further study.

---

58) W. J. COURTENAY, in *Traditio*, 28 (1972) 185–209.

II

SACRAMENT, SYMBOL, AND CAUSALITY
IN BERNARD OF CLAIRVAUX

THE AUTHORITY OF BERNARD OF CLAIR-
VAUX holds an unique place in the late medieval discussion of sacramental causality. His was the only pre-
thirteenth-century name consistently associated with the view
that the sacraments cause grace on the basis of an ascribed
rather than an inherent virtue or power, a view usually termed *sine qua non* causality and generally in disrepute since the
Council of Trent. The association of Bernard and *sine qua non*
causality in the sacraments was based on a passage from Bernard's sermon *In cena domini* in which he suggested that the
sacraments are signs of the investiture of grace and compared
their action to the way a canon is invested into office through
a book, an abbot through a crozier, and a bishop through a
crozier and ring.[1] The early opponents of sacramental causality based on ascribed virtue alone (for example, Peter of Tarantasia or Thomas Aquinas) claimed the Bernard was misinterpreted on this issue. But several supporters of ascribed virtue in the fourteenth century (for example, John of Bassoles
and Durand of St Pourçain) continued to enlist the authority
of Bernard on their side. Opponents of ascribed virtue accepted the association of Bernard with the denial of effective cau-

---

1. V HM 2 (5, 68-69): "*Sicut enim in exterioribus sunt diversa signa et, ut coepto immoremur exemplo, variae sunt investiturae secundum ea de quibus investimur, —verbi gratia, investitur canonicus per librum, abbas per baculum, episcopus per baculum et anulum simul—, sicut, inquam, in huiusmodi rebus est, sic et diviones gratiarum diversis traditae sunt sacramentis.*"

sality in the sacraments and simply rejected what they mistakingly regarded as Bernard's view.

To the modern historian of medieval thought it is apparent that both sides in this discussion were interpreting the passage from Bernard in light of the more highly developed sacramental theology of the late thirteenth and fourteenth centuries. The limited late medieval understanding of the development of dogma and of the broader twelfth-century milieu in which Bernard was writing made a balanced interpretation of the Bernard passage difficult. However, the disagreements over Bernard's meaning do provide the later historian with considerable material on how later generations of theologians interpreted him on this issue, a topic interesting in itself. Perhaps with the increased understanding of twelfth-century thought and of the development of sacramental theology in the high and late Middle Ages we are now in a better position to evaluate the Bernardine passage and its subsequent medieval interpretation. Did the idea that the sacraments are the *sine qua non* causes of grace originate with Bernard?[2] How should the often cited quotation from Bernard be understood in its original context and in later applications?

Carefully argued theories concerning sacramental causality were not developed before the thirteenth century, although analogies describing the nature and efficacy of the sacraments can be found as early as the second quarter of the twelfth century. The eucharist and, more especially, baptism had received considerable attention in patristic theology, but it was only in the twelfth century that theologians attempted to formulate an integrated, internally consistent, and complete examination of the sacraments. Thus Bernard stands within the first generation of theologians who addressed themselves to the issue of

---

2. To my knowledge this problem has not received direct treatment, although it is obliquely referred to by Joseph Lortz when he considers the *Asakramentalität* of Bernard in *Bernhard von Clairvaux. Mönch und Mystiker*. Internationaler Bernhardkongress, Mainz, 1953 (Wiesbaden, 1955), pp. xlvi-xlvii. For background and related issues see: F. Heiler, *Das Gebet* (München, 1920); G. Frischmuth, *Die paulinische Konzeption in der Frömmigkeit Bernhards von Clairvaux* (Beiträge zur Forderung christl. Theologie, 37/4; Gütersloh, 1933); R. Linhardt, *Bernard von Clairvaux* (Regensburg, 1937); D. R. Hesbert, "Saint Bernard et l'Eucharistie," *Mélanges Saint Bernard* (Dijon, 1953), pp. 156-176.

the relation of the sacramental elements to their principal effect, the infusion of grace. The analogy he used to describe that relationship alongside the more frequently repeated analogy of Hugh of St Victor formed the foundation for the theological exploration of sacramental causality.[3]

Bernard did not set out to explain sacramental causality in his Maundy Thursday sermon in 1139. Instead, he was explaining to his listeners the various effects that accrued from baptism, the eucharist and the ceremony of the washing of feet. In that context he defined the sacraments (including what are now called sacramentals) as signs or mysteries that bestow a hidden benefit.[4] In a passage that precedes the one referred to above, Bernard suggests that the sacraments are common, ordinary things or actions that have a special value and significance attached to them. If a person gives a ring to another as a present, the ring has no significance beyond being an expression of the affection of the giver for the recipient. If, however, the ring represents a claim to the future inheritance of some property, then the ring has a value and significance far greater than its intrinsic value. The ring itself remains unchanged; an added value is simply ascribed to it by those party to the agreement, an agreement sufficiently public so that there will be no question of rightful succession at the time of inheritance.[5]

It is this passage that forms the background and clarifies the subsequent passage that received so much attention by later theologians. While pursuing the same analogy Bernard

3. Hugh of St Victor defined the sacraments as vessels or receptacles of God's grace, as a doctor's vial would contain the medicine for the patient. *De sacramentis*, I, part ix, ch. 4; H. Weisweiler, *Die Wirksamkeit der Sakramente nach Hugo von St Victor* (Freiburg i. B., 1932).

4. V HM 2 (5,68): "*Sacramentum dicitur sacrum signum, sive sacrum secretum.*"

5. Ibid.: "*Multa siquidem fiunt propter se tantum, alia vero propter alia designanda, et ipsa dicuntur signa, et sunt. Ut enim de usualibus sumamus exemplum, datur anulus absolute propter anulum, et nulla est significatio; datur ad investiendum de hereditate aliqua, et signum est, ita ut iam dicere possit qui accipit: 'Anulus non valet quidquam, sed hereditas est quam quaerebam.' In hunc itaque modum, appropinquans passioni Dominus, de gratia sua investire curavit suos, ut invisibilis gratia signo aliquo visibili praestaretur.*" Landgraf is the only one who has commented on the importance of this passage for the development of what he terms intentional causality. A. M. Landgraf, *Dogmengeschichte der Frühscholastik*, III.1 (Regensburg, 1954), pp. 171-172.

argues that a diversity of graces are caused or communicated by different sacraments, just as investiture into particular offices is effected through different signs or symbols, a book in the case of a canon, a crozier for an abbot, and a crozier and ring for a bishop. In this second passage, as it was later pointed out, Bernard is not principally arguing for ascribed virtue or value but is comparing the effects of different sacraments. When viewed against the background of the previous passage, however, it seems to be Bernard's position that the sacraments are, like the signs used to invest in office, common things that receive their new significance by having an additional value applied or ascribed to them by some person (in the case of the sacraments, Christ), by some agreement or covenant, or by their recognized use in a particular ceremony. The implication is that intrinsically the signs remain what they were before; no special virtue is infused into them that alters their nature. The new or additional virtue is applicable only when these signs or symbols are used properly in a particular ceremony. Moreover, grace does not seem to be communicated directly in and through the sacraments but, like the ring that represents a claim to an inheritance, follows as a direct result of the reception of the sacraments. The sacraments, therefore, are legitimate and efficacious claims or titles to grace, given on the occasion of the proper reception of the sacraments.

In order to understand Bernard's view of the efficacious nature of signs in regard to the promise of future reward it is necessary to look first at Bernard's view of the administration of grace within the plan of salvation and, second, at the meaning of sign and symbol for Bernard's generation.

On first glance Bernard's soteriology seems to be dominated by an active, unrestricted, and possibly unpredictable God, a view which, if true, would make all covenants and agreements between God and man, including the efficacious nature of the sacramental signs, meaningless and undependable. Bernard shared with others within the monastic tradition (such as Peter Damian[6] or Anselm of Canterbury[7]) a high assessment of divine

---

6. *De divina omnipotentia*, 4 (PL 145:601 C).
7. Anselm's statements on the omnipotence of God are scattered throughout his

omnipotence and the extent of divine freedom before creation. Because of that belief Bernard criticized Abelard for maintaining that God's power to act was limited to those things that God in fact did do.[8] Even after creation and the establishment of a system of salvation God's freedom is not entirely restricted by the ordained order. For example, God remains free to accept one to eternal life who has not been baptized, and thus God can save apart from the normal channels of grace.[9]

In general, however, the freedom of God to save or to damn is limited by the divine nature, by the system of salvation that has been ordained, and by the human will. Whatever freedom may exist outside the ordained order (and there is little of it), is the freedom to be more beneficent and forgiving than the ordained order permits.[10] For Bernard, it is the nature of God, as a father, to forgive all those who place themselves in the

---

works. His position changed between *Proslogion* (1078) and *Cur Deus Homo* (1098). For a description of Anselm's development on this issue see: W. J. Courtenay, "Necessity and Freedom in Anselm's Conception of God," *Die Wirkungsgeschichte Anselms von Canterbury*. Acts of the International Anselm Congress, Bad Wimpfen, Sept. 1970 (to appear in 1973).

8. *Capitula Haeresum Petri Abaelardi* (PL 182:1049C - 1050A).

9. Bernard had in mind those who lived before the establishment of the sacrament of baptism or those to whom the gospel has not been preached. His position should not be confused with later *de potentia Dei absoluta* speculation, which discussed God's freedom to accept a sinner who rejected Christianity. Bapt (PL 182: 1033D-1034A): "*Sed forte aliquis dicat, eos quidem qui non audierunt, etsi non de contemptu judicari, damnari tamen propter originale peccatum, a quo utique nisi per lavacrum emundari minime potuerunt. At vero quis nesciat et alia praeter Baptismum contra originale peccatum remedia antiquis non defuisse temporibus? Abrahae quidem et semini eius, circumcisionis sacramentum in hoc ipsum divinitus traditum est* (Gen 17:10). *In nationibus vero, quotquot inventi sunt fideles, adultos quidem fide et sacrificiis credimus expiatos, parvulis autem solam profuisse, imo et suffecisse parentum fidem. Porro hoc ita quidem usque ad Baptismi tempora perdurasse: quo uno substituto, vacasse caetera.*" Ibid., 1034A-B: "*Quaerimus itaque Baptismi tempus ex quo coeperit. Ex quo, inquit, primum dictum est:* Nisi quis renatus fuerit, *etc. Tene ergo firmiter dictum hoc ad Nicodemum, utique amicum Jesu, occultum tamem propter metum Judaeorum; occultumque illud de nocte requisisse colloquium. Quanta autem putas obisse interim (ut de gentibus taceam) millia circumcisorum, cum necdum in lucem prodierit quod de Baptismo tunc in tenebris dicebatur? Quid ergo? damnatos illos omnes dicimus, quia baptizati non sunt? Fit ergo iniuria antiquo illi Dei aeque mandato, si novo adhuc furtive quodammodo superveniente, non tamen subveniente, illud ita subito evanuisse putetur, ut prodesse deinceps non valeret.*" cf. Ibid., 1031C-1033B.

10. This is also the implication of the parable of the laborers in the vineyard, Mt 20:1-16.

116   *Bernard of Clairvaux*

position of being sons of God.[11] Sonship results from acknowledging God as father and willing to be saved, a desire on the part of the human will that cannot be coerced by God.[12] For the one who strives after God, who does his best or, in later terminology, does what is in him, God will not deny him grace and final salvation.[13] According to Bernard, God is not free to reject those who have been baptized and who desire salvation.[14] Nor is he free to accept those who have heard about baptism but have refused it.[15] In sum, God cannot, or at least will not and does not, save men against their own wills. It is in all cases necessary that a man will to be saved, and he must cooperate with God to the extent of willing to be saved. When that has happened, God will perfect that desire through grace. In fact, God is obliged to accept those who turn to him and who partake of the sacraments in the form in which they were instituted.

11. SC 66. *Opera*, II, 184: *"Ita ergo clamant haec omnia, sanguis fratris, fides matris, destitutio miseri, et miseria destituti. Et clamatur ad Patrem; porro Pater seipsum negare non potest: Pater est."* Cf. Epi 3, *Opera*, IV, 309, 5-18; V Nat 1, *Opera*, IV, 201, 20 -202, 15.

12. Gra 11, *Opera*, III, 191, 13-24: *"QUOD DEUS NEMINEM IUDICAT SALUTE DIGNUM, NISI QUEM INVENERIT VOLUNTARIUM.—Nam quod legitur in Evangelio: NEMO VENIT AD ME, NISI PATER MEUS TRAXERIT EUM, item in alio loco: COMPELLE INTRARE, nihil impedit, quia profecto quantoscumque trahere vel compellere videatur ad salutem benignus Pater, qui omnes vult salvos fieri, nullum tamen iudicat salute dignum, quem ante non probaverit voluntarium. Hoc quippe intendit, cum terret aut percutit, ut faciat voluntarios, non salvet invitos, quatenus dum de malo in bonum mutat voluntatem, transferat, non auferat libertatem. Quamquam tamen non semper inviti trahimur: nec enim caecus aut fessus contristatur cum trahitur. Et Paulus ad manus tractus est Damascum, utique non invitus. Trahi denique spiritualiter volebat, quae et hoc ipsum magnopere falgitabat in Canticis: TRAHE ME, ait, POST TE; IN ODOREM UNGUENTORUM TUORUM CURRIMUS."* Cf. V Nat 1, *Opera*, IV, 201-202.

13. For the later development of this view and for the meaning of the phrase *"facere quod in se est"* see: Paul Vignaux, *Justification et prédestination au XIVe siècle* (Paris, 1934); Werner Dettloff, *Die Lehre von der Acceptatio Divina bei Johannes Duns Scotus* (Werl i.W., 1954); Werner Dettloff, *Die Entwicklung der Akzeptations und Verdienstlehre von Duns Scotus bis Luther* (Münster i.W., 1963); Heiko Oberman, "Facientibus quod in se est Deus non denegat gratiam, Robert Holcot, O. P. and the Beginnings of Luther's Theology," *Harvard Theological Review* LV (1962): 317-342; Heiko Oberman, *The Harvest of Medieval Theology* (Cambridge, Mass, 1963); W. J. Courtenay, "Covenant and Causality in Pierre d'Ailly," *Speculum* XLVI (1971): 94-119.

14. Gra 11, *Opera*, III, 191; V Nat 1, *Opera*, IV, 201-202.

15. Bapt (PL 182:1036B-C).

The grace made available to man through the sacraments, therefore, operates according to a pact or covenant. If the sacraments are taken as a sign of the desire of the recipient to be saved, if a bad will or disbelief does not place a barrier in the way of their effectiveness, then grace will be effected in the recipient. The sacraments are thus visible signs that call forth the gift of grace on the basis of a value attributed to them by God.

When viewed against the background of Bernard's soteriology and the covenantal nature of man's relationship with God, the efficacy as well as the importance of the sacraments become apparent. But does this not mean that, for Bernard, the sacraments are only the accidental causes of grace, the signs or symbols that accompany or declare the gift of grace? [16]

To answer this question one must examine the language used by Bernard in the context of the early twelfth century. The investiture controversy, which came to a formal close in 1122, centered in part around the effective power of symbols and material substances of ascribed value. From the conceptual standpoint the reformers within the Hildebrandine party believed that the symbols of office used in the investiture ceremony possessed an efficacious power that should not be sullied by laymen's hands. If the solution to the investiture controversy lay in the ability to distinguish the temporal and spiritual aspects of ecclesiastical office and to attach particular symbols to those separate aspects, it nevertheless remained true that the valid possession of those symbols or the valid application of them automatically and irrevocably granted the recipient the right to the office and the power which that entailed. Although the symbols of office (unlike the relics of the saints) possessed no inherent 'virtue that caused their effect, they did infallibly cause or effect a particular result. From the standpoint of the world in which Bernard lived, ascribed virtue could be as effective as inherent virtue, and in the sacraments it was considered effective. The view that ascribed virtue was not sufficiently efficacious, a view held by many theologians

16. For the origin and development of the idea of accidental causality in the sacraments see: W. J. Courtenay, "The King and the Leaden Coin: The Economic Background of *Sine Qua Non* Causality," *Traditio* XXVIII (1972): 185-209.

in succeeding generations, resulted from an intellectual transformation that removed from the symbols of investiture the
power and significance they once had.

There is no direct line of continuity that runs from Bernard
to the major theories of sacramental causality developed in
the period from 1225 to 1250. The analogy constructed by
Bernard in his sermon was forgotten or ignored, even by those
who, like Richard Fishacre and Robert Kilwardby, adopted a
theory of covenantal, contractual or juridical causality that
closely approximated the ideas of Bernard. Bernard was not,
therefore, the inspiration for the theory of *sine qua non* causality that developed around 1240 in opposition to the physical-dispositive theory espoused by William of Auxerre, Alexander of Hales, Roland of Cremona, William of Melitona and
Albert the Great, and in opposition to the physical-instrumental theory of Stephen Langton and Hugh of St Cher. Even
Bonaventure, who extensively examines the various positions
and eventually subscribes to covenantal, or *sine qua non,* causality, does not refer to the passage in Bernard.[17]

The earliest appearance of the quotation from Bernard in
the context of sacramental causality occurs in the fourth book
of the *Sentences* commentary of Thomas Aquinas (a supporter
of inherent virtue) and thus seems to be introduced by the
opponents of *sine qua non* causality rather than its defenders.[18]
The Bernard quotation is given prominence as the first authority and first argument used to support the idea that the
sacraments are not causes of grace. After providing his solution to the problem, Thomas responds to the Bernardine quotation by saying that Bernard intended to show the similitude
of the sacraments to the symbols of investiture only in regard
to signification, for as signs of grace they are also (and Thomas
assumes Bernard shares his opinion) causes of grace.[19]

---

17. The development of theories of sacramental causality in the thirteenth century is traced elsewhere: W. J. Courtenay, "The King and the Leaden Coin."
   18. *Sent.* IV, d. 1, q. 1, a. 4, qu. 1 (Parma, 1858), VII.1, 460-463.
   19. Ibid., 463: "*Bernardus, ut ex praecedentibus ibidem patet, non intendit ostendere similitudinem sacramentorum ad illa, nisi quantum ad significationem:
quia anulus est signum et baculus, et similiter sacramenta; sed sacramenta ulterius
sunt causae.*"

It may well be that Thomas was the first to introduce the Bernard quotation and to associate it with a rejection of sacramental causality. The pro and con arguments used at the beginning of a question by a *sententiarius* did not necessarily reflect or accurately present the positions of certain contemporary or earlier theologians. These initial arguments were often of artificial design, a creation of the bachelor and purposely couched in extreme language to make the two sides of the question seem authoritative and mutually exclusive. It is certain that Thomas did not view Bernard as a supporter of either *sine qua non* causality or the view that the sacraments were not causes at all, two theories that were in Thomas' mind identical. But making Bernard initially *seem* to reject sacramental causality altogether, Thomas colored the way in which that quotation was read by succeeding theologians.

Two years after Thomas commented on the *Sentences*, Peter of Tarantasia, a fellow Dominican who later became Pope Innocent V, treated sacramental causality in his *Sentences* commentary and repeated the Bernard quotation.[20] He introduced the passage in a form almost identical with Thomas' presentation. Later in his discussion he stated that those who reject *sine qua non* causality in favor of instrumental causality (the position with which he agrees) would deal with the authority of Bernard by saying that Bernard was speaking about a difference between the various types of sacraments, not in the way they act.[21]

In his *Summa theologiae* Thomas returned to the problem of sacramental causality and again referred to the quotation from Bernard, this time with one important difference: the Bernard passage does not occur among the arguments at the beginning of the question but rather in the body of the solution, where it is directly associated with the theory of covenantal causality.[22] Moreover, Thomas makes no attempt to explain the passage or put Bernard in a better light. Perhaps

20. *Sent.* IV, d. 1, q. 1, a. 6, qu. 1 (Toulouse, 1651), IV, 11.

21. Ibid.: "*Similitudo beati Bernardi attenditur quoad differentiam sacramentorum agentium, non quoad modum agendi.*"

22. *Summa theologiae*, P. III, q. 62, a. 1 (Ottawa, 1944), IV: 2821b-2822a.

120   *Bernard of Clairvaux*

on rereading the Maundy Thursday sermon Thomas decided that Bernard had supported *sine qua non* causality.

Thomas's association of the Bernard quotation with the complete rejection of sacramental causality influenced subsequent discussion. No one after 1260, regardless of the stand they took on sacramental causality, tried to disassociate Bernard and the *sine qua non* view. Because of the association, *sine qua non* causality seemed like an ancient view, that is, a view maintained in the twelfth century. Moreover, the idea was repeated, from Thomas on, that the signs or symbols of investiture have no serious causal power but are only declarative signs, and thus if the sacraments were similar signs they also would have no causal power.

These views were maintained by those Thomists at the beginning of the fourteenth century who referred to the passage in Bernard and associated it with *sine qua non* causality. Peter Palude, reciting four opinions on sacramental causality, quotes Bernard as an authority who supports the *opinio antiqua* that the sacraments are the *sine qua non* causes of grace because they operate out of a pact or divine ordination.[23] John of Naples follows the same procedure as Peter Palude.[24]

Among the supporters of *sine qua non* causality, however, were those who happily used the authority of the Mellifluous Doctor in support of their theory. These included John of Bassoles[25] (normally considered a Scotist but, on this issue, a more enthusiastic supporter of *sine qua non* causality than was Scotus) and Durand of St Pourçain.[26] Durand was one of the few who did more than simply quote the passage from Bernard. He analyzed the passage and rejected the construction that Thomas had placed upon it in his *Sentences* commentary, arguing that Bernard had meant more than simply signification and had indeed described the whole relationship between the

23. *Sent.* IV, d. 1, q. 1 (Venice, 1493), IV, 2r-3v.
24. *Quaestiones variae Parisiis disputatae*, q. 33 (Naples, 1618), 284.
25. *Sent.* IV, d. 1, q. 1 (Paris, 1517) IV, 8v, 11v.
26. *Sent.* IV, d. 1, q. 4 (Venice, 1571), 290r.

sacraments and grace through his investiture analogy.[27] Peter Aureol used the Bernard quotation in the counterargument at the beginning of his discussion of sacramental causality in his *Sentences* commentary, and it seems to be this counterargument that most closely resembles the position he eventually favored.[28]

When the Bernard quotation occurs in discussions of sacramental causality from the middle of the fourteenth century on, it is used in ways that would have seemed strange in the thirteenth or early fourteenth centuries. For example, Peter of Aquila (Scotellus), writing around 1334, rejected *sine qua non* causality along with the quotation from Bernard, only to turn around and support a causality that operates *ex pactione virtus divina*.[29] Michael Aiguani, a mid-fourteenth-century Carmelite from Bologna, supported *sine qua non* causality and looked with favor on the passage from Bernard. However, he regarded the signs of sacramental and canonical investiture as signs that had only an exemplary value, a view that would have horrified most supporters of *sine qua non* causality.[30]

The majority of those who defended convenantal causality in the fourteenth and fifteenth centuries did not use the Bernardine passage, possibly because Thomas and others had brought it into disrepute, or possibly because they agreed with Thomas that the signs and symbols of investiture to office did not possess sufficient causal power, even ascribed power, to provide a good analogy for the operation of the sacraments. Among those espousing covenantal causality who did not refer to Bernard were: William of Ockham, Robert Holcot, Thomas of Strasbourg, Conrad of Ebrach, Marsilius of Inghen, Pierre d'Ailly and Gabriel Biel—in short, many of the major figures associated with late medieval Nominalism. Perhaps, had they had

27. Ibid.: *"Nec fit [Bernardus] ibi comparatio solum quantum ad significationem (ut quidam [i.e., Thomas and the Thomists] dicunt) sed quantum ad omnem habitudinem, quam habent sacramenta respectu gratiae, ut patet diligenter intuenti verba beati Bernardi, in illo sermone."*
28. *Sent.* IV, d. 1, q. 1, a. 1 (Rome, 1605) IV, 9.
29. *Sent.* IV, q. 3 (Speyer, 1480).
30. *Sent.* IV, d. 2, q. un., a. 1 (Venice, 1622), 344.

a more sophisticated understanding of the context in which Bernard was writing and of the world in which he lived, they might have found in his analogy an appropriate expression of the efficacy of *sine qua non* causality in the sacraments.

University of Wisconsin
Madison, Wisconsin

Reprinted by permission from
Bernard of Clairvaux: Studies presented to Dom Jean Leclercq.
© *Copyright Cistercian Publications Inc.,*
Kalamazoo, Michigan, 1973.

III

NATURE AND THE NATURAL
IN TWELFTH - CENTURY THOUGHT

Since the publication in 1927 of Charles Homer Haskins' The Renaissance of the Twelfth Century, the idea of revival has become something of a cliché in the description of twelfth-century society. Economic historians have seen in the period from 1050 to 1250 the commercial revolution that gave birth to the western European economy and ultimately dissolved the social and political structures of feudal society. Similarly, cultural historians have placed within those same years achievements of importance not only for medieval civilization but for the modern age as well. One need only recall the expansion of cathedral schools and the emergence of universities; the growing appreciation for the Latin classics or the translation of the philosophical works of Greek and Arabic civilizations, particularly the recovery of the Aristotelian corpus; the rise of dialectic and scholasticism; the development of medieval science; the growth in statutory law, political thought, and eventually representative institutions; the appearance of courtly literature; the art and architecture of the Romanesque and Gothic; and the gradual adoption of polyphonic music. The list is impressive and by no means exhaustive.

One theme that links several of these cultural achievements and reveals some underlying assumptions, perhaps even preconditions of change, is the more positive attitude toward nature and the natural in twelfth-century society. Behind the growing vitality of that society and economy lay an interest in and self-confidence about nature, both in the sense of immediate physical environment as well as the awesome canopy of the heavens and the entire macrocosm. It was a society that met the challenge of the forces of nature through technological innovations and architectural daring.[1] Yet at the same time the ways of nature were true and beautiful, worth observing and emulating. The joyful odes to spring, or the compatibility of human moods and seasonal change, or the positive, unabashed depiction of sexual pleasure found in Goliardic verse and romance literature are only the most striking examples. The tendency toward naturalism and realism in Gothic sculpture and the increased accuracy in manuscript illuminations of plant and animal life by the mid-thirteenth century are further evidence.[2]

As those examples suggest, the theme of twelfth-
century naturalism, has usually, and correctly, been
tied to the themes of humanism and humanness. Man as
measure and model has been found almost everywhere: in
art, literature, philosophy, even theology and political
thought. Well before the recovery of Aristotle's
Politics there was, as Gaines Post long since pointed
out, a concept of the naturalness of the state and the
use of the human form as an analogy for the body
politic.[3] R. W. Southern has made Anselm's theory of
atonement, with its heightened, active role for man, a
telling, early feature of the new age.[4]

Certain changes in the philosophical and theological understanding of the interaction of God, nature,
and man form the foundation for this new appreciation of
nature and the natural in the twelfth century. Moreover, the last years of the eleventh and the first half
of the twelfth century was the period in which these
conceptual changes were formulated. Some features of
the story are familiar territory, especially after the
work of Chenu.[5] But other features may be new to the
reader, particularly the stages in the conceptual
conquest of nature.

Changing Attitudes Toward Nature

The medieval view of nature before the twelfth
century had elements in common with the animism of more
primitive societies. Even within the educated circles
of early medieval society nature possessed a numinous,
mythopoeic quality. Nature was a mixture of forces
beyond human understanding and control from which the
realm of man was not always clearly distinguished.
These forces inhabited the forests and wilderness that
surrounded villages and separated one community from
another. They could reduce the food supply through
drought and flood. They could strike at the family
through the death of infants or the barrenness of wives.
The forces of nature, awesome and terrifying in the
extent of their power, erratic and unpredictable in
their behavior, dwarfed human activity and made life
precarious. Apart from the regularity of the seasons
(which did not by itself guarantee the fecundity of the
soil), there was little idea of an orderly course of
nature. Natural forces were to be feared and appeased
through religious cult and the benevolent activity of

the saints. What later generations would consider natural phenomena, from the birth of a child to the growth of plants and crops, were objects of wonder and mystery. Nature was the realm of the marvelous; it was semi-divine.[6]

By the opening years of the twelfth century a different conception of man's physical environment began to emerge. The element of wonder and mystery remained, but it was gradually reduced to the level of respect, or admiration. The new element was the increased appreciation for the regularity of nature, the orderly working of what appeared to be fixed principles, or laws, that could be studied and whose behavior could be predicted.

There were many works within the legacy of the late antique and early medieval periods that served to reinforce the idea of an ordered and orderly universe, and twelfth-century writers did not fail to repeat and rephrase the ideas found in those works. The concept of the harmony of the spheres, musica mundana, was readily accessible in the sixth book of Cicero's Republic or Boethius' De musica and De consolatione philosophiae. The relation of mathematics and musical harmony, supported by the authority of Pythagoras, remained the principal model for the orderliness and homogeneity of nature.

One of the best expressions of that idea in the twelfth century comes from the pen of Honorius of Autun (active 1098-1140).

> For the supreme craftsman constructed the universe like a great lute on which, as it were, he placed various strings to produce a multiplicity of different sounds, for he divided his universe into two parts contrary to each other. For spirit and body join together in the essence of good, like a chorus of men and boys who, while different in nature, blend their bass and treble voices.
>
> Similarly, material things imitate different voices; while they are separated into various genera and species, into individuals, forms, and numbers, they blend harmoniously, for they serve laws implanted within them. The sound of harmony: spirit and body, angel and devil, heaven and hell, fire and water, air and earth, sweet and bitter, soft and hard, and the rest in this manner.[7]

The proportion and harmony of the physical universe
were not based solely on the relationship of mathematics
and music. They were also part of a hierarchical view
of the created order in which each element had its
proper place and function. Neoplatonism, the predominant philosophical tradition within early medieval
society (albeit limited to a clerical elite), was the
major source of this hierarchical view of the universe.
It was passed on to the twelfth century through a
variety of works, the most significant being those of
Augustine, Boethius, and Dionysius the Pseudo-Areopagite
(as translated by John Scotus Erigena). Within the Neoplatonic hierarchy evil was reduced to the status of
non-being, a turning-away from the Good toward which all
creation properly yearned. The ultimate purpose of
creation, therefore, was to be reunited with the Good,
and this understanding, in turn, gave an ontological and
teleological dimension to the orderliness of nature.
After the appearance of Scotus Erigena's De divisione
naturae, composed around 865, no single term better
summarized the grand design of the Neoplatonic vision
than the term Natura.

1. The Personification of Nature

Some elements compatible with an earlier animism
are in evidence in the newer attitude toward nature.
Nature remained alive and active, and man's contact with
nature still possessed aspects of an "I-Thou" relationship. The autonomous and irrational forces of
nature were, however, reduced in number, and nature
became one rather than many. As the pattern of nature
became more apparent, it seemed less a strange force,
antipathetic to man. It came to have a personality, the
personality of a woman, a mother.[8]
The direction of this development was dictated by
several factors. The Pelasgian heritage of fertility
religion and mother-cult thrived easily in a peasant,
agricultural society, and it is hard to imagine that
nature could have been personified apart from female
characteristics. Moreover, inasmuch as the concept of
nature in the twelfth century was articulated by an
educated and literate group, "Dame Nature" inherited the
role of the benevolent, semi-divine, spiritual adviser,
Sophia from Boethius' Consolation of Philosophy. The
dialogue structure of that and similar works -
contrived dialogues between one who was wise,

knowledgeable, sympathetic, and one who was younger in
years and learning - helped cast Nature into the role
of master and tutor to man, the willing and eager pupil.
Nature thus became man's teacher, a Sophia in other
dress.

The most important element in dictating the personality and behavior of Dame Nature, however, was her
association with the Neoplatonic World-Soul, the third
person of the Plotinian triad. As the human soul
inhabited and animated the body, so too the World-Soul
inhabited and animated the physical universe. The world
was not inanimate but alive. Nature, as World-Soul, was
both creator and creature. Through natura God had
created the universe, and the presence of the World-Soul
in nature made it both active and semi-divine. [9]

If certain elements of the Neoplatonic world view
continued to support the early medieval idea of nature
as a living force (although in a more sophisticated
form), other elements helped establish the orderliness
and predictability of nature. The hierarchical view of
the universe and the reduction of evil to non-being
certainly aided in this task. Even the personification
of nature gave to it a personality and a behavior that
could be studied with regard to motivation, intention,
repetition of action, and predictability. Nature was
not only a living person; nature was an orderly,
consistent, and predictable friend.

Personification reshaped and focused answers to the
question of what caused or lay behind physical change.
Change was not haphazard and chaotic, nor was it the
product of multiple capricious wills, acting in
different ways at different times. Nature was orderly
and unified, the result of forces working harmoniously
under the direction of a superior power. The personification of nature can be viewed as the first stage
in the desacralization of nature, in the movement from
an animistic to a scientific attitude toward the
physical environment. The numinous, divine qualities of
nature were reduced. Dame Nature was not God, but
rather God's vicar. The basic difference between God
and the created order, so strongly stressed in the
Augustinian tradition, was generally acknowledged.

But for most twelfth-century thinkers, God was not
the sole creator. Creation was a shared activity,
transferred down through the hierarchy of being. As
late as Alan of Lille's Anticlaudianus (written between
1181 and 1184) it is Natura, not God, who initiates the
plan to create the "perfect man," and the capacity to

create everything but the soul lies with the powers of nature.[10] This delegated power to create had a venerable history. It was an assumption encountered throughout Neoplatonic metaphysics and enshrined in Erigena's formulation: that which is created and creates. Despite the incompatibility between that view and the idea of the direct and exclusive creativity of God, it was not fully · abandoned until the Aristotelianism of the early thirteenth century provided scholars with a different model.[11] Yet misgivings were voiced already by the second quarter of the twelfth century by those more firmly attached to the Augustinian tradition. Objections to the perceived erosion of God's direct, creative control of the universe were first voiced not in the context of delegated creativity but because of the gradual removal of any volitional personality from behind the events and sequences of everyday life.

The personification of nature persisted throughout the twelfth century. Toward the end of that period it found one of its most forceful expressions in Alan of Lille's De planctu naturae, where Nature rails against those who misuse her bounty through unnatural acts. But even as that work reflects, Dame Nature was becoming more of a literary device than a conceptual tool useful in understanding the physical universe. Within the area of natural philosophy, for which nature was the direct object of study, the predominant tendency was toward the depersonalization and objectification of nature.

2. The Objectification of Nature

The desacralization of nature, a process through which man came to believe he could understand, predict, and control nature, can be found at levels of twelfth-century society below that of the intellectual elite. A more positive and optimistic attitude toward the physical environment, the belief that initiative would be rewarded more often than frustrated, was a conceptual presupposition for the agricultural and commercial revolutions. If nature thus became less mysterious, it also became less superior to man. Nature as God, then as master and teacher, was on the way to becoming the servant of man. The development of a scientific attitude and the assimilation of a body of knowledge that can be called science was one of the major products of the desacralization and objectification of nature.

At the heart of this objective view of nature lay the recognition of ordered sequences that repeated themselves and conformed to what were understood as laws of nature. Whatever the original connection between God's will and these laws, the latter were often seen to operate by themselves, devoid of divine participation. Earth was the realm of "cursus naturae nostrasque vices," as Alan of Lille expressed it.[12] Divine activity was limited to the initial stage of creation and to miraculous interventions that suspended the "common course of nature". The laws of nature needed no internal volitional power to effect their operation. They were self-sufficient, self-contained.

Regularity and order were the aspects of nature that permitted it to become an object of scientific study -- and eventually robbed it of its personal qualities and threatened to rob it of divine causality. The order established by God and reflected in nature was contrasted with the unorderliness of the chaos that supposedly pre-existed the divine creative action. Ex inordinata iactatione redegit in ordinem.[13] The thought is Plato's, but it is also twelfth century. How primordial matter and chaos were to be understood, however, was another question. In some versions unformed matter had its own laws and structure built into it, and the process of creation was seen as a natural development that produced actuality from possibility and aptitude. God was not so much creator as arranger of the inherent potentialities of the universe, orchestrating the unfolding drama of creation. The view of the physical world as an ordered whole, the domain of repetitive sequences, of laws of nature, patterns of causality, behind which stood in some sense the original causal power of God, found additional support with the recovery of the physical and biological works of Aristotle.

The universe could at times be viewed as a machine, an intricate contrivance by God, having no volition or motivation of its own but operating according to fixed laws, or principles. The term machina, whether applied to the universe (mundana machina) or to the human body (machina corporea), primarily described the intricacy of the structure. But the term also suggested a certain degree of self-sufficiency. It implied that the working parts, so beautifully and cleverly wrought, appeared to operate without the continual and direct presence and activity of the designer. Although the references to

III

- 8 -

nature as a **machina** can be found throughout the twelfth
century, sometimes occurring side by side with
references to Dame Nature, the view of nature as a
machina becomes more frequent in the course of the
century and in some circles, under the influence of the
writings of Avicenna, takes on aspects almost of Deism
by the opening years of the thirteenth century.[14]

3. **Deo nihil detraho**: The Contest of Nature and God

The birth of scientific inquiry in the twelfth
century and the explanation of natural phenomena as
simple cause-effect relationships, not actions of a
volitional spirit, did not develop without misgivings
and criticism. As the frequent defenses of a rational
explanation of natural phenomena reflect, there were
those strongly opposed to the study of nature,
especially the type of study that seemed to remove
direct, divine action from the daily life of man. If
the events and changes of nature were not the result of
the miraculous action of God, then where was God's
presence in the world observable? If one carried the
explanation of phenomena to a naturalistic extreme,
would that not make divine causality and creativity
unnecessary? Where would God's actions become visible?
Where would divine power and will interact with man in a
personal way?
It is difficult to know how serious or real was the
threat of natural determinism, where a rational explanation of nature excluded all forms of divine action.[15]
Many of the discussions of creation and nature utilized
Plato's **Timaeus** which gave at least a semi-autonomous
role to Nature. The frequent attempts to understand
Plato's **Timaeus** in light of Genesis seem from the view
of a later age to compromise both texts. Despite the
Augustinian affirmation of creation **ex nihilo**, one
encounters in the texts of the early twelfth century a
notion that nature and primordial matter coexisted with
God although beneath and dependent on him in the order
of being. Before creation there was the unformed chaos
of primal matter: necessary and unwilled. God was, in a
sense, confined from the very beginning within the
limits of the properties possessed by pre-existing
matter. God's creative activity, expressed through
Noys, may have consisted only in ordering things that
already existed. Divine creativity could be viewed as
analogous to human decision-making and creative

activity, where the boundaries of the problem and the possible solutions are limited. Even the theme of the music of the spheres suggests that God only harmonized things that had their own pre-existing properties.

Moreover, elements persisted of the Neoplatonic view of "creation" as impersonal, unwilled emanation in which the important creative forces are passed downwards in the hierarchy of being to the World Soul, sometimes identified with the Holy Spirit.[16] One might even enlist the support of Augustine's rationes seminales through which the plan of God for creation is worked out. The world so viewed is as much the product of the creative activity of nature as of God. Once the process of creation had begun, subsequent events and subsequent changes were in the hands of Nature, which oversaw the working out of God's plan and which ultimately might be viewed less as a personal force and more as an impersonal machina that operated according to immutable, involuntary laws.

It is equally difficult to determine who were the critics of all forms of rational, natural explanation. Some contemporaries referred to them as theologians with a peasant mentality.[17] This group may have included members of the School of Anselm of Laon, which considered theology to be the exegesis of Scripture and which took a biblicistic approach to nature. Theologians of this tradition concentrated on the supreme cause and on miracles (both biblical and contemporary) and discredited inquiries into "natural causes" or the reasons for the regularity and proportionality of the physical universe. The Cistercian critic of William of Conches, William of St. Thierry, should probably be placed within this group.[18] But it is difficult to know even in the case of William of St. Thierry whether one is dealing with theologians who refused to examine nature or speculate on secondary causality, or with theologians who were just attacking the more extreme idea that the laws of nature are absolute and eternal, uncreated by God, sufficient in themselves, both as a rational explanation for the operation and origin of things and as a principle that makes God into an arranger rather than a creator.

In defense of the rational investigation of nature and natural phenomena a number of formulations or conceptual tools were worked out to solve the seeming conflict between natural causality and divine action. The first of these was the idea of double causality, simultaneously operating in the same event. Discussions

of natural, secondary causality in no way detracted from
the ultimate power and dignity of God. There were,
indeed, two causes of events: an immediate natural
cause, which we observe, and the ultimate sustaining
causality of God, which lies behind the natural cause,
hidden from our eyes. Furthermore, even the most ardent
supporters of rational explanations admitted the possibility of direct, miraculous action as well, although
they tended to limit it severely. Thus, in addition to
the orderly course of nature, whose behavior could be
understood and predicted, God could temporarily suspend
some natural operation for a purpose in keeping with his
overall, providential design. The concepts of an
orderly universe and the possibility of miracles were
not contradictory, and that realization was not an
achievement of the thirteenth century but of Christian
thinkers a century earlier.

Both of these ideas are entailed in the famous
reply of Adelard of Bath:

> I do not detract from God. For whatever is, is
> from Him and because of Him. But nature is
> not confused and without system, and so far as
> human knowledge has progressed it should be
> given a hearing. Only when it fails utterly
> should there be recourse to God i.e.,
> explaining phenomena through direct divine
> intervention .[19]

William of Conches made a similar reply to his
critics:

> But someone will say: "Is it not the Creator's
> work that man is born from man?" To which I
> reply: I do not remove anything from God.[20]

The same approach was applied to the exegesis of
Scripture by Andrew of St. Victor:

> If he resort to the argument that divine
> omnipotence can do what nature cannot, enable a
> man to direct his gaze through the heavens and
> beyond them, we know that with God nothing is
> impossible and in no wise gainsay it. But he
> should realize this: in expounding Scripture,
> when the event described admits of no natural
> explanation, then and only then should we have
> recourse to miracles.[21]

The distinction between primary and secondary causality, however, did not completely solve the conflict occasioned by the natural, rational explanation for a miraculous event. To solve this difficulty a distinction was made between Nature, understood as the providential plan of God, coterminous with his will, and the common course of nature, understood as the way things normally, or usually, operate. God never acts against nature in the first sense, since what he has willed, he has willed from all eternity. But God, as part of that providential plan, can intervene .occasionally in the common course of nature to reveal his power and grace. Miracles in this sense do not upset the orderliness of the larger plan of nature, since they are only occasional and always part of God's design. Miraculous interventions are planned by God from eternity but hidden from man; they do not represent any change in God's will. Miracles, therefore, are not against nature or contrary to nature in the larger sense because they suspend only the operation of a particular law of nature and only temporarily; the full plan of nature is consonant with the total will of God.[22]

In order to further protect the orderly operation of the physical world while yet acknowledging the full freedom of divine omnipotence, early twelfth-century theologians developed a third distinction, namely between capacity and volition. The structure of the world in which we live, the ways God has chosen to act, did not exhaust divine capacity, the possibilities open to God. That idea, partially or dimly formulated by Anselm in Cur Deus Homo, was refined in the early twelfth century and codified by Peter Lombard in the text of the Libri quatuor sententiarum.[23] It was an idea attractive even to the more philosophizing of that age. William of Conches, after attacking those who did not adequately distinguish between those things that lie within the ability of God (those things he could have done or theoretically could do) and those things God has done, is doing, and will do, stated: "God does not do everything he is able to do. To use a peasant's words, Can God make a calf from a tree trunk? Has he ever done it?"[24] In contrast to those theologians who were overly concerned about protecting divine omnipotence, William suggests that to postulate contradictions of nature outside the context of a recorded miracle (although theoretically possible) is a waste of time.

The importance of these distinctions for the development of medieval theology was crucial. A new understanding of the relationship of God and nature had emerged and would continue to dominate the thinking on these issues throughout the thirteenth and fourteenth centuries. The orderliness of the universe was now seen as the result of an order God had imposed, an ordination based on the volitional but consistent plan of God. Even miracles were brought within the control of God's ordained will, which was immutable and eternal. Outside the ordination stood the possibilities God might have chosen; at the heart of that ordination was the common course of nature which could be relied upon, even when temporarily disturbed. As Arnold of Bonneval, a friend of Bernard of Clairvaux and a firm believer in the possibility of miracles, remarked: "the entire fabric of the world continues in its lawful and ordered way, solid, harmonious, and with no dread prospect of ruin."[25]

The Validation of the Natural Man

The restructuring of views on physical nature was only part of the naturalism of the twelfth century. Equally important was the understanding of human nature, of man in nature, and of what was natural to man. The exploration of the physical universe was inevitably conducted in consort with an exploration of human nature and of the relationship of man and his environment.

What was natural, in the sense of being orderly and customary, about the physical world -- the natural as opposed to the supernatural or preternatural -- was echoed in what was natural to man. Miraculous and preternatural explanations both in physical nature and in human relations gave way to more rational explanations. For man himself, there was an increasing appreciation for what was "natural" in human behavior apart from grace, an appreciation for the basic drives and desires of men. In spite of the reluctance of the Augustinian tradition to recognize much value in human life and institutions after the Fall, apart from grace, there was sufficient support in the twelfth century for an upward re-evaluation of the natural man in a natural world.

At first glance it would seem that there was much in the philosophical and theological heritage of the early Middle Ages that would have discouraged any such optimism and concentration on the natural. Both Augustinianism and the Neoplatonic tradition -- the two most

important parts of that intellectual heritage -- had
something of an anti-natural bias. The Platonic and
Augustinian epistemology downgraded the world of sense
experience in favor of innate ideas that are perceived
within the human mind, aided by divine illumination.
Moreover, the stress on contemplation and mystical
ascent was strong in these traditions, encouraging man
to separate himself from matter and the evils of this
world in order to ascend toward mystical union with God,
or the One. Although tempered somewhat in his later
writings, Augustine was associated with the view that
sexual desire was in itself sinful and a punishment for
sin, the burden of concupiscence that had been placed on
man after the Fall. What virtue had man apart from
divine grace? What chance of salvation apart from the
predestination of God? Even the state, the governing
institution of man, was a necessary evil, a negative
blessing, instituted by God to curb the worst instincts
of man's corrupt nature after the Fall.

There were aspects of the Neoplatonic and
Augustinian traditions, however, that encouraged a more
optimistic evaluation of nature and man. We have
already seen in the discussion of physical nature how
that optimistic view was built in part on elements in
the Neoplatonic worldview, especially the theme of an
ordered hierarchy of beings directed ultimately toward
the good, as found in the writings of Dionysius the
Pseudo-Areopagite and John Scotus Erigena. We should
not forget that the investigation of nature in the early
twelfth century was not anti-religious or irreligious.
Rather, it was an inquiry conducted with great piety,
based on the principle that to detract from the per-
fection of creation was to detract from the Creator.
God had given man senses and a mind through which he was
to inquire into the things that God had created and the
laws that God had established for governing the universe. A new evaluation of nature thus was inextricably
tied up with a new evaluation of man.

1. <u>Macrocosm - Microcosm</u>: Nature as Image of Man

For the twelfth century, man and nature, man and
the cosmos, were joined together through direct continuity. Man not only studied nature; man <u>was</u> nature.
At the heart of the recognition that man was part
of nature lay the realization that man was body, matter,
as well as spirit. If Neoplatonism tended to dema-

terialize the process of the return of all creation
toward union with the One, the opening chapter of
Genesis and the belief in the resurrection supported the
basic goodness of matter and its final inclusion within
the redemptive process. As Alan of Lille, toward the
end of the century, expressed it: "It was fitting that
corporeal as well as incorporeal nature should
participate in the divine goodness, should enjoy it and
live happily."[26]

The structure, the symmetry of the human body,
established a second point of contact, or continuity,
with nature. Man found in himself the same order of
parts to the whole, the same purposeful harmony, that he
found in external nature. Man was not only the imago
Dei; he was also the imago mundi.

It was particularly in the mind of man, in his
rational faculty, that he most closely resembled the
order of God's universe. It was that very unity,
continuity, or similarity that permitted man to study
the nature that surrounded him. The laws of nature,
according to which the physical world operated, were
paralleled by the law of nature within man, written upon
his heart. The understanding of natural law in man,
with its foundation in Roman law and patristic theology,
began to receive a more definitive and detailed
treatment in the twelfth century.

The symbiotic relationship between man and nature
extended even into the arena of moral action, since for
many writers, especiallly the Porretani (the disciples
of Gilbert de la Porree), it was Dame Nature who granted
virtue to men. Seen in this way, the moral life was yet
another instance of the life of nature, of the universe.

Although the theme of man as a little cosmos, man
as microcosm, was not treated in the writings of the
more traditional theologians of the early twelfth
century, such as those connected with Laon or Rheims,
nor by the so-called Augustinians, such as Hugh of St.
Victor, Peter Lombard, and Peter of Poitiers, it had
numerous exponents. One of the earliest references to
the concept occurs in the Elucidarium of Honorius of
Autun.

> Whence came the corporeal substance used in
> man's creation? From the four elements, and for
> this reason man is called a microcosm, that is,
> a lesser world; for from the earth he has his
> flesh, from water his blood, from air his
> breath, and from fire his warmth.[27]

In addition to the references to man as microcosm
found in William of Conches, Bernard Silvester, Gilbert
de la Porree, and the _Porretani_, especially Alan of
Lille, one of the last major theologians of the
Victorine school, Godfrey of St. Victor, wrote an entire
work entitled _Microcosmos_.[28]

2. _Viator in naturalibus_: The Natural Man in Theology

The natural virtues, namely those virtues that man
possesses on the basis of his created nature apart from
grace, took on new status in the twelfth century. The
Augustinian tradition, which defined true virtue only in
terms of man redeemed, infused by the supernatural gift
of grace, continued to find spokesmen within monastic
communities and among the heirs to the teaching of
Anselm of Laon and William of Champeaux: the Victorines
at Paris, the influential Peter Lombard, and Peter of
Poitiers.[29] Other theologians, however, took a more
favorable view of the virtues exemplified in un-
regenerated pagans, men unredeemed. Man as originally
created was not fully corrupted by the Fall, in spite of
what the Augustinian heritage might suggest. The
natural virtues of temperance, fortitude, magnaminity,
prudence, or justice were virtues that pagans possessed
and through which even man unredeemed could con-
structively contribute to the life around him. These
natural virtues might be enhanced through the supernatural infusion of charity when one became a Christian,
but they existed as part of the natural state of man and
did not require divine renewal in order to operate for
the improvement of society.
     The elevation in status of the natural virtues owed
much to the teaching activity of Peter Abelard. During
the 1130s in a number of works Abelard scrutinized the
ethical teaching of the pagan philosophers and developed
the notion that virtue was a habit of the mind, acquired
by individual effort, which in turn transforms the human
soul.[30] Despite the criticisms leveled by William of
St. Thierry, Thomas of Morigny, Bernard of Clairvaux,
and eventually Peter Lombard, the views of Abelard on
ethics and virtue were circulated and given continued
life by his disciples, particularly by Roland Bandinelli
and Omnebene of Verona.[31] Similar views on natural
virtue were held by the disciples and "school" of
Gilbert de la Porree, particularly Simon of Tournai,
Alan of Lille, Godfrey of Poitiers, Stephen Langton, and

Praepositinus.[32] How much of this teaching came
directly from Gilbert or was borrowed directly or
indirectly from Abelard is hard to determine, since the
extant writings of Gilbert include very little on the
subject of political and moral virtues. Among the
Porretani these natural virtues come to be known as the
political virtues in contrast to the Christian (or
theological) virtues of faith, hope, and love. One
should not gain the impression that there are two sets
of virtues, one natural and the other supernatural.
Political virtues become Christian virtues under the
influence of grace. There is one habitus of virtue
which at times is directed toward rational motives --
and as such is completely the work of man -- and at
other times, under the influence of grace in the
infusion of love, or charity, is directed toward God and
is meritorious of eternal life.

The reappraisal of human virtue was only part of a
more naturalistic ethical theory. Almost universal to
theologians of the twelfth century, whether imbued with
Augustinian perspectives or not, was the attempt to
explain human psychology in rational terms, to explain
why man felt himself to be the author of his own
actions, and to give those actions value with regard to
their motivation or intent. Both Abelard and the
Porretani stressed intent in their analyses of moral
behavior.[33] Motivation for action, the intention to do
good or evil, was more important to God than the act
itself, although church and society looked closely at
the deeds performed. Good deeds done by accident,
without just intention, were morally worthless. Evil
deeds done unintentionally would be forgiven, at least
by God if not by the state, church, or the kindred of
the one injured. Even Peter Lombard, who refused to
acknowledge any meritorious moral act that was not a
result of the indwelling Holy Spirit in the Christian,
argued that we feel ourselves to be the author of our
own moral actions because the Holy Spirit, the gift of
uncreated grace, lies within us and is not a force from
outside man.[34]

The concern for the natural man in Abelard and the
Porretani can also be seen in their attitude toward the
process of salvation. Against the Augustinian teaching
that man could never, in and of himself, initiate the
return to God (although once grace were given he could
cooperate with it), these theologians took a more
human-centered approach. For Abelard the desire for the
supreme good and the human effort that creates virtue

and leaves its mark on the soul are crucial elements in
man's ability to earn eternal life.[35] These views were
worked out in more juridical detail by the Porretani.
Ex puris naturalibus (out of man's pure nature apart
from grace) man could complete morally good acts which,
in turn, would require, through a debt of moral
obligation on God's part, the divine gift of grace and,
through cooperation with God, the ultimate gift of
eternal life. Within this teaching the dignity of man
was raised to a level that appalled Peter Lombard and
other twelfth-century "Augustinians". But, regardless
of opposition, this teaching attracted a wide following
in subsequent centuries, particularly among Franciscan
theologians.[36]

The doctrine of atonement is another area of
twelfth-century theology in which one can witness the
validation of the natural man. It was Anselm who
revived the view of the early Latin Father, Tertullian,
that the Fall of Man resulted not in the enslavement of
man by the Devil but in the broken pact or covenant
between man and God, an act of betrayal through which
man affronted the dignity and honor of God.[37] Anselm
understood the atonement for that sin -- an atonement
through the crucifixion of Christ -- to be an act of man
repaying God as much as it was an act of God forgiving
and saving man. With Anselm the Devil ceased to be a
significant character in the drama; man and God faced
each other directly in a legal dispute whose solution
was as predictable as it was necessary. Man was no
longer the inactive prize in a contest between God and
the Devil. Man had grown considerably in stature and
played his part in the drama of redemption through the
human nature of Christ.

The emphasis on the human and natural dimensions of
the redemptive act increased in the course of the
twelfth century. As the supernatural event of the
resurrection of Christ receded in significance in
Anselm's teaching before the more corporeal and human-
centered events of the incarnation and crucifixion, so
in both Peter Abelard and Bernard of Clairvaux one finds
increased attention given to the redemptive function
(through moral persuasion) of the human life of
Christ.[38] Although the image of the crucifixion
remained a major religious symbol for the twelfth and
thirteenth centuries and even grew in visual and
ritualistic importance in the late medieval period (one
should not forget that it depicts Christ's human
suffering), the acts and moral teaching from the life of

Christ as recorded in the Gospels exercised a force in
lay and urban piety, a potential model for the life of
love and virtue. Man returns to God through practicing
the forms of love expressed in Christ's earthly
ministry.

The foundations for the scholastic views on the
interaction of God, nature, and man were established in
the first half of the twelfth century. Most aspects of
that achievement were passed on to the thirteenth and
fourteenth centuries -- even the conflicting views over
the moral capacity of man after the Fall. Yet the
Neoplatonic assumptions on which much of that inquiry
was based were suppressed in the early thirteenth
century, partly because they were out-of-keeping with
much of Aristotelian philosophy then being studied and
assimilated for the first time, partly because the
pantheistic and emanationist elements could no longer be
easily fused with Christian theology or ignored. In
1210 at Paris pantheism was condemned along with John
Scotus Erigena's De divisione naturae -- an event that
condemned certain elements in the Neoplatonic view of
the universe, of creation, and of nature that had been
common to many writers of the early twelfth century.
The Parisian condemnation of 1210 was reflective of
change rather than a determining factor. It coincided
with several other important events or intellectual
shifts. Between 1197 and 1210 a generation of pro-
ductive and influential theologians died, men whose
views reflected many of the achievements and tensions of
twelfth-century approaches to nature: Peter Cantor,
Joachim of Fiore, Alan of Lille, Stephen of Tournai,
Peter of Poitiers, and Praepositinus. The idealization
of the Apostolic life, with its accent on poverty and
Christian witness to and within a secular and increasingly urbanized world (anticipated already in the
views of Atonement taken by Peter Abelard and Bernard of
Clairvaux) altered religious sentiment and monastic life
in the thirteenth century. 1210 is, significantly, the
date of the approval of the Franciscan order by Innocent
III. The opening years of the thirteenth century also
saw a change in the curriculum of the Arts Faculty at
the University of Paris along with a change in the style
and method of scholastic treatises -- both precipitated
and nourished by the introduction of Aristotle's
writings. After 1210 one finds few vestiges of the idea
of creation through emanation, the hymns to nature and

to the harmony of the spheres, the poetic approach to
philosophical writing, or the attitude toward nature so
characteristic of the twelfth century. The increased
sophistication of philosophic and theological speculation produced a specialization that discouraged the
continuing development of teachers of philosophy who
were also men-of-letters. Literature, whether the
product of a St. Francis, a Jean de Meun, a Gottfried
von Strassburg, or a Petrarch, was produced by men who
had neither training nor insight into the development of
logic and scholastic theology, as these came to be
handled in the schools and universities of Europe.
Apart from such rare instances as Thomas Aquinas'
sequence, Lauda sion salvatorem, it is hard to think of
a thirteenth- or fourteenth-century scholastic whose
writings might also be considered literature. Alan of
Lille, who died in 1203, was perhaps the last
"schoolman" who was also a capable and respected poet.

Although the understanding of man and nature became
increasingly more complex in the thirteenth and fourteenth centuries, the themes and conceptual advances of
the twelfth remained the foundation. The continuity of
physical nature and human nature remained a literary
theme and had its own following in the realm of science
and the occult. The objectification of nature and the
theories of causality, particularly those aimed at
resolving the conflicts between divine omnipotence and
the orderly course of nature were never abandoned. By
the late thirteenth century few scholastics would
recognize the extent of their debt in this regard to the
writers of the early twelfth century. Anselm was
pillaged for authoritative statements; Abelard was
forgotten; the Porretani were theologically suspect from
all sides. It is nevertheless true that later
scholastics would not have written as they did without
the conceptual framework achieved in the years between
Anselm of Bec and Alan of Lille.

III

Notes

1. For the early stages in the process of "harnessing nature" see Lynn White, Jr., Medieval Technology and Social Change (London, 1965), and Jean Gimpel, The Medieval Machine (New York, 1976).

2. An excellent though somewhat later example of naturalistic illumination is the Vatican Codex Ms. Pal. Lat. 1071: The Falcon Book, De arte venandi cum avibus, of Frederick II, now available in a facsimile edition with commentary by C. A. Willemsen, Das Falkenbuch Kaiser Friedrichs II, Codices e Vaticanis Selecti, Vol. 31 (Graz, 1969; separate printing Dortmund, 1980). On the subject of gothic realism see Max Dvořák, Idealism and Naturalism in Gothic Art (Notre Dame, 1967).

3. "The Naturalness of Society and the State," in G. Post, Studies in Medieval Legal Thought (Princeton, 1964), pp. 494-561.

4. In particular see R. W. Southern, The Making of the Middle Ages (New Haven, 1953) and Medieval Humanism and Other Studies (New York, 1970).

5. M.-D. Chenu, La théologie au douzième siècle (Paris, 1957), translated by Jerome Taylor and Lester Little as Nature, Man, and Society in the Twelfth Century (Chicago, 1968). Among the earlier literature see: E. Gilson, "Humanisme médiéval et renaissance," in Les idées et les lettres (Paris, 1932), 171-196; J. M. Parent, La doctrine de la création dans l'école de Chartres (Paris, 1938). A larger number of texts have subsequently become available through the efforts of M.-T. d'Alverny, Nicholas Häring, and Theodore Silverstein.

6. On earlier conceptions of nature see Marc Bloch, Feudal Society (Chicago, 1961), pp. 72-75; G. Boas, Essays on Primitivism and related ideas in the Middle Ages (Baltimore, 1948); William J. Brandt, The Shape of Medieval History: Studies in Modes of Perception (New Haven, 1966); Joel L. Bender, "Religion and Causality in Three Chroniclers of the First Feudal Age," unpublished master's thesis, University of Wisconsin (Madison, 1974).

7. Honorius of Autun, Liber XII quaestionum, ch. 2 (PL 172, 1179). Honorius also excerpted a large section of Scotus Erigena's De divisione naturae under the title Clavis physicae, ed. P. Lucentini (Rome, 1974).

8. See the discussion of Dame Nature in Chenu, Nature, Man, and Society, 18-24.

9. Manuscript illuminations of the anima mundi show a female figure. See for example Paris, Bibl. nat. lat. 6734, fol. 1ᵛ.

10. Alain de Lille, Anticlaudianus, ed. R. Bossuat (Paris, 1955); Engl. transl. by J. Sheridan (Toronto, 1973). Earlier in Bernard Silvester's Cosmographia one finds the view that the initial decision for creation comes from Natura and the yearnings of matter (Silva); see Brian Stock, Myth and Science in the Twelfth Century (Princeton, 1972), and Winthrop Wetherbee, The "Cosmographia" of Bernardus Silvestris (New York, 1973).

11. The question of whether the power to create could be communicated to a creature continued to receive attention well into the late Middle Ages. It was discussed by, among others, William of Ockham (Quodl. II, q. 9; Sent. II, q. 7), Walter Chatton (Sent. II, q. 1 = Principium quarti), Robert Holcot (Sent. IV, q. 1, ad 3 prin.), Adam Wodeham (Sent IV, q. 1), Marsilius of Inghen (Sent. IV, q. 1, a. 3), and Pierre d'Ailly (Sent. IV, q. 1, a. 2).

12. Anticlaudianus, VI, vv. 173-74 (p. 146). The idea of a "solitus cursus naturae" was available to twelfth-century writers in Augustine's Contra Faustum and elsewhere.
Earlier William of Conches had restricted direct divine creativity to the first moment of creation ("sine praeiacente materia ut est creatio elementorum et spirituum") or to miraculous events ("contra consuetum cursum naturae"). The physical features of our universe are inherent and work themselves out of matter through the agency of nature. See William of Conches, Glossae super Platonem, ed. E. Jeauneau (Paris, 1965), pp. 104, 116-19, 122-23. Clarembald of Arras affirmed that primordial matter descends from God and therefore is not coeternal with him; Tractatulus super librum Genesis, ed. N. Häring in Life and Works of Clarembald of Arras (Toronto, 1965), pp. 237-39.

13. Plato, <u>Timaeus</u>, 30 A.

14. Bernard Silvester, <u>Cosmographia</u>, L. II, chs. 10, 12; Hugh of St. Victor, <u>De arca Noe morali</u>, L. IV, ch.7 (PL 176, 672): "Sicut duo opera, id est opera conditionis et opera restaurationis distinximus, ita duos mundos esse intelligamus visibilem et invisibilem. Visibilem quidem hanc . machinam universitatis quam corporeis oculis cernimus; invisibilem vero cor hominis, quod videre non possumus." <u>Liber de stabilitate animae</u> (attributed by Chenu to a Benedictine author, c. 1130), ch. 7 (PL 213, 917): "Cum enim universitatis pulchritudinem, coeli terraeque machinam, opus mirabile delectabileque homo inspicit, opificem et auctorem operis ratio perquirit." See also the section of the <u>Liber Hermetis de vi rerum principiis</u> entitled "De machina mundi que sit," edited and discussed in T. Silverstein, "Liber Hermetis mercurii triplicis de vi rerum principiis," <u>Archives d'histoire doctr. et littér.</u> du moyen âge, 30 (1955), 217-302; Clarembald of Arras, <u>Tractatus super librum Boetii "De trinitate"</u>, ed. N. Häring in <u>Life and Works</u>, p. 127: "quoniam quod mundanae machinae tam pulchre tamque rationabiliter ordinatae in contrariis ...;" Alan of Lille, "Sermo de sphaera intelligibili," in <u>Textes inédits</u>, ed. M.-T. d'Alverny (Paris, 1965), 302-305; Peter of Poitiers, <u>Sententiae</u> II, ch. 7, ed. Moore, Garvin, and Dulong (Notre Dame, 1950), pp. 34-36; E. J. Dijksterhuis, <u>The Mechanization of the World Picture</u> (Oxford, 1964).

15. Manegold of Lautenbach took seriously the threat of a rationalistic naturalism: <u>Opusculum</u> 22 (PL 155, 170-71). Clarembald of Arras attacked those who in this way denied the virgin birth and transubstantiation, <u>Life and Works</u>, p. 239. On the anti-miracle movement in the twelfth century see Chenu, <u>Nature, Man, and Society</u>, pp. 14-15.

16. The identification of the World Soul and the Holy Spirit was one of the charges brought against William of Conches by William of St. Thierry. For a discussion of this issue see: William of St. Thierry, <u>De erroribus Gulielmi de Conchis</u> (PL 180, 333-340); Parent, <u>Doctrine de la creation</u>; T. Gregory, <u>Anima mundi: La filosofia di Guglielmo di Conches e la scuola di Chartres</u> (Firenze, 1955); Chenu, <u>Nature, Man, and Society</u>, p. 16; E. Jeauneau, "L'Usage de la notion d'<u>integumentum</u> à travers les gloses de Guillaume de Conches," <u>AHDL</u>, 24 (1957), 35-100.

17. William of Conches, De philosophia mundi, L. I,
ch. 23 (PL 172, 56): "Sed quoniam ipsi nesciunt vires
naturae, ut ignorantiae suae omnes socios habeant,
nolunt eos aliquid inquirer, sed ut rusticos nos credere
nec rationem quaerere.... Nos autem dicimus, in omnibus
rationem esse quaerendam, si autem alicui deficiat, quod
divina pagina affirmat, sancto Spiritui et fidei est
mandandum.... Sed isti...si inquirentem aliquem sciant,
illum esse haereticum clamant, plus de suo caputio
praesumentes quam sapientiae suae confidentes."

18. J. M. Déchanet, Oeuvres choisies de Guillaume
de Saint-Thierry (Paris, 1944), transl. R. Strachan as
William of St. Thierry (Spencer, Mass., 1972).

19. Adelard of Bath, Quaestiones naturales, 4, ed.
M. Müller, Beiträge zur Geschichte der Philosophie und
Theologie des Mittelalters, XXXI,2 (Münster i.W., 1934),
p. 8: "Deo non detraho. Quidquid enim est, ab ipso et
per ipsum est. Idipsum tamen confuse et absque discre-
tione non est, quae, quantum scientia humana procedit,
audienda est. In quo vero universaliter deficit, ad
Deum res referenda est." See also ch. 6, pp. 11-12.

20. William of Conches, Glossa in Boetium: "At
dicet aliquis: Nonne hoc est opus creatoris quod homo ex
homine nascatur? Ad quod respondeo: Nihil detraho Deo;
omnia quae in mundo sunt Deus fecit praeter malum, sed
alia fecit operante natura rerum quae est instrumentum
divinae operationis et ea dicuntur opera naturae quae a
Deo fiunt natura subserviente; alia fecit non ex aliqua
materia sed ex sola voluntate quae, ut ait Plato, major
est omninexu naturae, et illa a philosophis dicuntur
opera creatoris." Cited from Parent, Doctrine de la
création, p. 92 and 128, and corrected according to
Chenu, Nature, Man, and Society, p. 11.

21. Andrew of St. Victor, translated by Beryl
Smalley, The Study of the Bible in the Middle Ages, (Oxford, 1952), p. 144, and edited pp. 388-89: "Sin autem
ad hoc confugerit ut dicat non per naturam sed per
divinam potentiam factum ut in terris homo positus ultra
caelos caelorum aciem dirigat, scientes Deo nihil esse
impossibile, nihil resistimus. Verumtamen in scriptu-
rarum expositione cum secundum naturam res de qua agitur
nullatenus fieri potest tunc demum ad miracula con-
fugienda noverit."

22. Clarembald of Arras, <u>Tractatulus super librum Genesis</u>, in <u>Life and Works</u>, p. 239: "Sunt enim duo causarum genera: unum genus causarum est quae insertae sunt elementis ex quibus alia ex aliis suo quaeque tempore consuete producuntur. Aliae vero causae sunt in mente Creatoris ab aeterno absconditae quas ipse rebus conditis non inseruit. Ex quibus miracula ad ostensionem suae gratiae quando vult depromit." "Nemo itaque impie cogitet, sicut quidam impii cogitaverunt, nihil contra naturam, scilicet contra solitum naturae cursum, provenire posse, cum ex quibusdam causis occultis, quae in mente Creatoris ab aeterno sunt absconditae, ad ostensionem gratiae Dei multa contra solitum naturae cursum proveniant, non contra naturam, quae est voluntas Dei, quia contra eam nihil in mundo potest evenire." See also N. Häring, "The Creation and Creator of the World according to Thierry of Chartres and Clarenbaldus of Arras," <u>AHDL</u>, 22 (1955), 137-216.

23. See elsewhere in this volume: essay I on Anselm and essay IV on divine omnipotence.

24. William of Conches, <u>De philosophia mundi</u>, L. II, ch. 3 (PL 172, 58): "Quid miserius quam dicere istud, est! quia Deus illud facere potest, nec videre sic esse, nec rationem habere quare sic sit, nec utilitatem ostendere ad quam hoc sit. Non enim quidquid potest Deus facere, hoc facit. Ut autem verbis rustici utar, potest Deus facere de trunco vitulum: fecitne unquam?"

25. Arnold of Bonneval, <u>De operibus sex dierum</u>, prol. (PL 189, 1516): "Cuius moderamine diversa et contraria in unitatem pacis conveniunt et immobilia et errantia ad certum ordinem revocantur: nec intumescunt maxima nec minima consumuntur: nec tota illa mundi fabrica sine ulla ruinae formidine ex tam dissimilibus partibus uniformis, ex tam diversis una, ex tam contrariis quieta, et solida et concors in sua lege perserverat et ordine."

26. Alan of Lille, <u>Contra haereticos</u>, L. I, ch. 14 (PL 210, 319): "Decens enim fuit, ut tam corporea quam incorporea natura divinae bonitatis particeps fieret, et ea frueretur, et feliciter viveret."

27. Honorius of Autun, <u>Elucidarium</u>, L. I, ch. 11 (PL 172, 1116), as translated by Taylor and Little in Chenu, <u>Nature, Man, and Society</u>, p. 33. Latin text also

available in Y. Lefèvre, L'Elucidarium et les lucidaires (Paris, 1954), p. 371.

28. Ph. Delhaye, Godefroy de Saint-Victor: Microcosmos, 2 vols. (Lille, 1951); Chenu, Nature, Man, and Society, p. 31. For Gilbert's use of the term see N. Häring, "Die Sententiae magistri Gisleberti episcopi Pictavensis. II: Die Version der Florentiner Handschrift," AHDL, 54 (1979), 102.

29. Hugh of St. Victor, De sacramentis, I, 6, 17, distinguishes two types of virtue: one produced by the will moved by nature, the other produced by the will moved by grace. Only the latter is meritorious of eternal life. Peter Lombard, Sent., L. II, dist. 27, c. 2-3, recognizes only the supernatural virtues, which he identifies with grace; Ph. Delhaye, Pierre Lombard: sa vie, ses oeuvres, sa morale (Montreal, 1961), pp. 30-35, 75-87. See also Peter of Poitiers, Sent., L. III, ch. 1 (PL 211, 1041).

30. Peter Abelard, Dialogus inter Philosophum, Judaeum et Christianum (PL 178, 1651-52): "Virtus est habitus animi optimus"; and in edition of Rudolf Thomas (Stuttgart, 1970), pp. 115-18. Also D. E. Luscombe, Peter Abelard's Ethics (Oxford, 1971); "The Ethics of Abelard: Some Further Considerations," in Peter Abelard, ed. E. M. Buytaert, Mediaevalia Lovaniensia, ser. 1, n. 2 (Louvain, 1974).

31. D. E. Luscombe, The School of Peter Abelard (Cambridge, 1970).

32. For a survey of the views and texts of this "Aristotelian" current in twelfth-century ethics see O. Lottin, Psychologie et Morale aux XIIe et XIIIe siècles, Vol. III (Louvain-Gembloux, 1949), pp. 107-125; G. Bullet, Vertus morales infuses et vertus morales acquises selon Saint Thomas d'Aquin, Studia Friburgensia, nouvelle serie 23 (Fribourg, 1958), pp. 47-50.

33. Luscombe, Peter Abelard's Ethics; O. Lottin, Psychologie et morale, III.

34. Delhaye, Pierre Lombard, pp. 30-35, 75-87.

35. Luscombe, "The Ethics of Abelard: Some Further Considerations," p. 72: "...Abelard's main intention is to elaborate a definition of the supreme good and the

supreme evil for man in terms of the highest inner state
which a man can achieve and in terms of what actually
earns for man his eternal reward, that is, supreme love
of God or the fault which renders him evil." A. M.
Landgraf, Dogmengeschichte der Frühscholastik, I,1
(Regensburg, 1952), p. 251.

36. On the development and meaning of ex puris
naturalibus see: H. A. Oberman, The Harvest of Medieval
Theology (Cambridge, Mass., 1963), pp. 47-50.

37. Anselm, Cur Deus Homo; Southern, Making of the
Middle Ages, pp. 219-37.

38. J. Burnaby, Amor Dei (London, 1938), pp.
255-63.

IV

THE DIALECTIC OF DIVINE OMNIPOTENCE

One of the great contributions of thirteenth-
century scholastics both to the problem of divine omnipotence and the contingency of events was the development of an analytical tool commonly, though perhaps
misleadingly, known as the distinction between the
absolute and ordained power of God. The fundamental
perception on which it was based, namely that what God
created or established did not exhaust divine capacity
or the potentialities open to God, was articulated by
Peter Damian in the third quarter of the eleventh
century, generally accepted by the middle of the twelfth
century, embodied in the formula of de potentia abso-
luta/ordinata by the early thirteenth, and had become
commonplace scholastic terminology by mid-century. But
what was generally acknowledged to be a useful distinction expressing an accepted theological truth supposedly
became, in the fourteenth century, a destructive vehicle
upsetting the certainties of the natural and supernatural orders and dissolving both scientific empiricism
and natural theology before the terrifying possibility
of arbitrary divine intervention. The twin specters of
skepticism and fideism, so repeatedly encountered in the
literature on late medieval thought a generation ago,
were grounded in no small measure on the assumption that
the scholastic distinction between absolute and ordained
power was misunderstood or misapplied in the fourteenth
and fifteenth centuries.

Within the last generation considerable strides
have been made in our understanding of this distinction.
We now have a far clearer picture of its origins and
early development than that constructed by Grzondziel
and Borchert earlier in this century.[1] We are certain
of the principal and standard meaning and application of
the distinction. We are aware that in the development
and use of the terminology Roman law and canon law
played a part alongside theology.[2] And, on the assumption that the distinction was well understood and
appropriately applied in the late thirteenth century, we
have what appears to be careless usage or misapplication
in the late medieval period. Whether that is in fact
the case is the topic of the present paper, which
requires a re-examination of the high as well as late
medieval understanding of the distinction.

I. Glossing Divine _Impotentia_, 1050-1150

In 1067, almost a decade before Anselm wrote his first work, Peter Damian composed a treatise in the form of a letter, the product of his reflections on a memorable dinner conversation at Monte Cassino with abbot Desiderius.[3] The treatise concerned two interrelated problems that remained major issues throughout the rest of the Middle Ages: divine omnipotence and the contingency of temporal events. Yet those issues were the ones at which Damian arrived in the course of his analysis. They were not his beginning point. In fact, Desiderius and Damian were addressing a different, more exegetical point. In light of the firm belief and almost daily affirmation of divine omnipotence in the opening line of the creed, how is a Christian theologian to understand or interpret authoritative statements that speak of things that God _cannot_ do?

That question, which occupied the attention of theologians for the next two generations, was solved by Desiderius and Damian in different ways. Desiderius, paraphrasing a line from Augustine's _Enchiridion_, defined omnipotence as the power to do what one wills.[4] Correspondingly, statements implying divine inability should be interpreted to mean non-volition. Damian found that answer insufficient. The problem with that approach was not that it placed no limits whatever on what God could will and therefore do, but that the Augustinian and Desiderian phrase, particularly as used by dialecticians contemporary with Damian, limited divine power to the boundaries of the divine will, which in turn conformed to the divine nature. God cannot do whatever he wills; he can _only_ do what he wills.[5]

Damian adopted a different approach. God _can_ do more than he actually _wills_ to do; divine capacity exceeds divine volition. Despite the fact that Damian did not explore the internal or external conditions that govern the way God acts, he did suggest that the realm of possibility open to God is not exhausted by or limited to what God has chosen to do.[6]

These alternative approaches, each having much to recommend it, formed the foundation for later discussion. Many theologians shared Desiderius' suspicion that it was a false problem and that statements about divine inability were either meaningless or conveyed some meaning other than the words suggested. St. Anselm initially favored that approach.[7] His definition of God as that being, a greater than which cannot be conceived,

also applied to the attributes of God. Since God was
the highest wisdom, goodness, truth, and justice, discussions of what God cannot do, such as lie, deceive, be
corrupted, or change the past are meaningless by definition. They are based on the poverty or peculiarities
of our language in which statements seeming to imply
ability, such as "I can lie," really imply a liability
and thus cannot be applied to God.[8] Abelard a
generation later also adopted this approach and made the
boundaries of divine power coterminous with the nature
of God.[9]
Damian's approach was not without its supporters.
It expressed a deeply felt religious belief, that our
created world, its relationships and events, are not
contingent simply because they derive from and are
dependent upon God, but because they were chosen by God.
If divine power and freedom mean anything, they mean
freedom of choice, not just freedom to implement one's
will. St. Anselm eventually arrived at this position,
not by analyzing the nature of God but by attempting to
understand and explain the Incarnation in his Cur Deus
homo.[10] If Christ was fully human, he had to have had
the ability to sin, the ability to lie, deceive, or do
any of the culpable acts within our power, even if the
ability was never and could never be actualized. And
since the properties of Christ's human nature must be,
through the doctrine of communicatio idiomatum, predi-
cated of the divine nature, one must acknowledge God's
ability to do things he does not do. Yet even here the
linguistic interests of Anselm provided a check, lest
the divine nature appear too volitional. Through his
distinction between posse and velle Anselm attributed to
Christ the ability to sin but not the ability to will to
sin, which made all undesirable actions an empty
capacity that could never be realized, nor could Christ
have ever wished or contemplated doing so.[11] In one
remarkable passage, however, Anselm laid the foundation
for the subsequent absoluta/ordinata distinction. God
does not act by any external, compelling necessity but
by an internal, self-imposed necessity, freely willed.[12]
This concept of a self-binding God, with the companion
concept of contingent, relative necessity as opposed to
absolute necessity had a major impact on the idea of
divine omnipotence, particularly on what came to be
conceived as ordained power over against power conceived
in the abstract, absolute sense.
Other late eleventh-century theologians shared
Anselm's eventual perception that God acts by choice

rather than by necessity, even if that choice is limited by the divine nature. Thus the school of Anselm of Laon, compiling the standard gloss on scripture, interpreted phrases implying divine inability as self-imposed limitations based on the nature or will of God. "God could according to his power, but not according to his justice."[13] By the early twelfth century this approach to statements of divine inability had received wide acceptance, and theologians generally acknowledged a sphere of potentiality open to God by reason of his power but not realized, indeed unrealizable, by reason of his nature -- a sphere of potentiality larger than those things God has in fact chosen to do. Desiderius' formulation, non potuit = noluit, had been replaced by potuit, sed noluit.

Abelard did not subscribe to that consensus. Influenced by his reading of Augustine, Anselm, and Plato's Timaeus, Abelard rejected any discussions of what God might have done or could do according to his power.[14] Since God's actions always conform to the divine nature and are expressions of it, God could not have acted in any way other than he did. This view, first expressed in his Theologia christiana in 1124 and expanded in his Introductio ad theologiam in or shortly after 1136, was vigorously attacked by Hugh of St. Victor, Odo of Ourscamp, William of St. Thierry, Bernard of Clairvaux, the anonymous author of the Summa sententiarum, and, finally, by Peter Lombard who, in his treatment of divine omnipotence in distinctions 42 and 43 of the first book of his Libri sententiarum, made the approach of the school of Laon, the Victorines, and the Cistercians practically dogma.[15]

II. Absolutely Speaking: the Development
of the Formula, 1150-1250

The concept that lies behind the potentia absoluta/ordinata distinction was well-established in the early twelfth century and epitomized by Lombard through the Augustinian expression "potuit, sed noluit."[16] It was a half-century, however, before the concept came to be expressed by the formula potentia absoluta/ordinata and even longer before that formula received wide acceptance. The crucial period for the development of the terminology was the end of the twelfth, the beginning of the thirteenth century. In an anonymous commentary on the Pauline Epistles written

around 1200 the author argues that we can speak of
divine power in two ways, either according to what God
has chosen to do or according to divine power considered
in itself, without regard for what God has decreed. To
this second approach the author applies the adverb
absolute.[17] Godfrey of Poitiers writing around 1210
further refined the language. Godfrey is the first
writer, to my knowledge, who uses the term absoluta as
an adjective modifying the divine power and who phrases
the distinction in the way that was to become standard.
Godfrey states that there are things that God has the
capacity to do, de potentia absoluta, that he does not
do and, indeed, cannot do, de potentia conditionali.[18]
Other theologians developed their own terminology.
William of Auxerre, around 1220, acknowledged God's
power to have acted otherwise, de potentia pure considerata, which added special meaning to the natural and
moral orders God actually chose to establish, de
potestate determinata.[19]

In the period from 1220 to 1245 the terms potentia
absoluta and potentia ordinata gradually came into
common use. For example, in William of Auvergne's De
trinitate, written about 1225, one sees that the term
absoluta is becoming the normal way to describe the
capacity of divine power without regard for what God has
in fact done.[20] Hugh of St. Cher who commented on the
Sentences between 1230 and 1238, argues that God is able
to do some things de potentia absoluta that he is unable
to do de potentia ordinata.[21] The same terms, used in
the same way, can be found in the Sentences commentaries
of Guerric of St. Quentin (c. 1240) and Albertus Magnus
(c. 1244) and the Summa Halensis (before 1245).[22]

By 1245, then, the formula had achieved its classic
shape and was being applied in a consistent manner
None of these authors speaks of two powers in God, but
rather of two ways of speaking about divine power. One
way of speaking is to discuss power in the abstract,
without regard for God's will and actions as revealed in
the present order. The other way is to view divine
power in terms of what God has in fact chosen to do.
Thus certain things that are theoretically possible to
God, de potentia absoluta, are impossible to God in
light of the chosen order de potentia ordinata. God
never acts and can never act in an "absolute" way, since
the discussion of power, viewed absolutely, leaves aside
the entire question of divine volition and action. (See
figure 1).

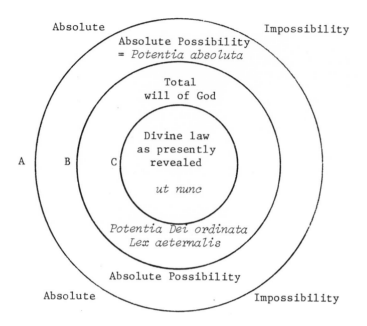

Figure 1: THE THEOLOGICAL MEANING

Beyond the standardization of terminology, the function or purpose of the distinction was altered in the first half of the thirteenth century. No longer were theologians attempting to gloss or reinterpret authoritative statements about divine inability. Instead the distinction came to embody a positive statement about God's relationship with the world, a relationship based on covenant and self-commitment. The distinction affirmed that what God does, including what he has done, is doing, and will do, is not done by necessity or external compulsion but by internal, voluntary choice. The order that God has established, therefore, is not necessary in any absolute sense but is only relatively or contingently necessary inasmuch as it has been established by God out of free choice. God is not bound, save in the sense that he has bound himself. We should, as good medieval christians, look at the world around us not as a world of necessary things and relationships, as did the uninformed Greeks and some of their Arab commentators, but as a contingent world, freely chosen and created by God.

Defined and applied in this way, the distinction sufficiently met the perceived needs of affirming the freedom of God and yet protecting the appropriateness and reliability of the established order of things. It was principally applied to theological issues (creation, incarnation, justification, and the sacraments) and stressed that what God has done (de potentia ordinata) was chosen from (i.e., lies within) the sphere of total possibility (de potentia absoluta). If one viewed God's actions from the standpoint of time, however, there was a secondary implication that the realm of potentia ordinata was what God has done (reality) and the realm of potentia absoluta what God has not done (counterfactuals). But whichever aspect one chose to stress, at the moment of its general acceptance the distinction began to create almost as many problems as it solved.

III.   Divine Temporality and Human Sovereignty, 1250-1300

Two groups of problems lay hidden within the potentia absoluta/ordinata distinction. The first group concern the difficulty of talking about the temporal acts of an eternal God. The procedure entails two hypothetical suppositions which, while false, seemed useful for the theoretical analysis. One supposition places God in a temporal framework, albeit only for purposes of discussion. It hypothesizes a time before God acted, even before he willed, a time when God was faced with total possibility, limited only by the impossibility of making contradictories simultaneously true or by denying his own nature. Moreover, the freedom of an eternal God is eternal and should be expressed by the present tense, no matter how uncomfortable that makes us. As Hugh of St. Cher expressed it, "God could and still can." Yet the divine posse, when viewed from the standpoint of our temporal order, translates as potuit, not potest, as Damian noted.[23] Since God has obliged himself to work in particular ways and, being omniscient and consistent, will not deviate from the divine plan for creation, the choices initially open to God are no longer real possibilities once the divine plan is established. Potentia Dei, concludes the Summa Halensis at one point, respicit res supra tem-

pus.[24] The second supposition ascribes to God a
rational process of deliberation, of choosing a course
of action out of a wider area of possibility. A God
with freedom of choice is a deliberating God, even if
only for an instant.

The second group of problems were not inherent in
the concept but stemmed from a failure to refine the
concept further or achieve an adequate consensus behind
attempted refinements. As long as theologians used the
distinction as a simple formula to attack divine
necessity, as a rewording of the sentiment potuit, sed
noluit, problems did not arise. But the fragile and
ambiguous nature of the distinction gradually became
apparent as more complex issues were assigned it. The
major problem was that miracles and changes in God's
laws were never fully integrated into the theory. They
did not belong with the potentia absoluta, since power
considered absolutely had nothing to do with action, and
no Christian theologian seriously wanted to entertain
the notion of God changing his mind and acting in a way
that he did not foreknow and foreordain. And yet most
discussions of potentia ordinata in the early thirteenth
century illustrated ordained power by reference to
natural and spiritual laws or ordinances now in effect,
which God has at times miraculously suspended and which
in the sacrament of the Eucharist he always suspends.
What was needed and what was attempted but never fully
developed in the thirteenth and fourteenth centuries was
a subdistinction within potentia ordinata between the
total ordained will of God (lex aeternalis or general
providence, an equivalent concept to the voluntas
beneplaciti consequens) and potentia ordinata as it is
expressed in specific laws (lex ut nunc) which have been
altered or suspended from time to time, thus creating a
home within potentia ordinata for the foreordained but
miraculous activity of God.[25]

In the third quarter of the thirteenth century the
predominant tendency among theologians was to equate the
ordained power of God with the total preordained, providential will. Beyond that there was little agreement.
Albertus Magnus, Bonaventure, and Richard Rufus of
Cornwall tended to identify God's wisdom, goodness, and
justice with the present order of things, so that the
hypothesis of a different order became an empty, theoretical construct.[26] Albert still found the distinction
useful as a defense against the Avicennian and
Averroistic idea of the absolute necessity of created
things. Bonaventure and Rufus, on the other hand,

rejected the distinction since, if the divine wisdom was identical with the present order, arguments de potentia absoluta would imply that God had the capacity to act in an unorderly, irrational, perhaps sinful way. Thomas Aquinas took a different approach. In his Sentences commentary he curiously ignored the language of potentia absoluta/ordinata in his treatment of the power of God, although some of the supporting concepts appear there.[27]   By 1260, however, he adopted the distinction and employed it marginally in his Summa contra Gentiles (1259-60), in his disputed questions De potentia Dei (1265-66), and in his Summa theologiae (begun around 1266).[28]   As with most of his generation, he principally identified the ordained power of God with the total divine plan, but he did not identify divine wisdom with the present order of things. God's wisdom, goodness, and justice could have found expression in some other preordained system. The present order is therefore a product of the divine will; it is not the necessary and only product of divine wisdom.

Peter of Tarantasia was one of the few mid-century theologians to attempt a distinction between God's total ordained will and the ordained laws presently in effect.[29]   If one considers things from the standpoint of ordo simpliciter, then God only acts de potentia ordinata. If one considers things from the standpoint of ordo ut nunc, then God can do things de potentia absoluta that he does not do de potentia ordinata. Peter was obviously sensitive to the problem and wished to affirm that God never acts without order, even in his miracles. Yet his formulation left the impression that actions in contradiction of the present order would be actions de potentia absoluta. That misinterpretation -- the hypothesis of arbitrary, extra-legal divine action that Bonaventure and Richard Rufus found so disturbing -- was reinforced by other factors in the thirteenth century.

One factor was the terminology eventually adopted. By replacing such phrases as potentia pure considerata or potentia accipi absolute with potentia absoluta, the gain in brevity was more than offset by a loss in clarity.[30]   The earlier phrases unambiguously referred to power viewed in the abstract; the later phrase misleadingly suggested a type of power. A second factor were the analogies drawn between divine power and human experience.

One analogy was inherent in the theological concept from the beginning: God's freedom to choose from a

larger sphere of possibility open to him is analogous to
our sense of freedom, our sense of a capacity far larger
than our actual choices. But instead of defining that
as a distinction between ability and volition, as did
Anselm, some theologians, such as Thomas, defined it as
the difference between ability and legitimate action.[31]
Thomas did not mean to imply that since we have the
freedom to act illegally or immorally, so does God; but
the parallel could leave that impression.

A second, more troublesome, analogy -- one between
divine power and forms of human sovereignty -- entered
theological discussion toward the end of the thirteenth
century. Canon lawyers in the early thirteenth century
sought a formula that would express the relation of
papal power to ecclesiastical law.[32] On the one hand
the pope was obliged to obey and uphold the fundamental
laws of the church (the status ecclesiae), which he
could in no way alter. On the other hand, through the
papal plenitudo potestatis, lesser, particular laws
could be suspended through dispensations or privileges
for the greater good of the church (the ratio ecclesiae). Here the theological distinction of absolute and
ordained power proved useful. Without altering the
concept in any way, it could be used to express the idea
that the pope conforms to the law by an internal,
self-imposed obligation, not by external compulsion or
necessity. The underlying Roman law principle that the
prince is bound by the law out of benevolence, not out
of necessity, (the lex digna of Emperor Theodosius)
provided further support.[33] Although the pope, de
potentia absoluta, is not bound by the law, he has bound
himself, de potentia ordinata, to act according to the
law. Moreover, in order to preserve and fulfil the
greater good, the total plan of God for his church, it
might on occasion be necessary to alter or suspend
particular laws. Just as alterations in the ordo ut
nunc do not contradict but rather implement the lex
aeternalis, so papal dispensations and privileges are
for the general good and implement God's higher will.
One might even consider the pope the means through which
God alters present law to bring it into conformity with
his general law.

Perhaps the earliest application of the theological
distinction to papal power is mentioned in Hostiensis'
Lectura in quinque decretalium in 1270. The context is
particularly interesting, since it carries us back to
the origin of the theological distinction. Hostiensis
was attempting to gloss an authoritative statement

implying papal inability to suspend or deviate from the
law. Moreover, the case under consideration entailed a
possibly inherent contradiction: whether the pope could
release a monk from his vows of chastity and poverty and
yet allow him to remain a monk, i.e., the degree to
which those vows were part of the very definition of
"monkness".

Hostiensis revealed a number of solutions that had
been developed by earlier or contemporary canonists.[34]
Some had adapted Jerome's approach to God's inability to
restore virginity: such an act would not be congruent
with papal power. Others argued the pope could
dispense, but the monk would no longer be a monk; or
that the pope could not do so except by divine
dispensation; or that he could if he wished (i.e., the
case falls within his capacity), but he does not by
custom do this. The most interesting solution in this
context is the argument that although the monastic vows
were part of the nature of the monastic state, the pope
could, through his _plenitudo potestatis_, change the
nature of the thing, _non de potestate ordinata, sed de
absoluta_. As the subsequent discussion in Hostiensis
suggests, he grants the right of the pope to suspend the
vow for the greater good, the _ratio status ecclesiae_.
Here as elsewhere Hostiensis recognized the ability of
the pope, through his _plenitudo potestatis_, to act outside the law in an emergency situation. Such extraordinary action comes to be described in Hostiensis as
the ability to act _de potestate absoluta_.

The analogy between divine power and human
sovereignty, particularly the identification of _potentia
absoluta_ with _plenitudo potestatis_, introduced a disturbing element into the dialectic of divine power inasmuch as it assumed a different model. (See figure 2).

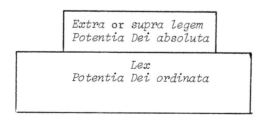

Figure 2: THE JURIDICAL/CONSTITUTIONAL MEANING

The realm of <u>potentia absoluta</u> was not conceived as simple capacity or total possibility but as a course of action, albeit occasional. Even if such action was ideally for the common good, the papal <u>plenitudo potestatis</u> did not reflect a preordained plan in the mind of the pope, nor was it in practice devoid of self-interest. Rulers are counseled and influenced. They have also been known to change their minds. The potential arbitrariness in the exercise of human sovereignty contained serious dangers if applied to the concept of divine power.

The canonistic interpretation of absolute and ordained power was already in circulation when the famous list of 219 articles were condemned in 1277 at Paris and Oxford. 1277 marked a victory for the concept of divine omnipotence, since many of the condemned articles restricted the freedom of God and affirmed the necessity of the world and the laws of nature. And yet that victory had little or nothing to do with the distinction of absolute and ordained power. Thomas Aquinas, part of whose thought was censured in 1277, accepted the distinction, while Henry of Ghent, viewed as a promoter of the condemnation, refused to apply the distinction to God because for him it implied the freedom to sin.[35] On the other hand, Henry was quite willing to apply the distinction to papal power and to equate <u>plenitudo potestatis</u> with <u>potentia absoluta</u>, even as he hoped a sense of propriety might restrain the pope's use of these extraordinary powers.[36]

The tendency toward the legal definition of absolute and ordained power met with a swift and strong response from some contemporary theologians. Petrus de Trabibus reaffirmed <u>potentia ordinata</u> as eternal fore-ordination and <u>potentia absoluta</u> as initial capacity or potentiality without regard to action.[37] God is <u>able</u> to do other things than those he has preordained, "yet it could never happen that he would act otherwise."[38]

Despite Trabibus' reaffirmation of the traditional, theological understanding of the distinction, the tendency to interpret <u>potentia absoluta</u> as a type of action rather than a neutral sphere of unconditioned possibility was unwittingly aided by Duns Scotus' treatment of the distinction.[39] In his desire to emphasize the unbound nature of God and the contingency of the orders of nature and grace, Scotus used the distinction of absolute and ordained power more than any previous scholastic. It formed the backbone of his theory of justification (<u>acceptatio divina</u>), of his view of sacra-

mental causality, and his ethical system.[40] Scotus
invariably equated _potentia ordinata_ with the present
order of things, _pro statu isto_, which God is obliged to
follow only insofar as he chooses. God could have acted
and still could act otherwise (_potest aliter agere_).[41]
But Scotus acknowledged that any other action would
result in another order (and thus God can never act
inordinate) not so much because of the consistency of
the divine nature but because whatever system God
institutes becomes right and just on the grounds that
God has chosen it.[42] The emphasis Scotus placed on
law-changing and on God's ability to act outside and
against his established law allowed _potentia absoluta_ to
appear as a form of extraordinary divine action, _supra
legem_. With Scotus the legal, constitutional definition
entered theological discussion. The _absoluta/ordinata_
distinction applied to any free agent, not just God.
Extending a line of argument in Thomas and not heeding
the warnings of Henry of Ghent or Petrus de Trabibus,
Scotus incorporated the analogy developed by the canon
lawyers: _potentia ordinata_ means acting according to
the law, _de iure_; _potentia absoluta_ is the ability to
act apart from the law, _de facto_.[43] Thus the phrases _de
potentia ordinata_ and _de potentia absoluta_ no longer
simply characterized two different senses of _posse_; they
now affirmed two different forms of action, one in
conformity with law and one outside and above the law.

IV. Doctors of the Absolute: The Fourteenth Century

It is well known that the _potentia absoluta/
ordinata_ distinction received far greater use in the
fourteenth and fifteenth centuries than it had in the
earlier period. Because of that it has been linked with
late medieval thought and sometimes seen as a major
component of nominalist theology and philosophy. But
the meaning and function of the distinction in the late
Middle Ages has as much to do with the conflicting
interpretations of the late thirteenth century as it
does with the new problems to which it was applied.
This is amply illustrated by the discussion and use of
the distinction in William of Ockham.
Ockham's understanding of absolute and ordained
power derives from the _Summa Halensis_, Thomas Aquinas,
Olivi, Trabibus, and Duns Scotus.[44] But despite the
parallel uses of the distinction in Scotus and Ockham
and the occasional parallels in language, Ockham's

repeated and lengthy insistence on the proper meaning of the distinction was directed as much at Scotus' juridical formulation as at John XXII's misunderstanding and rejection of the distinction.[45]   Ockham was adamant that these terms do not refer to two powers in God (_potentiae Dei_) but to two ways of considering the one power of God. _Absoluta_ considers power alone, without regard to divine action or will. _Ordinata_ considers God's power from the standpoint of his decrees, his revealed will. As did the _Summa Halensis_, Olivi, and Trabibus, Ockham locates much of the confusion on this issue in the ambiguous nature of the verb "can". _Potentia absoluta_ is simply the realm of total possibility, and to state that God or anyone could _act_ absolutely involves a contradiction. It is in this context, not in the context of hypothetical new orders (as with Scotus), that Ockham declares that God _only_ acts in an ordained manner.[46]   The persuasiveness of Ockham's definition of the distinction as well as the continuing threat of misunderstanding are underscored by Ockham's approach being repeated by Gregory of Rimini, Pierre d'Ailly, and Gabriel Biel.[47]

As had already become the pattern by the middle of the thirteenth century, Ockham used the distinction to point up the contingent, non-necessary character of our world and its relationships. His goal was always to prove non-necessity, not actual possibility. Most of Ockham's labors in this matter were, if you will, on the outer frontier between impossibility and possibility (figure 1, circle A) in order to establish the necessary or contingent status of the opposite proposition within the case at hand. For example, if the statements "two bodies can exist in the same place at the same time" or "one can receive eternal life without the habit of grace" are absolutely impossible, then the opposite negative propositions become absolutely necessary. If, however, the former propositions are not absolute impossibilities, then the latter propositions are not absolutely necessary. In other words, in order to establish contingency vs necessity one must establish possibility vs impossibility, which is not done at the point of real possibility (figure 1, circle B) but at the point of absolute or logical possibility (figure 1, circle A). The ultimate goal is to determine the necessity or contingency of the case at hand, for which the _absoluta_ speculation on possibility and impossibility is simply the means.

Ockham never confuses <u>potentia absoluta</u> speculation
with the possibility of divine intervention, which he
considered a separate issue. The miraculous biblical
examples Ockham frequently cites in the context of
<u>potentia absoluta</u> argumentation are not used to prove
that God acts absolutely. They are divinely ordained
acts, albeit special as opposed to normal, which prove
that the case under consideration, which appears to
involve a contradiction, is not contradictory and
therefore falls within the area of possibility viewed
abstractly. The miraculous example (<u>ordinata specialis</u>)
proves the case possible; the case does not make the
example <u>absoluta</u>.

Ockham's use of the human analogue is similar. As
did Thomas and Scotus before him, he found the freedom
of the human will, the sense that one can do far more
than one chooses to do or than one can legally do, a
helpful analogy in distinguishing divine capacity from
divine activity. At most, the papal example in Ockham
serves to underscore the belief that papal conformity to
law results from a self-imposed obligation, not from
necessity. Ockham, far more than Thomas or Scotus, was
disturbed by the idea of a pope acting contrary to
Scripture and Tradition. The whole problem of
contemporary church government, as Ockham saw it, was
exactly the attempt of John XXII and his successors to
contradict the accepted teaching of Scripture and
Church. Ockham would never have applied the distinction
to the papacy if he thought it would encourage
absolutist behavior.

But what of developments after Ockham? Not only
was there more frequent and extensive use made of the
distinction in the late Middle Ages; it was particularly
employed as a tool for analyzing the necessity or
non-necessity of causal relationships (both physical and
spiritual) or of states of affairs in the world around
us.[48] The language of the agent, namely God, was still
used, but the analysis was not of the actor but of that
which is acted upon. Secondly, although the distinction
still functioned as an expression of antinecessi-
tarianism, <u>potentia ordinata</u> increasingly became the
realm of the realized, and <u>potentia absoluta</u> the realm
of the unrealized possibilities, counterfactuals, hypothetical arguments, <u>secundum imaginationem</u>. Thirdly,
the distinction was increasingly applied to propositions
in logic and physics. First in England, then at Paris
and elsewhere on the Continent, theologians became
fascinated with the interplay between divine decrees and

moments of time, while devoting little attention to the
distinction between specific decrees and the eternal,
preordained plan of God (figure 1, circle C). They were
interested not so much in those regular suspensions of
the natural order, such as transubstantiation, which
engaged their attention in other ways, but in those
temporary suspensions or changes across time which could
make what was once false, true, and what was once true,
false.[49] In the contemplation of such moments one was
instantaneously transported from one part of God's
foreordained plan to another, from one type of order --
familiar, reassuring, known as the present state of
things or the common course of nature and grace -- to
another type of order in which the old rules did not
apply. For a brief time as the Israelites were leaving
Egypt theft and extortion were part of the ordained plan
of God. For those days in which Abraham and Isaac
journeyed to the appointed place of sacrifice, it was
part of the revealed plan of God for a father to kill
his only son. And for thousands of years circumcision
had been the gateway to salvation by divine ordination,
while for our authors, for over thirteen centuries,
baptism had been so ordained. Fictive royal examples
might also be used. A king might decree that all those
found in the treasury room before noon would be
rewarded, and all those discovered in the afternoon
would be put to death. Again the parallel between the
law-giving God and the legislative power of the king.
But to the degree that such examples illustrate the
transcendent power of God, answerable to no one, they
also suggest the image of a capricious, arbitrary
lord.[50]
     Similarly, fourteenth-century thinkers explored
situations or states of affairs that had seemed to
previous generations to be impossible, such as the
ability of God to deceive or the ability of God to
command someone to hate him. As long as attention was
focused on the nature of God, as it generally was from
the late eleventh to the late thirteenth centuries,
those hypotheses were self-contradictory. But when they
were looked at from the standpoint of propositions about
revealed future contingents, or the ability to will
one's own damnation for the love of God, some theologians felt that these cases did not involve a logical
contradiction and were therefore possible de potentia
absoluta.[51]
     Most theologians in the fourteenth century were
careful not to allow their discussion of God's power

considered absolutely to become a discussion of God's
acting absolutely. As long as the concept was being
applied in the traditional manner, excessive use could
never undermine the present order of things or produce
uncertainty and skepticism. Yet not all theologians
were that careful, and we find that the vocabulary
through which the distinction was expressed varied in
the fourteenth century, sometimes in ways that obscured
the earlier meaning. De potentia ordinata was sometimes
used interchangeably with de potentia naturali, placing
the emphasis on nature and man rather than God.[52] The
distinction was not only applied to sovereign rulers but
to anyone who acts according to law and nature (thus de
potentia ordinata) as opposed to participation in a
non-natural event which, since not impossible de
potentia absoluta, could be realized through a special,
miraculous ordinance.[53] In an unpublished paper Paul
Streveler has called attention to the use of the phrase
"ex privilegio speciali," which Robert Holcot used
interchangeably with potentia absoluta.[54] The technical
juridical language reveals that Holcot is thinking about
papal dispensation, and that in such an instance absolute power is a form of extra-legal action. The same is
true for Marsilius of Inghen, who preferred the phrase
de lege absoluta in place of de potentia absoluta.[55]
    A number of factors probably influenced this shift
from absolute capacity to absolute action: (1) the
syntactical structure of the terms themselves, which led
to ambiguity; (2) the failure of most theologians to
distinguish two senses of potentia ordinata; (3) the
fact that any hypothetical case, if it were ever
realized, would occur as a special miracle or a new
ordinance; (4) human conceptual weakness, much as the
idea of eternity is often misconceived as perpetuity or
perduration; and finally, (5) the influence of the human
analogy, particularly the analogy with the sovereignty
of the ruler. Popes and kings did on occasion act
outside, above, or contrary to the established laws of
society and church. Their actions might be justified on
the grounds of "reason of state" (necessitas legem non
habet), but it was expected that they would conform to a
higher good for society. Analogous to the distinction
between God's general will and his specific laws, one
might idealistically view royal or papal absolutism as
the implementation of a general, beneficent plan from
which those very laws, now suspended, were derived. In
fact, however, human sovereigns, even medieval ones,
have little foreknowledge or effective preordination;

they <u>do</u> change their minds. Law making and law suspending are new responses to unforeseen conditions. And as a social group university scholars -- the very writers of our arguments -- were among the principal recipients of papal privilege and dispensation in the late Middle Ages.

Thus it was with a new but by then not uncommon meaning that Henry VIII in 1528 employed the distinction of absolute and ordained power in his appeal for a dispensation from his first marriage. "A thing that the pope perhaps cannot do in accordance with the divine and human laws already written, using his ordinary power," he might possibly be able to do "of his mere and absolute power, as a thing in which he may dispense above the law."[56] After all, if an all-knowing, foreordaining, unchanging God can be moved by prayer, how much easier to influence Christ's vicar to implement a possibility that lay within his power, considered absolutely.

[1] H. Grzondziel, Die Entwicklung der Unterscheidung zwischen der potentia Dei absoluta und der potentia Dei ordinata von Augustin bis Alexander von Hales, Inaugural-Dissertation (Breslau, 1926); M. Grabmann, Die Geschichte der katholischen Theologie seit dem Ausgang der Väterzeit (Freiburg i.B., 1933); E. Borchert, Der Einfluss des Nominalismus auf die Christologie der Spätscholastik, Beiträge zur Geschichte der Philosophie und Theologie des Mittelalters, XXXV, 4/5 (Münster i.W., 1940), pp. 46-74. On the meaning of the term in high and late scholasticism see: P. Vignaux, "Nominalisme," in Dictionnaire de théologie catholique, XI (Paris, 1930), 769-775; Justification et prédestination au XIVe siècle (Paris, 1934), pp. 97-140, 177-189; Luther Commentateur des Sentences (Paris, 1935), pp. 71-86; Nominalisme au XIVe siècle (Montreal and Paris, 1948), pp. 22-28; H.A. Oberman, The Harvest of Medieval Theology (Cambridge, Mass., 1963), pp. 30-56; R. P. Desharnais, The History of the Distinction between God's Absolute and Ordained Power and Its Influence on Martin Luther (Unpublished doctoral dissertation, Catholic University of America, Washington, 1966); M. A. Pernoud, "Innovation in William of Ockham's References to the 'Potentia Dei'," Antonianum, XLV (1970), 66-97; "The Theory of the Potentia Dei According to Aquinas, Scotus and Ockham," Antonianum, XLVII (1972), 69-95; W. J. Courtenay, "Convenant and Causality in Pierre d'Ailly," Speculum, XLVI (1971), 94-119; "Nominalism and Late Medieval Religion," in The Pursuit of Holiness in Late Medieval and Renaissance Religion (Leiden, 1974), pp. 37-43; G. Gál, "Petrus de Trabibus on the Absolute and Ordained Power of God," in Studies Honoring Ignatius Charles Brady, Friar Minor, Franciscan Institute Publications, Theol. ser. 6 (St. Bonaventure, N.Y., 1976), pp. 283-292; B. Hamm, Promissio, Pactum, Ordinatio: Freiheit und Selbstbindung Gottes in der scholastischen Gnadenlehre (Tübingen, 1977).

[2] F. Oakley, "Jacobean Political Theology: The Absolute and Ordinary Powers of the King," Journal of the History of Ideas, XXIX (1968), 323-346; "The 'Hidden' and 'Revealed' Wills of James I: More Political Theology," Studia Gratiana, XV (1972), 365-375.

[3] Peter Damian, De divina omnipotentia in reparatione corruptae, et factis infectis reddendis (Epist. 2, 17), in J. P. Migne, Patrologiae cursus completus... series latina (Paris, 1844 ff.) (Henceforth cited as

PL), Vol. 145, col. 596: "Nam dum aliquando, ut meminisse potes, uterque discumberemus ad mensam, illudque beati Hieronymi sermocinantibus deveniret in medium...." For a thorough examination of Damian's treatise see Lettre sur la toutepuissance divine, ed. & transl. with introduction by A. Cantin, Sources chrétiennes, CXCI (Paris, 1972). For the later influence of one dimension of Damian's thesis see my "John of Mirecourt and Gregory of Rimini on Whether God Can Undo the Past," Recherches de Théologie ancienne et médiévale, XXXIX (1972), 224-256; XL (1973), 147-174.

4 PL 145, 597: "Deum non ob aliud hoc non posse, nisi quia non vult." Desiderius' wording is similar to the statement of Augustine, Enchiridion, c. 96 (PL 40, 276): "Non ob aliud veraciter vocatur omnipotens, nisi quoniam quidquid vult, potest."

5 PL 145, 597: "Si nihil, inquam, potest Deus eorum, quae non vult: nihil autem, nisi quod vult, facit; ergo nihil omnino potest eorum facere, quae non facit. Consequens est itaque, ut libere fateamur, Deum hodie idcirco non pluere, quia non potest; idcirco languidos non erigere, quia non potest; ideo non occidere injustos; ideo non ex eorum oppressionibus liberare sanctos. Haec, et alia multa idcirco Deus non facit, quia non vult, et quia non vult, non potest; sequitur ergo, ut quidquid Deus non facit, facere omnino non possit. Quod profecto tam videtur absurdum, tamque ridiculum, ut non modo omnipotenti Deo nequeat assertio ista congruere, sed ne fragili quidem homini valeat convenire. Multa siquidem sunt quae nos non facimus, et tamen facere possumus. ... Si quid igitur tale divinis paginis reperitur insertum, non mox passim procaci ac praesumptiva vulgari debet audacia, sed sub modesta sobrii sermonis proferendum est disciplina; quia si hoc diffunditur in vulgus, ut Deus in aliquo, quod dici nefas est, impotens asseratur, illico plebs indocta confunditur, et Christiana fides non sine magno animarum discrimine perturbatur." Cf. PL 145, 601.

6 PL 145, 600-601; 618-619

7 Anselm, Proslogium, ch. 7 (Opera Omnia, ed. F. S. Schmitt; Edinburgh, 1946), Vol. I, p. 105.

8 Ibid., 105: "Sed et omnipotens quomodo es, si omnia non potes? Aut si non potes corrumpi nec mentiri

nec facere verum esse falsum, ut quod factum est non
esse factum, et plura similiter: quomodo potes omnia?
An haec posse non est potentia, sed impotentia? Nam qui
haec potest, quod sibi non expedit et quod non debet
potest. Quae quanto magis potest, tanto magis
adversitas et perversitas possunt in illum, et ipse
minus contra illas. Qui ergo sic potest, non potentia
potest, sed impotentia. Non enim ideo dicitur posse,
quia ipse possit, sed quia sua impotentia facit aliud in
se posse; sive aliquo alio genere loquendi, sicut multa
improprie dicuntur. Ut cum ponimus 'esse' pro 'non
esse', et 'facere' pro eo quod est 'non facere', aut pro
'nihil facere'." Cf. De casu diaboli, 12 (Opera Omnia,
I, 253). For an extensive examination of Anselm's
position see my "Necessity and Freedom in Anselm's
Conception of God," Analecta Anselmiana, 4.2 (1975),
39-64.

9 Abelard, Theologia christiana, V (PL 178,
1321-1330); Introductio ad theologiam, III, 4-5 (PL 178,
1091-1102).

10 Anselm, Cur Deus homo, II, 5 (Opera Omnia, II,
100); II, 10 (Opera Omnia, II, 107); II, 17 (Opera
Omnia, II, 122-126); "Necessity and Freedom," pp. 53-60.

11 Cur Deus homo, II, 10 (Opera Omnia, II, 107):
"Omnis potestas sequitur voluntatem. Cum enim dico quia
possum loqui vel ambulare, subauditur: si volo. ...
Possumus itaque dicere de Christo quia potuit mentiri,
si subauditur: si vellet. Et quoniam mentiri non potuit
nolens nec potuit velle mentiri, non minus dici potest
nequivisse mentiri. Sic itaque potuit et non potuit
mentiri." Cf. also chs. 16 (II, 120-121) and 17 (II,
122-126).

12 Cur Deus homo, II, 5 (Opera Omnia, II, 100):
"Non enim haec est dicenda necessitas, sed gratia, quia
nullo cogente illam suscepit aut servat, sed gratis.
Nam si quod hodie sponte promittis cras te daturum,
eadem cras voluntate das, quamvis necesse sit te cras
reddere promissum, si potest, aut mentiri: non tamen
minus tibi debet ille pro impenso beneficio cui das,
quam si non promisisses, quoniam te debitorem ante
tempus dationis illi facere non es cunctatus." "Quare
multo magis, si deus facit bonum homini quod incepit,
licet non deceat eum a bono incepto deficere, totum
gratiae debemus imputare, quia hoc propter nos, non

propter se nullius egens incepit. Non enim illum latuit quid homo facturus erat, cum illum fecit, et tamen bonitate sua illum creando sponte se ut perficeret inceptum bonum quasi obligavit. Denique deus nihil facit necessitate, quia nullo modo cogitur aut prohibetur facere aliquid."

13 Glossa ordinaria on Gen. 19: "poterat de potentia, non poterat de iustitia."

14 Introductio ad theologiam, III, 4 (PL 178, 1092): "Posse itaque Deus omnia dicitur, non quod omnes suscipere possit actiones, sed quod in omnibus quae fieri velit, nihil eius voluntati resistere queat." (PL 178, 1094): "Hinc est illa Platonis verissima ratio, qua scilicet probat Deum nullatenus mundum meliorem potuisse facere qua fecerit; sic quippe in Timaeo suo ait: 'Dicendum', inquit, 'cur conditor fabricatorque geniturae omne hoc instituendum putaverit. Optimus erat. Ab optimo porro invidia longe relagata est, itaque consequenter sui similia cuncta, prout cujusque natura capax beatitudinis esse potuerit, effici voluit'." (PL 178, 1095): "Patet itaque quidquid Deus faciat ac dimittat, justam ac rationabilem causam subesse, ut sola faciat aut dimittat; quae fieri vel dimitti oporteat atque ipsum deceat. Quod si quidquid facit eum facere oportet, justum est ubique ut faciat quidquid facit, ac sine dubio quidquid facit facere debet. Omne quippe quod justum est fieri, injustum est dimitti, et quisquis non facit id quod ratio exigit, aeque delinquit, ac si id faciat quod rationi minime concordat." (PL 178, 1096): "Hac itaque ratione id solum posse facere videur Deus quod facit, vel illud solum dimittere posse quod dimittit. ... Ex his itaque tam de ratione quam de scripto collatis, constat id solum posse facere Deum quod aliquando facit."

15 Bernard of Clairvaux, Epist. 190; William of St. Thierry, Disputatio (PL 180, 270); Odo of Ourscamps, Quaestiones Magistri Odonis Suessionensis, II, 298, in Analecta novissima Spicilegii Solesmensis II, ed. by I. B. Card. Pitra (Tusculum, 1888), 113; Hugh of St. Victor, De sacramentis, I, 2, 22 (PL 176, 214-216); Summa sententiarum, I, 14 (PL 176, 68-70); Peter Lombard, Sententiae in IV Libris Distinctae, L. I, dist. 42-44 ("Spicilegium Bonaventurianum," IV; Grottaferrata, 1971), 294-306. Cf. Peter Comestor on Matthew 19, Historia Scholastica (PL 198, 1588): "Potest enim Deus

facere, ut camelus transeat per foramen acus, nullo ob-
stante. Avarum vero, qui hic nomine divitis intelligitur, ponere in gloria, si potest de potentia, de justi-
tia non potest."

[16] Augustine, De natura et gratia, c. 7, n. 8 (PL
44, 250; CSEL 60, 237); Lombard, Sent. I, dist. 43 (I,
303).

[17] Quaestiones in epistolam ad Romanos, q. 91 (PL
175, col. 457): "Quaeritur an Deus potuit facere
convenientiorem modum redemptionis? Si dicatur quod non
potuit, videtur quod potentia Dei terminum habeat, et
non sit immensa; si dicatur quod potuit, quomodo iste
convenientissimus est? Solutio: Licet in hoc terminum
habeat, non tamen simpliciter concedendum, quod terminum
habeat. Vel licet iste modus nostrae miseriae sit
convenientissimus, non tamen est necesse, quod sit
convenientissimus absolute."

[18] Godfrey of Poitiers, Summa (Avranches, Bibl. de
la ville, Cod. lat. 121, fol. 137^r: "Dico quod de
potestate absoluta potuit ei dare. Quis enim auderet de
potestate eius et immensitate disputare? Sed non potuit
de potentia conditionali, scilicet manentibus decretis,
quae ipse constituit." In A. Landgraf, Dogmengeschichte
der Frühscholastik, II, 2 (Regensburg, 1954), p. 103.

[19] William of Auxerre, Summa Aurea (Paris, 1500),
fol. 27^v: "Ad primo objectum dicimus, quod Deus de
potentia pure considerata potest damnare Petrum, et
habito respectu ad potentiam Dei et potentiam Petri
naturalem qua potuit peccare et non peccare. Sed non
sequitur: ergo, potest damnare Petrum, quia hoc verbum
'potest' in conclusione respicit merita."

[20] William of Auvergne, De trinitate, c. 10 (Opera
omnia, Paris, 1674), p. 14.

[21] Leipzig, Universitätsbibliothek, Cod. lat. 573,
fol. 223^r: "Distingui tamen debet, quod duplex est
potentia Dei, absoluta et ordinata. De absoluta potentia potuit Deus et potest adhuc dare puro homini
potestatem cooperationis. De potestate ordinata non
potest, id est non mutato ordine rerum. Idem enim
omnino est potentia absoluta Dei et ordinata. Sed
potentia ordinata respicit ordinem rebus a Deo inditum."
Cited from Landgraf, Dogmengeschichte, III, 1 (Regens-

burg, 1954), 207.

[22] For Guerric see Paris, Bibl. nat. lat. 15 603, fol. 11ʳ: "Potestate absoluta potuit dare, sed non potestate ordinata, quae respicit ordinem rerum;" cited from Landgraf, Dogmengeschichte, III, 1, p. 207. Albertus Magnus, Sent. I, dist. 42, a. 6 (Opera omnia, ed. A. Borgnet), Vol. XXVI (Paris, 1893), 362-366; dist. 43, pp. 377-380. The Summa theologiae, attributed to Albert and on which Borchert relied for his interpretation of Albert, is of doubtful authenticity; see A. Hufnagel, "Zur Echtheitsfrage der Summa Theologiae Alberts des Grossen," Theologische Quartalschrift, CXLVI (1966), 8-39. Summa Halensis, Pt. I, inq. I, Tr. 4, q. 1, m. 2, c. 2 (Quaracchi, 1924), I, 207: "Tamen comparando absolute potentiam voluntati, sic potentia in plus est quam voluntas; secundum vero quod intelligitur potentia ordinata, quae quidem ordinatio intelligitur in ratione praeordinationis, coaequantur potentia et voluntas. Distinguitur ergo potentia absoluta [a] potentia ordinata. Potentia absoluta est eorum quorum non est divina praeordinatio; potentia vero ordinata est eorum quorum est divina praeordinatio, hoc est eorum quae a Deo sunt praeordinata sive disposita." Cf. pp. 220-222, 228, 234-235.

[23] Peter Damian, De divina omnipotentia (PL 145, 619): "... non inepte possumus dicere quia potest Deus facere, in illa invariabili et constantissima semper aeternitate sua, ut quod factum fuerat apud hoc transire nostrum, factum non sit, scilicet ut dicamus: Roma, quae antiquitus condita est, potest Deus agere ut condita non fuerit. Hoc quod dicimus: potest, praesentis videlicet temporis, congrue dicitur quantum pertinet ad immobilem Dei omnipotentis aeternitatem; sed quantum ad nos, ubi continuata mobilitas, et perpes est transitus, ut mos est, potuit convenientius diceremus ...." "Potuit secundum nos, potest secundum se."

[24] Summa Halensis, Pt. I, Inq. I, Tr. 4, q. 1, m. 4 (I, 228). The Summa Halensis identifies potentia ordinata with total divine preordination, possibly influencing usage in the second half of the thirteenth century. It also established a trend by defining potentia absoluta not as the realm of total possibility out of which God chose but specifically those things that he did not choose.

[25] A number of authors distinguished two types of order or two categories within the ordained order. Already in the mid-twelfth century Clarembald of Arras argued that while miracles suspend the "common course of nature," they are not "contra naturam, quae est voluntas Dei" (Tract. super librum Genesis in N. Häring, Life and Works of Clarembald of Arras (Toronto, 1965), p. 239. Thomas Aquinas and Peter Aureoli distinguished the natural order from the order of justice, while Duns Scotus distinguished general decrees from those that applied to particular persons. Thomas was well aware of the distinction between the general will of God and the present order of things. In question 19, a.7, of the first part of his Summa theologiae Thomas affirmed the unchanging nature of the divine will despite the changes in divine decrees. Later, in article 6 of question 105 he cited Augustine's distinction between the common course of nature and the higher law of God (Contra Faustum, c. 26): "Deus contra solitum cursum naturae facit; sed contra summam legem nullo modo facit, quia contra seipsum non facit." For Thomas changes in God's ordinances do not represent changes in his will: "Unde cum praeter hunc ordinem agit, non mutatur." And yet Thomas did not employ this distinction in his discussion of divine power in question 25, and Peter of Tarantasia's attempt was largely unsuccessful.

A few writers made this distinction in the context of their discussions of divine omnipotence. In the course of an extensive treatment given to absolute and ordained power by Francis Mayronnes, Sent. I, dists. 43-44, q. 6, he noted that "potentia ordinata potest dupliciter accipi: vel quae actualiter est ordinata, vel quae aptitudinaliter vel possit esse ordinata. Licet enim Deus non ordinaverit quod revelet mihi hodie incarnationem, tamen posset oppositum ordinare de potentia absoluta. Ergo Deus de potentia absoluta multa potest quae non potest de potentia ordinata actualiter; sed tamen nihil potest nisi quod potest de potentia ordinata vel actualiter vel aptitudinaliter." Pierre d'Ailly made a similar distinction within ordained power; Sent. I, q. 13, a. 1: "Sed Deum aliquid posse de potentia ordinata potest dupliciter intelligi. Uno modo stricte, quod potest stante sua ordinatione qua aeternaliter voluit se sic vel sic esse facturum, et sic solum potest illa quae ipse ordinavit se facturum. Alio modo potest intelligi magis large, quod potest stante veritate legis seu scripturae divinae. Et sic

possibile ordinate potest dici illud quod est possibile
et non obviat alicui veritati legis ordinatae vel scripturae sacrae. ... Aliquid est impossibile de potentia
ordinata primo modo et non secundo modo ...." For the
full text see article XI 41.

As unfortunate as it seems in retrospect, it is
understandable why that distinction between normal order
and special order was never fully developed in the thirteenth century. The absoluta/ordinata distinction was
designed to establish necessity or contingency by
proving impossibility or possibility. They were less
concerned with the questions of whether God might act
arbitrarily, and what conditions the actions of God.
But because the latter issues were handled separately
and not built into or accommodated by the absoluta/-
ordinata distinction, that could leave the erroneous
impression that if miracles or special decrees were not
in the normal order of things, they must be in the area
of power considered absolutely.

26 Albertus Magnus, I Sent., dist. 42, a. 6 (Opera
omnia, ed. A. Borgnet, Vol. XXVI; Paris, 1893), p. 366:
"Ad aliud dicendum, quod potentia absolute considerata
generalior est, quam est ars vel scientia practica: et
ideo illa objectio non procedit, nisi de potentia
exsequente, et non de potentia absolute considerata." I
Sent, dist. 43, arts. 1-3 (XXVI, 377-380), where Albert
contrasts potentia absoluta with potentia conjuncta
actui. I Sent., dist. 44, arts. 2-4, where Albert seems
to restrict the divine wisdom to the present order of
things (XXVI, 391-395). Bonaventure, Commentaria in
quatuor libros Sententiarum, I, dist. 43, dub. 7 (Opera
omnia, Vol. I; Quaracchi, 1883), p. 778: "Aliqui
distinguunt hic potentiam Dei dupliciter, dicentes, Deum
posse aut de potentia absoluta, et sic potest Iudam
salvare et Petrum damnare; aut de potentia ordinata, et
sic non potest. Sed haec distinctio non videtur esse
conveniens, quia nihil potest Deus, quod non possit
ordinate. Posse enim inordinate facere est 'non posse',
sicut posse peccare et posse mentiri." Elsewhere
Bonaventure seems to allow some validity to the
distinction of divine capacity and volition; cf.
Breviloquium, p. 1, c. 7; Sent. I, dist. 43, q. 4 (I,
775); Sent. I, dist. 43, dub. 2 (I, 776-777); Sent. II,
dist. 7, p. 1, a. 1, q. 1, ad 1. Richard Rufus, In
comm. Sent. Bonav. abbreviatio, I, dist. 43 (Vat. lat.
12 993, fol. 117rb, cited from Gál, "Petrus de
Trabibus," p. 285): "Responsio: quidam dicunt quod Deus

potest de potentia absoluta et Iudam salvare et Petrum damnare, sed de potentia ordinata non potest. Sed haec distinctio potentiae non videtur conveniens, quia nihil potest Deus quod non possit ordinate. Posse enim inordinate facere est non posse, sicut posse peccare."
Henry of Ghent later repeated Bonaventure's reservations about applying this distinction to God's power. It is curious that those most responsible for perfecting the distinction in the thirteenth century were Dominicans: Hugh of St. Cher, Guerric of St. Quentin, Albertus Magnus, and Thomas Aquinas, while those most suspicious of its value have usually been associated with the Augustinian tradition: Bonaventure, Richard Rufus, and Henry of Ghent. The latter were reluctant to apply to God a distinction that to them suggested a difference between the way God normally acts and the way he occasionally acts.
Albert's position on this issue has usually (Borchert, Desharnais) been extracted from the possibly inauthentic **Summa theologiae** (see above, note 22). There **potentia absoluta** was defined as total possibility, unchecked even by the principle of non-contradiction; **potentia ordinata**, on the other hand, meant that God cannot make contradictories true at the same time. Albertus Magnus(?), **Summa theol.**, Pt. I, Tr. 19, q. 78, m. 2, solutio (**Opera omnia**, XXXI; Paris, 1895), p. 832: "Ad hoc dici consuevit, quod potentia Dei potest accipi absolute, et potest accipi ut disposita et ordinata secundum rationem scientiae et voluntatis. Si accipitur absolute: tunc, ut dicit Damascenus, accipitur ut pelagus potestatis infinitae, et tunc nihil est quod non possit. Si autem accipitur ut potentia disposita et ordinata secundum providentiam et bonitatem: tunc dicitur quod potest facere ea quae potentiae sunt, et non ea quae impotentiae. Unde sic non potest facere majorem se, nec potest facere contra ordinem veritatis suae, et sic non potest facere esse et non esse simul de eodem, vel alia opposita esse simul, quia faceret contra veritatem ordinationis suae."

27 Thomas Aquinas, **Scriptum**, I, dist. 42, q. 2, arts. 2-3 (**Opera omnia**, Vol. VI; Parma, 1856), pp. 344-346; **Scriptum**, I, dist. 43, q. 2, arts. 1-2 (VI, 350-351).

28 Thomas Aquinas, **Quaestiones disputatae de potentia Dei**, q. 1, a. 5 (**Opera omnia**; Parma, 1856), VIII, 10: "Respondeo dicendum, quod hic error, scilicet Deum

non posse facere nisi quae facit, duorum fuit. Primo
fuit quorumdam Philosophorum dicentium Deum agere ex
necessitate naturae. Quod si esset, cum natura sit
determinata ad unum, divina potentia ad alia agenda se
extendere non posset quam ad ea quae facit. Secundo
fuit quorumdam Theologorum considerantium ordinem divinae justitiae et sapientiae, secundum quem res fiunt a
Deo, quem Deum praeterire non posse dicebant; et
incidebant in hoc, ut dicerent, quod Deus non potest
facere nisi quae facit." "Ex his ergo colligitur quod
id quod ex necessitate natura agit, impossibile est esse
principium agens, cum determinetur sibi finis ab alio.
Et sic patet quod impossibile est Deum agere ex
necessitate naturae; et ita radix primae positionis
falsa est.
    Sic autem restat investigare de secunda positione.
Circa quod sciendum est, quod dupliciter dicitur aliquis
non posse aliquid. Uno modo absolute; quando scilicet
aliquod principiorum, quod sit necessarium actioni, ad
actionem illam non se extendit; ut si pes sit con-
fractus; posito enim opposito alicuius actionis, actio
fieri non potest; non enim possum ambulare dum sedeo."
"Sicut enim manifestatur divina bonitas per has res quae
nunc sunt et per hunc rerum ordinem; ita potest manifestari per alias creaturas et alio modo ordinatas; et
ideo divina voluntas absque praeiudicio bonitatis,
iustitiae et sapientiae, potest se extendere in alia
quam quae facit. Et in hoc fuerunt decepti errantes:
aestimaverunt enim ordinem creaturarum esse quasi
commensuratum divinae bonitatis quasi absque eo esse non
posset. Patet ergo quod absolute Deus potest facere
alia quam quae fecit. Sed quia ipse non potest facere
quod contradictoria sint simul vera, ex suppositione
potest dici, quod Deus non potest alia facere quam quae
fecit: supposito enim quod ipse non velit alia facere,
vel quod praesciverit se non alia facturum, non potest
alia facere, ut intelligatur composite, non divisim."
Summa theologiae, Pt. I, q. 25, a. 5, ad 1 (Ottawa,
1945), I, 177: "... quod attribuitur potentiae secundum
se consideratae, dicitur Deus posse secundum potentiam
absolutam." "Quod autem attribuitur potentiae divinae
secundum quod exequitur imperium voluntatis iustae, hoc
dicitur Deus posse facere de potentia ordinata.
Secundum hoc ergo dicendum est quod Deus potest alia
facere de potentia absoluta, quam quae praescivit et
praeordinavit se facturum; non tamen potest esse quod
aliqua faciat, quae non praesciverit et praeordinaverit
se facturum. Quia ipsum facere subiacet praescientiae

et praeordinationi; non autem ipsum posse, quod est
naturale." Cf. Summa theologiae, I, q. 19, a. 3; Summa
contra Gentiles, II, chs. 23-30.

29 Peter of Tarantasia (Innocent V), Sent. I, dist.
43, q. 1, a. 4 (In IV. Libros Sententiarum Commentaria,
Vol. I; Toulouse, 1652; repr. 1964), pp. 360-61:
"Respondeo: est ordo simpliciter et est ordo ut nunc.
Nihil potest Deus nisi de potentia ordinata, primo modo
loquendo de ordine; sed multa potest de potentia,
circumscripto hoc ordine, scilicet ut nunc. Primo modo
dicitur posse de potentia absoluta; secundo modo dicitur
posse de potentia ordinata. Ergo multa potest primo
modo quae non potest secundo modo. Ideo quaedam dicitur
posse de potentia absoluta, quae non potest de ordinata,
quia multa subsunt suae potentiae quae non congruit sibi
ut nunc facere; posset tamen ea facere convenientia, et
sic ea facere." Thomas Aquinas distinguished between
present law and total divine will (Summa theol., Pt. I,
q. 19, a. 6-7) but not in the context of his discussion
of omnipotence.

30 If an adjectival construction was to be
substituted for the adverbial, absoluta might better
have modified 'possibility' than 'power'.

31 Thomas Aquinas, Summa theol., Pt. I, q. 25, q.
5, ad 1 (I, 176): "... in nobis ... potest esse aliquid
in potentia, quod non potest esse in voluntate iusta,
vel in intellectu sapiente."

32 G. Post, Studies in Medieval Legal Thought:
Public Law and the State, 1100-1322 (Princeton, 1964),
pp. 264-269. See also Brian Tierney, Origins of Papal
Infallibility, 1150-1350 (Leiden, 1972).

33 Corpus iuris civilis, C. 1, 14, 4, ed. P.
Krueger, T. Mommsen, and R. Schoell (3 vols., Berlin,
1899-1902), II, 68, cited in F. Oakley, "Jacobean
Political Theology," 330. The mid-fourteenth-century
civilian and canonist, Baldus de Ubaldis, glossed the
lex digna by using the absoluta/ordinata distinction to
underscore the self-binding nature of human sovereignty;
Oakley, p. 330. Giles of Rome used the same analogy in
his De ecclesiastica potestate, ed. R. Scholz (Weimar,
1929), III, 9, pp. 190-195. It should be noted that
Giles does not equate plenitudo potestatis with potentia
absoluta either for pope or God. Actions within the law

and outside the law are both ordained, but in different ways. In concluding a passage on the self-binding nature of papal conformity to the law (III, ch. 7, pp. 181-182) Giles states: "Verumtamen huiusmodi iurisdictio, quod sit sic casualis non est referenda ad suum posse absolutum, sed ad suum posse, ut est quibusdam regulis regulatum." It is interesting that this analogy was not taken one step further in the constitutional structure of medieval society. One could argue that all human obedience to the law is in some sense self-imposed by way of an earlier social contract. One might view Marsilius of Padua's legislator humanus as a corporate personality who has voluntarily bound himself to obey the law.

34 Hostiensis, Lectura in quinque Decretalium Gregorianarum libros, Ad 3, 35, 6 (Venice, 1581; repr. 1965), III, fol. 134r: "dixerunt quod super his non potest Papa dispensare cum monacho, quamdiu monachus est, potest tamen facere de monacho non monachum .... Alii dicunt, quod licet votum sit de substantia monachatus, tamen hoc potest de plenitudine potestatis, quasi dicant, non de potestate ordinata, sed de absoluta, secundum quam potest mutare substantiam rei .... Nec obstat, quod hic dicitur, quia quod sequitur possit exponendum est, id est, potentiae suae non congruit, sic exponitur illud Hieronymi . . . Vel de solito cursu, quia non consuevit hoc facere, posset tamen si vellet, sic expone et hic. Vel hoc non potest Papa sine causa, sed ex magna et Deo magis placente hoc posset. ... Alii tamen quam Papae contra iura sine causa dispensare non licet, quod si praesumpserit non valet dispensatio, vel revocatur .... Sed et ex causa potest Papa dispensare cum monacho, ut proprium habeat. Quid enim si tota Christianitas, vel etiam aliqua pars ipsius esset in periculo, nisi monachus fieret rex. Forte, quia non est alius qui posset vel sciret regnum regere. Nonne dices, quod monachus fiat rex in hoc casu?" Hostiensis' reference in this context to the famous passage in Jerome suggests that his analogy was derived from the theological tradition we have examined, not from the commentaries on the Decretum, where Jerome's text occurs in a different context.

J. Marrone, "The Absolute and the Ordained Powers of the Pope: an Unedited Text of Henry of Ghent," Mediaeval Studies, XXXVI (1974), 7-22, has called attention to another passage in Hostiensis where papal

dispensation is described as de potestate absoluta.
Lectura, Ad 5, 31, 8 (V, fol. 72^V): "... quia Papa hoc
potest facere sine concilio ecclesiarum, ... sed
episcopus hoc non potest absque laudatione clericorum
suorum, et consensu ambarum ecclesiarum .... Sed nec
Papa haec, vel alios casus sibi specialiter reservatos,
ut in praemissis versibus, consuevit expedire sine
consilio fratrum suorum, id est Cardinalium, nec istud
potest facere de potestate ordinaria, referring to his
discussion of papal dispensation in 3, 10, 4 and 3, 8,
4, licet secus sit de absoluta." See also F. Oakley,
"Jacobean Political Theology," 323-346, who first called
attention to the Hostiensis text.

35 Paris, Bibl. Nat. 3120, fol. 139^V; Marrone, "The
Absolute and Ordained Powers of the Pope," p. 17: "...
de potentia absoluta et ordinata. Licet enim circa Deum
non contingat distinguere inter potentiam absolutam et
ordinatam; Deus enim, eo quod peccare non potest, nichil
potest de potentia absoluta nisi illud possit de
potentia ordinata. Omnis enim potentia sua quocumque
modo vadit in actum ordinata [est]." As Marrone concluded, p. 18: "since Henry of Ghent identified absolute
power with power used sinfully and unjustly, he thus had
to deny that God possessed such absolute power." In
light of the views of Henry of Ghent, there is a need to
examine how the distinction was understood and used by
Robert Kilwardby, John Pecham, Giles of Rome, and
Godfrey of Fontaines.

36 Although Henry of Ghent rejected the absolute/-
ordinata distinction as it applied to God's power, he
did equate papal plenitudo potestatis with potestas
absoluta. Paris, Bibl. Nat. lat. 3120, fol. 140^r
(Marrone, p. 18): "Ecce plana distinctio inter potentiam
absolutam et ordinatam circa dominum papam. Quando
beatus Bernardus aliquid factitando ostendit se habere
plenitudinem potestatis, quam appelo potentiam absolutam, super quo dubitat an habeat potentiam iusticie,
quam appelo potentiam ordinatam."

37 Gál, "Petrus de Trabibus." Trabibus' contemporary, Richard de Mediavilla, also established the
boundaries of potentia absoluta by the principle of
non-contradiction, as did Thomas; Sent. I, dist. 43, q.
7, as cited by E. Hocedez, Richard de Middleton (Paris,
1925), 245: "Respondeo, quod si dicam posse de potentia
ordinata illud quod ipse facturum proposuit et rationa-

biliter disposuit, sic dico quod aliqua potest de
potentia absoluta, quae non potest de potentia ordinata:
quia absolute potest quidquid non includit contradictionem."

[38] Trabibus, as cited in Gál, p. 290: "Si loquamur
de potentia ordinata, quia ille rerum ordo et numerus
aeternaliter a divina sapientia et voluntate est
praefixus et praeordinatus et non aliter, ideo licet
alia possit facere et alia omittere, numquam tamen
eveniret quod aliter fiat." For a similar discussion in
Trabibus' master, Petrus Johannis Olivi, see the
latter's Quaestiones in secundum librum Sententiarum,
ed. B. Jansen, Bibliotheca Franciscana Scholastica Medii
Aevi, Vol. IV (Quaracchi, 1922), pp. 63-65. It may well
be that Franciscan polity encouraged Olivi and Trabibus,
in applying the absoluta/ordinata distinction, to adopt
the position of the infallibility (unchangeability) of
God's "past tradition"; see Tierney, Origins of Papal
Infallibility.

[39] John Duns Scotus, Opera Omnia, Vol. VI, ed. A.
Sépinski (Vatican, 1963), Ordinatio I, dist. 44, q. un,
pp. 363-369.

[40] Among the numerous works on these aspects of
Scotus' thought, see: W. Dettloff, Die Lehre von der
Acceptatio divina bei Johannes Duns Scotus (Werl i.W.,
1954); A. B. Wolter, "Native Freedom of the Will as a
Key to the Ethics of Scotus," in Deus et Homo ad mentem
I. Duns Scoti; Acta Tertii Congressus Scotistici Inter-
nationalis Vindebonae, 1970 (Rome, 1972), 359-370.

[41] Scotus, Ordinatio I, pp. 364-366.

[42] Ibid.: "Quando autem illa lex recta -- secundum
quam ordinate agendum est -- non est in potestate
agentis, tunc potentia eius absoluta non potest excedere
potentiam eius ordinatam circa obiecta aliqua, nisi
circa illa agat inordinate; necessarium enim est illam
legem stare -- comparando ad tale agens -- et tamen
actionem 'non conformatam illi legi rectae' non esse
rectam neque ordinatam, quia tale agens tenetur agere
secundum illam regulam cui subest. Unde omnes qui
subsunt legi divinae, si non agunt secundum illam,
inordinate agunt.
    Sed quando in potestate agentis est lex et
rectitudo legis, ita quod non est recta nisi quia

statuta, tunc potest aliter agens ex libertate sua
ordinare quam lex illa recta dictet; et tamen cum hoc
potest ordinate agere, quia potest statuere aliam legem
rectam secundum quam agat ordinate. Nec tunc potentia
sua absoluta simpliciter excedit potentiam ordinatam,
quia esset ordinata secundum aliam legem sicut secundum
priorem; tamen excedit potentiam ordinatam praecise
secundum priorem legem, contra quam vel praeter quam
facit. Ita posset exemplificari de principe et sub-
ditis, et lege positiva." "Ideo sicut potest aliter
agere, ita potest aliam legem rectam statuere, -- quae
.si statueretur a Deo, recta esset, quia nulla lex est
recta nisi quatenus a voluntate divina acceptante est
statuta; et tunc potentia eius absoluta ad aliquid, non
se extendit ad aliud quam ad illud quod ordinate fieret,
si fieret: non quidem fieret ordinate secundum istum
ordinem, sed fieret ordinate secundum alium ordinem,
quem ordinem ita posset voluntas divina statuere sicut
potest agere."

[43] Ibid.: "... potest agere praeter illam legem vel
contra eam, et in hoc est potentia absoluta, excedens
potentiam ordinatam. Et ideo non tantum in Deo, sed in
omni agente libere -- qui potest agere secundum dictamen
legis rectae et praeter talem legem vel contra eam --
est distinguere inter potentiam ordinatam et absolutam;
ideo dicunt iuristae quod aliquis hoc potest facere de
facto, hoc est de potentia sua absoluta, -- vel de iure,
hoc est de potentia ordinata secundum iura." The
distinction to which Scotus refers appears in Decretales
Greg. IX, 1, 3, 13 where lack of power (impotentia) can
result from legal condition (de iure) or from physical
impediment (de facto). The positive corollary, the
distinction between potentia de iure and potentia de
facto can be found in Hostiensis, Lectura, Ad 1, 3, 13
(I, fol. 14vb) and Ad 2, 28, 65 (II, fol. 200vb). The
juridical flavor of Scotus' treatment of divine
omnipotence has been noted by Pernoud, "The Theory of
the Potentia Dei," 84-86.

[44] Ockham's discussion of the ambiguity of 'posse'
was anticipated by the Summa Halensis, Pt. I, Inq. I,
Tr. 4, q. 1, m. 4 (I, 228): "... sic nos loquimur de
divino 'posse' duobus modis: habere potentiam vel uti
potentia." Cf. Petrus Johannis Olivi, Quaest. in
secundum librum Sent., I, 64; Gál, "Petrus de Trabibus,"
286, 290. Ockham's reaffirmation of the traditional
theological meaning of the distinction parallels that of

Thomas at various points. Ockham followed the thirteenth-century practice, found both in Thomas and
Scotus, of using human analogies to explain divine
power; e.g., Quodl. VI, q. 1 (Opera theologica, IX, ed.
J. C. Wey; St. Bonaventure, N.Y., 1980), p. 586: "Sicut
Papa aliqua non potest secundum iura statuta ab eo, quae
tamen absolute potest." Ockham also followed the main
lines of Scotus' ethical .teaching, including the belief
that God never acts inordinate but would, by a change of
decree, establish a new order; see W. Kölmel, "Das
Naturrecht bei Wilhelm von Ockham," Franziskanische
Studien, XXXV (1953), 39-85; David Clark, "Voluntarism
and Rationalism in the Ethics of Ockham," Franciscan
Studies, XXXI (1971), 72-87; A. Wolter, "Native Freedom
of the Will."
    The traditional character of Ockham's teaching on
this issue has been frequently noted in the last decade.
See, for example, H. A. Oberman, Harvest of Medieval
Theology, 30-56; Pernoud, "Innovation in William of
Ockham's References;" "The Theory of the Potentia Dei;"
Courtenay, "Nominalism and Late Medieval Religion," pp.
37-43. K. Bannach, Die Lehre von der doppelten Macht
Gottes bei Wilhelm von Ockham (Wiesbaden, 1975) provides
a somewhat different interpretation.

    [45] On John XXII's views see Ockham, Opus nonaginta
dierum, ch. 95 (Lyons, 1495): "Quia iste impugnatus ut
quidam istorum impugnatorum dicunt se audivisse ab ore
eius, et ipse postea in sermonibus suis declaravit,
negat illam distinctionem theologorum de potentia Dei
ordinata et absoluta intendens multis rationibus
ostendere quod quicquid potest Deus de potentia absoluta
potest etiam de potentia ordinata, et quicquid non
potest de potentia ordinata non potest de potentia
absoluta." Ockham, Tractatus contra Benedictum, ch. 3;
Opera politica, Vol. III (Manchester, 1956), pp.
230-234.

    [46] Ockham, Quodlibeta, VI, q. 1 (ed. cit.,
585-586): "... quaedam potest Deus facere de potentia
ordinata et aliqua de potentia .absoluta. Haec
distinctio non est sic intelligenda quod in Deo sint
realiter duae potentiae quarum una sit ordinata et alia
absoluta, quia unica potentia est in Deo ad extra, quae
omni modo est ipse Deus. Nec sic est intelligenda quod
aliqua potest Deus ordinate facere, et aliqua potest
absolute et non ordinate, quia Deus nihil potest facere
inordinate. Sed est sic intelligenda quod 'posse

[facere] aliquid' quandoque accipitur secundum leges ordinatas et institutas a Deo, et illa dicitur Deus posse facere de potentia ordinata. Aliter accipitur 'posse' pro posse facere omne illud quod non includit contradictionem fieri, sive Deus ordinaverit se hoc facturum sive non, quia multa potest Deus facere quae non vult facere ...." Summa logicae, III-4, c. 6 (Opera philosophica, I, ed. Ph. Boehner, G. Gál, & S. Brown; St. Bonaventure, N.Y., 1974), 779-780: "Item, talis propositio 'Deus per suam potentiam absolutam potest aliquem acceptare sine gratia sed non per suam potentiam ordinatam' multiplex est. Unus sensus est quod Deus pe unam potentiam, quae est absoluta et non ordinata, potest acceptare aliquem sine gratia, et per unam aliam potentiam, quae est ordinata et non absoluta, non potest acceptare eum, quasi essent duae potentiae in Deo per quarum unam posset hoc et non per aliam. Et iste sensus est falsus. Aliter accpitur improprie, ut ponatur ista propositio pro ista oratione: Deus potest acceptare aliquem sine gratia informante, quia hoc non includit contradictionem, et tamen ordinavit quod hoc numquam est facturus. Et iste sensus verus est." Opus nonaginta dierum, c. 95 (Opera politica, II; Manchester, 1963), pp. 726-727: "Et ita dicere quod Deus potest aliqua de potentia absoluta, quae non potest de potentia ordinata, non est aliud, secundum intellectum recte intelligentium, quam dicere quod Deus aliqua potest, quae tamen minime ordinavit se facturum; quae tamen si faceret, de potentia ordinata faceret ipsa; quia si faceret ea, ordinaret se facturum ipsa. Quia igitur, ut dicunt isti, iste impugnatus nescivit videre aequivocationem huius verbi 'potest', ideo male intellexit illam distinctionem theologorum de potentia Dei absoluta et ordinata." "Rationes vero, per quas probare conatur quod praemissa distinctio de potentia Dei absoluta et ordinata non est approbanda, facile dissolvuntur. Prima enim ex falso intellectu procedit, quasi haec esset possibilis secundum sic distinguentes: 'Deus aliquid facit de potentia absoluta, quod non facit de potentia ordinata'. Haec enim de inesse secundum eos est impossibilis et contradictionem includit; quia eo ipso quod Deus aliquid faceret, ipse faceret illud de potentia ordinata." Cf. Gál, "Petrus de Trabibus," 287-288.

47 Gregory of Rimini, Super primum et secundum sententiarum, L. I, dist. 42-44, q. 1, a. 2 (Venice, 1522; repr. 1955), I, fol. 162^v-163^r. D'Ailly, Quaes-

tiones super libros sententiarum cum quibusdam in fine adjunctis, L. I, q. 13, a. 1 (Strasbourg, 1490; repr. 1968), D. Gabriel Biel, Sent. I, dist. 17, q. 1, a. 3; Biel, Sent. IV, dist. 1, q. 1, a. 3, dub. 2. The texts are provided in article XI 40-42.

[48] Fire is not necessary or contingent; the relationship of fire and combustion is necessary or contingent. It is not charitas that is necessary or contingent but the relationship of the habit of charity to the gift of eternal salvation that is necessary or contingent.

[49] In terminist logic there is a great deal of interest in the way in which the truth value of propositions changes with the circumstances in which it is spoken, thought, or written. This was particularly true in the fourteenth century for the time context. To give a present example, the statement "I am in Columbus" is true (at the time this paper was delivered), as is the statement "I was in Columbus" (at some previous time), but the statement "I was in Columbus last week" is true only if thought, spoken, or written during the week after I was in Columbus.

[50] Some of the parables of Christ pose that same time/reward problem, e.g. that of the laborers in the vineyard, or the parable of the talents. These also formed a source for fourteenth-century discussion and were so explored.

[51] Fourteenth-century discussions of certitude in light of the possibility of intuitive cognitions of non-existents provided another context for discussions of absolute and ordained power. See in particular K. H. Tachau, "The Problem of the Species in medio at Oxford in the Generation after Ockham," Mediaeval Studies, XLIV (1982), 394-443.

[52] Gregory of Rimini, Super Primum et Secundum Sententiarum (Venice, 1522; repr. 1955), I, 165 F: "... et non solum de potentia Dei, sed etiam naturali, quia in casu non ponitur Deum specialiter agere nisi quantum ad dationem praecepti." Pierre d'Ailly, Quaestiones super Libros Sententiarum (Strassburg, 1490; repr. 1968), Sent. IV, q. 1 N: "Tercia conclusio probatur, circa quam sciendum est quod sicut dicitur quod Deus aliquid potest de potentia absoluta quod non potest de

potentia ordinata, ita dico de creatura. Ideo concedo probabiliter quod licet creatura de potentia naturali seu naturaliter ordinata non possit creare vel annihilare ut dictum est. Tamen ista potest de potentia simpliciter absoluta, sive supernaturaliter seu miraculose."

[53] D'Ailly, Sent. IV, q. 1 N.

[54] Paul Streveler, "God's Absolute and Ordained Power in the Thought of Robert Holcot." Much of Holcot's usage is traditional, despite his fascination for time/place/decree problems of law-changing.

[55] Marsilius of Inghen, Questiones super quattuor libros sententiaaum (Strassburg, 1501; repr. 1966), L. I, q. 20, a. 2 (fol. 84^r): "Potest uno modo intelligi de potentia Dei absoluta, scilicet agendo praeter legem quam promulgavit. Alio modo agendo secundum legem quam ordinavit et promulgavit, scilicet agendo secundum potentiam ordinatam." "Deus de lege absoluta alicui posset dare salutem nullam habenti charitatem creatam." Sent. III, q. 9, a. 3 (fol. 405^V): "... et ex consequente potest non velle ea conservare de lege absoluta, ergo possunt ab anima Christi tolli." By the phrase de lege absoluta Marsilius meant nothing other than power or possibility considered absolutely, hypothetice (fol. 84^r). Yet the phrase betrays the model of law-making and sovereign power, paralleling Scotus' observation that all actions of God outside the normal course of nature and grace are simply other forms of law and order: ordo simpliciter as opposed to ordo ut nunc. Marsilius in Sent. I, q. 43, a. 1 (fol. 183^r) distinguishes between the common course of nature and potentia ordinata: "... quae secundum cursum naturae possunt esse, vel etiam secundum potentiam Dei ordinatam."

[56] Letters and Papers, Foreign and Domestic, of the Reign of Henry VIII, ed. J. Brewer et al. (22 vols., London, 1862-1932), IV, Pt. 2, 2158 (No. 4977); cited in Oakley, "Jacobean Political Theology," p. 335, n. 61.

V

THE CRITIQUE ON NATURAL CAUSALITY
IN THE MUTAKALLIMUN AND NOMINALISM

ONE of the most significant developments in medieval Islamic thought was the emergence in the ninth and tenth centuries of a theological reaction against some of the rationalistic and deterministic elements of Greek philosophy that had begun to influence Islamic life and thought. Alongside the assimilation of Greek ideas and the development of Arabic philosophy by al-Kindi, al-Farabi, and Avicenna, a counter-movement arose, among the Mutakallimun (speculative theologians), that rejected any attempt to view nature as a closed, eternal, and necessary system or to view God as limited by human conceptions of justice or by human free will.

Parallels have frequently been drawn between the teaching of the Mutakallims in Islam and the teaching of William of Ockham and his followers in late medieval Christian thought.[1] While important differences have been acknowledged, both systems have been seen as a return to a Biblical or Koranic emphasis on the total omnipotence, creativity, and causality of God; both systems have been credited with rejecting the possibility of a rationally demonstrable metaphysics or at least reducing within metaphysics the number of propositions that can be established by reason alone; both supposedly held an atomistic view of nature, matter, and time in which individual particulars were isolated from one another; both allegedly reduced the limits of human reason and knowledge through an extreme skepticism; and both were supposedly marked by a strong fideistic tendency to ground human certainty in the dogmas of religion accepted by faith alone.

The parallel that has received the most attention is the sup-

[1] Cf. MAJID FAKHRY, *Islamic Occasionalism and its Critique by Averroës and Aquinas* (London, 1958), 9–20; M. R. HOLLOWAY, Occasionalism, in *New Catholic Encyclopedia*, X (1967), col. 624–25; E. GILSON, *History of Christian Philosophy in the Middle Ages* (New York, 1955), 184–85.

posed rejection of the principle of causality by interpreting the causal nexus as simultaneity or succession which has the appearance of causality only on the basis of past observation. By maintaining such a view, al-Ghazali, a leading example of the Mutakallimun position, and Ockham, the principal representative of late medieval nominalism, have been seen as precursors of David Hume. Moreover, by replacing natural causality with direct, divine intervention, these same two figures have been seen as the founders of metaphysical occasionalism which was later raised to the level of a system by the disciple of Descartes, Malebranche.

Recent discussions have not only accepted this parallel between Islamic and Christian thought as proven but have attempted to establish that the nominalist version may have depended on or have been influenced by Mutakallimun theories already known to the West either directly [2] or, indirectly, through one or more sources available in the thirteenth and early fourteenth centuries, e.g., through Maimonides' description of the Mutakallimun in *Guide of the Perplexed*; [3] through Thomas Aquinas' *Summa contra Gentiles*,[4] which seems to depend on Maimonides; through Raymond Martin's *Pugio Fidei*,[5] which refers to the thought of al-Ghazali through Averroes' critique; or, finally, the Latin translation in 1328 of Averroes' *Tahafut al-Tahafut*,[6] which summarizes long sections of al-Ghazali's *Tahafut al-Falasifah*.[7] Regrettably for those seeking an Islamic "cause" of nominalist occasionalism, the 1328 translation of Averroes' work postdates the

---

[2] HARRY A. WOLFSON, Nicolaus of Autrecourt and Ghazali's Argument against Causality, *Speculum* XLIV (1969), 234–38.

[3] MAIMONIDES, *Guide of the Perplexed*, translated with introduction and notes by S. Pines (Chicago, 1963), P. I, ch. 73.

[4] THOMAS AQUINAS, *Summa contra Gentiles*, Book III, ch. 69.

[5] RAYMOND MARTIN, O. P., *Pugio Fidei adversus Mauros et Judaeos* (Lipsiae et Francofurti, 1687), Pt. I, chs. 6–12, pp. 213–28.

[6] AVERROES, *Tahafut al-Tahafut* (Arabic text), *Bibliotheca Arabica Scholasticorum*, III, ed. M. Bouyges (Beyrouth, 1930); Arabic text translated into English by Simon Van den Bergh, 2 Vols. (London, 1954); the early sixteenth-century Latin translation of the Hebrew translation from the Arabic: *Averroes' Destructio Destructionum Philosophiae Algazelis in the Latin Version of Calo Calonymos*, ed. with intro. by B. H. Zedler (Milwaukee, 1961).

[7] AL-GHAZALI, *Tahafut al-Falasifah* (Arabic text), in *Bibliotheca Arabica Scholasticorum*, II, ed. M. Bouyges (Beyrouth, 1927); English translation by S. A. Kamali, *Al-Ghazali, Tahafut al-Falasifah*, Pakistan Philosophical Congress (Lahore, 1958).

completion of Ockham's *Commentary on the Sentences* as well as his *Quodlibeta* and, in any case, omits the four disputations on the natural sciences which contain the best discussion of al-Ghazali's critique on natural causality. But the materials included by Maimonides and Aquinas, although drawn from the Mutakalli-mun tradition in general rather than al-Ghazali in particular, provide a sufficient Islamic source around which to build a Western theory of occasionalism.

The question of when and in what form the West became aware of the Islamic critique on natural causality is difficult to answer with certainty. One of the underlying assumptions of that discussion, however, has been the belief that al-Ghazali and Ockham taught occasionalism. It is to this issue that the present paper addresses itself.

Before we begin an examination of either the Islamic or Christian theories of occasionalism, some initial consideration needs to be given to the structure and terminology of the problem in general. No medieval writer with whom I am familiar doubted that everything (excluding God) must have one or more causes, although this thesis was not always stated in causal language. When we speak of critiques on the "principle of causality," there-fore, we are referring to questions about the necessity, demon-strability, validity, and knowability of particular causal relation-ships (especially within the natural order), that is, that events have definable causes, or that causal sequences are predictable. Furthermore, the mention of David Hume should make us aware that the critique on the demonstrability of the principle of cau-sality does not necessarily entail the substitution of divine for natural causality. These are two separate issues, and one must be careful to distinguish which is under discussion by a particular author.

In regard to the critique of the principle of natural causality several different questions might be raised. One question is whether the principle of causality can be demonstrated in the technical, Aristotelian sense of *demonstratio*, that is, according to a syllogistic proof where the premises are absolutely necessary, universal, and self-evident, or deduced from such. It was difficult, if not impossible, for any medieval Christian theologian to argue for the demonstrability of particular causal sequences in this strict sense, for the created order was neither eternal nor absolutely necessary, and the Bible contained episodes in which normal causal relationships were temporarily suspended (thus proving that these relationships were not in all cases necessary). The difficulty of demonstrating the necessity and universality of causal sequences, however, in no way prevented most medieval theologians from asserting the general validity and dependability of the principle of causality. Where God did not intervene, causal sequences operated of necessity (i.e., through a relative necessity within the contingent, established order).

A second question is how we come to know the principle of causality, either in the sense that things and events in general have causes or that there are predictable causal sequences. Is the principle of causality an *a priori* category of the mind or known through experience? If the principle is based on experience, is the certainty of the causal sequence based on anything more than repeated occurrence? Is there some quality or aspect to things and events that reveals them to be effects of some cause and through which that cause can be discovered?

A third question is what it is about the cause that produces the effect. Is it some inherent virtue, or nature, some divine ordination, or some combination of circumstances? One might attack the idea of inherent virtue without questioning either the validity or knowability of the causal principle.

In addition to understanding exactly which question or issue is under discussion, it is important to understand the sense in which certain terms are used, for example, the terms "possible," "can," or "able" when applied to divine action or to the operation of causality. This last issue is of great importance. The West, at least since the time of Anselm's *Cur Deus Homo*,[8] was familiar, when considering divine action, with the distinction between

---

[8] ANSELM, *Cur Deus Homo*, II, 5; II, 10 in *Opera Omnia*, ed. F. S. Schmitt (Edinburgh, 1946–61), Vol. II, pp. 100, 107. The development of this distinction in ANSELM has been examined at length by the author in a forthcoming article: Necessity and Freedom in Anselm's Conception of God, to appear in the Proceedings of the International Anselm Congress (Bad Wimpfen, Germany, 13–16 September, 1970) in 1973.

ability and will (or, for Anselm, between the ability to act and the ability to will), between what God is theoretically capable of doing, or able to do, on the basis of his omnipotence and what God has done and will do on the basis of his nature and will. This does not mean that God can sometimes act according to his omnipotence and sometimeš according to his revealed will. It rather means that God retains the ability or power to do many things which he does not desire to do and consequently will never do. With slight variations this distinction was accepted by every theologian of the high and late Middle Ages, save possibly one (Autrecourt), and it permitted them to affirm the omnipotence of God and the contingency of the universe while, at the same time, to affirm the orderly, rational, and consistent behavior of God in dealing with his creation. This distinction, eventually known as the distinction between the absolute and ordained powers of God, became in the late Middle Ages a device for analyzing the degree of necessity possessed by or attributed to a wide variety of philosophical and theological propositions.

The Islamic and Christian discussions of natural causality must be seen in light of this distinction. When an author states that God "could" do something, one should not automatically infer that the author believes that this possibility might actually take place unless, in addition to not being contradictory, and thus to be included within the power of God viewed absolutely, the author should indicate that such a possibility would not contradict the nature and revealed will of God.

A further problem arises in determining what an author means by the concept of divine causality. It may refer to a causality that operates *in place of* secondary, natural causality (the idea of occasionalism). It may, however, refer to a divine causality that operates or cooperates *alongside* the secondary, instrumental cause in every event. Moreover, divine causality may be the result of direct intervention, or it may be the result of a system whereby when certain conditions are present, certain results will take place, not out of an inherent power in the cause but out of an ordination that whenever 'a' is present, 'b' will occur.

Many of these distinctions have been ignored in past discussions of occasionalism. At times the radicalism of the Mutakallims and the nominalists has been assumed rather than established, so that when al-Ghazali and Ockham state that God "could" do certain things outside the normal order, arbitrary, capricious, and disastrous results of divine intervention are envisaged as possible at any moment. But when Thomas Aquinas states that God "could" act in ways other than those he has chosen, it is assumed that he is referring to God's power viewed absolutely, and that God in no sense would do these things. When al-Ghazali and Ockham speak of divine causality, it is often assumed that they refer to a causality that operates in place of natural causes. When Thomas refers to divine causality, it is assumed that he refers to a cooperative action, or ultimate dependency on a first cause, or a temporary suspension of the natural action, as in the case of a miracle.

Although a definitive answer to this problem would require a reexamination of the leading thinkers within the Mutakallimun and nominalist traditions, the following analysis is limited to the two figures most frequently mentioned in this regard: al-Ghazali and Ockham. It is my hope that through a study of their views on natural causality others will be stimulated to test my interpretation against a broader sample.

Modern descriptions of Islamic occasionalism have been based almost exclusively on sources unsympathetic to the Asharite Mutakallimun.[9] One of the most quoted of these sources is

---

[9] The sources for the Mutakallimun teaching on atomism and occasionalism are of four types: (1) those antagonistic to the Mutakallimun (possibly more of a caricature than a description), such as IBN HAZM's *Kitab al-Fisal*, AVERROES' commentaries on Aristotle, or MAIMONIDES' *Guide of the Perplexed*; (2) those that were produced by Asharite orthodoxy after AL-GHAZALI (which do not necessarily reflect the teaching of Asharite Mutakallims before 1150), such as FAKHR AL-DIN AL-RAZI's *Kitab al-Arab'in*, SANUSI's *Maqaddimat*, and LAQANI's *Jawharat al-Tawhid*; (3) the "histories" of doctrine (which describe atomism and occasionalism but do not always indicate the position of the author), such as AL-ASHARI's *Maqalat* and AL-BAGHDADI's *Kitab al-Farq bayn al-firaq* and *Kitab usul al-din*; and (4) works of the early Asharites, such as AL-BAQILLANI's *Kitab al-Tamhid*. Of these the most frequently cited are *Guide of the Perplexed* and *Maqalat*, the former unsympathetic and the latter a secondhand account of pre-Asharite atomism. The teaching of AL-ASHARI himself, as described by AL-JUWAYNI or IBN ASAKIR, does not appear so extreme. What is needed is a rereading of AL-ASHARI and AL-BAQILLANI, without Aristotelian and Thomist presuppositions, and with a more sophisticated appreciation for the terminology of such discussions.

Maimonides' *Guide*, which influenced Aquinas' view of the *loquentes in lege Maurorum*. According to Maimonides, the Mutakallims affirmed direct, divine action within every event in the natural order in place of any natural or intrinsic causality. Not only does God directly cause the color black to appear whenever white cloth is brought into contact with black dye, but God also moves the pen and the hand when someone writes. Indeed, natural causality and human volition have both been sacrificed in favor of intensifying divine omnipotence and thus honoring God. Nothing happens in this world except by God's action alone, and what we normally call a cause is simply the occasion for divine action.[10]

The major studies of Islamic occasionalism are: D. B. MacDonald, Continuous Recreation and Atomic Time in Muslim Scholastic Theology, *Isis* IX (1927), 326–44; S. Pines, *Beiträge zur islamischen Atomenlehre* (Berlin, 1936); L. Gardet and M.-M. Anawati, *Introduction à la théologie musulmane* (Paris, 1948); and M. Fakhry, *Islamic Occasionalism* (London, 1958). See also H. A. Wolfson, The Controversy over Causality within the Kalam, in *Mélanges Alexandre Koyré*, Vol. II: *L'aventure de l'esprit* (Paris, 1964), 602–18; M. E. Marmura, Ghazali and Demonstrative Science, *Journal of the History of Philosophy* III (1965), 183–204; H. A. Wolfson, Judah Halevi on Causality and Miracles, in *Meyer Waxman Jubilee Volume* (1966), 137–53.

[10] Maimonides, *Guide of the Perplexed*, II, 73, Sixth Premise (Pines transl., 201–02): "What led them to this opinion [that an accident does not last during two units of time] is that it is not to be said that there is a nature in any respect whatever and that the nature of one particular body may require that this and the accident be attached to that body. Quite the contrary, they wish to say that God, may He be exalted, created the accidents in question now, without the intermediary of nature — without any other thing. . . . In accordance with this premise, they assert that when we, as we think, dye a garment red, it is not we who are by any means the dyers; God rather creates the color in question in the garment when the latter is in juxtaposition with the red dye, which we consider to have gone over to the garment. They say that this is not the case, but that God has instituted [*de potentia ordinata*] a habit according to which, for example, black color does not appear except when a garment is juxtaposed with indigo. However, this blackness, which God creates when an object about to turn black is juxtaposed with blackness, does not last, but disappears instantly, and another blackness is created. . . . In conformity with this assumption, they have drawn the corollary that the things we know now are not identical with the contents of the knowledge known by us yesterday. . . . They assert that when a man moves a pen, it is not the man who moves it; for the motion occurring in the pen is an accident created by God in the pen. Similarly the motion of the hand, which we think of as moving the pen, is an accident created by God in the moving hand. Only, God has instituted the habit that the motion of the hand is concomitant with the motion of the pen, without the hand exercising in any respect an influence on, or being causative in regard to, the motion of the pen. . . . According to them, there is no body at all endowed with the power of action. On the other hand, the ultimate agent is God; and it is He who, in view of the fact that He has instituted such a habit [*sine qua non*

Leaving to other scholars the issue of whether Maimonides accurately described the general teaching of the Mutakallims on causality, let us examine the view of al-Ghazali, written almost a century earlier, to which Maimonides' description is often compared and on which, some have felt, it may have been based. The critique on natural causality found in al-Ghazali is motivated by a similar desire to protect the concept of divine omnipotence. Al-Ghazali believes that the connection between cause and effect, whatever it be, is not a necessary relationship. It obtains because God so established it, and it remains within God's power to alter or temporarily hinder the normal operation of that relationship. It does not imply a contradiction for the relationship between cause and effect to operate in ways other than normal, as occasional miracles recorded in the Koran have shown. By stating in this way that the relationship of cause to effect is not a necessary relationship, al-Ghazali implies that such a relationship generally, or normally, exists. Al-Ghazali seems to presuppose the distinction between the absolute and ordained powers of God. God retains the ability to act in ways other than those ways in which he has chosen to act.[11]

Moreover, al-Ghazali maintains that the principle that the effect results from something in the cause cannot be rationally demonstrated. Observation does not prove causality, understood in this sense, but only proves simultaneity or coexistence of cause and effect.[12]

---

causality, *d.p.o.*], has created the blackness in the body that is the garment when the latter was juxtaposed with indigo. To sum it up: it should not be said in any respect that this is the cause of that. This is the opinion of the Mutakallimun."

[11] *Tahafut al-Falasifah,* Probl. XVII (Kamali translation, 185): "In our view, the connection between what are believed to be the cause and the effect is not *necessary.* . . . They are connected as the result of the Decree of God [*ordinata*], which preceded their existence. If one follows the other, it is because He has created them in that fashion, not because the connection in itself is necessary and indissoluble. He has the power [*absoluta*] to create the satisfaction of hunger without eating, or death without the severance of the head, or even the survival of life when the head has been cut off. . . . We admit the *possibility* of a contact between the two [cotton and fire] which will not result in burning, as also we admit the possibility of the transformation of cotton into ashes without coming into contact with fire. And they reject this *possibility.*" Cf. the sections of AL-GHAZALI quoted by AVERROES in *Tahafut al-Tahafut,* Pt. II, disc. 1 (Van den Bergh, I, 316). The italics and the bracketed additions are my own.

[12] Kamali transl., 186: "The only argument is from the observation of the fact of

It should be noted that al-Ghazali is not making a positive statement on the issue of causality. He is attacking the position (opposed to the religious thought of Islam) that the principle of causality is a necessary rather than contingent truth. In order to show the nonnecessary, or "chosen," quality of causal relations, al-Ghazali points to miraculous suspensions of the normal operation of causality and argues that the idea of an inherent nature in the cause that produces the effect, while it may be believed, cannot be rationally demonstrated, in the strict sense referred to above.

In order to undermine the notion that causality is a necessary principle, al-Ghazali offers two alternate theories on what it is about 'a' that normally produces 'b'. The first theory, similar to the position of the Mutakallims as described by Maimonides, maintains that natural causality does not operate on the basis of any inherent quality, virtue, or power; rather, the cause is the occasion or *sine qua non* for the effect, normally present but not directly active.[13] The causal nexus is to be understood in the sense that where certain conditions are present, God or his angels will directly intervene in the natural order to produce the effect. Consequently, there is no such thing as natural causality in the sense of inherent virtue but only divine causality. Indeed, there is no such thing as a natural order but only the orderly action of God.[14]

The second theory, which al-Ghazali also feels is viable (but which has been ignored by scholars), states that God has created

---

burning at the time of contact with fire. But observation shows that one is *with* the other, not that it is *by* it and has no other cause than it." Cf. Van den Bergh transl., I, 317.

[13] The term *sine qua non* should not be confused with accidental causality, as was done by THOMAS (*Comm. in IV Lib. Sententiarum*, IV, dist. 1, q. 1, a. 4, qu. 1, and *Summa theologiae*, P. III, q. 62, a. 1). An accidental cause of a building, to repeat THOMAS' example, would be the color of the builder, which has nothing to do with the building. A *causa sine qua non* is a cause whose presence results in the effect and whose absence prevents the effect. The latter is usually associated in medieval thought with a type of causality that operates on the basis of a pact or ordination rather than on some inherent virtue in the cause itself.

[14] Cf. footnote 12. Kamali transl., 186: "We say that it is God who — through the intermediacy of angels, or directly — is the agent of the creation of blackness in cotton, of the disintegration of its parts, and of their transformation into a smouldering heap or ashes." Cf. Van den Bergh transl., I, 316-17.

within the cause a nature or quality that produces the effect and, unless otherwise impeded, it will do so in every instance. That relationship, however, is a result of God's ordination and not a necessary relationship. God could and occasionally has altered that relationship, not by replacing natural with supernatural causality nor by breaking the connection of cause and effect but by adding to the normal properties of the agent or patient an additional property that will prevent the normal operation, as, e.g., the addition of talc or asbestos to the body hinders the burning operation of fire.[15]

These two theories are quite different. Not only does the second theory espouse a causality that operates *ex natura rei*, but apparent interruptions of the natural order in the case of miracles are given a rationalistic or "scientific" explanation. The first theory, on the other hand, does not limit direct divine causality to miracles but instead posits exclusive divine activity in every change and motion of the universe. However, the two theories share at least one presupposition: whatever the nature of the causal relationship, it is one chosen by God and not a necessary relationship.

The lack of necessity in the causal relationship raises a question in regard to both of al-Ghazali's substitute theories. Whether God

---

[15] Kamali transl., 190–91: "We agree that fire is so created that when it finds two pieces of cotton which are similar, it will burn both of them, as it cannot discriminate between two similar things. At the same time, however, we can believe that when a certain prophet was thrown into the fire, he was not burnt — either because the attributes of fire had changed, or because the attributes of the prophet's person had changed. Thus there might have originated — from God, or from the angels — a new attribute in the fire which confined its heat to itself, so that the heat was not communicated to the prophet. Hence, although the fire retained its heat, its form and its reality, still the effect of its heat did not pass onwards. Or there might have originated a new attribute in the prophet's body which enabled it to resist the influence of fire, although it had not ceased to be composed of flesh and bones.

"We see that one who covers himself with asbestos sits down in a blazing furnace, and remains unaffected by it. He who has not observed such a thing will disbelieve it. Therefore, our opponents' disbelief in God's power to invest fire or a person's body with a certain attribute which will prevent it from burning, is like disbelief on the part of a man who has not observed asbestos and its effect. Things to which God's power extends include mysterious and wonderful facts. We have not observed all those mysteries and wonders. How, then, can it be proper on our part to deny their possibility, or positively to assert their impossibility?" Cf. Van den Bergh transl., I, 326–27.

is present and active in every normal operation of nature or whether he simply reserves to himself the right to intervene and upset the normal operation when he so chooses, the order of nature becomes precarious and mysterious in such a view. How is one able to have scientific knowledge or even to plan for the immediate future in a world where divine action may at any moment suspend, rearrange, or transform any and all aspects of that world?

Al-Ghazali was aware that his position seemingly led to the acknowledgment of man's inability to depend upon or predict the course of nature. He even mentions some of the possibilities his critics might suggest in order to make his position look absurd. If the causal relation is not necessary, al-Ghazali remarks, then might it not be true that "one who left a book in his house might return to find it transformed into a slaveboy, intelligent and resourceful; or into an animal. Or having left a slaveboy in the house, one may return to find him transformed into a dog. Or having left ashes, one may find musk in their place. Or one may find stone transformed into gold, or gold into stone. And when asked concerning the change, he might say: 'I do not know what is now in the house. All I know is that I left a book there. Perhaps it has turned into a horse, defiling my library with its excrement.' Or he might say: 'I left a jar of water in the house. Perhaps it has changed into an apple tree.' " [16]

Skeptical inferences of this variety are, according to al-Ghazali, unwarranted. Although the relationship of cause and effect is not necessary, it operates consistently, and God does not alter that operation by whim or caprice. God will never interrupt the normal operation of cause and effect without good intention and concomitant revelation. We know, says al-Ghazali, either through the repeated uniformity of nature or through special revelation, that God will not do certain things which are possible for Him. Throughout the discussion it is al-Ghazali's assumption that God only acts for the good and in conformity with his wisdom.[17]

[16] Kamali transl., 189.

[17] *Ibid.*, 189–90: "If you could prove that in regard to things which 'can exist' there cannot be created for man a knowledge that they 'do not exist' then these absurdities would be inescapable. We have no doubt in regard to the situations

At one point, however, al-Ghazali undermines the limitations which the revealed nature and will of God place upon the omnipotence of God. He states that if God should "change his mind" and act in a way contrary to his revealed will, he would be able to alter the memory and expectations of men so that no inconsistency would be experienced. If that is true, then the continuity of human knowledge and divine activity has been destroyed.[18]

Let us now turn to Ockham's treatment of natural causality, which has often been identified with the more extreme theory of al-Ghazali. I will consider, in turn, three aspects of Ockham's critique: the demonstrability of the principle of causality; the operation of causality in the natural order; and possible motivations for Ockham's position.

Ockham believed that the principle of causality could not be demonstrated, although it could be proved. This statement is not as contradictory as it might seem. Demonstration for Ockham, as for Aristotle, refers to a syllogistic proof, the conclusion of which is necessary because it is deduced from evident and absolutely necessary premises.[19] Very few things can be established

---

described by you. For God has created for us the knowledge that He *would not do these things*, although they are *possible*. We never asserted that they are necessary. . . . It is only when something possible is repeated over and over again (so as to form the Norm), that its pursuance of a uniform course in accordance with the Norm in the past is indelibly impressed upon our minds. . . . Therefore, there is nothing to prevent us from believing that: (a) something may be possible, and may be one of those things to which God's power extends; (b) in spite of its being possible, it might have been known *as a rule* in the past that God *would not do it*; and (c) God may create for us a knowledge that He would not do it in *this* particular instance." Cf. Van den Bergh transl., I, 324. *Ibid.*, 327: "And the best method according to both you and us is to relate these things [miracles] to God, either immediately or through the intermediation of the angels. But at the time these occurrences become real, the attention of the prophet turns to such facts, and the order of the good determines its appearance to ensure the duration of the order of religion, and this gives a preponderance to the side of existence. The fact in itself is possible, and the principle in God is His magnanimity; but such a fact *only* emanates from Him when *necessity* gives a preponderance to its existence and the *good* determines it, and the *good* only determines it when a prophet needs it to establish his prophetic office for the promulgation of the good." The italics and the bracketed additions are my own. Cf. Kamali transl., 191–92.

[18] Van den Bergh transl., I, 324: "They [the prophets] know the possibility of an event, but know that it will not happen. And if God interrupts the habitual course by causing this unusual event to happen, this knowledge of the habitual is at the time of the interruption removed from their hearts and He no longer creates it." Cf. Kamali transl., 190.

[19] The best study of OCKHAM's understanding of *demonstratio* is by DAMASCENE

V

89

in this way, certainly not the principle of causality, the terms of which are contingent creatures and exceptions to which are recorded in the Scriptures.[20] However, the principle of causality is, for Ockham, valid and can be established inductively by experience.[21] Although we never intuitively perceive the internal relation between cause and effect, we are justified in inferring that such a relationship exists through repeated experience.[22] For

WEBERING, *Theory of Demonstration according to William Ockham* (St. Bonaventure, 1953).

[20] OCKHAM, *Sent.* I, dist. 1, q. 6 (*Opera Philosophica et Theologica; Opera Theologica*), I (St. Bonaventure, 1967), 497: "Dico quod necessarium simpliciter non potest dependere a non necessario. Sed isto modo nulla creatura est necessaria, nec aliquis effectus sic necessario dependet a quacumque causa. Non est tamen inconveniens aliquem effectum necessario elici ab aliqua causa. . . ."

[21] *Summa Totius Logicae* III, II, ch. 41: "Per praedicta potest faciliter sciri, quomodo terminatur quaestio quid est. Dupliciter enim potest terminari, scilicet per experientiam et intuitivam notitiam. Sicut si aliquis videret terram interponi inter solem et lunam; aliter potest terminari a posteriori per effectum per demonstrationem; quia sicut astrologus sciens quod luna illuminatur a sole nisi sit aliquid opacum medium, concludit, quod terra interponitur inter solem et lunam et quod illa interpositio est causa, ita est de multis aliis principiis, quod dupliciter notificari possunt." *Sent.* I, Prol., q. 4 (St. Bonaventure ed., I, 154–55): "Unde demonstratio dicitur particularis vel quia praedicatum non concluditur de omnibus contentis sub subiecto, sicut si demonstraretur quod aliqua figura habet tres angulos etc.; vel quia, quantum est ex forma conclusionis, non concluditur praedicatum pro semper inesse sed pro aliquo tempore determinato. Et communiter tales demonstrationes, si sint ex simpliciter necessariis, sunt hypotheticae, condicionales vel temporales, non categoricae. Verbi gratia, per nullam demonstrationem concluditur quod luna est eclipsabilis, quia ista non potest sciri nisi per experientiam, sicut non potest sciri nisi per experientiam quod luna est illuminabilis a sole. Sed postquam ista est scita per experientiam, demonstratur quod tali tempore vel tali eclipsabitur, sic arguendo: quandocumque terra interponitur inter solem et lunam tunc luna eclipsatur; sed quandocumque sol est in tali situ et luna in tali tunc terra interponitur inter solem et lunam; ergo tunc luna eclipsatur. Et isto modo fit demonstratio per causam extrinsecam."

[22] OCKHAM, *Quodlibeta* VI, q. 12: "Si productio activa sit alia res, aut ergo est prior natura ipso effectu producto, aut simul natura, vel posterior natura. Non primo modo, quia relatio, si sit alia res essentialiter, dependet tam a fundamento quam a termino, et per consequens neutro est prius natura. Effectus autem productus est terminus productionis activae. Ergo non est prior natura termino. Praeterea correlationes sunt simul natura cuiusmodi sunt effectus respectus et causa. Sed respectus effectus non est prior natura ipso effectu. Ergo nec respectus causae ad effectum est prior natura effectu. Et eodem modo probatur quod respectus causae ad effectum non est simul natura cum effectu, nec est posterior natura ipso effectu, quia tunc prior natura esset effectus in rerum natura quam produceretur. Et sic effectus in primo instanti naturae in quo secundum modum loquendi aliorum esset effectus, non esset productus, et certum est quod nihil producitur de novo postquam est. Ergo numquam effectus produceretur de novo, quod est absurdum." *Sent.* I, dist. 1, q. 3 (St. Bonaventure ed., I, 416–17): "Ad primum istorum respondeo, quod quamvis respectu eiusdem effectus possint esse plures

Ockham, the principle of causality can even be termed universal and necessary as long as one recognizes the contingent and ordained quality of the relationship. Natural causes of the same species always produce the same effects, if no free cause, divine or human, interferes.[23]

Granting that Ockham believes that the principle of causality can be validly inferred from experience and that the secondary cause is necessary (not absolutely but by ordination) in order for the effect to occur, what is it about the secondary cause that produces the effect? Does Ockham believe, as did Thomas, that God has given to the secondary cause a creative power of its own, out of which the effect is produced immediately and in cooperation with God's primary causality? · Or does Ockham reaffirm the Augustinian conception that the secondary cause facilitates the appearance of the effect which results from primary causality through the system of *rationes seminales*? Or does Ockham make the secondary cause only the occasion for direct and exclusive action by God?

In his discussions of natural causality, Ockham never specifically indicates what it is about the cause that produces the effect. Generally, he is satisfied with the definition that a cause is that

---

causae, hoc tamen non est ponendum sine necessitate, puta: nisi per experientiam possit convinci, ita scilicet quod ipso posito, alio destructo, sequitur ille effectus, vel quod ipso non posito, quocumque alio posito, non sequitur effectus. Exemplum primi: probatur quod ignis est causa caloris, quia ipso igne posito — omnibus aliis amotis — sequitur calor in calefactibili approximato; eodem modo probatur de sole quod est causa caloris, quia igne amoto et sole approximato sequitur calefactio. Exemplum secundi: probatur quod obiectum est causa intellectionis intuitivae, quia omnibus aliis positis, ipso solo amoto, non sequitur notitia intuitiva; ergo obiectum est causa notitiae intuitivae. Et tenet tale argumentum per talem propositionem quod 'quaecumque res absoluta requiritur in esse reali ad esse alicuius, est causa illius in aliquo genere causae.' Primum argumentum tenet per istam propositionem 'omne illud quo posito sequitur aliud, est causa illius.' Aliter aliquid esse causam alterius potest probari sine tali experientia per rationem. Et isto modo probatur quod voluntas est causa effectiva actus sui, quia omnis potentia libera quae non potest necessitari est causa effectiva sui actus. Et forte ista ratio sola est convincens voluntatem esse causam effectivam alicuius actus sui." (418): "Ad secundum dico quod ex tali ordine semper contingit inferre causalitatem in priori respectu posterioris, maxime si prius potest esse sine posteriori et non e converso, naturaliter etiam."

[23] OCKHAM, *Quodlibeta* IV, q. 2: ". . . actio talis agentis sine variatione agentis vel passi vel alicuius concurrentis ad actionem numquam variatur sed semper uniformiter sequitur actio." Cf. *Quodl.* I, 17 and *Sent.* I, d. 1, q. 6 for similar statements.

thing, the presence of which results in the effect and the absence of which prevents the effect, a definition that would suit all of the above types of causality and exclude only accidental causality.[24] *How* the cause produces an effect can be seen when we compare the operation of causality in the natural order with causality in the economy of salvation.

Within the area of theological (as opposed to natural) causality, e.g., the way in which the crucifixion of Christ effected the redemption of mankind, the way in which good acts done in a state of grace merit eternal life, the way in which the sacraments produce grace, Ockham taught that the cause possessed no infused quality or virtue that necessarily produced the effect; rather, the cause operated effectively because it was *ordained* to have such an effect. For example, Ockham maintained that the sacraments cause grace not on the basis of some inherent virtue but rather on the basis of an ordination or pact that where the sacraments are validly administered, grace will be produced in the recipient, *ex opere operato*.[25] This *ex pacto* causality, which Ockham defines as *sine qua non* causality, is not simply within the power of God but is, for Ockham, the way in which God operates, *de facto*, or *de potentia ordinata*.[26]

It is in this context that Ockham asserts that the very *ex pacto*,

---

[24] OCKHAM, *Sent.* I, d. 45, D: "Quod autem hoc sufficit ad hoc quod aliquid sit causa immediata alterius videtur esse manifestum. Quia si non, perit omnis via ad cognoscendum aliquid esse causam alterius immediatam. Nam si ex hoc quod hoc posito sequitur effectus et hoc non posito non ponitur effectus non sequitur illud esse causam illius effectus, nullo modo potest cognosci quod ignis est causa immediata caloris in ligno, quia potest dici quod est aliqua alia causa illius caloris, quae tamen non agit nisi in potentia ignis." Cf. quotations in footnote 19.

[25] OCKHAM, *Sent.* IV, q. 1, G-H: "Ideo ad quaestionem primo praemittam unam distinctionem propter dicta sanctorum et auctorum, quod cum causa sit illud ad cuius esse sequitur aliud, dupliciter potest accipi. Uno modo quando ex natura rei ad praesentiam et esse unius sequitur naturaliter esse alterius. Alio modo quando ad esse et praesentiam unius non ex natura rei sed sequitur aliud ex sola voluntate divina aliquid instituentis, et isto modo dicimus quod actus meritorius dicitur causa praemii ex sola voluntate divina et causa sine qua non dicitur secundo modo causa. Primo dico quod sacramenta non sunt causa gratiae. Circa quod probandum primo ostendam quod sacramenta per virtutem naturalem non causant gratiam nec aliquid praevium instrumentaliter gratiae. Secundo quod nec per virtutem eis collatam. . . . Secundo dico quod sacramenta sunt causa gratiae, quia Deus sic instituit quod non conferatur gratia nisi positis sacramentis et sacramento posito conferatur; et ideo causa sine qua non."

[26] *Ibid.*: "Deus sic instituit."

or *sine qua non*, operation of the sacraments marks an important difference between causality in the economy of salvation and causality in the natural order. God could have, *de potentia absoluta*, created in the natural order a system that where 'a' is present 'b' will occur, where 'a' would only be the *sine qua non* that occasioned or precipitated situation 'b'. But Ockham is clear that God does not, *de potentia ordinata*, act this way in nature. Causality in nature is not only a result of God's ordination and primary causality but is also, simultaneously, the result of a power in the secondary cause. Causality in the natural order operates *ex natura rei*.[27] Secondary causes, therefore, are true causes and not simply occasions. The only exceptions to this rule are miracles, which are experienced as exceptions, and, far from upsetting or undermining the natural order, they reveal the benevolence and the dependability of the God that created and upholds that order.

Ockham's understanding of divine activity in the natural order is surprisingly close to that of Thomas Aquinas. God is the immediate cause of everything that happens, not in place of but in cooperation with secondary causality.[28] This is in sharp contrast with the traditional picture of the Mutakallims, who saw divine and natural causality as being mutually exclusive. Thus in Ock-

---

[27] *Ibid.*: "Unde in naturalibus non est dare aliquam causam sine qua non nec mediatam nec immediatam respectu alicuius effectus, sed in voluntariis bene potest esse talis causa." OCKHAM made the same point in an earlier passage, where he compared natural causality with sacramental causality, *Sent.* II, q. 4 & 5: "Ad aliud dico quod licet Deus agat mediantibus causis secundis vel propinquius cum eis, non tamen dicitur Deus mediate agere, nec causae secundae frustra, cum sit agens voluntarium non necessarium, et si esset agens necessarium adhuc ageret immediate. . . . Deus enim est tale agens quod potest esse causa totalis effectus sine quocumque alio; quia tamen Deus sic res administrat ut eas motus proprios habere sinat secundum Augustinum, ideo non vult totum solus producere sed coagit cum causis secundis tamquam causa partialis licet sit principalior. Ita quod ipse est causa immediata omnium quando agit cum causis secundis, sicut quando agit sine illis. Nec propter hoc superfluunt causae secundae, quia Deus non agit in qualibet actione secundum totam potentiam suam. Et ex hoc sequitur quod non potest demonstrari quod aliquis effectus producitur a causa secunda, quia licet semper ad approximationem ignis ad combustibile sequatur combustio; cum hoc tamen potest stare quod ignis non sit eius causa, quia Deus *potuit ordinasse* quod semper ad praesentiam ignis passo approximato ipse solus causaret combustionem, sicut *ordinavit* cum ecclesia quod ad prolationem certorum verborum causetur gratia in anima." See also note 25.

[28] THOMAS AQUINAS, *Summa contra Gentiles*, III, ch. 66–67.

ham and Thomas, every event has two causes, one divine and one natural. In order for God to act apart from the natural cause, no fresh intervention is necessary but only a temporary suspension of the natural cause, which permits God to maintain the same effect without its natural cause or to substitute some different effect.

Although Ockham's conclusions on natural causality do not approximate those of al-Ghazali, either in meaning or vocabulary, a similar motivation pervades their discussions. Ockham shares the thesis, common to Islamic and Christian theology, that the created universe is contingent, and therefore absolute necessity cannot be ascribed to the principles that regulate its operation, including the principle of cause and effect. If Ockham stresses this belief more than most scholastics, it is not with the idea of destroying the relative necessity or dependability of these principles. Ockham wishes to protect the historicity of miracles taught in Scripture, to defend the omnipotence of God, and to maintain the *chosen* quality of creation and its laws. As is becoming increasingly apparent, Ockham, by emphasizing the power of God, was not concerned with attacking Thomas Aquinas but rather thinkers nearer to his own time who used ideas borrowed from Thomas, Scotus, and others to support a system of nature in which divine activity was effectively excluded or reduced to one creative act at the beginning of time.[29] Exactly against whom Ockham was arguing has not yet been clearly determined, but his opponents on this issue seem to fall within a type of Aristotelianism or Averroism that saw nature as a closed, eternal, and necessary system.

In summary, neither al-Ghazali nor Ockham have been properly evaluated on the question of natural causality. Al-Ghazali, in order to describe a natural order in which miracles were possible, attacked the ideas of the necessity and demonstrability of the principle of causality. In describing the causal relationship, he offered two theories, the first occasionalistic and the second ratio-

[29] E.g., cf. E. A. Moody, Ockham, Buridan and Nicholas of Autrecourt: The Parisian Statutes of 1339 and 1340, *Franciscan Studies* VII (1947), 113–46; E. A. Moody, Ockham and Aegidius of Rome, *Franciscan Studies* IX (1949), 417–42; H. Schepers, Holkot contra dicta Crathorn, *Philosophisches Jahrbuch* LXXVII (1970), 320–54; LXXIX (1972), 106–36.

nalistic. When these theories are properly seen as problematic formulations meant to refute the Islamic philosophers rather than positive statements of al-Ghazali's thought, one is led to conclude that, regardless of the occasionalistic and skeptical arguments used by al-Ghazali, his main intention was to preserve the contingency as well as the dependability of the natural order.

As has already been indicated, Ockham shared that motivation, although he was considerably more careful in excluding any occasionalistic or skeptical implications. In spirit and in method, Ockham stands much closer to Thomas Aquinas and the constructive traditions of the thirteenth century than was once thought. If he was aware of the teaching of the Mutakallimun as reflected in Maimonides and Thomas — and he surely must have been — it made only a marginal impact upon his thought. Ockham's position can be described by these words which Etienne Gilson wrote on Thomas: "It is a question of understanding how one and the same effect can proceed simultaneously from two different causes: God and the natural agent which produces it. . . . At the head of this series is God, the total and immediate cause of all the effects produced and of all the activity released therein. At the foot comes the natural body, the immediate cause of the proper action which it performs, even though it only performs it by virtue of the efficacy conferred upon it by God. . . . God's operation is clearly necessary to produce natural effects, since second causes owe all their efficacy to the first cause, God. But it is not superfluous that God, who can [de potentia absoluta] produce all natural effects Himself, should accomplish them by the mediation of certain other causes [de potentia ordinata]. These intermediaries which He has willed, are not necessary to Him in that He is unable to do without them. . . . The existence of second causes points to no lack in His power but to the immensity of His goodness." [30]

Perhaps, instead of searching for the avenues through which Islamic occasionalism entered and influenced Western thought, we should be encouraged by the past misinterpretations of al-Ghazali and Ockham on this issue to reexamine in greater detail the arguments of the Mutakallims.

[30] *The Christian Philosophy of St. Thomas Aquinas* (New York, 1956), 182–83.

VI

THE KING AND THE LEADEN COIN:
THE ECONOMIC BACKGROUND
OF 'SINE QUA NON' CAUSALITY*

In 1255, in his commentary on the fourth book of Peter Lombard's *Sentences*,[1] Thomas Aquinas rejected a solution to the problem of sacramental causality, one that was enjoying a certain degree of popularity in the mid-thirteenth century. The opinion that Thomas rejected was that the sacraments effect grace not through an inherent, created virtue but rather through a pact, covenant, or ordination of God that guarantees grace to the person who receives the sacraments, if the latter are properly administered and the recipient places no obstacle in the way of their effectiveness. This type of sacramental causality, termed causality *sine qua non*, was usually illustrated, Thomas informs us, with the following example. A king might decree that any person possessing a certain leaden coin would receive 100 pounds. In such a case, it would not be the leaden coin that causes the reception of the 100 pounds, but rather the arbitrary acceptation of the token by the king. For Thomas, the leaden coin would be only the occasion for the reward, not its cause. Therefore Thomas rejected this solution which, it seemed to him, would make the sacraments nothing more than the occasion or accidental cause of grace. He sealed his rejection by equating such causality with the way in which the racial color of the builder of a house could be said to be

---

* An earlier version of this paper was presented to the Late Medieval Colloquium, meeting in conjunction with the American Historical Association, in New York City on December 29, 1968.
[1] Thomas Aquinas, IV *Sent.* dist. 1 q. 1 a. 4, qc. 1: 'Quidam enim dicunt, quod non sunt causae quasi facientes aliquid in anima, sed causae sine quibus non: quia increata virtus, quae sola effectus ad gratiam pertinentes in anima facit, sacramentis assistit per quamdam Dei ordinationem, et quasi pactionem. Sic enim ordinavit et quasi pepigit Deus, ut qui sacramenta accipiunt, simul ab iis gratiam recipiant, non quasi sacramenta aliquid faciant ad hoc. Et est simile de illo qui accipit denarium plumbeum facta tali ordinatione, ut qui habuerit unum de illis denariis, habeat centum libras a rege: qui quidem denarius non dat illas centum libras, sed solus rex accipienti ipsum. Et quia pactio talis non erat facta in sacramentis veteris legis, ut accedentes ad ipsa gratiam acciperent, ideo dicuntur gratiam non conferre, sed promittebant tantum. Sed hoc non videtur sufficere ad salvandum dicta sanctorum. Causa enim sine qua non, si nihil omnino faciat ad inducendum effectum vel disponendo vel meliorando, quantum ad rationem causandi, nihil habebit supra causas per accidens; sicut album est causa domus, si aedificator sit albus; et secundum hoc sacramenta essent causae per accidens tantum sanctificationis.'

the cause of the house. Thomas maintained this position throughout his life, and, although he altered his solution to the problem of sacramental causality, he in no way altered his rejection of the type of causality based on the example of the king and the leaden coin.[2]

Thomas' treatment of the problem has dominated the discussion of sacramental causality down to our own day. It is largely on the basis of his opinion and reputation that the Nominalist[3] solution to this problem, a solution which talks of covenant and ordination and which frequently uses the example of the leaden coin, has been dismissed as occasionalism, suspect if not actually heretical according to the canons of Trent.[4] It has also been suggested that the Nominalist solution, which seems to make the sacraments only the signs of grace rather than their effective cause, prepared the way for the Protestant rejection of the efficacy and causality of the sacraments as these are normally understood in the Roman Church.[5]

---

[2] Cf. Thomas Aquinas, *Summa theologiae* III q. 62 a. 1: 'Quidam tamen dicunt quod non sunt causa gratiae aliquid operando, sed quia Deus, sacramentis adhibitis, in anima gratiam operatur. Et ponunt exemplum de illo qui afferens denarium plumbeum, accipit centum libras ex regis ordinatione; non quod denarius ille aliquid operetur ad habendum praedictae pecuniae quantitatem, sed hoc operatur sola voluntas regis. Unde et Bernardus dicit in quodam sermone *De cena Dom.*: Sicut "investitur canonicus per librum, abbas per baculum, episcopus per anulum, sic divisiones gratiarum diversae sunt traditae sacramentis." — Sed si quis recte consideret, iste modus non transcendit rationem signi. Nam denarius plumbeus non est nisi quoddam signum regiae ordinationis de hoc quod pecunia recipiatur ab isto. Similiter liber est quoddam signum quo designatur traditio canonicatus. Secundum hoc igitur sacramenta novae legis nihil plus essent quam signa gratiae; cum tamen ex multis Sanctorum auctoritatibus habeatur quod sacramenta novae legis non solum significant, sed causant gratiam.'

[3] In keeping with present scholarly practice in the late-medieval field, the term 'Nominalist' is used in this paper to refer to the thought of William of Ockham and those most directly influenced by him. Accordingly, it is most applicable in late-medieval theology to such figures as Ockham, Pierre d'Ailly, Marsilius of Inghen, Gabriel Biel, and, to a lesser degree, Robert Holcot, Adam Wodeham, and Gregory of Rimini. It does not include Peter Aureol or Durand of St. Pourçain, in spite of their similarity to Ockham on certain issues. The concept of covenantal causality is not a small point in sacramental theology but rather one of the fundamental principles of the Nominalist worldview. Although not created by the Nominalists, it was utilized by Ockham and his followers to solve a wide variety of theological problems. For a further discussion of this issue see: W. J. Courtenay, 'Covenant and Causality in Pierre d'Ailly,' *Speculum* 46 (1971) 94-119.

[4] For example see: Pierre Pourrat, *Theology of the Sacraments: A Study in Positive Theology* (3rd ed.; London 1924) 167-169; Antonius Piolanti, *De sacramentis* (Collectio theologica Romana VI; Rome 1945) I 69; Emmanuel Doronzo, *De sacramentis in genere* (Milwaukee 1946) 163-164; Bernard Leeming, *Principles of Sacramental Theology* (London 1956) 287, 290-294.

[5] For example see: Erwin Iserloh, *Gnade und Eucharistie in der philosophischen Theologie des Wilhelm von Ockham: ihre Bedeutung für die Ursachen der Reformation* (Wiesbaden 1956) 134-147.

Regardless of present and future assessments of the orthodoxy and implications of the Nominalist theory of sacramental causality, the immediate economic background of the example of the king and the leaden coin suggests that no occasionalism was intended by the theory of covenantal causality,[6] nor could such be easily inferred unless one were unaware of certain contemporary economic practices, unwilling to acknowledge their validity, or unwilling to acknowledge the general applicability of the concept that lay behind them. The covenantal theory of sacramental causality was based on a belief that certain causal relationships need depend for their efficacy on nothing more than a contract or a more general ordination, agreement, or understanding that is accepted by all persons concerned. Such contractual agreements could be effective apart from any inherent value residing in the items used. This theory had a certain theological, even Biblical background to it, as will become apparent in the following discussion. What is of more immediate interest is the increasing importance in the thirteenth century of analogies drawn from commercial activity, although the instances are limited and isolated. What those practices were, the causal validity of their operation, and their potential impact on the theory of monetary value will be one of the major concerns of this paper. The other concern will be the development of the covenantal theory of causality and Thomas' reaction to it.

Thomas' rejection of covenantal causality when applied to the sacraments raises several questions. Did he simply fail to note the economic implications of the example of the king and the leaden coin? Did he feel that what was valid in commerce was not valid in theology, at least not in sacramental theology? Or was Thomas so limited by the Aristotelian categories of inherent virtue and causality that he was unable or unwilling to recognize a causality based solely on the nature of contract itself, wherever it occurred?

---

[6] I have chosen the term 'covenantal' since this type of causality operates on the basis of a covenant, pact, or contract. The Latin term most frequently used in describing such causality is *pactum*. This type of causality is equivalent to what is called 'juridical causality' in modern Catholic discussions of the sacraments, that is, the way in which a legally binding contract causes the observance of the terms of that contract or the way in which paper currency buys goods and services. The similarity of this last example, the major example of juridical causality in modern discussions, with the king and the leaden coin will become apparent in the course of this paper. In general, I have avoided using the modern Catholic terminology, since such terms are based on the post-Tridentine theories of sacramental causality and do not exactly correspond to the medieval discussions. In fact, the grouping of the various medieval opinions under the categories of recent theological debate has been one of the major barriers prohibiting our understanding of this area of medieval thought.

It is the thesis of this paper that the example of the king and the leaden coin was more than one example among many of the principle of covenantal causality. Indeed it was a carefully developed analogy whose power to convince rested on familiarity with and acceptance of the validity of certain economic practices in the thirteenth century. Behind the initial argument for *sine qua non* causality and Thomas' rejection of it lay two conflicting theories of monetary value within a metallistic system. One theory, supported by Thomas and dominant throughout the Middle Ages, maintained that money must consist of a precious metal or other substance having, because of its composition, a value equivalent to the commodities for which it is exchanged, allowance being made for shifts in market value as a result of supply and demand. The second theory, appearing toward the middle of the thirteenth century and distrusted by Thomas, maintained that money need not 'consist of' but need only be 'covered by' a commodity having value apart from its monetary role. Thomas' rejection of that theory in the economic order as well as in theology was based on his adherence to the theory of inherent value. An examination, therefore, of Thomas' discussion of sacramental causality against the background of thirteenth-century economic practices not only throws light on the meaning and function of *sine qua non* causality but also suggests the prevalence, at least in theological circles, of an interesting and, as far as I know, hitherto unnoticed medieval monetary theory, a theory of ascribed value based on the ability and willingness of the government to stand behind its currency.

I. SACRAMENTAL CAUSALITY BEFORE 1250

Sacramental theology, the foundations for which were only partially begun in the patristic age,[7] developed rapidly in the twelfth and thirteenth centuries under the threat of various heterodox movements.[8] Gnostic influences, such as were present in the Petrobrusians and the Albigensians, rejected the Catholic sacraments, which at best seemed to be unnecessary and useless and which, more frequently, were viewed as evil practices that reinforced the imprisonment of the soul in flesh. Moreover, lay movements

---

[7] As a result of the Pelagian and Donatist controversies, Baptism was the only sacrament that was extensively treated in the ancient Church.

[8] See A. M. Landgraf, *Dogmengeschichte der Frühscholastik*: III. *Die Lehre von den Sakramenten* (Regensburg 1954); D. Van den Eynde, 'The Theory of the Composition of the Sacraments in Early Scholasticism (1125-1240),' *Franciscan Studies* 11 (1951) 1-20, 117-144; D. Van den Eynde, *Les Définitions des sacrements pendant la première période de la Scholastique* (Louvain 1950).

for apostolic poverty, such as the Waldensians and the Arnoldists, rejected priestly control over the sacraments. Against these attacks, theologians attempted to defend the importance of the priest, as mediator between God and man, and to define the number and general efficacy of the sacraments. This effort concentrated primarily on baptism, which had already achieved a thorough examination and defense in the writings of Augustine, and on the eucharist, the meaning and efficacy of which was affirmed in the decree on transubstantiation in 1215.

Neither the Fourth Lateran Council nor the Albigensian Crusade, however, was successful in re-establishing the Catholic Church's exclusive control over the channels of grace and salvation.[9] A further explication and defense of sacramental efficacy were needed in the thirteenth century in order to counteract doctrinally such movements as the Brethren of the Free Spirit as well as the sacramental theology of the Greek Church with which the West was coming into closer contact, a sacramental theology even less well-defined than the Roman.

Several barriers to an effective doctrinal defense of sacramental efficacy stood before the early-thirteenth-century theologian. One barrier was the Augustinian affirmation that only God could create and give grace, no creature having the power to create *ex nihilo*. Secondly, it was difficult philosophically to explain how a physical action could result in a spiritual effect. Thirdly, there was a growing mistrust of the Neoplatonic view of creation as emanation, which seemed to imply, in the versions of Avicenna and Averroës, the power of creatures to create. Fourthly, there was the tradition of Hugh of St. Victor,[10] so popular in the late-twelfth century, that defined the sacraments as vessels or receptacles of God's grace, as a doctor's vial would contain the medicine for the patient. Beyond a mere containing, theologians felt compelled to assert a causality that would guarantee the efficacy of the sacraments. Finally, there were differences among the sacraments of the new law, e.g. between the eucharist, in which there are material elements, and marriage, in which there are not; as well as similarities to the' sacraments' of the old law, e.g. between baptism and circumcision. Since baptism was the first sacrament to be treated, discussions of sacramental causality generally took it as the model.

The earliest solution, one which commended itself to several generations of theologians, made a distinction between creation and causality. Only God creates grace; the sacraments cause it. The efficacy of the sacraments and the divine prerogatives over grace were further protected by developing

---

[9] See H. Grundmann, *Religiöse Bewegungen im Mittelalter* (Berlin 1935).
[10] Hugh of St. Victor, *De sacramentis* I part ix ch. 4.

the idea of a material cause or disposition and by dividing the activity of the sacraments into two successive operations. The sacraments were considered to be direct, efficient causes of only the character or ornament created in the soul. On the other hand, the sacraments were material causes, *causae sine quibus non*, or dispositive causes of sanctifying grace. The sacraments, therefore, effected grace only indirectly; they caused a disposition which, in turn, required the presence of grace. This theory was developed by William of Auxerre,[11] Alexander of Hales,[12] Roland of Cremona,[13] William of Melitona,[14] and was adopted by Albertus Magnus[15] and by Thomas Aquinas (in his Sentence-Commentary). It remained the accepted theory for the Thomist school of the fourteenth and fifteenth centuries.

Some theologians felt, however, that this dispositive theory did not sufficiently underline the effective and causal nature of the sacraments. Therefore, another theory was devised that defined the sacraments as the instrumental causes of grace. This second theory related divine activity to sacramental activity as principal cause to instrumental cause. As the human hand, acting as principal cause, moves a hammer, pickaxe, or saw, so God, as principal agent, moves the sacraments and acts through these instruments to cause grace. It is the hammer that drives the nail or the saw that cuts the wood, thus causing whatever new form they receive; yet these instruments cannot act apart from the principal cause. This theory of physical, instrumental causality, devised first by Stephen Langton[16] and developed by Hugh of

---

[11] William of Auxerre, *Summa aurea* IV tr. 1-2. Cf. M. Gierens, *De causalitate sacramentorum seu de modo explicandi efficientiam sacramentorum Novae Legis* (Rome 1935) 27-29; F. Gillmann, *Zur Sakramentenlehre des Wilhelm von Auxerre* (Würzburg 1918); A. Van Hove, 'Doctrina Gulielmi Altissiodorensis De causalitate sacramentorum,' *Divus Thomas* 33 (1930) 305-324. William of Auxerre has, incorrectly, been placed in support of occasionalism by some modern Catholic theologians, e.g., Antonius Piolanti, *De sacramentis* (Rome 1945) I 69.

[12] Alexander of Hales, *In IV Sententiarum* dist. 1 sect. 1-4.

[13] Roland of Cremona, *Sent.* IV dist. 1; cf. H. D. Simonin and S. Meersseman, *De sacramentorum efficientia apud theologos Ord. Praed.* Fasc. I: 1229-1276 (Rome 1936) 1-5.

[14] K. F. Lynch, 'Texts Illustrating the Causality of the Sacraments from William of Melitona, *Assisi Bibl. Comm.* 182, and *Brussels Bibl. Royale* 1542,' *Franciscan Studies* 17 (1957) 238-272. The fourth book of the *Summa Halensis*, or *Summa Alexandri*, was compiled for the most part from William of Melitona's *Qq de sacramentis*: cf. Alexandri de Hales *Summa theologica IV lib.*, III proleg. (Quaracchi 1948) ccxl-ccxliii; cf. also the texts in Gierens, *op. cit.* (above note 11) 30-33, and W. Lampen, *De causalitate sacramentorum iuxta scholam Franciscanam* (Bonn 1931) 6-17.

[15] Albertus Magnus, *In IV Sententiarum* dist. 1 B, art. 5.

[16] Texts in D. Van den Eynde, 'Stephen Langton and Hugh of St. Cher on the Causality of the Sacraments,' *Franciscan Studies* 11 (1951) [141]-[155]. Cf. J. F. Veal, *The Sacramental Theology of Stephen Langton and the Influence upon him of Peter the Chanter* (Rome 1955) 16-21.

St. Cher[17] and Peter of Tarantasia,[18] was adopted by Thomas Aquinas later in his life, in his *Summa theologiae*.

There were those, however, who felt that these theories (the physical-dispositive and the physical-instrumental) were unsatisfactory in two respects. First of all, they did not really explain how a material agency could be the cause or even the disposition of a spiritual quality or substance such as grace. Secondly, these explanations seemingly made the sacraments too mechanical and denied to God His proper role in the creation and administration of grace. Therefore, a reaction set in against what were felt to be the excesses of the dispositive and instrumental theories which, in order to defend adequately the efficacy of the sacraments, had sacrificed the activity and freedom of God.

This reaction seems to have begun around 1240,[19] perhaps at Oxford, for it is there that we find its earliest defenders: Richard Fishacre[20] and Robert Kilwardby.[21] It is probable that Fishacre is the author of this new theory

---

[17] Texts in D. Van den Eynde, *Franciscan Studies* 11 (1951) [141] - [155].

[18] Texts in Simonin and Meersseman 108-117.

[19] It has been suggested, e.g. by Doronzo, *De sacramentis in genere* (Milwaukee 1946) 164, that this reaction, which grows into what I have termed 'covenantal causality' and which has been incorrectly called occasionalism, originated with William of Auvergne (1180-1249). The passage in William on which this is based, *De sacramentis in speciali* (ed. Paris 1674) I 418 b, is too brief and too vague to support this. My own conjecture is that William intended only to repeat the position of Hugh of St. Victor, that God is the author of grace and acts directly to produce grace in the recipient. Such direct action is not covenantal.

[20] Richard Fishacre, *Sent.* IV dist. 1 (Simonin and Meersseman 18-20): 'Est enim haec relatio non a natura aliqua — in natura autem est — sed a voluntate, ut denarius fit pretium, nulla in eo facta mutatione vel superadditione alterius quam relationis. Foedus ergo quod pactum est inter Deum et homines, in sacramentis est. Unde ratione talis relationis est in signis illis sanctitas et eis, quod Dei est, attribuitur.' '. . . si tunc stetisset, quod nunc baptismus, sicut si aliquis minister regis distribueret signa stanea pauperibus, quae si servarent, per illa reciperentur ad prandium regis, sed non statim, sed cras, quando comedet rex, et deinde minister alius regis daret, hora prandii, consimilia vel alia signa aliis pauperibus, posset dici quod signa prius data essent eiusdem efficaciae cum ultimo datis, quia utraque faciunt intrare et eodem tempore, scilicet ad horam prandii.'

[21] Robert Kilwardby, *Sent.* IV dist. 1 (Simonin and Meersseman 27-28): 'Secundi dicunt quod sacramentum sensibile vere dicitur iustificare et vere dicitur causa et vere dicitur disponere ad iustitiam sed extendendo nomina ista. Non enim disponit vel efficit vel causat tamquam qualitatem vel potentiam activam in se habens qua alteret et qualificet animam, sicut ignis agit per inditum vel innatum calorem, sed tamquam habens sibi assistentem virtutem divinam, quae ad eius praesentiam facit et causat iustitiam et haec habet ex institutione divina et pactione eius, qua instituit, ut qui rite susciperet suum sacramentum, susciperet internam occultam operationem virtutis divinae iustificantis. Nihil igitur in se habet sacramentum sensibile nisi quandam relationem qua associatum est, ex divina pactione, virtuti divinae iustificativae, per quod vel propter quod dicitur iustificare vel disponere ad iustitiam vel huiusmodi. Et ponunt [Fishacre and others] exemplum tale:

inasmuch as we can find no earlier mention of it,[22] its earliest defenders are at Oxford, and Fishacre does not credit the opinion to *aliqui* or *quidam*, as was the custom. This new theory, as it is developed by Fishacre, places the operation, efficacy, and causality of the sacraments (all of which it strongly defends) in a covenant or pact between God and His Church rather than in some supernatural virtue, infused into the sacrament itself. Fishacre terms this type of causality *sine qua non* or *a voluntate Dei*. By way of illustration Fishacre refers his reader to the Old Testament example of Elisha's cleansing of Naaman, the leper, through the command for Naaman to wash himself seven times in the Jordan river. By this example, Fishacre attempted to show that in the sacraments, especially in baptism for which this example is most appropriate, something is conferred not through some innate virtue but through a covenanted virtue, a divine, uncreated virtue, effective in the sacraments through the ordination of God. Their value is not inherent in them but is rather ascribed.[23]

Fishacre adds a second example of covenanted virtue to point up the difference between the sacraments of the old law and those of the new, an example that is partially Biblical, partially monetary. Against the background of the parables of the king's wedding feast and the laborers in the vineyard,

---

Litterae regis liberant de carcere non per aliquam virtutem activam illis insitam, quae procedit ad liberandos solvendos et extrahendos, sed per significativam potentiam quae est relativa et instituta ad hoc. Similiter si institueret rex signum aliquod obtinendi coronam vel primatum, illud signum causaret habenti ipsum coronam vel dignitatem non efficiendo in ipsum aliquid per influentiam sed significando per regiam institutionem, cui scilicet significationi adnexa est vel sociata alia virtus a rege ordinata ad efficiendum, quod ex pactione signi debet fieri. . . . sed secunda [opinio] verisimilior est. . . .'

[22] Some advocates of covenantal causality quoted a passage from one of Bernard of Clairvaux's sermons that seemed to support their position, a fact that has led some historians to see Bernard as the originator of this opinion. Bernard, however, does not refer to a pact or covenant — a concept crucial to this theory. The significance of Bernard for the theory of covenantal causality and ascribed value will be discussed in more detail toward the end of this paper.

[23] Fishacre, *Sent.* IV dist. 1 (Simonin and Meersseman 17): 'Si diceret tibi Deus: Quacumque die sic te permiseris immergi et cum tali verborum prolatione, sanabo te ab infirmitate tua, si hoc faciens deinde curareris, dicere posses te curatum per aquam et talia verba et per Deum, et proprie efficiens sanitatis fuisset Deus. Sed aqua et verbum sunt sine quibus non fecit, et actio aliquando attribuitur per se agenti et hoc proprie; aliquando autem ei, sine quo non egit agens, et hoc per quandam consuetam extensionem sermonis. Sic Naaman septimo mersus in Iordane, quod et typum gessit baptismi, ad verbum prophetae sanatus est a corporali lepra, et dici poterat, quod eum sanasset aqua; item quod propheta; item verissime quod Deus ad verbum prophetae per aquam. Sic propriisime Deus baptizat et iustificat; per extensionem sermonis aqua sanctificata verbo et sacerdos; et sicut ibi nihil unum ex verbo vocali prophetae et aqua, nec fuit aliquid in illa aqua tunc, quod non prius, nec aliud quam in alia aqua.'

Fishacre gives the example of a minister of a king who might give to certain paupers a token made of tin or a silver-lead alloy that, after the completion of some specified work, would admit them to the meal of the king. This meal, however, would not immediately follow their service but would be on the next day. If, on the morrow, another minister of the king gave a similar token to another group of paupers, both would eat the same meal at the same time, in spite of the fact that they had received tokens at different times. Such, for Fishacre, is the difference between the sacraments of the old law and those of the new. It is essentially the difference between the sacraments which promise or signify future grace and the sacraments which confer immediate grace.[24]

While Fishacre used this example to distinguish the sacraments of the old and new laws, it also describes the type of causality operative in the sacraments. There is no inherent virtue or natural virtue in the sacraments that could cause grace, just as there is little intrinsic or natural value in the token of tin. The value or virtue arises in both cases from a certain value denoted or ascribed by the king. The token is more than the occasion or accidental cause of the meal, since without the token no food would be given. Moreover, the token represents work completed and is therefore similar to being paid in scrip, redeemable for a specific amount of food at a specific time in the king's commissary. The tokens have the value of promissory notes. Once in the possession of the pauper, the token represents a legal claim on the king for food and is as effective as gold or silver coinage. The example implies that certain valid transactions depend not on the inherent or natural value of the unit of exchange, but rather on the nominal value and on the ultimate redeemability of such a sign, a redeemability that depends on the good faith, the trustworthiness of the person or agency issuing it.[25]

II. The Medieval Economic Uses of Ascribed Value

The example of the king and the pauper's token was, in all probability, not an imaginative construct of Fishacre unrelated to any practice with which he was familiar. Behind this example lay several economic practices or credit instruments which permitted commercial transactions to be completed without the exchange of gold or silver coinage.

---

[24] Cf. footnote 20.

[25] Assigning a nominal value to a coin, higher than the market value of the precious metal it contains, may lead to almost immediate inflation in an economic system based on the commodity theory of money. If, however, that coin can be eventually converted into precious metal in the amount of its nominal value, no inflation need take place.

The first practice, familiar to students of medieval economic development, was the use of credit instruments, such as promissory notes, letters of credit, and bills of exchange — all common to international trade by 1200. Commerce in the early-thirteenth century depended upon credit methods that assumed the ability and willingness of merchants to stand behind their financial agreements. Equally recognized was the right of the king, in an emergency situation, to issue promissory notes, or even substitute money, which could be redeemed at face value at some future date. The promissory notes of an international figure, whose ultimate ability and willingness to fulfill obligations was unquestioned, might be passed around in multiple transactions before returning to him for redemption, as happened with the notes of St. Louis that effected his ransom in 1250. The leather coinage issued by Frederick II at Faenza in 1241 and during several other sieges operated in a similar way.[26] Apart from the ancient examples of the use of leather coinage mentioned by Aristides,[27] Aeschines,[28] Seneca,[29] and others[30] (most of which seem to refer to currencies that developed out of primitive money and should not, therefore, be confused with either emergency money or fiduciary currency[31]), there may have been more immediate precedents within the Italian economy that would tie Frederick's action to the leather coinage issued by the Venetian Doge Domenico Michiele in 1122.[32]

The limited and temporary issuing of substitute money in the thirteenth century, based as it was on the principle of a promissory note, suggests a

---

[26] Villani, *Chronicle* VI 21. Cf. Ernst Kantorowicz, *Frederick The Second, 1194-1250* (London 1931) 541; William Charlton, 'Leather Currency,' *The British Numismatic Journal and Proceedings of the British Numismatic Society* Ser. 1 III (1906) 316; Paul Einzig, *Primitive Money in its Ethnological, Historical and Economic Aspects* (London 1949) 268-299. The occasional practice, referred to by Charlton and Einzig, by which the French monarchy issued leather pieces containing a small, silver nail, e.g. during the reigns of Philip I, Louis IX, John the Good, and Charles the Wise, differed somewhat from the case of Frederick II. The presence of the silver nail added some intrinsic value to the 'coin,' although not as high as its nominal value.

[27] Aristides, *Orat. Platon.* II 145. Cf. François Lenormant, *La Monnaie dans l'Antiquité* (Paris 1878) I 220.

[28] Aeschines, *Dial. Socrat.* 78. Cf. R. Bosworth Smith, *Carthage and the Carthaginians* (London 1913) 31.

[29] Seneca, *De beneficiis* V 14 4. Seneca attributes leather currency to Sparta, but he may have been confusing it with Carthage. According to Plutarch (*Lycurgus* 9; *Lysander* 20) and archaeological evidence, Sparta used iron bars as currency.

[30] Charlton, *op. cit.* 312-313, mentions Eusebius and Isidore in this regard, but I have been unable to find references in their works.

[31] For the distinction between primitive money and substitute money see Einzig, *op. cit.* esp. 268-269, 319-339.

[32] Cf. Fulcher of Chartres, *Gesta Francorum Iherusalem peregrinantium* III 27 (ed. H. Hagenmeyer [Heidelberg 1913] 694-695).

second economic practice that is less familiar, namely token coinage.[33]   In spite of the abundance of late-medieval tokens that are now extant in European collections, little attention has been directed to their economic significance. Apart from the nuisance caused by the ecclesiastical and trading tokens supplementing small change in areas of France and England in the sixteenth, seventeenth, and eighteenth centuries, it is generally assumed that tokens never substituted for money in the regular economy, nor were they used in transactions or for purposes normally handled by money. In addition, having been struck from base metals, they were of less interest to the numismatist.[34] However, in light of the accumulated data of numismatic and literary sources of the late Middle Ages, it would seem that certain tokens did possess economic significance, some of them even as early as the thirteenth century.

References to the use of tokens before the fifteenth century are rare, and few of the surviving tokens can be attributed to the thirteenth or fourteenth century with any degree of certainty.[35]   The earliest medieval references to tokens, called *merelli, marelli,* or simply *signi,* date from the third quarter of the twelfth century, where they functioned as symbols of some specific privilege.[36]   Such recognition signs were unique or few in number and always remained in the possession of the person or persons exercising such authority or privilege.

In the middle of the thirteenth century, however, other tokens, differing in nature and function from the earlier symbols, began to make their appearance.

---

[33] The remarks made here on the economic importance of token coinage are introductory to a longer study on medieval tokens yet to be completed. For further discussion see: W. J. Courtenay, 'Token Coinage and the Administration of Poor Relief During the Late Middle Ages,' *Journal of Interdisciplinary History* 3 (1972).

[34] Typical in this regard is the comment of Philip Grierson in his *Coins and Medals: A Select Bibliography* (London 1954) 78-79: 'The lists that follow include works dealing with coin-weights and jettons, whose importance for the student of coinage is obvious, but omit continental tokens (*méreaux, Gildepfenningen,* etc.), which are mainly of antiquarian interest.' The opinion that tokens seldom if ever served as a substitute for real money can be found in such a major work as A. Luschin von Ebengreuth, *Allgemeine Münzkunde und Geldgeschichte des Mittelalters und der neueren Zeit* (Berlin 1926) 30-31.

[35] *Tesserae,* or tokens of lead, were used in the Roman period as tax receipts, sales receipts, religious souvenirs, etc. There seems, however, to be no direct connection between the Roman *tesserae* and the medieval *merelli.* For an examination of the type and function of the Roman *tesserae* see: F. Ficoroni, *Piombi antichi* (Rome 1740); L. Dancoisne, 'Tessères romaines de plomb,' *Revue belge de numismatique* 47 (1891) 210-218; R. Mowat, 'Contre marques sur les tessères romaines de bronze et de plomb: les spintriennes,' *Rivista italiana di numismatica* 11 (1898) 21-42; M. Rostovtsew and M. Prou, *Catalogue des plombs de l'antiquité du moyen âge et des temps modernes conservés au département des médailles et antiques de la Bibliothèque nationale* (Paris 1900); M. Rostowzew [= Rostovtsew], 'Tessere di piombo,' *Rivista italiana di numismatica* 15 (1902) 151-164.

[36] See charters of 1167 and 1173 from William, Count of Nevers, in Du Cange IV 364-365.

196

One type, known as jettons or counters, were used with an abacus or a counting table to facilitate calculation and bookkeeping.[37] These counters bore the symbols of the organization or sub-agency that used them. The minting of such counters for use in the respective households of the king and queen of France seems to date from the reign of St. Louis,[38] although there are 'leads' of an even earlier date that may have served as counters.[39]

A second type, probably later and properly designated as *méreaux* or tokens, were used in the internal administration of monasteries, cathedral and collegiate chapters, and the royal household.[40] Rather than keeping written accounts of the flow of goods and services among the various parts or persons of the household or organization, tokens were transferred and accounts balanced on the basis of the possession of such tokens. Where the staff of the household or the clergy of a cathedral received 'accounting' tokens in return for services rendered, whether these tokens were redeemed daily for food and drink or weekly for money, such tokens took on the appearance of wages. Moreover, in situations where personnel were expected to care for some of their daily needs outside the palace or church, it was natural that some of these

---

[37] See Jules Rouyer and Eugène Hucher, *Histoire du jeton au moyen âge* (Paris 1858); J. Rouyer, 'Des jetons du moyen âge au type de l'ours,' *Mélanges de Revue numismatique* 1 (1875) 473-484; J. de Fontenay, *Nouvelle étude de jetons* (Autun 1850); J. Rouyer, 'Les méreaux des offices de l'hôtel du Roi considérés surtout dans ce qui concerne l'office de la fourrière,' *Revue numismatique* 63 (1898) 519-527; J. Rouyer, 'Miscellanea en fait de jetons et de méreaux,' *Revue numismatique* 64 (1899) 356-373; Paris, Bibliothèque nationale, *Catalogue de la Collection F. Feuardent: Jetons et méreaux, depuis Louis IX jusqu'à la fin du consulat de Bonaparte* (3 vols.; Paris 1904-1915); Bernard, 'Italian Jettons,' *Numismatic Chronicle* (1920) 216-272; M. Hoc, 'A propos de jetons des anciens Pays-Bas,' *Numisma* 15 (1965) 31-43.

[38] See Rouyer and Hucher, *Histoire du jeton au moyen âge*; Rouyer, *Revue numismatique* 63 (1898) 519-527; *Catalogue de la Collection F. Feuardent*; E. Hucher, 'Second supplément à l'essai sur les monnaies du Maine,' *Revue numismatique* 13 (1848) 364.

[39] Jules Rouyer, 'Notes pour servir à l'étude des méreaux,' *Revue numismatique* 14 (1849) 358.

[40] Alexandre Hermand, 'Recherches sur les monnaies, médailles et jetons, dont la ville de Saint-Omer a été l'objet,' *Mém. de la Société des antiquaires de la Morinie* 2 (1834); J. Rouyer, *Revue numismatique* 14 (1849) 356-377; E. Hucher, 'Méreaux de plomb,' *Revue numismatique* 23 (1858) 338-350; J. Rouyer, 'Méreaux de la Sainte Chapelle de Paris,' *Revue numismatique* 27 (1862) 481-497; L. Dancoisne, *Numismatique béthunoise, recueil des monnaies, méreaux, médailles et jetons de la ville et de l'arrondissement de Béthune* (Arras 1859) and the review by J. Rouyer, *Revue numismatique* 27 (1862) 318-322; J. Rouyer, 'Notes concernant des méreaux et d'autres pièces du même genre,' *Revue numismatique* 29 (1864) 444-463; Arthur Forgeais, *Collection de plombs historiés trouvés dans la Seine et recueillis par Arthur Forgeais* 3rd ser. (Paris 1864); Adrien Blanchet and A. Dieudonné, *Manuel de numismatique française* (Paris 1930) III 511-520.

tokens should find their way into the local economy on a limited and temporary basis as substitute money.[41]

A similar development accompanied the issuance of charity tokens. Before the thirteenth century alms were administered by the church or private persons in kind, namely clothing, food, and fuel, or in money, sometimes minted specifically for such eleemosynary purposes.[42] Beginning in the thirteenth century, however, charity tokens were produced for ecclesiastical institutions and religious confraternities to be distributed to the poor on special feast days or anniversaries.[43] Such tokens would permit the recipient to receive food or clothing from the church or confraternity at a specified time. A simpler system, which came into common use in the fourteenth and fifteenth centuries, allowed the needy to use these tokens, marked with a nominal value of one or more *denarii*, to take care of their own needs through the merchants of the community, who could, in turn, redeem these tokens from the cathedral treasury. These tokens were sometimes marked with the type of goods being distributed and the name of the donor but always with an indication of the agency issuing the tokens and the value ascribed to them.[44] Thus the charity tokens, unlike those used for the internal administration of various organizations, quickly became substitutes for goods or money and were used by the poor to purchase their basic necessities from the almsgiver, either directly or through local merchants.

Apart from the jettons, most of the late-medieval tokens that have survived were issued by churches or religious confraternities.[45] Some of these tokens were little more than religious souvenirs, similar to good-luck charms. Most, however, represent an attempt on the part of prominent ecclesiastical agencies to conduct much of their daily and weekly economic activity by

---

[41] See discussion in *Revue numismatique* 1 (1836) 43, 132-133; J. Rouyer, *Revue numismatique* 14 (1849) 357; Charles Robert, 'Monnaies de Mâcon,' *Revue numismatique* 25 (1860) 481; J. Rouyer, *Revue numismatique* 27 (1862) 319-320; A. Blanchet and A. Dieudonné, *Manuel* III 513-518.

[42] Alms money has survived from the reigns of Pepin the Short and Alfred the Great. See Friedrich Frhr. von Schrötter, *Wörterbuch der Münzkunde* (Berlin and Leipzig 1930) 22.

[43] Giovannina Majer, 'Le tessere delle scuole religiose di Venezia,' *Rivista italiana di numismatica e scienze affini* 38 [Ser. 3 II] (1925) 17-18.

[44] O. Eklund, 'Charity Tokens of the Netherlands,' *The Numismatist* 60 (1947) 867-876; 61 (1948) 19-28; Piero Vandoni, 'Tessere Milanesi di beneficenza,' *Rivista italiana di numismatica e scienze affini* Ser. 5 nr. 56 (1954) 112-139.

[45] In addition to those issued by churches and confraternities, some tokens have survived that were issued by noblemen or municipal governments. These tokens seem to have served functions similar to those issued by the churches. Cf. Adrien Blanchet and A. Dieudonné, *Manuel* III 521ff.

means of tokens rather than real coinage. The theory behind the promissory note and the precedent of substitute coinage established the economic principle.

Some of the motivations for adopting a system of tokens can be seen by looking at the most common issuing agency in northern France in the late-medieval period, the cathedral or collegiate chapter. The major factor seems to have been the increasing complexity of ecclesiastical economic commitments, especially the multiplicity of economic transactions that stood between the church's revenue and the ultimate distribution of that revenue. Much of the income that went to pay the clergy resulted from legacies or endowments that brought an income to the church only at certain times in the year. That income had to be divided among those members of the clergy who actually performed the services for which the legacy was given, and attendance at such offices often varied. Consequently a system was needed that would facilitate and simplify the distribution of those revenues as well as bridge the gap between an annual income and a weekly expenditure.

A second factor was the heavy burden of charity to which the Church was committed. Much of the charity resulted from the same endowments that supported the cathedral clergy and therefore suffered from the same administrative problems. The system of tokens not only provided a solution to these problems but permitted the Church to delay the payment of real money for weeks, months, or perhaps even years, thus enabling it to apply some of its accumulated wealth to other activities.

The ease with which tokens could be passed around in multiple transactions as coins of small denomination before returning to the issuing agency for redemption is evident. It is not clear, however, on the basis of our present knowledge, when and under what circumstances administrative and charity tokens began to be used in this way. There is no written evidence before 1401 that incontestably supports the practice of distributing lead tokens to the clergy as a means of recording their presence at the various offices and Masses and thus their share of the income from endowments given for those divine services.[46] Most numismatists feel that the practice is at least as old as the late-fourteenth century and may possibly go back to the thirteenth century, inasmuch as it is not out of keeping with token practices that can be dated to the thirteenth century.[47]

---

[46] The document of 1401 outlines the distribution of the *méreaux* at Sainte Chapelle in Paris. For the discussion about whether the distribution of *nummi matutinales* at Tours in 1216 refers to the *méreaux* see the comments of J. Rouyer and E. Cartier, *Revue numismatique* 15 (1850) 84, 241-242.

[47] Cf. Robert, *Revue numismatique* 25 (1860) 481-483; Forgeais, *Collection de plombs*; *Revue numismatique* 68 (1903) 68-69; Blanchet and Dieudonné, *Manuel* III 512; Jean Tricou,

The practice of charity tokens can be documented from the late-thirteenth century.[48] Moreover, there is evidence which suggests that tokens were used to pay workers and were being used as a form of fractional currency in local economies as early as 1251.[49] By the middle of the thirteenth century the production of tokens was important enough to be a jealously guarded privilege of the guild of tin and pewter makers.[50] Tokens in the thirteenth century, as in the fourteenth and fifteenth, were issued in and used by those areas of Europe that were most developed commercially: northern France, the Low Countries, and northern Italy. By the fifteenth century many churches in northern France had converted their administration of salaries and charity to a token coinage system that had increasingly important implications for the local economy.[51] As in so many areas, the practices of the Church preceded and set the precedent for secular usages, and the abuses of the ecclesiastical token coinage in the fifteenth and sixteenth centuries form the background to the tradesmen tokens of the sixteenth and seventeenth centuries.

On the basis of this discussion of token coinage, especially of charity tokens, we are now better able to evaluate the meaning and significance of Fishacre's analogy. The analogy is of considerable numismatic importance, since we have here the earliest medieval example of a distribution of tokens for any purpose whatsoever. Moreover, it is interesting that the tokens are used for charity and that Fishacre's example precedes by only a few years or decades other references to the use of tokens in the administration of charity. This would suggest that charity tokens probably emerged around the middle of the thirteenth century. If Fishacre's example casts any light on the operation of these eleemosynary tokens in his day, it suggests that they were normally redeemed directly from the issuing agency in food or other necessities.

'Un moule a méreaux Lyonnais du xiiie ou xive siècle,' *Revue numismatique* Sér. 4 34 (1931) 97-100.

[48] From the statutes of the school of San Teodoro in Venice: 'Et avanti si faccia essa elemosina sia dato un Bollettin a cadaun delli poveri doveranno ricever dita elemosina. E non possa esser data se non a chi farà mestier per necessità' (Archivio di Stato, Venezia, Rubrica universale di tutte le parti, ordini e terminazioni della Venetiana Scola di San Teodoro, ecc. c. 208). Cf. Majer, *Rivista italiana di numismatica* 38 (1925) 17-18. For the earliest evidence from northern France see: J. Rouyer, 'Quelques anciens méreaux de Tournai et souvenirs qui s'y rattachent,' *Revue belge de numismatique* 40 (1884) 165-189.

[49] L. Dancoisne and R. Delanoy, *Recueil de monnaies, médailles et jetons, pour servir à l'histoire de Douai et de son arrondissement* (Douai 1836); J. Rouyer, *Revue numismatique* 14 (1849) 361; Blanchet and Dieudonné, *Manuel* III 517.

[50] R. de Lespinasse, *Les métiers et corporations de la ville de Paris* (Paris 1892) II 524ff.; Blanchet and Dieudonné, *Manuel* III 512.

[51] Cf. Blanchet and Dieudonné, *Manuel* III 512-520.

The most striking feature of Fishacre's analogy is that the issuing agency is not a cathedral chapter or a religious confraternity but rather the king. Although the distribution of royal alms was an ancient custom, well organized by the mid-thirteenth century,[52] the use of tokens for the administration of royal alms cannot be dated with accuracy before the late-thirteenth century.[53] Further research will be necessary before we can decide whether Fishacre based his example on the contemporary practice of Henry III or Louis IX or whether this aspect is an important innovation on his part; for, it is only on the basis of the authority and prestige of the crown that a system of ascribed-value coinage could be effective over a wide area. As will be evident through the subsequent development of Fishacre's analogy, the person and authority of the king is as necessary to the argument as the quality of the token or the benefits it might purchase.

III. BONAVENTURE AND ASCRIBED VALUE FOR MONEY AND THE SACRAMENTS

Promissory notes, substitute currency, or token coinage issued by the king, in view of a belief in the future wealth of the royal treasury and in the king's good faith, need never have returned to the king for redemption, but could have operated as did our paper currency at one time. Such a step, however, was never taken in practice, and its theoretical justification had not yet appeared in 1250. Fishacre's example supports the theory of scrip and not the theory of an inherently valueless coinage based on the value ascribed to it and supported by a royal or national treasury. The discussion of covenantal causality at Oxford in the 1240s was still at the formative stage.[54] The development of Fishacre's analogy into a theory of a negotiable currency of

---

[52] The office of royal almoner seems to have been introduced in France in the second half of the twelfth century. The office was expanded considerably under Louis IX.

[53] The distribution of 'maundy money' by the English kings was probably a medieval practice, although most references to the institution are from the eighteenth century. For medieval examples of French royal maundy tokens, see: Paris, Bibliothèque nationale, *Catalogue de la Collection Rouyer* comp. Henri de la Tour; I: *Jetons et méreaux du moyen âge* (Paris 1899) 19-20.

[54] Unlike Fishacre, Kilwardby, writing some five years later, ascribes the theory of covenantal causality to an unnamed group of theologians, which may possibly have included Robert Grosseteste. That Kilwardby is not relying specifically on Fishacre is indicated by the markedly different examples chosen to illustrate the theory. Although Kilwardby does not use the example of the king and the leaden coin, he gives an example of a royal token or sign which, like Fishacre's, has limited applicability. Cf. footnote 20.

ascribed value was effected not by Oxford Dominicans, such as Fishacre and Kilwardby, but by Parisian Franciscans, most notably Bonaventure.[55] As with Fishacre, the example of Elisha, Naaman, and the waters of the Jordan forms the best example for Bonaventure. He alters it, however, to insist that to be really applicable to the sacraments God would have to command that at the word of Elisha not only Naaman but anyone approaching the waters of the Jordan would be cured. In a similar way Bonaventure improves upon or alters the example of the tin token given to paupers by the king's ministers. In Bonaventure's version the king commands that those who have a *signum*, or token, would have a hundred marks or pounds, that is, that tokens might be issued with a nominal value of 100 pounds.

---

[55] Gierens, *op. cit.* (above note 11) 33-37; Lampen, *op. cit.* (above note 14) 18-32. Cf. P. Remy, 'La Causalité des sacrements d'après Saint Bonaventure,' *Études franciscaines* 42 (1930) 324-339; W. Lampen, 'De causalitate sacramentorum iuxta S. Bonaventuram,' *Antonianum* 7 (1932) 77-86. Lampen, *op. cit.* (above note 14) 25-26: 'Sacramento enim dicunt assistere divinam virtutem, quae est causa gratiae, et fidem et devotionem suscipientis, quae disponit ad gratiam. — Et adducunt simile: quoniam ad verbum Elisei, Naaman se lavante, astitit virtus divina effectiva sanitatis et devotio et obedientia Naaman dispositiva; nulla tamen causalitas fuit nec in verbo Elisei nec in aqua Iordanis. Si ergo Dominus ita instituisset, ut ad verbum Elisei non solum ipse Naaman, sed ceteri accedentes curarentur, et hoc ex quadam pactione, ita quod semper assisteret vis divina, aqua illa diceretur curare et sanare lepram et esse causa curationis et habere virtutem curandi. Sic in sacramentis dicunt, quod ad prolationes verbi assistit virtus divina aquis et infundit gratiam et regenerat, dum homo subicit se per fidei professionem et obedientiam. Dicunt ergo, quod sacramenta dicuntur habere virtutem et dicuntur causa et dicuntur efficere secundum communem modum loquendi propter assistentiam divinae virtutis.

'Et si tu quaeras, utrum habeant virtutem aliquam creatam super increatam, respondent, quod praeter virtutem increatam est dicere aliquam virtutem habere sacramentum, sed extenso nomine virtutis. Si enim virtus dicat aliquam qualitatem vel naturam sive essentiam advenientem sacramento, sicut virtus proprie dicitur, sic secundum eos non est dicendum, quod habeat virtutem, sed extenditur nomen virtutis ad aliquam ordinationem, ut quando aliquid habet efficacem ordinationem ad aliquid, dicitur habere virtutem respectu illius. — Et ponunt hoc exemplum: rex statuit, ut qui habent tale signum, habeant centum marcas. Post istam institutionem signum illud non habet aliquam proprietatem absolutam, quam non haberet prius; ad aliquid tamen est ordinatum, ad quod non erat prius. Et quia habet efficacem ordinationem, dicitur habere virtutem, ut faciat aliquem habere centum marcas, et tamen nihil plus habet de bonitate nunc quam prius. . . . Sic dicunt, quod sacramenta sunt talia signa a Deo instituta, ut qui ea susceperit debito modo habeat tantum de gratia vel habeat gratiam ad hunc actum; illa, inquam, ordinatio efficax secundum istos virtus est sacramenti, et ratione illius disponit hominem, ut habeat gratiam, quia efficaciter ordinat ad habendam et suscipiendam gratiam.'

Bonaventure gradually changed from an undecided position in the Commentary on the fourth book of the *Sentences* to a more energetic support of covenantal causality in his Commentary on the third book and in his *Breviloquium*.

It is interesting to note that in both of these examples Bonaventure has removed the restrictions or limitations on the applicability of the sign. The waters of the Jordan would, if God so decided, be cleansing for anyone at any time. The token is now worth 100 marks or pounds anywhere in the king's realm; that is, the token no longer has to be redeemed directly from the king or his ministers, but is negotiable currency anywhere in the kingdom.

The final stage in the development of this inherently valueless coinage, based on and redeemable out of the wealth of the king, was achieved by an unknown contemporary of Bonaventure. Since Thomas credits his opponent with the term 'lead *denarius*' and since that term is unknown before Thomas, it must have been developed by a theologian, contemporary with Thomas and Bonaventure, who shared the position of Bonaventure, Kilwardby, and Fishacre. By substituting the term *denarius* for *signum* our unknown theologian clearly underlined the universal negotiability of the sign which, as currency, could be used to buy — and thus effect the purchase of — anything up to the amount of 100 pounds. By changing the metallic composition of the sign to lead and by making the purchasing power 100 pounds, the author underlined the lack of any inherent or natural value in the unit of exchange. Like paper currency which, although only paper, has a stated purchasing power and supposedly can be redeemed for a stated amount, the lead *denarius*, although relatively worthless as metal, has a stated purchasing power and redeemability of 100 pounds. This unknown theologian attacked by Thomas has, on the basis of the credit practices of the mid-thirteenth century, devised the theory that would eventually support the currency issues of modern nations.

It should perhaps be remarked that this group of theologians supporting covenantal causality, of whom we know only a few, was not attempting to create a new monetary theory. They were only perfecting an analogy that would accurately describe the way in which the sacraments were the cause of grace. In so doing they developed the idea of the leaden coin that argued for the efficacy of substitute money. While their analogy suggests that such currency would be valid by ordination of the king, apart from an emergency situation, it does not really envision a whole system based on substitute money, such as began to emerge in the seventeenth century. It only provided the theoretical justification for such a system, but that in itself is significant.

IV. THOMAS AND INTRINSIC VALUE FOR MONEY AND THE SACRAMENTS

In light of the frequent association of covenantal causality in the sacraments with various economic practices of the thirteenth century, may it not be that opposition to the covenantal theory, such as we find in Thomas Aquinas, was based on an unwillingness to recognize value apart from intrinsic or inherent value? May not the rejection of *sine qua non* causality depend as much on economic presuppositions as theological ones? And, if so, should Thomas be seen, as is sometimes done, as a friend of the commercial revolution who attempted to ease its conflict with theological doctrine?

Thomas' theory of monetary value depended heavily on that of Aristotle, as can be seen through a comparison of the relevant passages in Thomas' commentary on Aristotle's *Ethics*[56] and the *Summa theologiae*.[57] According to Aristotle, value is always in direct relation to demand.[58] Where need or desire for a given item is lacking, that item is worthless. Viewing exchange value from the standpoint of commutative justice, Aristotle supported a theory of equivalence in barter and commercial transactions as set by a free market. Each item in such a transaction had to have a natural value that made it desirable to one of the parties, slightly more desirable than what he was trading.

Money, to be effective, had to be a commodity whose natural value was mutually recognized as equivalent to the goods exchanged. The purpose of money, indeed its very origin according to Aristotle, grew out of an agreement among men to designate one item in relation to which the value of all other items could be reckoned. This one item should have two functions. It should act as a standard or measure of value and, secondly, as a means of payment or exchange. The most necessary quality, however, was that money have a use, function, or desirability apart from its monetary role, that is, that it be a commodity.

All the arguments used in the course of the fourteenth and fifteenth centuries to establish, on the foundation set by Aristotle, that gold or silver coinage best served the purposes of money need not concern us here. What is important for our consideration is that monetary value, as it was understood in the thirteenth century on the basis of Aristotle, depended on three factors: intrinsic value or *bonitas intrinseca*; extrinsic or nominal value as determined by the government or general custom, i.e., the *valor impositus*;

---

[56] Thomas Aquinas, *In decem libros Ethicorum Aristotelis ad Nicomachum expositio* V lect. 9 sect. 978-991. Cf. also Thomas Aquinas, *In libros Politicorum Aristotelis expositio* I lect. 7 sect. 111-121.

[57] Thomas Aquinas, *Summa theologiae* II-II q. 78.

[58] Aristotle, *Nicomachean Ethics* V 8; *Politics*, I 9-10. For discussions of Aristotelian and Thomistic monetary theory see: Joseph A. Schumpeter, *History of Economic Analysis* (ed. E. B. Schumpeter; New York 1954); Walter Taeuber, *Geld und Kredit im Mittelalter* (Berlin 1933); Edmund Schreiber, *Die volkswirtschaftlichen Anschauungen der Scholastik seit Thomas v. Aquin* (Jena 1913); A. E. Monroe, *Monetary Theory before Adam Smith* (Cambridge, Mass. 1923); and J. T. Noonan, Jr., *The Scholastic Analysis of Usury* (Cambridge, Mass. 1957).

204

and supply and demand. The meaning of these terms or factors, however, has not always been clearly understood.[59]

By the *bonitas intrinseca* Thomas did not understand the absolute inherent value of a thing within the natural order. If such were the case, a mouse, inasmuch as it is an animal endowed with sense, would have a higher value than a pearl, which is inanimate and thus further down the scale of being.[60] Value is rather determined by the usefulness of the item for man. However, that usefulness is based on something within and inherent to the object itself. Consequently, the *bonitas intrinseca* is not an arbitrary value that may be altered from time to time. It is based on the presence within the coinage of a commodity that is desired and useful apart from its monetary role. The recognized value of the gold or silver *in* the coin establishes the value and buying power *of* the coin.

The meaning of the term *valor impositus* in the thirteenth century has been subject to some misunderstanding.[61] Although the scholastic use of the term was not always precise, in no instance did it imply ascribed value or any arbitrary determination of the buying power of the currency.[62] Rather it referred to the right of the head of state to establish an exact relationship among different currencies or, in some cases, the relationship between one commodity (in this case gold) and other commodities. Supply and demand would itself establish an approximate ratio. To establish a more exact ratio among coins of various denominations or types as well as to establish the approximate buying power of the coins, a more exact value was required. It was the prerogative and responsibility of the prince on behalf of the commonwealth to determine that value.

---

[59] Particularly misleading in this regard is the assertion of A. E. Monroe that the *valor impositus* was considered in partial opposition to the *bonitas intrinseca*, so that to stress one automatically decreased the importance of the other; see Monroe, *op. cit.* 25-31. Similar difficulties occur in the monographs of Ernst Stampe; see his *War Carolus Molinaeus Nominalist? Eine Untersuchung über seinen Valor extrinsecus monetae* (Sb. Akad. Berlin [1926] nr. 9) and *Zur Entstehung des Nominalismus: Die Geldgesetzgebung Frankreichs von 1547 bis 1643 und ihre treibenden Kräfte* (Abh. Akad. Berlin [1932] nr. 3).

[60] Thomas Aquinas, *In decem libros Ethicorum* V lect. 9 sect. 981: 'Non enim appretiantur secundum dignitatem naturae ipsorum: alioquin unus mus, quod est animal sensibile, maioris pretii esset quam una margarita, quae est res inanimata: sed rebus pretia imponuntur, secundum quod homines indigent eis ad suum usum.'

[61] I intend to examine this concept in more detail in a separate article.

[62] This is also true for the covenantal theory. The king is not arbitrarily determining the value or buying power of the hundred marks; rather he is determining the ratio between the lead token and regular currency. The buying power of the token is determined not by the fiat of the king or the number of tokens in circulation but rather by its redeemability in 'hard' currency.

Supply and demand, the third factor affecting the value of money, was
acknowledged by Thomas, but it disturbed him the most. He recognized the
fact that the scarcity or abundance of coinage affected its buying power and
thus its value, but he felt that ideally such should not be the case. The value
of the money should at all times and in all places be the same because of its
intrinsic value and because the buying and selling of money, which gave opportunity for the sin of usury, was associated with just such supply and demand.
Thomas took comfort in the theory that the value of money, among all other
commodities, changed less under the pressures of supply and demand.[63]

Thomas not only followed Aristotle in placing strong emphasis on the standard
of value and the store of value functions of money, but he also adopted the
Aristotelian suggestion that money originated as an agreement among men
and that it therefore rests on convention.[64] This has led some historians to
assert that for Thomas money and monetary value are human conventions
and that the *valor impositus*, or *bonitas extrinseca*, is more important than the
bonitas intrinseca.[65] Such an inference, however, is misleading. Human agreement or convention establishes which commonly desirable object or useful
commodity should serve as a standard of value and a medium of exchange.
Convention does not establish the relationship of intrinsic and extrinsic value.
Thomas does not believe that society at some early date rationally chose
one object or group of objects to act in this way. Human agreement means
nothing more than that certain items are generally considered very desirable,
not on the basis of any absolute value within the order of being, but only
within the pragmatic order of human usefulness.

To what degree should Thomas' position be characterized as a commodity
theory of money, and to what degree does his rejection of the example of the
king and the leaden coin represent a monetary theory as well as a sacramental
theory? In his discussion of the problem of usury in his *Summa theologiae*,
Thomas defines money in such a way that its use and ownership cannot be

---

[63] Thomas Aquinas, *In decem libros Ethicorum* V lect. 9 sect. 987: 'Verum est autem
quod etiam denarius patitur hoc idem quod aliae res, quod scilicet non semper pro eo accipit homo quod vult, quia non semper potest aequale, idest non semper est eiusdem va-
loris; sed tamen taliter debet esse institutus, ut magis permaneat in eodem valore quam
aliae res.'

[64] *Ibid.*, sect. 982: 'Et quod secundum rei veritatem indigentia omnia mensuret, manifestum est per hoc, quod numisma factum est secundum compositionem, idest secundum
conventionem quamdam inter homines, propter commutationem necessitatis, idest rerum
necessariarum. Est enim condictum inter homines quod afferenti denarium detur id quo
indiget. Et inde est quod denarius vocatur numisma: *nomos* enim lex est, quia scilicet
denarius non est mensura per naturam, sed *nomo*, idest a lege: est enim in potestate nostra
transmutare denarios et reddere eos inutiles [i.e., as currency].'

[65] Cf. Monroe, *op. cit.* (above note 58) 25-31.

separated.[66] With some goods, he tells us, the use and ownership can be sold separately. Thus in giving immovable property, such as land or a house, the use can be sold apart from ownership (in which case the owner can legitimately charge rent) or the ownership can be sold apart from the use (as in usufruct in which case the original owner pays the rent). Money, however, is like food in that use and ownership cannot be sold separately. Money is a commodity with intrinsic value that is consumed in the use.

In spite of the fact that Thomas does not accord to money any absolute value in the order of being, that he recognizes the necessity of the *valor impositus* and the pressures of supply and demand, he does consider the value of money to be based on the intrinsic value, the commodity value, of the precious metal it contains. For money to lack such precious metal would make the commercial transactions in which it was used fraudulent and unjust.

The restraints that Thomas placed on a 'just' commercial transaction represent an attempt to curb what he saw as the worst aspects of a bad situation. The life of the merchant, for Thomas, was particularly subject to evil and brought all sorts of corruption into human life. The ideal city should rely on commercial activity as little as possible and, moreover, should have a very small population. In fact, Thomas' ideal city is not really a city at all, as is obvious from his discussion in *De regno*.[67] It is a glorified village where human contact and commercial activity are reduced to a minimum. Born to the lesser aristocracy, Thomas was by disposition anti-urban. Although most of his life was lived within city walls he never seems to have accepted the movement of the twelfth and thirteenth centuries toward an increasingly commercial and urbanized society. While Thomas attempted to understand and answer the commercial problems of his age, his ideal remained that of an earlier one.

Just as Thomas believed in the economic necessity of intrinsic value rather than ascribed value, so also there was no way of giving validity and efficacy to the sacraments apart from affirming some created virtue, albeit supernatural, that inheres in the sacrament itself and that causes its effect. Behind the idea of an infused, supernatural virtue in the sacraments lies the idea of a natural value in money, in the sense that the 'coin' used in any transaction must have a basic, inherent value accepted as equal to what is purchased or sold.

It should be noted here that the advocates of covenantal causality are not precursors of modern, Keynesian theories of monetary value, as attractive

---

[66] Thomas Aquinas, *Summa theologiae* II-II q. 78 a. 1.
[67] Thomas Aquinas, *On Kingship* II 7 (transl. and ed. by G. B. Phelan and I. T. Eschmann [Toronto 1949] 74-78).

as that idea may appear. The difference between Thomas and Bonaventure on this question is not the difference between the commodity theory and the nominalist theory of monetary value in modern discussions.[68] The covenantal theory restricts the function of the *valor impositus* to establishing the ratio among currencies. The convention on which the tokens rest is not a social contract but rather the will of the king[69] backed up by a currency as real as the concept of eternal life in the thirteenth century. Bonaventure and the other supporters of covenantal causality did not acknowledge the right of the king to set a nominal value on his coins considerably higher than the market value of the gold or silver they contained. Nor are they suggesting that the king could establish a coinage of no intrinsic value that would also not be based on precious metals. The king establishes that his lead tokens have a buying power of a hundred marks *because* he will redeem them on demand at that price. Many of the advocates of covenantal causality in the fourteenth and fifteenth centuries, e.g., Buridan, Oresme, and Biel, were among the strongest supporters of a close approximation of intrinsic and extrinsic value when it came to gold or silver coinage.[70] Substitute currency, as a means of meeting an economic crisis, protected the intrinsic value and buying power of real money. Debasement of the real currency would be as invalid and damaging to the covenant between king and people as would God's failure to give grace to the recipients of his sacraments or his failure to reward sufficient merit with eternal life.

Thomas' idea of the natural, inherent value of currency or units of exchange represents no new development in economic theory but is similar to the approach of the early Middle Ages which used cloth, pepper, and spices in exactly this way. This theory simply found support in the thirteenth century through the revival of Aristotle. In other respects, however, the theory of Thomas on sacramental causality, specifically his rejection of *sine qua non* causality, represents an important break with the early Middle Ages. Defenders of covenantal causality sometimes made use of a quotation from Bernard of Clairvaux that compares the causal efficacy of the sacraments to the way

---

[68] For an exposition of the position of what modern economists call the nominalist school, see the work of its leading exponent, J. M. Keynes, *A Treatise on Money* (London 1930). For the position of the materialist school, which maintains the commodity theory of monetary value, see: Karl Helfferich, *Money* (London 1927); Karl Menger, *Grundsätze der Volkswirtschaftslehre* (Vienna 1871); J. Laurence Laughlin, *Principles of Money* (New York 1903).

[69] The application of the theory of covenantal causality to the ideas of social contract and royal absolutism in Nominalist political thought will be the subject of a future paper.

[70] The subsequent development of covenantal causality and its impact on sacramental and monetary thought in the fourteenth and fifteenth centuries will be traced in a later article.

208

in which a canon is invested in his office through a book, an abbot through a crosier, and a bishop through a ring.[71] Bernard, writing at the close of the investiture controversy and in many respects sharing the outlook of an even earlier age, saw a real causal power within the symbols, an inherent or at least a collated virtue which directly conferred the authority and power of the office. These symbols of office could not be handled or controlled by the laity because they were so efficacious, because they operated with a virtue and power similar to the relics of the saints.

It is difficult to know how much power these symbols had for the advocates of covenantal causality. Those few who used the quotation from Bernard seem to have attributed some ascribed value to these symbols that 'caused' the possession of the office. Fishacre, Kilwardby, and Bonaventure, however, did not use the quotation and may have felt, as did Thomas, that these symbols of office were only declarative signs having no causal value or efficacy.[72] The ability to conceive of a sign that is effective rather than declarative or representative and yet does not possess an infused, inherent virtue is the key idea separating Thomas and his opponents. For Thomas, if a sign causes, it must be on the basis of an inherent or infused virtue; otherwise such a sign would be only declarative, like a trademark on a product or the sign outside the shop of a cobbler or smith. For Bonaventure, certain signs are effective without any inherent virtue; such an effective sign is to a declarative sign as a system of token coinage would be to membership tokens or commemorative medals struck from lead.

The shift whereby the symbols of investiture ceased to be effective signs and became merely declarative is indicative of the enormous transformation that took place within educated society in the four generations that separate Bernard and Thomas. Although the ability to distinguish the temporal and spiritual aspects of an office may have provided a solution to the investiture controversy, that distinction did not radically alter the early-medieval worldview.[73] A more far-reaching intellectual shift came in the century from 1150

---

[71] Bernard, *Sermo in coena Domini* (*PL* 183, 271-272): 'Sicut enim in exterioribus diversa sunt signa, et, ut coepto immoremur exemplo, variae sunt investiturae secundum ea de quibus investimur: verba gratia, investitur canonicus per librum, abbas per baculum, episcopus per baculum et annulum simul: sicut, inquam, in huiusmodi rebus est, sic et divisiones gratiarum diversis sunt traditae sacramentis.'

[72] Thomas, *Summa theologiae* III q. 62 a. 1: 'Unde et Bernardus dicit in quodam sermone *De cena Dom.*: Sicut "investitur canonicus per librum, abbas per baculum, episcopus per anulum, sic divisiones gratiarum diversae sunt traditae sacramentis." — Sed si quis recte consideret, iste modus non transcendit rationem signi. . . . Similiter liber est quoddam signum quo designatur traditio canonicatus.'

[73] A slightly different view and an earlier dating of this transformation has been suggested by R. W. Southern, *The Making of the Middle Ages* (London 1953).

to 1250 through the restriction of inherent virtue, be it natural or supernatural, to the market value of material objects or to the spiritual force present
within an ever-decreasing number of ecclesiastical objects. For Bernard, as
for earlier generations, symbols *qua* symbols caused the effect of the action
in which they were used. For Thomas, symbols *qua* symbols only declared
or 'symbolized' an action or effect that was achieved through other causes.

The general intellectual shift of the early-thirteenth century of which Thomas
was a product, a shift from a world dominated by the mysterious and miraculous to a world ordered according to natural and divine laws, where most
phenomena could be understood in terms of cause and effect, made it all
the more difficult for Thomas and others like him to understand a causality
based on ascribed value and covenant. In spite of the innovations in credit
in the world of the merchant, the general view supported the idea of natural
value. In Thomas, the needs of a strong, apologetic defense of sacramental
efficacy, fused with earlier, less sophisticated ideas of commercial contract
and currency value (especially as reinforced by his study of Aristotle), caused
him to support first the dispositive and then the instrumental theory of sacramental causality. This is why Thomas dismissed the example of the lead
denarius as nothing more than *occasio* or *per accidens* causality, similar to
the causality which the color of the builder would have with regard to the
building itself.[74]

In conclusion, therefore, it can be said that *sine qua non* causality had a
different meaning for many in the thirteenth century than is normally understood, a meaning taken from the realm of royal writs and commercial contracts
and applied to theology. *Sine qua non* did not imply occasionalism or accidental causality save for those who, like Thomas, failed to see the effective nature
of contract and sign in the commercial world. The concept of covenant or pact
stands behind the concept of *sine qua non* causality in theology, a causality
resting on the good faith and recognized wealth of a human king like St. Louis
or, in the case of the sacraments, on the trustworthiness and beneficence of
God.

The University of Wisconsin
Madison

---

[74] The strong Aristotelian character of Thomas' attack on covenantal causality is further
reflected in Thomas' utilization not only of Aristotle's distinction between *per se* and *per
accidens* causality but also of Aristotle's explanation of accidental causality in terms of
the incidental attributes of a housebuilder. See Aristotle, *Physics* II 3-5 (194b-197a); *Metaphysics* V 2 (1013a-1014a). Moreover, Thomas may have seen in the example of the king
and the leaden coin the same type of chance or intentional causality expressed in Aristotle's
example of the man collecting subscriptions for a feast (197a).

VII

Token Coinage
and the Administration of Poor Relief
During the Late Middle Ages
Among the aphorisms collected by Erasmus and circulated through his *Adages* are two references to *nummi plumbei*,[1] lead coins of no intrinsic value that provided, apart from their religious or economic significance in the Roman world,[2] the opportunity for Plautus in several of his plays to question the mental gifts of persons who would accept at face value such "fool's money."[3] In the second reference to these coins, Erasmus added his own comment, with what degree of regret or sarcasm it is difficult to determine, that in his own day copper coins were recognized in Flanders and lead coins in England.[4]

English numismatists have traditionally seen in Erasmus' reference to "English leads" the early stages of the private issue of small change for commercial activity that eventually developed into the tradesmen

William J. Courtenay is Professor of History at the University of Wisconsin, Madison. He is coeditor of the critical editions of Gabriel Biel, *Canonis Misse Expositio* (Wiesbaden, 1963–67), 4v. and *Defensorium Obedientiae Apostolicae et Alia Documenta* (Cambridge, Mass., 1968), and has written numerous articles on Medieval theology and philosophy.

1 [Desiderius] Erasmus, *Collectanea Adagiorum Veterum* (Strasbourg, 1517; 4th ed.), Chil. III, Centur. VII, Prov. 52; Chil. V, Centur. I, Prov. 9. See also *idem.*, *Opera Omnia* (Leiden, 1703; repr. London, 1962), II, cols. 895 C, 1183 C–D.
2 Francesco Ficoroni, *Piombi antichi* (Rome, 1740); A. Belfort, "Essai de classification des tessères romaines en bronze," *Annuaire de la société française de numismatique et d'archéologie*, XIII (1889), 69–92; XVI (1892), 127–133, 171–179; Louis Dancoisne, "Tessères romaines de plomb," *Revue belge de numismatique*, XLVII (1891), 210–218; Joseph Scholz, "Römische Bleitesserae," *Numismatische Zeitschrift*, XXV (1893), 5–122; Michael Ivanovich Rostovtsew, "Étude sur les plombs antiques," *Revue numismatique*, I (1897), 462–493; II (1898), 77–102, 251–286, 457–477; III (1899), 22–61; Michael Rostovtsew and Maurice Prou, *Catalogue des plombs de l'antiquité du moyen âge et des temps modernes conservés au départment des médailles et antiques de la Bibliothèque nationale* (Paris, 1900); Michael Rostowzew [Rostovtsew], "Tessere di piombo," *Rivista italiana di numismatica*, XV (1902), 151–164; *idem.*, *Römische bleitesserae* (Leipzig, 1905); J. Grafton Milne, "The Leaden Token Coinage of Egypt under the Romans," *Numismatic Chronicle*, VIII (1908), 287–310; Rudolf Herzog, *Aus der Geschichte des Bankwesens im Altertum. Tesserae nummulariae* (Giessen, 1919); Denis van Berchem, "Tessères ou calculi? Essai d'interprétation des jetons romains en plomb," *Revue numismatique*, XXXIX (1936), 297–315.
3 Plautus, *Casina* II, 3; *Mostellaria* IV, 2; *Trinummus* IV, 2.
4 Erasmus, *Collectanea Adagiorum Veterum*, Chil. V, Centur. I, Prov. 9 (II, 1183 C–D): "*Aereos nummos et hodie novit Flandria, plumbeos Anglia.*"

276

tokens of the seventeenth and eighteenth centuries.[5] Since tradesmen tokens had no intrinsic value or general negotiability throughout England, their proliferation in the early modern period was considered an affront to royal prestige, in particular royal control of the monetary system, and especially harmful to the poor, who, in order to realize the value of the tokens they received in place of small change, were obliged to trade with the issuing company without regard to the quality or cost of its products. One might assume, on the basis of Erasmus' remark, that the use or abuse of lead tokens in the sixteenth century was something which, if not peculiarly English, was at least predominantly so. Such, however, was not the case. The origin of the lead token was medieval, not modern; its geographical domain was more continental than English; and its earlier functions contrasted sharply with those of the tradesmen tokens of the seventeenth century.

Tokens have attracted only moderate interest since they came to the notice of numismatists in the second quarter of the nineteenth century. Composed of base material, lacking the stamp of a recognized public authority, seldom bearing a date, and often lacking sufficient markings to indicate with certainty the place of their origin, issuing agency, or function, these pieces have remained second-class citizens in the world of numismatics. The number of extant tokens, however, has grown enormously in the course of the last century. The quantity of tokens that have survived is amazing when one considers the soft and destructible quality of the material of which they were made (usually lead, but sometimes copper, leather, or tin) and the small value ascribed to such coins, which made them unlikely candidates for hoarding.

5 On the leads of the sixteenth century see Robert Shiells, "Penny tokens of Great Britain," *American Journal of Numismatics and Bulletin of American Numismatic and Archaeological Societies*, X (1876), 49–50; J. B. Caldecott and G. C. Yates, "Leaden Tokens," *British Numismatic Journal*, IV (1907), 317–326; Adrien Blanchet, "Monnaie et Méreau de Paris en 1590–1591," *Revue numismatique*, VIII (1945), 152–155; R. H. M. Dolley and A. Hocking, "'Plumbei Angliae' A Find of Sixteenth-Century (?) Lead Tokens from Huntington," *Numismatic Circular*, LXXI (1963), 206–207. The literature on tradesmen tokens is too vast to be included here. The reader may find helpful the following general studies: Soleirol, "De la refronte des monnaies de cuivre," *Revue numismatique*, IX (1844), 140–144; William Boyne, *Trade Tokens issued in the Seventeenth Century in England, Wales, and Ireland by Corporations, Merchants, Tradesmen* ... (London, 1889–91), 2v.; George C. Williamson, "Historical Evidence and Information Gathered from the Traders' Tokens of the Seventeenth Century and from the Minor Currency," in *Transactions of the Royal Historical Society*, IV (1889), 171–196; M. Perkins, *Dudley Tradesmen's Tokens of the Seventeenth, Eighteenth, and Nineteenth Centuries* (Dudley, 1905); Cecil A. Meadows, *Trade Signs and Their Origin* (London, 1957); C. Wilson Peck, *English Copper, Tin and Bronze Coins in the British Museum 1558–1958* (London, 1964; 2nd ed.).

Most of the tokens were used up in the activities for which they were created, and consequently have not survived. Of those that have been preserved, many were found while dredging new river channels through towns, especially in northern France and Belgium. It should not be supposed that these tokens were discarded because of their lack of value or thrown into the Rivers Seine or Schelde by tourists to ensure their return to Paris or Ghent. Such tokens were found most frequently in that portion of the river bed beneath or adjacent to an area of commercial or charitable activity. In Paris, for example, the most extensive finds were the result of dredging the bed of the Seine immediately below the Hôtel-Dieu, the leading charity hospital in Paris and a short distance from the Pont au Change, the bridge upon which, until the modern era, the money-changers and goldsmiths had their shops similar to those on the Ponte Vecchio in Florence.[6]

The tokens that have survived have been the subject of local studies describing for collectors, in traditional numismatic fashion, the obverse and reverse of the tokens that can be assigned to a particular town or institution within a town. Moreover, many tokens have been classified according to function, although the ability to recognize a particular type has usually taken precedence in the available literature over an examination of the uses and implications of token coinage. It is now generally recognized (among those few numismatists who have studied this problem) that tokens date back well into the medieval period and that they were issued by different agencies for a variety of purposes.[7] Ranked according to the number of tokens that have survived, the issuing agencies were primarily ecclesiastical, followed by guilds and confraternities, and, finally, municipal governments. The functions that have been ascertained range from a means of paying workers, tax or merchandise receipts, membership passes, means of internal accounting, means of recording the performance of duties, to a means of facilitating the distribution of charity.

6   Arthur Forgeais, *Notice sur les plombs historiés trouvés dans la Seine* (Paris, 1858); *idem.*, *Collection des plombs historiés trouvés dans la Seine* (Paris, 1862–66), 5 ser.; Eugène Hucher, "Méreaux de plomb," *Revue numismatique*, III (1858), 338–350.

7   Cf. Alexandre Hermand, *Recherches sur les monnaies, médailles et jetons, dont la ville de Saint-Omer a été l'objet, suivies de quelques observations sur l'origine et l'usage des méreaux ...* (Saint-Omer, 1834), also in *Mémoires de la société des antiquaires de la Morinie*, II (1834); Jules Rouyer, "Notes pour servir à l'étude des méreaux," *Revue numismatique*, XIV (1849), 356–377; Hucher, "Méreaux de plomb," 338–350; Jules Rouyer, "Méreaux de la Sainte Chapelle de Paris," *Revue numismatique*, VII (1862), 481–497; *idem.*, "Notes concernant des méreaux et d'autres pièces du même genre," *ibid.*, IX (1864), 444–463;

The social and economic significance of these tokens has yet to be examined. It is this issue, especially as it concerns the origin and function of charity tokens, that will be the subject of this paper. In particular, I wish to provide some tentative solutions to the following questions: What role did tokens play in the distribution of charity in the late medieval period? Did their use alter current conceptions of the act of charity, either in regard to the one giving or to the one receiving? What role did tokens play in the two most significant changes in the operation of charity in the late Middle Ages—the increasing centralization and secularization of charitable institutions, and the attack on begging and vagrancy which presupposed and eventually popularized a distinction between the deserving and the undeserving poor? Finally, what was the impact of such tokens on the European economy?

Apart from the tokens used in Roman society (which seem to have had no influence upon the development of medieval tokens), the earliest medieval references to what were termed *signi, merelli, marelli,* or in French, *méreaux,* occur in the second half of the twelfth century.[8] These tokens had no ascribed value, nor were they passed from one person to another in repeated transactions. They remained in the possession of the persons to whom they were originally given, and each token attested to the fact that the bearer possessed a certain privilege or had already met a required payment. For example, the seal or sign of office, which was carried and displayed by a wine seller to indicate that he had official permission to sell wine in the town, was called a token.[9] Similarly, the receipt given to acknowledge that a toll had been paid was also termed a sign or *méreau.*[10] In no case until the middle of the thirteenth century

---

Forgeais, *Collection de plombs* (1864; 3rd ser.); Adrien Blanchet and Adolphe Dieudonné, *Manuel de numismatique française* (Paris, 1930), III, 511–520.

8 Examples of medieval token coinage issued before the middle of the twelfth century have been reported, but they are not well documented. For example, siege money, or obsidional money, a form of credit money or substitute currency used in emergencies, has been attributed to the Byzantine emperor Constantine V Kopronymous in 743 and to the Venetian Doge, Domenico Michieli, in 1122. Both of these examples were issues of leather currency which, even if true, may have been pierced with a nail of precious metal to give them value, as was done later. These pieces were not necessarily tokens of ascribed value. Cf. William Charlton, "Leather Currency," *British Numismatic Journal and Proceedings of the British Numismatic Society,* III (1906), 311–328; Paul Einzig, *Primitive Money in its Ethnological, Historical and Economic Aspects* (London, 1949).

9 See charters of 1167 and 1173 from William, Count of Nevers, in Charles DuCange, *Glossarium mediae et infimae latinitatis* (Paris, 1845), IV, 364–365.

10 E.g., at Cologne in 1204 (Rouyer, "Notes pour servir à l'étude," 373). Possibly also at Rouen around 1150 (Blanchet and Dieudonné, *Manuel,* 512; Ch. de Beaurepaire,

do we have an uncontested instance where a token with ascribed value was passed from one person to another.[11]

The earliest reference that I have been able to locate occurs around 1240 in what might appear to be the most unlikely place, a discussion of sacramental causality in the *Sentences* commentary of Richard Fishacre, a Dominican theologian at Oxford.[12] In order to distinguish the sacraments of the Old and New Law, both of which for Fishacre operated on the basis of a pact or covenant rather than on the basis of an inherent, intrinsic virtue or power, Fishacre presented the following analogy. A king, through one of his ministers, might give certain paupers a token made of tin which would admit them to a meal at the king's table at a future date. If, on the day of the meal, another minister of the king gave similar tokens to another group of paupers, both groups would partake of the king's charity on the same day in the same way in spite of the fact that the tokens had been given at different times.

Fishacre's analogy was, from the theological point of view, of considerable interest. It stressed a principle of Augustinian theology— that man is always a beggar in regard to the favors bestowed by God. Moreover, it indicated a way in which there could be an effective relation between the sacrament and the reward of grace bestowed by the sacrament without attributing to the sacrament a natural, inherent virtue of its own that produced such an effect. Finally, it differentiated

---

"Méreaux de la vicomté de l'Eau et des chanoines de N.-D. de Rouen," *Bulletin de la Commission des Antiquaires de la Seine-Inferieure*, III (1873-75), 399). Rouyer, however, rejects the idea of tax or merchandise receipts as early as 1150 ("Notes pour servir à l'étude," 360-361). For a further discussion of *méreaux* of this kind, see DuCange, *Glossarium*, 365; Rouyer, "Notes concernant des méreaux," 444-463.

11 Ecclesiastical tokens distributed to cathedral and collegiate clergy during the office as a control on the performance of duties and as an administrative convenience to facilitate payment would be an exception to this statement if the practice could be established for the early thirteenth century. The evidence, however, is not persuasive. The reference that Etienne Cartier found for *nummi matutinales* at Tours in 1216 may be a reference to distributions in real currency; *Revue numismatique*, XV (1850), 84, 241-242. Tokens attributed to the twelfth century have been identified for the bishopric of Beauvais and the monastery of Cluny, but their function is uncertain. Rouyer, "Notes pour servir à l'étude," 358; Eugène Hucher, "Second supplément à l'essai sur les monnaies du Maine," *Revue numismatique*, XIII (1848), 364. Cf. also DuCange, *Glossarium*, 365.

12 Richard Fishacre, *Sent.* IV, dist. 1, in H. D. Simonin and S. Meersseman (eds.), *De sacramentorum efficientia apud theologos ord. praed.*, Facs. I: 1229-1276 (Rome, 1936), 18-20. The development of this analogy and its implications for the thought and institutions of the thirteenth century has been examined in William J. Courtenay, "The King and the Leaden Coin: The Economic Background of *Sine Qua Non* Causality," *Traditio*, XXVIII (1972), 185-209.

sufficiently, at least for Fishacre, between the sacraments of the Old and New Testaments and indicated how the reward promised to the patriarchs and prophets was effective only after the coming of Christ.

The numismatic, economic, and social implications of the analogy are even more striking. A token of tin representing a future claim on a meal was passed, as an act of royal charity, from one person to another. Did Fishacre simply imagine this scene or was it based upon contemporary practices or concepts? There is considerable evidence to suggest the latter, as will be seen in a moment. At the very least, Fishacre had to assume that his audience would grant that royal charity could be administered in this way, or else he could not have persuaded them of his theological conclusion.

Fishacre's token is not far removed in function from the twelfth-century examples known to us. A person received a token which he later displayed upon request. As earlier tokens declared the right to sell wine or to be exempted from further payment of a toll, so Fishacre's token declared the right to a meal. There are, however, differences. None of the earlier examples represented a *future* claim on goods, disassociated from a specific holder, which would permit the token to be exchanged one or more times before being redeemed. Moreover, none of the earlier examples concerned charity of any variety.

It might be objected that Fishacre's token did not possess ascribed value but only identified the bearer as one worthy to receive a designated reward. It is therefore a recognition sign, similar to the twelfth century examples, rather than a claim on goods. Nor was the token passed around in multiple transactions. It was equivalent to an entrance ticket, valid only for one activity at one specific time, and it lost all value once the king's meal had taken place, whether it was used or not.

The objections, it seems to me, miss the characteristics of a metallic token whose distinguishing marks would identify the benefactor and the nature of the future reward, not the bearer. It is the assumption of the one collecting or verifying the tokens for purposes of entrance that the possessor had a valid claim to the token and, therefore, to the reward. A token of ascribed value meant that the bearer was entitled to whatever reward was indicated by the token within the restrictions that occasioned its issue. The restrictions on the time and place at which one might share the meal of the king seem less significant when one recalls that Fishacre was speaking about the reward of eternal life which, as long as one is living, remains future.

A coin of ascribed value representing a future claim on the beneficence of a king seems to have been the aspect of Fishacre's analogy that caught the imagination of his contemporaries. His analogy was adopted and developed in the period from 1240 to 1255 by several theologians, among them Robert Kilwardby (a fellow Oxford Dominican and, later, Archbishop of Canterbury), Bonaventure, and an unknown theologian attacked by Thomas Aquinas.[13] They revised the analogy so as to concentrate not on the distinction between the Old and New Law, but on the question of whether the sacraments cause grace through a supernatural virtue inherent in them and controlled by the priest, or whether they cause grace on the basis of an ascribed value, a value conferred upon them by God through a covenant or pact with the Church. In the perfected form, the analogy states that a king could issue a token of lead and ascribe to it an amount vastly in excess of its inherent value, namely 100 pounds or marks of silver. As long as the king were willing to redeem such a token at that figure, it could operate as negotiable currency and have a buying power of £100.[14] In the later versions, such tokens were not given specifically to beggars nor did they have to be redeemed directly from the king or his ministers. The origin of the analogy, however—a fact that is not forgotten in some later versions—lies in the practice of the administration of charity.[15]

Although this theological example is the earliest reference to tokens of ascribed value being exchanged, it is not the only instance of such tokens in the middle of the thirteenth century. The leather coinage issued by Frederick II at Faenza in 1241, and during several other sieges, was a form of token coinage or substitute currency for a limited purpose and time.[16] A more lasting form of token coinage was instituted in 1251 at Douai, on the southern edge of Flanders, when the

---

13 Robert Kilwardby, *Sent.* IV, dist. 1, in Simonin and Meersseman, *De sacramentorum,* 27–28. For the texts of Bonaventure, see Michael Gierens, *De causalitate sacramentorum seu de modo explicandi efficientiam sacramentorum Novae Legis* (Rome, 1935), 33–37; Willibrord Lampen, *De causalitate sacramentorum iuxta scholam franciscanam* (Bonn, 1931), 18–32. For a discussion of Bonaventure's position, see P. Remy, "La causalité des sacrements d'après Saint Bonaventure," *Études franciscaines,* XLII (1930), 324–339; Willibrord Lampen, "De causalitate sacramentorum iuxta S. Bonaventuram," *Antonianum,* VII (1932), 77–86. Cf. Thomas Aquinas, *Commentum in quatuor libros Sententiarum,* L. IV, dist. 1, q. 1, a. 4, qu. 1; *Summa theologiae,* P. III, q. 62, a. 1.
14 For an examination of some of the economic implications of this theological analogy, see Courtenay, "The King and the Leaden Coin."
15 The later development of the analogy of the king and the leaden coin will be traced in a future article.
16 Giovanni Villani, *Chronicle,* VI, 21. Cf. Ernst Kantorowicz, *Frederick The Second, 1194–1250* (London, 1931), 541; Charlton, "Leather Currency," 316; Einzig, *Primitive Money,* 268–269.

282

municipal government solved the problem of the rate of exchange between Artesian currency, which was used at nearby Arras, and the money of Douai, by issuing a *méreau*, or token, that could serve as a coin of small denomination into which currency of higher denominations could be divided.[17]

Were tokens being used in the middle of the thirteenth century to facilitate the administration of charity? It is my belief that they were, although the evidence on which that judgment is based is not conclusive. We should not be hastily led to a negative conclusion by the fact that few charity tokens have survived that can be attributed with absolute certainty to the thirteenth century. Given the composition and function of tokens, it is surprising that any have survived. Although the numismatic evidence for charity tokens is almost negligible, it is equally scarce for all types of tokens, in spite of the fact that we have sufficient documentary evidence for the types of tokens described above and know, as at Douai, that they were circulated in significant quantities. Token molds, made of slate or stone, have survived from the thirteenth century at Paris, Lyon, and elsewhere.[18] We also know that the manufacture of lead tokens was, by the middle of the thirteenth century, a coveted monopoly of the pewter makers.[19] There must have been a wider use and circulation of tokens than the numismatic evidence would lead us to believe.

The earliest tokens with which I am familiar whose function can be tied to the administration of charity date from the end of the thirteenth century.[20] Around 1400, the examples become more numerous, and fifteenth century charity tokens are plentiful. The vast majority of these

17 Louis Dancoisne and A. Delanoy, *Recueil de monnaies, médailles et jetons, pour servir à l'histoire de Douai et de son arrondissement* (Douai, 1836), 48–49; Rouyer, "Notes pour servir à l'étude," 361; Blanchet and Dieudonné, *Manuel*, 517.

18 Cf. Forgeais, *Collection des plombs* (1866; 5th ser.), 249–254. Three of the four examples listed by Forgeais date from the fourteenth century. Cf. also Jean Tricou, "Un moule a méreaux Lyonnais du xiiie où xive siècle," *Revue numismatique*, XXXIV (1931), 97–100.

19 Etienne Boileau, *Livre des Métiers*, title XIV, published as *Réglements sur les arts et métiers de Paris, rédigés au XIIIe siècle, et connus sous le nom du Livre des Métiers d'Étienne Boileau* ("Collection de documents inédits sur l'histoire de France" (Paris, 1837), 43–44; René de Lespinasse, *Les métiers et corporations de la ville de Paris* (Paris, 1892), II, 524 ff.; Blanchet and Dieudonné, *Manuel*, 512.

20 The earliest charity tokens were discovered and/or authenticated by Rouyer, the nineteenth-century French numismatist who made the history of medieval tokens his life's work. Royer himself possessed several royal alms tokens, one dated to the thirteenth or early fourteenth century; *Bibliothèque nationale. Catalogue de la Collection Rouyer léguée en 1897 au Département des Médailles et antiques rédigé par Henri de la Tour*. Part I:

tokens come from northern France and northern Italy, and some of the earliest and most informative documentary evidence of the use of charity tokens comes from the Italian confraternities. The *Marigole*, or statutes, of most of these lay, mutual-aid societies not only place an obligation to pay an annual or monthly sum to the society for purposes of charity, but also reveal that tokens were used to facilitate the redistribution of that portion of the societies' wealth designated for charity. The earliest descriptions of the use of charity tokens bare a marked resemblance to Fishacre's analogy. Before the time of the annual chapter meeting and feast of the confraternity, tokens were to be given to the poor who were to receive alms, and these tokens, in turn, were collected from each of the poor when the alms were distributed. The poor were selected on the basis of need, and the tokens were thus used as a means to ensure that only those designated as "deserving" by the standards of the confraternity (and only a specified number) would receive charity.[21] Although there is no way to determine whether the fourteenth-century statutes of a confraternity founded in the thirteenth century reflect thirteenth-century practice, the close similarity with

---

Jetons et méreaux du moyen âge (Paris, 1899), 19–20. Rouyer also called attention to some tokens from the end of the thirteenth and the beginning of the fourteenth centuries that were used by the Bassin du Saint-Esprit, a lay beneficent institution at Tournai that operated separately from the so-called tables of the Holy Spirit. Jules Rouyer, "Quelques anciens méreaux de Tournai et souvenirs qui s'y rattachent," *Revue belge de numismatique*, XL (1884), 165–189. For examples and discussion of charity tokens in northern France and the Low Countries, see Dancoisne and Delanoy, *Recueil de monnaies*; Louis Dancoisne, *Numismatique béthunoise, recueil historique des monnaies, méreaux, médailles et jetons de la ville et de l'arrondissement de Béthune* (Arras, 1859), 60–64; Forgeais, *Collection des plombs* (1864; 3rd ser.); De Schodt, "Méreaux de bienfaisance, ecclésiastiques et religieux de la ville de Bruges," *Revue belge de numismatique*, XXIX (1873), 321–380; XXX (1874), 75–96; XXXIII (1877), 84–133, 245–279; XXXIV (1878), 293–365; Jules Rouyer, "Méreaux of the Fourteenth Century Relating to the Miracle of the Holy Sacrament at Brussels, and Others," *American Journal of Numismatics*, XXXIII (1898–99), 8–13, 37–42; Joseph de Beer, "Méreaux anversois," *Revue belge de numismatique*, LXXXI (1929), 151–173; O. P. Eklund, "Charity Tokens of the Netherlands," *The Numismatist*, LX (1947), 867–876; LXI (1948), 19–28. An equally early development seems to have taken place in Italy and is associated with the religious confraternities. For the Italian evidence, see Giovannina Majer, "Le tessere delle scuole religiose di Venezia," *Rivista italiana di numismatica e scienze affini*, Ser. 3, II (1925), 17–40; Piero Vandoni, "Tessere milanesi di beneficenza," *Rivista italiana di numismatica e scienze affini*, Ser. 5, III (1954), 112–139; IV (1955), 139–147; V (1956), 149–164.

21 From the statutes of the school of San Teodoro in Venice: "Et avanti si faccia essa elemosina sia dato un Bollettin a cadaun delli poveri doveranno ricever dita elemosina. E non possa esser data se non a chi farà mestier per necessità," Archivio di Stato, Venezia, Rubrica universale di tutte le parti, ordini e terminazioni della Venetiana Scuola di San Teodoro, ecc. c. 208. Cf. Majer, "Le tessere," 17–18.

284

Fishacre's example suggests that they did, especially since the function of charity tokens was beginning to change by the second half of the fourteenth century.

Apart from Fishacre's analogy, there is some evidence to suggest that royal charity was occasionally administered in the mid-thirteenth century by means of tokens. The institution of maundy money goes back at least to the beginning of the thirteenth century, and, although this seems to have been normally dispensed, like most royal charity, in coins of intrinsic value, a French charity token of the royal almonry produced for the *Mandé* has survived from the thirteenth or early fourteenth century.[22] It might be possible that Saint Louis, who enjoyed that form of charity in which he dined with and sometimes waited on the poor, and who permitted tokens to be introduced into the household administration as a means of keeping accounts, used tokens on occasion for the distribution of charity.[23]

Just as most of the tokens of the twelfth and thirteenth centuries whose use we can ascertain were related to commercial activity and were issued by a secular authority, so the earliest evidence surrounding the appearance of charity tokens suggests the background of lay society in the form of religious confraternities, municipal governments, and royal administration. Tokens thus played a role in the transformation of the distribution of poor relief in the thirteenth and fourteenth centuries, a transformation as significant as that which took place in mid-sixteenth-century Europe, for which it prepared the way. In general, this transformation may be called, to borrow a term from Strayer, the laicization of poor relief.[24] It was also, as the use of charity tokens re-

22 *Bibliothèque nationale. Catalogue de la Collection Rouyer*, 19. On royal charities and the maundy, see Helen Farquhar, "Royal Charities," *British Numismatic Journal*, II (1916), 39–135; III (1917), 93–163; IV (1918), 89–120; V (1919–20), 141–184; VI (1921–22), 195–228; VII (1923–24), 133–164; VIII (1925–26), 63–91; IX (1927–28), 109–129; X (1929–30), 215–250; Robert Shiells, "Maundy Money," *American Journal of Numismatics*, XIII (1878–79), 3–4.

23 The royal maundy token referred to above may date from the reign of Saint Louis. The earliest *jetons* used in the royal administration date from the second quarter of the thirteenth century. For a description of the counters used in the households of Blanche of Castile and Margaret of Provence, see *Bibliothèque nationale. Catalogue de la Collection Rouyer*, 33–34. For additional discussion, see Jules Rouyer and Eugène Hucher, *Histoire du jeton au moyen âge* (Paris, 1858); Jules Rouyer, "Les méreaux des offices de l'hôtel du Roi considérés surtout dans ce qui concerne l'office de la fourrière," *Revue numismatique*, II (1898), 519–527; *Catalogue de la collection F. Feuardent: Jetons et méreaux depuis Louis IX jusqu'à la fin du Consulat de Bonaparte* (Paris, 1904–15), 3v.; Hucher, "Second supplément," 364.

24 Joseph Strayer, "The Laicization of French and English Society in the Thirteenth Century," *Speculum*, XV (1940), 76–86.

veals, a simplification and a rationalization of the process of giving assistance to the needy. How this developed can best be seen by looking at the administration of charity before the thirteenth century.

Most of the charity in the early Middle Ages was distributed through ecclesiastical institutions in the form of alms to the poor. Each monastery or parish church served the needs of those who lived in the immediate vicinity and of pilgrims who occasionally passed through the area. Gifts were usually in kind (bread, clothing, or fuel), were normally distributed at the gate of the monastery or the door of the church, and were paid for out of the revenues of the Church or out of some specific endowment in the name of and for the benefit of the soul of the departed benefactor.

By the early thirteenth century, if not before, the charity administered by the parish churches of northern France and Flanders was known as the *mensa Sancti Spiritus*, or table of the Holy Spirit. In its origin, it was literally a table of the type that could be seen outside of many parish churches until early modern times. It stood near the door of the church and from it food and other necessities were distributed to the poor on Sundays, after high mass. There, more frequently in winter months, they received bread, fish, clothing, and occasionally meat and some fuel, such as charcoal, peat, or wood. In a way analogous to the development of the term *mensa canonica* (the canons' portion of episcopal revenues), the term *mensa Sancti Spiritus* was used to describe the fund or portion of revenues set aside for the poor, regardless of the specific means of distribution. Donations and bequests were made in favor of the "table of the Holy Spirit," so that in time this form of charity came to rely upon a broad and sometimes substantial economic base.

With the advance of the money economy in the twelfth and thirteenth centuries, it became possible to provide for the needs of the poor through gifts in currency with which they could buy what they needed themselves. Monetary alms were not unknown in the earlier period; in fact, royal alms were particularly associated with this type of charity.[25] Most alms, however, were given in kind, even by the king,

25 Royal charity took several forms: portions of the king's food given to beggars at the gate, known as the food dole; daily alms, or privy alms, also given at the gate and supplementary to food and clothing; the Maundy on Holy Thursday, associated with the washing of feet; touchpieces for healing; largesse scattered on progresses; and pensioners. Friedrich von Schrötter, *Wörterbuch der Münzkunde* (Berlin, 1930), 22, believes that there were eighth and ninth century coins specifically minted for gift to the poor, and he points to the reigns of Pepin the Short and Alfred the Great. His claim, however, is not supported by recent research.

and the Church as well as other charitable institutions never abandoned gifts in kind in the later period.[26] The commercial revolution of the twelfth and thirteenth centuries simply made monetary alms more common. Indeed, the thirteenth century experienced a sharp increase in the number of issues of real currency for alms money.[27]

One of the major results of this growing monetization of charity through gifts in small currency was that it facilitated the process of distribution and reduced the need of churches and confraternities to traffic extensively in comestibles and combustibles. As a supplement to gifts in kind, it made the stocking, transporting, and dispensing of quantities of food, clothing, and fuel unnecessary. Instead of always inviting the poor to the Lord's feast and running the risk of providing too much for too few or, more likely, too little for those who came, many of the poor could be provided with the means of supplying their own feast, albeit on a small scale.

Monetary alms, like gifts in kind, might be given indiscriminately and out of proportion to the needs of the individual. Where charity was carelessly administered, as in the dole or in gate alms, gifts in currency simplified but did not necessarily rationalize the process. In some forms of charity, however, such as in visiting the homes of the parish poor and sick, almoners were relieved of the need to carry items that might or might not be needed and, instead, could give coins that would buy exactly what would be needed by each family in the proper amount. To the degree that they were used in this way, they represented not only a simplification, but also a rationalization of charity which matched gift and need and permitted to the poor the dignity of purchasing what they required when they so chose.

The monetization of charity was only one aspect of the transformation of poor relief. An equally significant factor was the more direct involvement of the laity in charitable activity and the new institutions that resulted from that movement. The late twelfth and early thirteenth centuries witnessed a remarkable trend on the part of the laity to take a more active interest in the religious life, especially as exemplified by the life of Christ and the Apostles. The two most significant elements within the apostolic life were preaching and the ministry to the poor and needy. In earlier centuries, both of these activities had been primarily ecclesiastical. Preaching was restricted to the bishop and to those clerics

---

26 The image of the man of charity recorded in Matth. 25: 34–40, who gives of his *own* food, clothing, and time, remained foremost in the minds of many Christians.
27 See Farquhar, "Royal Charities," for the minting of royal alms.

appointed by him to that privilege and responsibility; alms were administered through ecclesiastical institutions, both monastic and episcopal. While many noblemen gave alms at the gate, especially at Christmas and Easter, the largest portion of lay wealth that went for eleemosynary uses was given to the Church for that purpose in the form of legacies and endowments. One of the major purposes of such an endowment was to establish perpetual prayers and masses for the soul of the donor; another was charitable activity that would be done in the name of the donor and for his benefit in the after-life in perpetuity.

In the late twelfth century, however, a new attitude developed toward the religious life (an attitude more typical of the new urban classes than of the older aristocracy) that sought to express commitment and devotion through preaching and direct acts of charity than through gifts to monasteries and churches. Some of these groups, like the Waldensians, found it difficult to remain within the structure of orthodoxy; others, like the Franciscans, were more successful in this regard and quickly became a model for one kind of the new piety. Another type may be seen in the confraternities that emerged in great numbers in the course of the thirteenth and fourteenth centuries. Primarily lay and urban, such groups provided a framework for religious zeal without abandoning a secular vocation; they provided a mechanism in which to express piety and engage in charitable activities.

In the thirteenth and fourteenth centuries, this new spirit resulted in a series of charitable institutions that functioned alongside those of the Church. Most of these new institutions were lay founded, lay endowed, often lay operated, and, in their initial stages, lay staffed. Perhaps the most striking example of this form of lay piety is the hospital movement, which had its origin in the twelfth century.[28] Although places for the care of the poor and sick existed in the early Middle Ages, such as the monastic infirmaries and episcopal hospitals like the Hôtel-Dieu in Paris, the real period of growth in medical care was after 1100. One need only recall the Knights of St. John of Jerusalem, Guy de Montpellier and the Hospitallers of the Holy Spirit, or St. Elizabeth of Hungary, to realize both the geographical dimensions and the lay

28   Of particular significance on the development of medieval hospitals are Rotha Mary Clay, *The Medieval Hospitals of England* (London, 1909); Wilhelm Liese, *Geschichte der Caritas* (Freiburg, 1922), 2v.; Dorothy L. Mackay, *Les hôpitaux et la charité à Paris au xiiie siècle* (Paris, 1923); Marie Thérèse Bassereau, *Hôtels-Dieu, hospices, hôpitaux et infirmeries au moyen-âge* (Paris, 1958); Ulrich Craemer, *Das Hospital als Bautyp des Mittelalters* (Köln, 1963); Dieter Jetter, *Geschichte des Hospitals. I: bis 1850* (Wiesbaden, 1966; "Sudhoffs Archiv," No. 5).

288

orientation of the movement. Beginning with the founding of the hospital in Montpellier and the reorganization of the Santo Spirito in Rome, scores of hospitals were established before the middle of the fifteenth century. These institutions, whose services were free, cared for the sick, aged, indigent, homeless, orphans, foundlings, unwed mothers, and the insane. Many of the associations that supported these institutions encouraged and sometimes required their members to give of their time as well as their money, participating more fully in the life of charity. Within the limited range of the medical knowledge of the time, the medieval hospitals were of enormous benefit to the poorer classes, whose economic condition made them more susceptible to disease and less able to combat it. It is one of the tragedies of the late medieval economic depression that it reduced the financial resources of such charitable institutions at the very time the number of the needy increased.

The introduction of the charity token represents a further stage in the process of rationalizing and simplifying the distribution of poor relief. The earliest use that can be ascertained indicates that the tokens were given out to those whose need was justifiable several days before the actual distribution of alms in order to exclude from that distribution those who were strong enough to work and whose need resulted from laziness. Eventually, in the fourteenth and fifteenth centuries, the charity tokens became a type of substitute currency, marked with a particular monetary value or item of necessity, such as bread, wine, meat, or charcoal, with which the poor could supply their future needs, when they so chose, from designated distribution centers or from institutions or merchants of the town, who, in turn, would redeem them in real money from the issuing agency.[29]

It is not surprising that the first evidence of the actual use of tokens for charitable activity should have come not from ecclesiastical institutions of the former age, but from the confraternities and municipal governments, from the ranks of men whose activity in the commercial world already provided them with the economic principles and devices on which to base such a practice, namely informal commercial papers,

29 Cf. Rouyer, "Quelques anciens méreaux de Tournai," 185–186, 189; *idem.*, "Méreaux of the Fourteenth Century," 9–10; De Beer, "Méreaux anversois," 156–159; Eklund, "Charity Tokens of the Netherlands," 867–876; Vandoni, "Tessere milanesi," III (1954), 112–139. There seems to have been an increasing tendency in the late medieval period to tie the charity token to some specific pious action that a poor person could render, such as attendance at a mass, taking part in religious processions, or attending a funeral.

such as bills of exchange, letters of credit, and promissory notes. Behind the idea of token coinage stand the credit instruments of the twelfth and early thirteenth centuries. The promissory note, in particular, functioned as a substitute for money, an I.O.U., which could be used in multiple transactions. Such notes were common in commercial activity and were accepted as a form of deferred payment in the areas of greatest economic growth and sophistication: northern France and northern Italy (the two areas from which our examples come).

There were several advantages that may have recommended the distribution of alms by means of tokens. First, tokens permitted some control on the number and character of those who received charity. The distribution of tokens attempted to ensure (perhaps unsuccessfully) that charity would go only to those whom the issuing institution considered worthy, whether the tokens were given as a reward for some pious activity, such as attendance at a funeral or an anniversary mass, or were given on the basis of need, either in place of alms in money or kind or before the actual distribution of alms. Where need was the issue, tokens helped to channel aid to the *poveri vergognosi*, the timid poor, who were otherwise too ashamed to compete successfully in the general distribution. Although not foolproof, the token system reduced indiscriminate charity. That the issuing agencies did not establish guarantees against tokens being subsequently sold or traded, lost or stolen, suggests either that they did not view the exclusion of the "undeserving" as the major purpose of poor relief, or they saw no satisfactory means of implementing this ideal.

Second, tokens distributed as a form of substitute currency, whether they were marked with a specific item of charity or a particular monetary value, also supplemented the supply of small change and meant that charity need not be withheld when small change was scarce, as it seems frequently to have been in the late Middle Ages and early modern period.

Third, where tokens represented substitute currency, they permitted a charitable institution to defer the expenditure of that portion of its resources earmarked for charity. This was especially important for an institution that engaged in activities other than charity, since ideally only a portion of the tokens would be turned in for redemption at any one time, and a certain portion of them might circulate within the town economy as small change before they were exchanged for real currency. Ultimately, such a system meant that an institution could coin more tokens (more substitute currency or claims on goods) than it had resources to cover, thus giving more aid to the poor at less cost to the institution.

It should not be forgotten, however, that a large number of charity tokens from the fifteenth century on were marked with a specific item of charity, such as bread or peat, and, unlike those marked with a specific value in real currency, they probably could not circulate for long at a fixed and recognized value before being redeemed. The practice of using tokens valued in kind may have been motivated by a desire to preserve a close tie between the act of charity and the particular need of the recipient. The token *represented*, for example, a gift of bread just as much as it represented a claim on bread. The practice had all the simplicity of monetary alms without the monetization of the charitable relationship. Moreover, tokens in kind made it difficult (although not impossible) for the gift to be used for any other purpose, such as wine or dice. Finally, tokens of this sort would guarantee to the recipient the item of charity indicated on the token, regardless of price fluctuations.

Although it is difficult to determine what particular advantage proved the strongest motivation, charity tokens became increasingly popular in the fourteenth and fifteenth centuries. The dramatic increase in the number of numismatic examples as one moves toward the sixteenth century cannot simply be a result of greater proximity to our own age (which would lessen the chance of destruction). The increased number of issuing agencies indicates the degree to which the system of charity distribution by means of tokens was becoming more common.

By the fourteenth century, some ecclesiastical institutions in northern France had begun to adopt the system of charity tokens as a further simplification of *their* system of poor relief. For the Church, it appears that the immediate benefits of deferred payment probably recommended the system. It solved one major problem in ecclesiastical finance: How to meet regular financial obligations with an income that varied and came in only at particular times of the year. The implications of such a system, however, were soon to become apparent. In the fifteenth century, the abundance of tokens in the local economies of various towns, not only in northern France and Belgium but, by then, in the Rhone valley and other areas, far exceeded the resources of the churches to redeem them immediately.[30]

30 On ecclesiastical charity tokens, see: J. Petit-de-Rosen, "Catalogue des méreaux, des médailles et des jetons de chapitres, des corporations et des familles de l'ancien pays de Liége," *Revue belge de numismatique*, VI (1850), 121–145; De Schodt, "Méreaux de bien-

The late medieval proliferation of tokens whose design allowed them to circulate as substitute currency included far more than those created for charitable purposes. Municipal tokens produced as fractional currency, or as currency of small value to supplement the amount of circulating small change, have been found in great number in northern France and Belgium—in particular at Arras, Bruges, Courtrai, Ghent, Tournai, and Ypres—and as far south as Nevers and Perigord.[31] As early as the second half of the thirteenth century, tokens were used to pay workers who repaired town walls or helped put out fires.[32] These tokens, ranging in value from a fraction of a *denarius* to two *denarii*, were expected to, and did, circulate in the town economy.

Another type of token coinage was developed in the late fourteenth century by which cathedral and collegiate chapters began recording the presence of the clergy at the holy office and anniversary masses by means of the distribution of lead tokens.[33] These ecclesiastical tokens facilitated the internal administration of the Church and were not intended as substitute currency, and, initially, they never functioned as such. In time, however, tokens of presence, on which were marked a nominal value in real money, found their way out of the churches and into the economy of the towns, functioning as a reservoir of small change in much the same way as the charity tokens.

The system of token coinage came under attack long before its inherent weakness was revealed, namely the inability of the issuing agencies to cover their substitute currency. The attack was not the result of a panic and run on the episcopal and fraternal bursars of the fifteenth century. It came from two different quarters in the sixteenth century,

---

faisance," as cited in n. 20, above; Rouyer, "Quelques anciens méreaux de Tournai," 165–189; Eklund, "Charity Tokens of the Netherlands," as cited in n. 20, above.

31 Of the more than 300 lead tokens recovered from Arras, some forty are of a type of fictive money and date from the thirteenth or fourteenth century. Cf. Louis Dancoisne, "Les petits méreaux de plomb d'Arras aux types de mailles," *Revue belge de numismatique*, XL (1884), 55–59; *Numismatique béthunoise*, 33–96; "Petits méreaux de plomb d'Arras," *Revue belge de numismatique*, XLIII (1887), 82–98; "Méreaux communaux d'Arras," *ibid.*, XLVI (1890), 49; ff. L. Deschamps de Pas, "Notice descriptive des méreaux trouvés à Therouanne," *ibid.*, XXVIII (1872), 53–65; De Schodt, "Méreaux de bienfaisance," XXXIV (1878), 293–294; Jules Rouyer, Review of Dancoisne's *Numismatique bethunoise* in *Revue Numismatique*, VII (1862), 318–320; idem., *Revue belge de numismatique*, XL (1884), 55–59; Blanchet and Dieudonné, *Manuel*, 514, 516–517.

32 De Schodt, "Méreaux de bienfaisance," XXXIV (1878), 294; cf. Dancoisne, *Numismatique béthunoise*.

33 Hermand, *Recherches*; Rouyer, "Notes pour servir à l'étude," 356–377; Blanchet and Dieudonné, *Manuel*, 511–520.

from townspeople who objected to the limited negotiability of the tokens, and from royal officials who saw in the system of token coinage an undermining of royal prestige and the royal control of the monetary system. Political authorities were all too aware of what later came to be called Gresham's law. The objections raised in the sixteenth century were frequent. Let me provide two examples.

In August 1557, two counselor-generals of the royal Cour des Monneyes, while passing through the town of Mâcon, abolished the system of ecclesiastical token coinage, much to the despair of the canons of the cathedral chapter and some of the townspeople.[34] The canons were told to cease minting such tokens under pain of being charged with counterfeiting. In the course of the investigation, so the account reads, a quantity of lead marks, vulgarly called *jettons de plomb*, was turned up which the dean, canons, and chapter of the cathedral distributed to the choristers and other priests serving the church. The problem, however, was that these leads were not used solely for the internal administration of the cathedral, but circulated throughout the whole town, some being worth six *deniers*, others valued at two *deniers*. In defense of the system, the cathedral clergy claimed long usage (300–400 years). In spite of that claim, the tokens were suppressed, at least to the degree that they substituted for real currency in the economy *extra ecclesia*. This incident was repeated throughout France in the sixteenth century, often arbitrarily and not always with complete success.

The second example takes us across the channel to the home of Erasmus' "English leads." Beginning with the European silver famine in the late fourteenth century, during which England, unlike other countries, refused to increase the value of silver in relation to gold, England experienced an acute shortage of halfpences and farthings that could be used for small transactions or for charity. From 1378 the Commons repeatedly petitioned the royal council to remedy this situation by which silver was drained out of England to be replaced by foreign pieces, such as the "galley halfpence," of almost no intrinsic value. The readjustment of the gold–silver ratio in 1411 considerably eased the situation, but the lack of small change of good quality occurred repeatedly across the next 300 years.[35]

Already in the early fifteenth century the lack of small change led

34 Rouyer, "Notes pour servir à l'étude," 362–363; Cf. Germains Constans, *Traité de la cour des monnoyes* (Paris, 1658), 270.
35 Charles Oman, *The Coinage of England* (London, 1967), 188–201.

to an influx of foreign counters and lead tokens. The tokens were especially prevalent in southeastern England, an area economically associated with Flanders and the cloth industry. The tokens that were marked with a value in real currency were particularly useful.

The Tudor monarchy was concerned over the spread and economic implications of the system of token coinage in England, not only for the sake of royal prestige and the control of the currency, but also because the limited negotiability of much of the token coinage worked a hardship on the poorer elements of the population. However, royal attacks on tokens in the sixteenth century, without a significant increase in coins of small denomination, proved useless.

In 1559, Elizabeth addressed herself to the reorganization of the coinage by lowering the value and finally demonetizing the base coinage of Henry VIII and Edward VI. At a later stage in the reorganization, it was proposed that the crown issue halfpences and farthings in copper, valued not on intrinsic worth in relation to silver or gold, but valued on ascribed worth as royal pledges or promises to pay. Possibly through a reluctance of the queen to place the royal seal on something so base as copper or lead, the system was never put into effect. However, it continued to be considered, and we possess test pieces from 1601 of pennies, halfpennies, and farthings that represented "pledges" of payment in real currency.[36]

In returning to the questions raised at the beginning of this paper, what changes occurred in the administration of and attitude toward charity in the late medieval period, and what role did token coinage play? As Tierney has pointed out, the transition from medieval to early modern poor law was not so dramatic as has been previously assumed.[37] The medieval system of ecclesiastical relief can no longer be characterized, as Ashley once termed it, as "the old pauperizing system of indiscriminate charity."[38] The civil authority began to assume more and more of the task of charity not because the Church had failed to meet the needs of the poor, but because that system was submerged under the increasing numbers of poor that resulted from the economic dislocations of the late Middle Ages. When the state stepped in to help

36 *Ibid.*, 286–288. Cf. Edgar Rogers, "The Rose Farthing Tokens," *British Numismatic Journal*, VIII (1925–26), 93–119.
37 Brian Tierney, *Medieval Poor Law: A Sketch of Canonical Theory and Its Application in England* (Berkeley, 1959).
38 William J. Ashley, *An Introduction to English Economic History and Theory* (London, 1909; 4th ed.), II, 340.

and, finally, to surpass the Church in the administration of charity, it adopted not only the Church's poor, but also many of the methods that had been devised in the late Middle Ages for dealing with the poor.

It is here that the system of token coinage is able to shed some light on the reorganization of charity in the fifteenth and sixteenth centuries. The turning point in the administration of and attitude toward charity has traditionally been seen in the writing of Jean-Louis Vives, *On the Relief of Paupers* (n.p., 1524), and the reform at Ypres in 1525 which suppressed begging and established a *Bourse Commune* for the centralized and secularized distribution of charity. The new system spread rapidly as a means of counteracting vagrancy, and Charles V, in a general ordinance of 1531, urged the establishment in every town in the Low Countries of a civil organization for the administration of charity according to the model of Ypres.

The real model for such a central agency, however, was at Antwerp in Brabant. In 1458, Antwerp established a Chambre des Pauvres, organized by parishes, to govern the administration of charity.[39] This new civil agency was fused with and depended upon the older institution of the tables of the Holy Spirit. Tokens, moreover, served as a major means of caring for the needs of the poor. The introduction of civil administration was nothing new. As early as the thirteenth century, charity had been a major concern of lay confraternities, and the distribution of charity by means of tokens arose through lay ingenuity and was later adopted by the Church. The new factor was centralization, not lay influence. The problem of vagrancy in the late Middle Ages, caused by the crises that depressed the economy in the fourteenth and fifteenth centuries and quickened the destruction of the affective ties that previously had maintained the units of family, manor, and commune, did effect a new attitude toward the poor. With the increasing polarization of society into the haves and havenots, with the increasing spirit of individualism, and with the decline in the confraternities and in that type of piety that patterned itself after the life of the Apostles—so important for the lay charitable movements of the thirteenth and fourteenth centuries—the relationship of giver and receiver was often understood more as an unpleasant task, a burden on society, than as a reliving of the relationship between Christ and those whose feet he washed.[40] Slowly the distinction between the deserving and the

39 De Beer, "Méreaux anversois," 151–153.
40 Charity in the form of maundy money was associated with the act of washing the feet of the poor.

undeserving poor grew as well as the distinction between "our poor" and "others." The concern for the poor evidenced by both Roman Catholics and Protestants in the sixteenth century, and supported by humanist ideals, was strong, although motivations were frequently mixed.[41] The intent of the rationalization and centralization of charity in the sixteenth century was to put an end to vagrancy and mendicancy. While it no doubt administered the available relief more equitably, it removed the Christian giver from direct, personal participation in the act of charity.

Like so many aspects of the medieval administration of charity that lived on under the new conditions of the sixteenth century, the charity tokens remained a useful device for meeting the needs of at least some of the poor. Unlike the trading tokens, which were useful only in trading with the issuing company, the charity tokens eventually had wide negotiability within the community where they were issued and used. As a means of simplifying and rationalizing the system of charity, tokens represent part of the tendency (met with increasing frequency in the period from the thirteenth to the sixteenth century) to place the relationship of giver and recipient on a more commercial basis and to remove from the relationship the fulfillment of the immediate basic needs of the poor through gifts of food or clothing. It might be said in their favor, however, that charity tokens, along with money alms, removed some of the patronizing aspects of the act of charity inasmuch as they allowed even to the beggar the individual freedom to choose when and where to purchase the things he needed, and the freedom to bestow his business, no matter how meager and insignificant, upon another—in short, the ability to be a giver and not always just a receiver.

41   Natalie Z. Davis, "Poor Relief, Humanism, and Heresy: The Case of Lyon," *Studies in Medieval and Renaissance History*, V (1968), 217–275.

Reprinted from The Journal of Interdisciplinary
History *III (1972), by permission of* The Journal of
Interdisciplinary History *and the MIT Press, Cambridge, Massachusetts.*
Copyright © 1972 by the Massachusetts Institute of Technology
and the editors of The Journal of Interdisciplinary History.

John of Mirecourt
and Gregory of Rimini
on Whether God Can Undo the Past

In spite of the crucial significance of the Parisian condemnations of 1347 for the history of fourteenth-century thought, we know surprisingly little about the ideas and intentions of the two principal figures associated with those condemnations : Nicholas of Autrecourt and John of Mirecourt. In the case of the former, about whom a number of studies have been made in the course of this century [1], the confusion over what he taught is somewhat understandable,

---

1. H. RASHDALL, *Nicholas de Ultricuria, a Mediaeval Hume*, in *Proceedings of the Aristotelian Society*, N.S. 8 (1907) 1-27 ; J. LAPPE, *Nicolaus von Autrecourt : sein Leben, seine Philosophie, seine Schriften (Beiträge zur Geschichte der Philosophie des Mittelalters*, VI, 2), Münster i.W. 1908 ; G. M. MANSER, *Drei Zweifler am Kausalprinzip im XIV. Jahrhundert*, in *Jahrbuch für Philosophie und spekulative Theologie* 27 (1912) 291-305 ; G. M. MANSER, *Die Geisteskrise des XIV. Jahrhunderts*, Freiburg i.B. 1915 ; C. MICHALSKI, *Les courants philosophiques à Oxford et à Paris pendant le XIVᵉ siècle*, in *Bulletin international de l'Académie polonaise des Sciences et des Lettres, Classe d'histoire et de philosophie*, 1919-1920, Cracovie 1922, 77-79 ; C. MICHALSKI, *Les sources du criticisme et du scepticisme dans la philosophie du XIVᵉ siècle*, in *International Congress of Historical Sciences : La Pologne au Vᵉ Congrès international des Sciences historiques*, Bruxelles 1924, 248, 267-268 ; C. MICHALSKI, *Le criticisme et le scepticisme dans la philosophie du XIVᵉ siècle*, in *Bulletin internat. de l'Acad. polon. des Sciences et des Lettres, Classe d'hist. et de philos.*, Cracovie 1927, 65-66, 106-109 ; P. VIGNAUX, *Nicolas d'Autrecourt*, in *Dictionnaire de Théologie catholique* XI (1931) 561-587 ; J. R. O'DONNELL, *The Philosophy of Nicholas of Autrecourt and his Appraisal of Aristotle*, in *Mediaeval Studies* 4 (1942) 97-125 ; E. A. MOODY, *Ockham, Buridan, and Nicholas of Autrecourt : The Parisian Statutes of 1339 and 1340*, in *Franciscan Studies* 7 (1947) 113-146 ; J. R. WEINBERG, *Nicolaus of Autrecourt : A Study in 14th Century Thought*, Princeton 1948 ; M. DAL PRA, *Nicola di Autrecourt*, Milan 1951 ; M. DAL PRA, *La fondazione dell'empirismo e le sue aporie nel pensiero di Nicola di Autrecourt*, in *Rivista critica di Storia della Filosofia* 7 (1952) 389-402 ; E. MACCAGNOLO, *Metafisica e gnoseologia in Nicolò d'Autrecourt*, in *Rivista di Filosofia neo-scolastica* 45 (1953) 36-53 ; T. K. SCOTT, *Nicholas of Autrecourt, Buridan, and Ockhamism*, in *Journal of the History of Philosophy* 9 (1971) 15-41.

since we do not possess his *Sentences* Commentary, which would survey his thought, but have been forced to extract his ideas from the lists of condemned and retracted propositions, his correspondence with Bernard of Arezzo, and his small work known as the *Exigit ordo* [2]. In the case of John of Mirecourt, the failure to give an adequate account of his thought is more surprising inasmuch as there exist multiple copies of the original redaction of his *Sentences* Commentary from which sixty-three suspected propositions were initially extracted and from which a reduced and altered list of forty-one propositions were finally condemned. Most of these manuscripts had been identified and knowledge of them circulated as early as 1925 [3]. An edition of the two defenses that Mirecourt composed, one for each list of propositions, has been available to scholars since 1933 [4]. However, in spite of such abundant sources, relatively few examinations of Mirecourt's Commentary have yet been made [5], and the textbooks on medieval

---

2. For the propositions extracted from Autrecourt's writings see : *Chartularium Universitatis Parisiensis*, ed. by H. DENIFLE and E. CHATELAIN (henceforth abbreviated as *CUP*), Vol. II, Paris 1891, pp. 505-507 (No. 1042), 576-587 (No. 1124), 587 590 (No. 1125) ; LAPPE, pp. 31*-48*. For Nicholas' letters to Bernard and Giles see : LAPPE, pp. 2*-30*. For the *Exigit ordo* and Nicholas' question on the beatific vision see : J. R. O'DONNELL, *Nicholas of Autrecourt*, in *Mediaeval Studies*, 1 (1939) 179-280.

3. The manuscripts of the first (authentic and longer) version of Mirecourt's *Sentences* Commentary known in 1925 were : *Erlangen 510 (370)* (Books II-IV) ; *Krakow 1184* (Book I) ; *Metz 211* (Books I-IV) ; *Naples, Bibl. Naz. VII C 28* (Books I-III) ; *Paris, Bibl. Nat. lat. 15882* (Book I) ; *Paris, Bibl. Nat. lat. 15883* (Books II-IV) ; *Prag, Univ. III B 10* (419) (Books II-IV) ; *Turin D IV 28* (Book I) ; *Vatican, Pal. lat. 340* (Book I). Manuscripts discovered since then include : *Bologna, Archiginnasio A 921* (Books I-IV) ; *Erfurt, Amplon. 2⁰ 127* (Book III, q. 1 & 8-10) ; *Florence, Laurent., Acquisti e Doni 347* (Books I-IV) ; *Lilienfeld 148* (Books I-IV) ; *Padua, Mus. Civico, CM 236* (Books I-IV) ; *Prag, Kapitel 428* (C XV 1) (Book III, q. 1) ; *Toledo, Cabildo XIII 39* (Book I).

4. F. STEGMÜLLER, *Die zwei Apologien des Jean de Mirecourt*, in *Recherches de Théologie ancienne et médiévale* 5 (1933) 40-78, 192-204.

5. The only two studies that have been devoted exclusively to John of Mirecourt have been rather inaccessible to western scholars. The work of C. MICHALSKI, *Wplyw Oksfordu na filozofja Jana z Mirecourt*, Krakow 1921, was never translated, and the thesis of Gilbert Ouy for promotion at the École des Chartes in 1946, entitled *Un commentateur des « Sentences » au XIVᵉ siècle, Jean de Mirecourt*, has never been published. For a resumé of this work see : *École Nationale des Chartes. Positions des Thèses soutenues par les élèves de la promotion de 1946 pour obtenir le diplôme d'archiviste paléographe*, Paris 1946, 117-122. The descriptions of the thought of Mirecourt found in the textbooks of medieval philosophy depend either on remarks found in the articles of Michalski or on the text of the first apology as reproduced by Stegmüller. For MICHALSKI's remarks see : *Les courants philosophiques...*, 78-81 ; *Les sources du criticisme...*, 242, 248, 263-265, 267-268 ; *Die vielfachen Redaktionen einiger Kommentare zu Petrus Lombardus*, in *Miscellanea Ehrle*, Vol. I, Rome 1924, 226-236 ; *Le criti-*

philosophy have based their description and evaluation of the thought of this important figure on the remarks of Michalski (which were never meant to be more than provisional) or on a hurried and sometimes inaccurate reading of the edition of the two apologies.

Some of the results of this improper approach can be seen by considering one of the most controversial and most quoted issues tied to the name of Mirecourt, namely his stand on the question of whether God's omnipotence extends to the power to change or erase the past. At present, one of the " sure " statements that scholars are willing to apply to Mirecourt is that he revived the theory of Peter Damian [6] that God could undo or annihilate the past, and that such action would not involve a contradiction (and thus be impossible even for God). A close examination of the original statement of Mirecourt and his defense of his position indicate that Mirecourt never taught that doctrine and constructed his original *quaestio* specifically against that position.

Since that conclusion, soon to be documented, calls into question some of the presuppositions and procedures according to which Mirecourt is " placed " in the history of medieval philosophy, it might be well to consider the present evaluation or evaluations of Mirecourt's thought.

The events leading up to the condemnation of Mirecourt can be briefly stated. In the academic year 1344-45 [7] John lectured on the

---

cisme et le scepticisme..., 46-47, 65-66, 69-71, 109-112 ; *Le problème de la volonté à Oxford et à Paris au XIVᵉ siècle*, in *Studia philosophica : Commentarii Societatis Philosophicae Polonorum*, Vol. II, Lvov 1937, 275-279, 326-331. Franz EHRLE, *Der Sentenzenkommentar Peters von Candia des Pisaner Papstes Alexanders V.*, (*Franziskanische Studien*, 9), Münster i.W. 1925, pp. 103-106 added little to the interpretation of Mirecourt's thought. Maurice DE WULF, *Histoire de la philosophie médiévale*, 6th ed., III, Louvain 1947, drew the material for his frequent references to Mirecourt from Michalski. The only recent analysis of any aspect of Mirecourt's thought (with which I am familiar) that has based itself on the manuscripts of the *Sentences* Commentary is : W. DETTLOFF, *Die Entwicklung der Akzeptations- und Verdienstlehre von Duns Scotus bis Luther mit besonderer Berücksichtigung der Franziskanertheologen* (*Beiträge zur Geschichte der Philosophie und Theologie des Mittelalters*, XL, 2), Münster i.W. 1963, pp. 325-328.

6. PETER DAMIAN, *De divina omnipotentia*, c. 4 (PL 145, 601C).

7. According to the *explicit* of the *Lectura in primum sententiarum* in the Bologna manuscript (fol. 62ᵛᵇ), Mirecourt completed these lectures in 1344 and thus commented on the *Sentences* during the academic year 1344-45. Evidence available from other sources supports this dating. A. BIRKENMAJER, in proposing the date of 1346-47, confused the dates of the Commentary and condemnation (*Vermischte Untersuchungen zur Geschichte der Mittelalterlichen Philosophie*) (*Beiträge zur Geschichte der Philosophie des Mittelalters*, XX, 5)

Sentences at the Cistercian College of St. Bernard at Paris, particularly attacking the position of one of his *socii* or fellow *baccalarii*
sententiarum, the Benedictine, John Normannus. Soon after these

---

Münster i.W. 1922, 110-111. Ehrle, Michalski, and Ouy based their argument
for the date of 1345-46 on the letter of Clement VI (*CUP* II, 568-69, No. 1111)
to John of Chaudemayo, abbot of Cîteaux, dated June 23, 1345, referring to
John of Mirecourt (who was a monk at Cîteaux), as the first in an order of Cistercian readers at Paris. This letter attempted to solve a dispute between Peter of
Serasaco, who had been designated by the General Chapter of the Cistercian
Order to read after John of Mirecourt, and Richard of Lincoln, who had originally
been designated to read before Peter but who had lost his place in line because
of questionable views. Richard, declared orthodox in 1343 (*CUP* II, 541-42,
No. 1076), had tried to force his way back into line before Peter, but Clement,
in the letter in question, permitted him to read after Peter. The document
nowhere states that John is about to read (i.e., in the academic year 1345-46).
Instead, the implication is that he has already read (i.e., 1344-45), and thus the
squabble between Peter and Richard over who was to begin reading in the
fall term, 1345. It would be interesting to know whether the renewed hostilities
between England and France, which culminated the following year at Crécy,
inclined Clement to prefer the priorities of Cîteaux and the candidacy of the
French Peter over the English Richard.

Two things follow upon the fact that Mirecourt read in 1344-45 and not
in 1345-46. First, a more realistic period of time existed between his lectures
and his condemnation in which a process against him could develop, a list of
suspect propositions be published, a defense be written by Mirecourt, and,
finally, a second list of propositions be drawn up for condemnation. Second,
we are able to identify (and in some cases have the writings of) several *baccalarii*
sententiarum who read in the same year as Mirecourt, for we know more about
the bachelors of 1344-45 than about those of the following year. This is of
considerable importance. By knowing those with whom and often against
whom Mirecourt debated, we are able to understand his thought and theirs
with greater precision, and in that process to understand more about the concerns and conflicts that dominated Paris at that time. Moreover, having multiple
references to the same debates and debators, incomplete or oblique references
can be identified.

In this regard, the most helpful figure who was reading at Paris in 1344-45
was the Spanish Augustinian, Alphonsus Vargas of Toledo. We know through
his references that among his *consocii* were : John Scot ; Fernandus Vargas of
Spain ; John Ferrati ; the Franciscan, Rudolf of Cornaco ; and the Italian Carmelite, Paul of Perugia. To that list we can add the Dominican, William Munerius,
and the Benedictine, John the Norman. The Johannes de Magno Monasterio
referred to by Alphonsus as a *consocius* might refer either to the *monachus niger*,
John the Norman, since the Latin for the Benedictine monasteries known as
Marmoutier is *Major Monasterium*, or to John of Mirecourt, who was a monk
from the mother house of the Cistercian order. H. HURTER, *Nomenclator*, 3rd ed.,
Vol. II, Innsbruck 1906, 239 mentions a *Jacobus monachus O. Cist. Majoris*
Monasterii, by which is meant James of Cîteaux. If the second conjecture is
correct, the original reference in Alphonsus might have read : *Johannes de*
Magno Monasterio Cisterciense. This problem could be solved by comparing
the position that Alphonsus ascribes to John de Magno Monasterio with the

lectures, a list of 63 suspect statements were extracted and officially reviewed with an eye toward censure or condemnation. In order not to leave matters totally in the hands of his adversaries, Mirecourt wrote a long defense, replying to each suspect proposition in turn, indicating where the examiners misquoted or misinterpreted his thought or intention. This apology was then sent to an official whose opinion would ultimately carry considerable weight in any inquisitorial proceeding, Pastor of ·Serrescuderio, O.F.M., Archbishop of Embrun, who was the papal legate in France in 1347 [8].

Mirecourt's counterattack was not without effect. A considerable number of the suspect propositions were dropped and never appeared among the list of condemned propositions. A condemnation did, however, take place in 1347 through the authority of Robert de Bardis [9], chancellor of the University, acting, so it seems, with the approval of a majority of the theological faculty. Mirecourt recanted but also authored a second, shorter defense in which he tried to show that even the reduced list of 41 propositions that were finally condemned, some of them new and not to be found among the original 63, could be understood in a harmless sense, and he examined each one in turn.

Mirecourt's defense must have been more successful than historians have led us to believe. His work was not burned nor destroyed; rather it has survived in a surprisingly large number of manuscripts, scattered all across Europe [10]. Mirecourt's request to have his " apo-

---

Lectura of Mirecourt, which includes the positions of Mirecourt and his opponent, John the Norman.

8. Since we do not know exactly when Mirecourt wrote to Pastor, it is not clear whether the latter was already papal legate. The purpose of Mirecourt's maneuver, however, was to enlist influential support, and the dedication to Pastor, therefore, must have been after his appointment as papal legate or shortly before when the eventuality of the appointment seemed certain. It would be interesting to know whether the *Sentences* Commentary of " Frater Pastor " (*St. Omer 239* ; F. STEGMÜLLER, *Repertorium commentariorum in sententias Petri Lombardi*, Würzburg 1947, No. 615,1) might belong to the Archbishop of Embrun.

9. Robert de Bardis, a Florentine by birth and a friend of Petrarch, was chancellor of the University of Paris from 1336 to 1349. His theological and humanistic interests are demonstrated by his edition of the sermons of St. Augustine, but his ability as a scholastic theologian as well as his particular theological persuasion are unknown. His interests in the condemnations of 1347 may not have exceeded the responsibilities of his office to authenticate the actions of the faculty. Cf. Giovanni POZZI, *Roberto de' Bardi e S. Agostino*, in *Italia medioevale e umanistica* I, 1958, 139-153.

10. Counting the later and shorter redactions of Mirecourt's Commentary, the greatest concentrations of manuscripts are at Paris, east-central Europe,

logy " added to his work as a clarification of his position was probably
accepted, which would explain why the apologies are found attached
to so many manuscripts of his work. If it were not felt that his defenses
were appropriate and sufficiently explanatory, they would probably
never have survived in such number nor, similarly, would his *Sentences*
Commentary.

When one surveys the available biographical evidence, one finds
that the case for Mirecourt's "radicalism" (apart from what may
or may not be found in his writings) is weak and circumstantial.
For example, the names of Mirecourt and Autrecourt are never
linked in the documents from 1340-1350. When Autrecourt first
appears in 1340, it is, indeed, in the company, among others, of a
Cistercian, Henry of England [11]. Before 1342 a second English Cistercian, Richard of Lincoln, was accused by Benedict XII of holding
erroneous views, although he was later cleared of this charge to the
satisfaction of Clement VI and was permitted to read the *Sentences*
at Paris after John of Mirecourt and Peter of Serasaco [12]. Although

---

and northern Italy. Outside Paris (where the greatest number are located),
only one town in France possesses a copy, namely Metz, in the area of Mirecourt's birth. There exist two manuscripts in central Spain, three manuscripts
at Krakow in southern Poland, two at Prague, and one each at Erfurt, Erlangen,
and the Cistercian monastery of Lilienfeld in Austria. In Italy there are six
manuscripts : Turin, Padua, Bologna, Florence, Rome and Naples. No manuscripts have been discovered in England, nor do any of the continental
manuscripts seem to have originated there. This is a little surprising, since
Mirecourt supposedly depended heavily on the English theologians, and one
might expect that he would have found a sympathetic audience at Oxford.
Several of the east European manuscripts combine in the same volume portions
of the *Sentences* Commentaries of Mirecourt and Holcot, e.g., *Erfurt, Amplon.
2º 127, Krakow 1378,* and *Prague, Univ. III B 10.* In the collection of the Bibliothèque nationale in Paris, a copy of Holcot's *Sentences* Commentary (ms. *lat.
15884*) follows immediately after two of the most important Mirecourt mss.
(*lat. 15882* & *lat. 15883*). The relation of Mirecourt to the thought of Holcot
and other English theologians must, however, be solved through a comparison
of the content of their writings.

11. *CUP* II, 505, No. 1041. Most of those listed in this summons were, like
Autrecourt, seculars : Helias de Corso, Guido de Veeli, and Petrus de Monteregali. Apart from Henry, the only religious was the Servite, John.

12. Richard had apparently recanted his *opiniones phantasticae* and was
reinstated by Clement VI in 1343 (*CUP* II, 541-542, No. 1076) : " ... licet olim
felicis recordationis Benedictus papa XII predecessor noster tibi, qui apud eum
de nonnullis opinionibus fantasticis quas in certis disputationibus in Parisiensi
studio te tenuisse delatus fueras, tibi ad suam presenciam propterea evocato
interdixisset, et inter cetera per eum injuncta ordinasset, quod tu ad lectionem
Sententiarum et alios gradus et honores bacallariatus et magisterii in eadem
theologia promoveri et assumi non posses in ipso studio sine licentia sedis
apostolice spetiali : tamen tu postmodum opiniones hujusmodi totaliter dese-

230

Richard and John are mentioned in the same document they are in no way associated ; in fact, the document in question was Clement's solution to the confusion occasioned by his earlier attempt (November, 1343) to insert Richard of Lincoln into the priority list of *baccalarii sententiarum* that had already been established by the General Chapter of the Cistercian Order. The compromise recognized the claim of Peter of Serasaco and forced Richard to wait his turn [13]. Mirecourt was not connected, in this document or any other, with the earlier views of Richard or Henry.

The lack of documentary evidence that ties Autrecourt and Mirecourt together seems, however, to have disturbed no one. Having established that there were Cistercians of questionable orthodoxy associated with Autrecourt in 1340, and knowing that Mirecourt, a Cistercian, was condemned at Paris within a few months of Autrecourt's public retraction there, the temptation was simply too great for historians not to assume that Mirecourt must have been part of the radical Cistercians and an associate or disciple of Autrecourt. But the documents do not support that view. If anything, they suggest that Mirecourt's orthodoxy was never questioned until shortly before his condemnation in 1347.

Moreover, the coincidence in timing and location between the condemnations of Autrecourt and Mirecourt should not lead one to conclude that they were condemned by the same theological commission for the same reasons. Autrecourt was first charged in 1340 and was tried and condemned at Avignon, although his sentence was carried out at Paris as well. Mirecourt was not questioned until 1346 and was tried by a theological commission at the University of Paris, not necessarily made up of those who questioned Autrecourt's orthodoxy in 1340 nor necessarily representative of the majority of the theological faculty at Paris. The fact is that we know little or nothing about

---

rendo ac etiam dimittendo, semper bone et sane doctrine inheseras et continue inherebas, propter quod te dignum reddebas gratia et misericordia dicte sedis. "
Since Benedict XII died before the process against Autrecourt, begun in 1340, was brought to completion, one might assume that Richard had been accused before 1340. The document of 1345 that mentions both Richard and Mirecourt is in *CUP* II, 568-569, No. 1111. Interestingly enough, Benedict XII (Jacques Fournier) was himself a Cistercian and had, in his earlier career, been a noted theologian.

13. Advancement in the Cistercian hierarchy in the fourteenth century was greatly facilitated by study at Paris, especially when crowned by the coveted degree of *magister theologiae*. Consequently, in the middle years of the century, there were many in line for this degree and the competition " to read " or to proceed to the *magisterium* was fierce. Cf. the references to this problem in the petition of John, abbot of Valoires, to Clement VI in 1343, *CUP* II, 540-541, No. 1075.

those who condemned Mirecourt, although historians have assumed that the theological commission that performed that task was composed of men of unquestionable orthodoxy, representative of the best philosophical and theological traditions within an otherwise decadent age. But rather than gain insight into the examining commission and the reasons for the condemnation by first looking at the available manuscripts of the *Sentences* Commentary, historians have preferred the shorter route to understanding Mirecourt and have concluded from the fact of Mirecourt's condemnation that his thought must have been extremely radical and destructive to the minds of young scholars and offensive to the pious ears of even more seasoned theologians.

The questions here raised over the nature and implications of Mirecourt's thought should be viewed in light of the research that has, across the last three decades, severely altered the traditional understanding of the development of philosophy from Ockham to Autrecourt. For many years the events leading up to the condemnations of 1347 fell together to form a clear and believable picture. William of Ockham brought to fruition a critical, skeptical movement in philosophy that destroyed metaphysics, separated faith and reason, questioned man's knowledge of himself, the world around him, and God, undermined ethical norms, and offered instead only a fideistic trust in the authority of the Church. Ockham was therefore a radical and escaped condemnation only because he fled Avignon before the completion of his trial. The destructive tendency known as Ockhamism, however, began to flourish at Oxford and Paris. It was attacked at Paris in 1339 as a growing cancer on the intellectual scene, and in 1340 Nicholas of Autrecourt, obviously an Ockhamist, was summoned to Avignon to answer charges of teaching heresy. Then, after a few years of seeming quiet (although things must not have gotten better), the issue of Ockhamism vs. Orthodoxy came to a head in 1347, and the two leading exponents of radical Ockhamism, Nicholas of Autrecourt and John of Mirecourt, were condemned ; an event which, in cooperation with the Black Death shortly afterwards, expunged that particular form of corrupt doctrine from the medieval universities, at least for half a century [14].

---

14. This view, although it has its background in the theological controversies of the early modern period, was not extensively developed until the end of the nineteenth century. Inadvertently it was built into the editing of the documents of the University of Paris by Denifle who, in some of his titles and notes, gave an interpretation rather than a description of the documents ; cf. e.g., *CUP* II, 505-507 (No. 1042), 592 (No. 1127), and MOODY, *Ockham, Buridan...* The view was a major thesis of such important works as EHRLE, *Der Sentenzenkommentar...*, DE WULF, *Histoire...*, III, and Michalski's articles. Although

Historical narratives with such a clear and consistent logic and such a dramatic conclusion live on long after the fragile and inaccurate evidence on which they were based has been overturned. Thus, in spite of the re-evaluation of Ockham's thought conducted primarily by Hochstetter [15], Boehner [16], and Moody [17] before 1950, the general outlines of which have been accepted by most scholars specializing in fourteenth-century scholastic thought, one still finds the older view prevailing in almost every textbook on medieval philosophy. On the level of primary research, however, Ockham presently appears far less radical. Although still acknowledged as a critical and gifted mind in philosophy who took exception to certain presuppositions, arguments, and conclusions of Thomas and, more frequently, of Giles of Rome, Henry of Ghent, and John Duns Scotus, Ockham is viewed as a continuation and, in some areas, a further refinement of thirteenth century thought rather than a radical rejection of past approaches. The description of " skeptical " when applied to Ockham's epistemology has proved unacceptable and is even doubtful when applied to his metaphysics. In most areas of theology Ockham was not truly innovative but belonged to the Franciscan tradition as it was developed in the thirteenth century.

One result of the revision in Ockhamist studies has been to separate Ockham and Autrecourt. Moody has been able to highlight a series of striking and significant differences between the two and has interpreted the Parisian decrees of 1339 and 1340 in a way that removes them as major documentary evidence for the earlier theory [18]. The Parisian decree of 1339 does not condemn Ockhamism, as Denifle suggested, but only states that Ockhamism should not be taught or dogmatized to the exclusion of other positions. If the decree of 1340 against Autrecourt is compared to Ockham's thought, one finds they have little in common. Two of the leading opponents of Autrecourt, namely Bernard of Arezzo and John Buridan, seem to

---

extensively qualified, it still lingers in the pages of Étienne GILSON, *History of Christian Philosophy in the Middle Ages*, New York 1955 ; Frederick COPLESTON, *A History of Philosophy*, Vol. III : *Ockham to Suárez*, London 1960 ; David KNOWLES, *The Evolution of Medieval Thought*, New York 1962 ; Gordon LEFF, *Medieval Thought from Saint Augustine to Ockham*, St. Albans 1958 ; and Armand MAURER, *Medieval Philosophy*, New York 1968.

15. Erich HOCHSTETTER, *Studien zur Metaphysik und Erkenntnislehre Wilhelms von Ockham*, Berlin 1927.

16. Philotheus BOEHNER, *Collected Articles on Ockham* (*Franciscan Institute Publications, Philosophy Series*, 12), St. Bonaventure, N.Y., 1958.

17. MOODY, *Ockham, Buridan...* ; *Ockham and Aegidius of Rome*, in *Franciscan Studies* 9 (1949) 417-442 ; *Empiricism and Metaphysics in Medieval Philosophy*, in *Philosophical Review* 67 (1958) 145-163.

18. MOODY, *Ockham, Buridan...*

VIIIa

have had more in common with Ockham than did Autrecourt, and they may have been attacking Autrecourt on the basis of Ockhamistic presuppositions. In the view of Moody, therefore, Ockhamism, or at least some of the Ockhamists, represented the conservative, orthodox, common opinion at Paris in the period from 1340 to 1350. Many of the leading theologians have been placed within this category, including those responsible for the condemnation of Autrecourt. Autrecourt, on the other hand, and, by association, Mirecourt, represented a new radicalism that was opposed to Ockhamism, and they in turn, were opposed by the Ockhamists [19]. This picture was, in a sense, solidified when Damasus Trapp claimed to have discovered that Gregory of Rimini, a leading *modernus* and heavily influenced by Ockham, was one of the major figures who authored the condemnation of Mirecourt [20].

These extensive reinterpretations of fourteenth-century thought have, if anything, bound Mirecourt and Autrecourt more closely together. Yet the portions of the *Sentences* Commentary that have been examined to date do not support that assumption [21]. In fact, most of the theories, both old and new, about Mirecourt and the condemnation of 1347 appear questionable in light of the new evidence. Toward the end of this essay, Mirecourt's relation to Ockham, Autrecourt, and Rimini will be re-examined and some suggestions made for

---

19. A slightly different evaluation of the relationship between Autrecourt and Ockham has been suggested by T. K. SCOTT, *Nicholas of Autrecourt...* In spite of the line of continuity that Scott attempts to construct between these two figures, the earlier assessment of Moody seems more accurate and balanced. For a more extensive discussion of this problem see R. PAQUÉ, *Das Pariser Nominalistenstatut zur Entstehung des Realitätsbegriffs der neuzeitlichen Naturwissenschaft*, Berlin 1970.

20. Damasus TRAPP, *Augustinian Theology of the 14th Century : Notes on Editions, Marginalia, Opinions and Book-Lore*, in *Augustiniana* 6 (1956) 146-274 ; *Peter Ceffons of Clairvaux*, in *Recherches de Théologie ancienne et médiévale* 24 (1957) 101-154 ; *Gregory of Rimini Manuscripts : Editions and Additions*, in *Augustiniana* 8 (1958) 425-443 ; and *Gregorio de Rimini y el nominalismo*, in *Augustinianum* 4 (1964) 5-20. The thesis of Trapp, and the evidence he has marshalled in support of it, will be considered later in connection with Gregory of Rimini.

21. Apart from the sections that may have been examined by Ouy in his unpublished thesis, the sections I have looked at are the first six questions of Book I (on epistemology) ; Book I, q. 39, which forms the material for this study ; and Book IV, q. 1 on sacramental causality, which I shall treat in a separate paper. Book I, q. 2-6 have been edited by A. FRANZINELLI, *Questioni inedite di Giovanni de Mirecourt sulla conoscenza*, in *Rivista critica di Storia della Filosofia* 13 (1958) 319-340, 415-449. The first six questions of Book I have recently been examined by Roy Van Neste in a doctoral dissertation at Wisconsin on Mirecourt's epistemology. The question of merit and the habit of grace have been discussed by DETTLOFF in *Die Entwicklung...*, 325-328.

234

constructing a theory that will better accord with what we now know. However, it should be kept in mind that the conclusions put forward there, although preferable to earlier evaluations, are based on only a small portion of Mirecourt's work and, therefore, are tentative, pending a more complete study of his thought, a task that could with ease and profit absorb the interests and labors of many scholars.

MIRECOURT'S FIRST APOLOGY.

Because the conclusions of the following study of Mirecourt's position on God's power to undo the past depart so sharply from earlier assessments, it may be helpful to begin by comparing those assessments with the texts of Mirecourt upon which they were based. The general interpretation of Mirecourt now current owes much to Michalski's articles, but the idea that Mirecourt expanded divine omnipotence by sacrificing the certainty of the past was given prominence by Frederick Copleston [22] and Étienne Gilson [23] as a result of their reading of Mirecourt's first apology. The relevant sections of Gilson and Copleston are as follows :

> John maintains that God can arrange that the world never existed, or more exactly that " it is neither evident nor imposed by faith, that God could not so make it that the world never existed " ; to which he adds that the contrary is no more evident, for he could not drive " the partisans of the contrary either to contradict themselves, or to deny faith, experiences or demonstrated conclusions. " Of course, he concludes, " I know that it follows from faith that this should be false. " This probably was a verbal precaution. How could a man accept by faith a thesis which he maintains does not necessarily follow from faith ? Commenting on the fifth of his condemned propositions : " For me, it is neither evident, nor evidently proven, nor resulting from faith, that it should be impossible for God so to arrange it that the world never existed ", John simply remarks : " My conclusion on this subject appeared to me to be true, because I did not wish to flatter myself that I had a knowledge I did not have [24]. "

> Similarly he [Mirecourt] seems, though extremely tentatively, to have favoured the opinion of St. Peter Damian that God could bring it about that the world should never have been, that is to say, that God could bring it about that the past should not have happened. He allows that this undoing of the fact cannot take place *de potentia Dei ordi-*

---

22. *History of Philosophy*, III, 127-134.
23. *History of Christian Philosophy in the Middle Ages*, 503-505.
24. *Ibid.*, 504-505.

nata ; but, whereas one might well expect him to appeal to the principle of contradiction in order to show that the undoing of the past is absolutely impossible, he says that this absolute impossibility is not evident to him. ' I was unwilling to lay claim to knowledge which I did not possess ' (first apology, proposition 5). He does not say that it is possible for God to bring it about that the past should not have happened ; he says that the impossibility of God's doing this is not evident to him. John of Mirecourt was always careful in his statements [25].

Just how careful and precise Mirecourt was in his statements can be seen when we compare these two descriptions with the text of Mirecourt's defense upon which the two historians based their judgment, namely Mirecourt's replies to the second and fifth suspect propositions in his first apology. Let us examine first Mirecourt's reply to the second suspect proposition.

Whence I say, and I have said, that God is not able to make it so that the world never existed, whether " to make " is taken positively [= to create] or in the sense of privation [= to annihilate]. And therefore all the things that follow from this [i.e., any other propositions that seemingly imply God's power to undo the past] I reckon to be impossible things and to imply a contradiction. I have even said that by taking " to make " in the sense of creation it is evident to me that God is not able to do this, because this would imply a contradiction.

I have said, however, that by taking " to make " improperly, in the way in which it might be said that before the world was [i.e., before creation] God was making the world not to be, *then it is neither evident to me nor does it follow from faith that God could not so make it that the world never existed* [i.e., it is not self-evident nor is it deduced from faith that God was not allowing or sustaining the non-existence of the world up until the instant of creation, nor is it evident or deduced from faith that God could not have sustained that non-existence, so that creation might not have taken place, had God so willed it], nor is even the opposite (evident or given by faith) [i.e., the non-necessity of creation], because I would not know how to lead those holding the opposite opinion into contradicting themselves or into denying the faith, experience, or a demonstrated conclusion. I know, however, that it follows from faith that these things are false [26].

---

25. COPLESTON, 133.

26. John of Mirecourt, First Apology, reply to the second " suspect " proposition (STEGMÜLLER, 48) : " Unde dico et dixi, quod Deus non potest facere mundum numquam fuisse, sive capiatur ' facere ' positive sive privative, et ideo omnia quae sequuntur ad hanc, reputo impossibilia et contradictionem implicare. Dixi etiam, quod capiendo ' facere ' positive, evidens est mihi, quod Deus non potest hoc facere, quia hoc implicaret contradictionem ; dixi tamen,

The first paragraph reveals Mirecourt's position on the central issue. He rejects as a logical contradiction the idea that God could undo or annihilate the past. What is past is necessarily true and no longer contingent, a situation that cannot be altered even by God, even *de potentia absoluta* [27]. The second paragraph addresses itself to an entirely different issue : the question of the necessity or non-necessity of creation. The only sense, Mirecourt states, in which it could be said that God could make what has happened not to have happened would be to consider the situation *before* it took place, before creation, when what we call past was in the future and, therefore, contingent. Then God had an option to act or not to act, to create or not to create, and in that sense only it was possible (or was at least a live option to God) that he might have sustained the non-existence of the world, and thus what is now past to us would never have happened. If one, speaking in a loose and improper way, says that before creation God was " making " the non-existence of the world, he is saying no more than that creation or any past thing was not absolutely necessary but something chosen freely by God, contingent upon his will and wisdom. Before God made the world it was possible for him not to have made it (assuming that such a discussion has meaning when applied to an a-temporal God).

---

quod capiendo ' facere ' improprie, eo modo quo diceretur quod antequam mundus esset Deus faciebat mundum non esse, tunc non est mihi evidens nec sequens ex fide, quod Deus non posset facere mundum numquam fuisse, nec etiam oppositum, quia tenentes oppositum nescirem deducere ad contradictoria nec ad negandum fidem nec experientiam nec conclusionem demonstratam. Scio tamen, quod est ex fide sequens haec esse falsa. "

27. The distinction between the absolute and ordained powers of God was common throughout thirteenth and fourteenth century thought. What God has done and what God will do are ordained, whether revealed yet or not, and because of the immutability and unity of the divine nature, including the divine will, God will never act otherwise. Since, however, it seems impious to deny to God the freedom to have done other than he did, a freedom seemingly possessed by every human, theologians acknowledged an area of initial possibility for divine action, limited only by the principle of contradiction, out of which the things God did do or is going to do were chosen. The distinction presupposes, although it does not pursue, the idea that God's choices and actions can, for purposes of discussion, be placed in a hypothetical temporal sequence ; a hypothesis that many in the modern age are unwilling to allow, either through an insistence on the a-temporality of God or through the belief that any freedom of choice, human or divine, is illusory. Medieval theologians, however, found it a useful distinction, and it is the historians task to understand their view, not to judge it. No thirteenth or fourteenth century theologian, with whom I am familiar, rejected the distinction for reasons of a-temporality or determinism, nor did they depart from the common usage, although one, Nicholas of Autrecourt, avoided using the distinction, seemingly because the supposition of nonintervention (i.e., *de potentia ordinata*) did not sufficiently insure certitude.

The italicized sentence extracted from the second paragraph by Gilson as representative of the true thought of Mirecourt is misleading when taken out of context. Mirecourt was only stating that the question of the necessity of creation cannot be finally or definitively decided on the basis of evident knowledge or Scriptural revelation. He was not saying that the impossibility of God's undoing the past was not evident to him. The issue of God's altering the past was treated in the first paragraph and was answered forcefully in the negative.

Thus far Mirecourt's meaning is clear, whether one believes him to be sincere or not. Against his accusers he claims to hold, even by evident knowledge, the opposite of the position he was credited with holding, and he claims that this was his earlier position as well (a statement the truth of which can only be determined by examining his *Lectura sententiarum*). He says, however, that the proposition " God can make the past not to have been " is ambiguous, and, if taken in the second, improper sense (God's power before the event), then it is not evident that God lacks such power. Consequently, he is forced to admit his inability to lead those affirming the truth of this proposition into a contradiction, a denial of experience, or a denial of faith, since they can always take refuge in the second interpretation of the proposition. Unlike the terms " undo ", " erase ", " alter ', " annihilate ", the term " make " does not imply there is something already in existence which is being changed, although it can be used in that way. If any of the former terms were used, then, Mirecourt believes, the proposition could be shown to be patently false and self-contradictory, but because the ambiguous term " make " is used and the time of action is not indicated, the proposition cannot be shown to be false in all its possible meanings. The concluding sentence, " I know that it follows from faith that these things are false ", was not a verbal precaution, as Gilson described it, nor does it contradict what Mirecourt said earlier. He is not referring to his own position but to that of the *tenentes oppositum*, and he is saying that although he cannot in a final sense prove them wrong by arguments from faith (arguments based on Scripture and defined doctrine), he does feel (his own inner conviction) that faith supports his position and not theirs. The doubts Mirecourt reveals in his second paragraph, therefore, are not doubts over what he believes but doubts over his ability to demonstrate what he believes in such a way that his opponents will concede his point. This last section was written in a personal and revealing manner and was expected to arouse sympathy and understanding from the reader, probably from Pastor, a theologian trained in the schools of Paris, to whom it was sent.

238

Not all of Gilson's and Copleston's description of Mirecourt's position on whether God can undo the past was based on Mirecourt's
reply to the second proposition. The reply to the fifth proposition
was also used and seems, on face value, to support the traditional
view, although Gilson erroneously refers to it as a " condemned proposition ". The proposition states : " For me, it is neither evident,
nor evidently proven, nor resulting from faith, that it should be
impossible for God so to arrange is that the world never existed. "
Mirecourt's only reply is that the conclusion appeared to him to be
true, because he did not wish to presume to have a knowledge he did
not possess [28]. When we compare this text with the original passage
in the *Sentences* Commentary (to which we shall turn in a moment),
we shall see why Mirecourt was willing to stand behind that statement
and why his accusers dropped the issue and did not include it among
the condemned propositions in the second list [29].

In order to ascertain the justice (or lack of justice) of Mirecourt's
frequent remark in his first apology that he was misquoted and misinterpreted, it is necessary to examine briefly the other propositions
and replies that concern the issue of God's power to alter the past
before turning to the question in the *Lectura* from which that material
was extracted. The first seven propositions were drawn from the same
question, although it was on propositions two and five that the modern
discussion has been based.

The first proposition was that it was possible for Christ to have
willed something by his created will and for that never to have come
about [30]. Mirecourt admits to having said this and claims that it is an
acceptable statement, when understood properly. He further remarks
that his interpretation or qualifications of this proposition are not
new to the apology but appeared in the text of the *Lectura* [31]. Essentially Mirecourt's reply is that the proposition is false *de potentia Dei*

---

28. STEGMÜLLER, 49 : « Quinta propositio est quinta conclusio illius eiusdem
quaestionis : ' Non est mihi evidens nec evidenter probatum nec ex fide sequens, quod impossibile sit, quod Deus faciat mundum numquam fuisse '. —
Quantum ad hoc apparebat mihi conclusio vera, quia nolebam praesumere me
scientiam habere quam non habebam. »

29. One suspect proposition (No. 1) extracted from Mirecourt's question
on whether God can undo the past was repeated in the final list of condemned
propositions (No. 1). The proposition concerns Christ's willing something
through his created will that might not come to pass and is thus a proposition
about future contingents, not the past. Even so, it seems far from heretical,
as the discussion in Mirecourt shows and as will become apparent in the following remarks.

30. STEGMÜLLER 47 : « Quod possibile erat, quod Christus aliquid voluit volitione creata, et numquam sic debuit evenire. »

31. *Ibid.* : « Quantum ad istam dixi et dico... »

ordinata but true when : (1) one understands "can" in the sense of
de potentia Dei absoluta ; (2) one remembers that it is the created
(human) will of Christ under discussion, not the uncreated will ;
and (3) one places the proposition in the context of future contingents
where, as Mirecourt views it, the future, although it happens necessarily as God foresees it, remains contingent [32].
This was the only proposition of the seven that remained in the
final, condemned list. In his second reply, Mirecourt again points
out that there are various ways in which the proposition can be understood. He states that he never intended the proposition to be read *de
potentia ordinata*, namely as something that did or could possibly
happen in reality [33]. He even states that he did not mean to imply
that the proposition was true *de potentia absoluta*, if one considers the
human will as conjoined with the divine will [34]. He only meant to
assert that the contingency of the future is not removed or falsified
because Christ, through his created will, wills some future event that
will happen, when it happens, necessarily [35].
Judging from the fact that this proposition and one similar,
extracted from another question [36], were condemned, it seems safe

---

32. *Ibid.* : « ... illud numquam fiet nec fiebat, nec est possibile fieri de potentia
Dei ordinata. ... Huiusmodi videbatur mihi esse talis propositio : ' Christus
voluit *a* volitione creata ', quia necessarium est illam volitionem fuisse in illa
anima, et animam Christi per illam voluisse *a*, et per consequens per communicationem idiomatum Christum voluisse *a*, et per consequens haec est simpliciter
necessaria : ' Christus voluit *a* volitione creata '. Quo concesso adhuc est contingens simpliciter *a* non esse, nam alias *a* esse verum esset necessarium, et *a*
non esse verum est compossibile praedictae necessariae, alias obligatus ad
sustinendum *a* non esse verum, quod est possibile, haberet negare praedictam
necessariam, videlicet propositionem de praeterito esse necessariam, et concedere
oppositam esse impossibilem, et sic in consequentia bona et formali ex vero
sequeretur falsum et ex possibili impossibile, quod Aristotelis logica non tenet
nec concedit. »
33. STEGMÜLLER, 193 : « ... quod hoc est possibile per potentiam Dei ordinatam ... numquam sensi ».
34. *Ibid.* : « Alius sensus est, quod hoc esset possibile per potentiam absolutam Dei, sic quod oppositum non implicaret contradictionem ; et tunc posset
esse sensus, quod hoc posset esse possibile cum hoc, quod ista volitio creata
esset conformis voluntati increatae, et hoc numquam sensi. »
35. *Ibid.* : « Alius sensus posset esse, quod ex quo de aliquo quod fuit non
est possibile illud numquam fuisse, et si aliqua volitio creata fuit in aliqua
creatura, qua voluit aliquid, videtur multis, quod non sit possibile quin et
illa creatura voluerit illud, et anima Christi est creatura, et ideo quandoque
videbatur mihi, quod haec esset necessaria : Christus voluit volitione creata,
quod antichristus esset futurus ; et si necessaria, non repugnaret alicui contingenti. Et ideo in illo sensu posui eam et expressi. »
36. *Ibid.* : « Quod Christus potuit dicere falsum et etiam asseruisse assertione
creata tam vocali quam mentali. » This proposition was extracted from the
previous question in Mirecourt's *Sentences* Commentary.

240

to conclude that the examining commission felt that to state that Christ could will or say something, even *de potentia absoluta*, that was or might later be proved to be false was impious and ill sounding. Yet the statement is hardly unorthodox and, in the way in which Mirecourt explained it, quite acceptable by the standards of the twelfth or thirteenth century. The examiners were either unfamiliar or unsympathetic with the famous passage from Anselm's *Cur Deus Homo* on which such discussions are based and which states that although Christ, because he was fully human, must have possessed the ability to lie, he did not possess the ability to will to lie [37]. While this thesis was reformulated in the thirteenth century in terms of the distinction between the absolute and ordained powers of God, Mirecourt's formulation is much closer to the conservative wording of Anselm.

In reply to the first proposition in both apologies, Mirecourt makes statements concerning God's power to undo the past that should be noted. In the first apology he states that it would appear to him, along with many subtle doctors, that God is *not* able to make the past never to have been, and that consequently any proposition concerning the past, whose truth is not dependent on some future contingent, is necessary [38]. Concerning anything that *was*, it is impossible for it never to have been [39].

Suspect propositions two, three, and four were all taken from Mirecourt's reply to the arguments against his fourth conclusion which stated that it is not evident that it be impossible for some past thing never to have been. The ambiguity of the phrase "it is possible for some past thing never to have been" has already been noted. In addition to clarifying his position, as he does in reply to proposition two, Mirecourt insists in each instance that he was misquoted and that his position is the opposite of the one attributed to him. In the

---

37. ANSELM, *Cur Deus Homo*, II, 10 (*Opera omnia*, ed. F. S. SCHMITT, Edinburgh 1946-1961, II, 107) : « Possumus itaque dicere de Christo quia potuit mentiri, si subauditur : si vellet. Et quoniam mentiri non potuit nolens nec potuit velle mentiri, non minus dici potest nequivisse mentiri. Sic itaque potuit et non potuit mentiri. » Cf. also chs. 16 (II, 120-121) and 17 (II, 122-126). For a discussion of this problem in Anselm see : W. J. COURTENAY, *Necessity and Freedom in Anselm's Conception of God*, in *Die Wirkungsgeschichte Anselms von Canterbury*. Acts of the International Anselm Congress, Bad Wimpfen, Sept. 12-18, 1970 ; to appear in 1974.

38. STEGMÜLLER, 47 : « Apparebat tamen mihi cum multis doctoribus subtilibus, quod Deus non potest facere praeteritum numquam fuisse ; et per consequens quaelibet propositio de praeterito, cuius veritas non dependet ex aliquo futuro, est necessaria. »

39. *Ibid*, 193 : « ... de aliquo quod fuit non est possibile illud numquam fuisse... »

second proposition Mirecourt was charged with saying that it was not evident to him that Christ was not crucified yesterday. Mirecourt's reply is, essentially, that it was not evident to him that Christ could not have been crucified yesterday, had God so willed it (i.e., willed to delay that event for some 1311 years) [40]. The same applies to the third proposition. Mirecourt was charged with saying that God could so arrange it that a father might not exist and yet the son would exist, that the son might exist without father or mother, and that the statement, " you are born of a virgin ", can be true. Mirecourt again claims that he did not say this, in the way in which it was taken, but instead holds the opposite. His position is that it is not evident to him that it would imply a contradiction for God to so have arranged it that these things could have happened in this way. When one reflects on the theological maxim, accepted throughout the thirteenth and fourteenth centuries, that God could (if he so chose) cause directly whatever he causes through secondary causality, and when one reflects on the historical event (or so the fourteenth century viewed it) of a son without a father, namely the virgin birth of Christ, one can appreciate why Mirecourt felt that this situation did not involve a logical contradiction, and thus that its impossibility for God, *de potentia absoluta*, was not evident [41].

In reply to the fourth proposition, Mirecourt again claims he was misinterpreted. He was accused of holding as possible the proposition that the world had lasted only one day. His answer is that although he did not maintain this (but said the opposite), such is the conclusion one might arrive at if one were to hold that God is able to make the past never to have been [42].

The fifth, sixth, and seventh propositions were all taken from Mirecourt's reply to the arguments against his fifth conclusion. The fifth conclusion, which is the subject of the fifth suspect proposition,

---

40. *Ibid.*, 47 : « Secunda propositio... est : Oppositum istius non apparet mihi evidens : Christus heri fuit crucifixus, natus de Virgine sicut a sua Matre, negatus sicut a Petro. » For Mirecourt's answer see footnote 26.

41. *Ibid.*, 48 : « Tertia propositio... est : Deus potest facere, quod pater tuus numquam fuerit te remanente, et potest facere, quod numquam habueris nec patrem nec matrem, et potest verificare istam : Tu natus es de virgine. — Secundum veritatem haec non dixi, immo dico totum oppositum. Sed dico, quod hoc non est mihi evidens haec esse possibilia nec haec esse impossibilia. »

42. *Ibid.* : « Quarta propositio... : Haec est possibilis : Mundus non duravit nisi per unum diem. — Quantum ad hoc etiam dixi totum oppositum ; sed bene dixi, quod hoc diceret ille (scil. adversarius), qui teneret, quod Deus potest facere mundum numquam fuisse. Unde dico, quod hoc non est mihi evidens nec oppositum. »

seems potentially damaging and, as was stated earlier, Mirecourt does not answer the charge directly but assumes his previous statements and his position in the *Lectura* are sufficient. Similarly, in reply to the sixth proposition he attributes to his adversary rather than himself the idea that God is able to arrange it so that the world never was [43]. His reply to the seventh proposition assumes that his position is clear on the basis of previous discussion and the *Lectura* [44].

MIRECOURT'S ' LECTURA '

If Mirecourt was sincere and truthful in his defense, why was his position ever called into question ? Have not Gilson and Copleston seen through Mirecourt's clever maneuver and exposed the position Mirecourt wanted to support and probably did support in the original text from which the inquisitors extracted these propositions ? Was he not attempting, as Copleston suggests, " to explain away in his apologies what he had said in his lectures on the *Sentences* " [45] ? The answer is no, but before examining the *Lectura*, it might be well to consider the authenticity and structure of Mirecourt's *Sentences* Commentary.

Are we sure, first of all, that the text of Mirecourt's Commentary is authentic in the sense that it represents his original teaching, before he came under attack ? Might it not have been tampered with, revised or rewritten by Mirecourt or his students in a milder form ? To apply the conspiracy theory of historical documentation in this case seems even less appropriate than usual. No scholar from Michalski to Copleston has ever questioned the authenticity of this text. After a careful comparison of the manuscripts available to him, Michalski concluded that they contained the original unexpurgated and unaltered text. All the suspect propositions charged against Mirecourt can be found in the *Sentences* Commentary, as can Mirecourt's quotations

---

43. *Ibid.*, 49 : « Sixta propositio... : Deus potest facere, quod mundus numquam fuit, et quod mundus nihil sit. Concederetur etiam, quod Deus posset facere patrem meum numquam fuisse sine omni mutatione non solum in sensu diviso, immo etiam in sensu composito, cuius oppositum dicunt aliquando tenentes etiam Deum posse facere mundum numquam fuisse. — Sine dubio hoc non dixi, sed dixi, quod sic diceret vel quod sic haberet dicere, qui teneret, quod Deus potest facere praeteritum numquam fuisse, sicut patet in Lectura. »
44. *Ibid.*, 49-50 : « Septima propositio... : Argumenta quae probant Deum non posse facere mundum numquam fuisse, vel non concludunt evidenter, vel assumunt antecedentia inevidentia, vel concludunt conclusiones quas non est evidens esse impossibiles. — Hoc credebam esse verum, si propositio bene inspiciatur. Hoc etiam positum est, ut appareat mens mea de praedictis. »
45. COPLESTON, 134.

from himself that he included in the two apologies. The amount of work and talent required to rewrite an entire *Sentences* Commentary, preserving all the quotations found in the apologies and suspect propositions, rearranging their context to make them seem milder, yet retaining the flow and logic of the argumentation so that the changes would not be evident, seems beyond the reach of any age.

Secondly, a word should be said about the structure of Mirecourt's *quaestiones* and the problem of deciding what statements in his text can be taken as representing his own opinion. The scholastic style of Mirecourt is deceptively simple. After the title of the question, the customary *videtur quod sic* or *videtur quod non* and the *in oppositum*, Mirecourt generally divides the question into four articles. The first article will usually contain a series of conclusions and proofs, normally six but sometimes five or seven. The second article will raise objections, in turn, to each of these conclusions. The third article will respond to the objections to the conclusions. Finally, the fourth article will respond to the arguments used in the brief introductory section preceeding the *in oppositum*.

On the basis of that style of organization, it would seem that the historian interested in establishing Mirecourt's position would concentrate primarily on the first and third articles. For the most part this is an acceptable procedure, although there are some dangers in this approach. The conclusions of Mirecourt are seldom final conclusions that unambiguously represent his thought. This is not because Mirecourt was trying to be overly clever or devious, but rather because he was adopting a style, common in the schools of his generation, in which conclusions were statements to be tested, not solutions to be uncritically accepted. These conclusions — and this applies to a significant number of fourteenth century authors who adopt this method — are, therefore, not conclusions in the normal sense of that word but are propositions, or theological theorems [46], that

---

46. A term coined by André Combes to describe a similar use of conclusions in the *Sentences* Commentary of John of Ripa. Although the development of this particular style of *Sentences* Commentary has not been studied in any detail, it would appear that it had its origins in the academic generation of 1315-1325. Occasional use of conclusions are present in the Commentaries of William of Ockham, Walter Chatton, John Baconthorp, Landulf Caracciolo, and Francis of Marchia, although the structure of every *quaestio* or *articulus* is not built around them and Ockham's use of *conclusiones* more closely resembles Peter Aureol's use of *propositiones* and stylistically can be termed Scotistic. By 1340, especially at Paris, the *conclusiones* have become a major structural feature of most *Sentences* Commentaries, e.g. those of Thomas of Strasbourg, Gregory of Rimini, Alphonsus Vargas of Toledo, John of Mirecourt, John of Ripa, James of Eltville, Gottschalk of Nepomuk, Peter of Candia, and Pierre d'Ailly. Within

244

might be (and often were) used in school exercises, both in teaching and in debate, to encourage and test critical thinking. When used as conclusions within the pages of a *Sentences* Commentary, they are propositions with at least one possible meaning that the author feels can be defended with a high degree of probability or that cannot be demonstrated to be false. The conclusions are worded in a precise manner and much depends on the reader's appreciation for the level of sophistication on which they are being proposed. Some conclusions unequivocally represent the position of the author and thus the subsequent discussion supports the obvious meaning. Others, however, may contradict or at least be incompatible with the majority of the conclusions, and these are being proposed not because the author agrees with their obvious meaning, but only because they can be interpreted or construed in at least one way that cannot be proven false by the standards of faith and reason. The discussion following conclusions of this second type does not show why the conclusion is true, but instead why it is not false in every possible meaning or construction that can be placed on it, and therefore cannot be totally disproven. Conclusions of this second type were not clever devices to cloak heretical or outrageous views in the guise of sophisticated argument. They were the common property of the schools, not the creation of a particular author, and they were intentionally worded in an ambiguous manner in order to serve as debatable theses or propositions. The conclusions of either type represent the thought of the author only as understood and qualified in subsequent discussion. Mirecourt will provide a good example of this scholastic style and will illustrate why one ought not to accept the conclusions at face value or read selectively, searching for a brief, clear summary of the author's position [47].

---

the *conclusiones* style there seem to be two separate forms. Some commentaries, such as those of Mirecourt, Eltville, and Nepomuk have a certain number of conclusions per question ; others, such as Strasbourg, Rimini, Vargas, Ripa, and d'Ailly divide each question into articles with a separate set of conclusions for each article. The *conclusiones* style was also used in the Arts Faculty. Cf., e.g., John Buridan's commentary on *De anima* and Albert of Saxony's commentary on the *Physics*. By contrast, the organization of the *Sentences* Commentaries of such prominent English theologians as Adam Wodeham, Robert Holcot, and Richard Fitzralph is not based on a *conclusiones* system.

47. Paul Vignaux and André Combes, in their introductory essays to the publication of Ripa's *Conclusiones* (Paris 1957), urge a similar caution in respect to the *conclusiones*. Vignaux (p. 7) : « ... propositions abstraites de leur contexte, évidemment liées les unes aux autres mais dont le sens précis ne peut apparaître qu'après publication de l'œuvre intégrale, après des recherches aussi sur le milieu contemporain. » Combes (p. 14) : « Ces *conclusiones* sont autant de théorèmes théologiques dont l'énoncé a été élaboré avec le plus grand soin. Sans doute,

A style of analysis in which a problem is clarified and its solution refined through a series of definitions, distinctions, conclusions, propositions corollaries, objections, and replies, and in which the position of the author is only gradually revealed on the basis of this interwoven fabric of arguments and the various levels of interpretation and meaning that are thus exposed, was generally termed *subtile*, a highly valued quality among most scholastics. Unlike the term *modernus*, which though not always a pejorative term was never complimentary, the term *subtile* was often joined with *pulchre* and was usually a compliment even when applied to the argument of one's worst adversary. *Subtilitas* did not exclude sincerity, conviction, or commitment, and this is certainly true of Mirecourt, as the text of the first apology shows and as a reading of his *Lectura* will reveal.

Beyond permitting a higher degree of precision and *subtilitas*, there lay another value in using in a question occasional conclusions that appeared, on first examination, to contradict the majority of conclusions, the intent of the author, or accepted opinion. The shock value of such conclusions could be useful in stimulating interest on the part of students and colleagues and, used in this way, this teaching technique was known as *aporia*. No doubt the method achieved its purpose and the students waited eagerly to see how the refractory conclusions could be shown to be valid and to be integrated with the others. For the less gifted or less patient students, however, this method had certain drawbacks. If the solution was difficult to understand, as frequently it was, someone might leave the classroom maintaining or reporting a false or ill-sounding proposition, forgetting the sense in which the proposition was interpreted and believing that the teacher had proven the proposition true in its most obvious sense.

To what degree this method was under attack in 1347 will be discussed later. In application to Mirecourt, however, it should be noted that the " shock " value of Mirecourt's abnormal, or refractory conclusions (at least in those case I have examined) was not that they contradicted commonly held assumptions or beliefs but that they seemingly contradicted the other conclusions. Moreover, in the texts examined to date, it was not particularly the refractory con-

---

on mutilerait la doctrine intégrale de Jean de Ripa si l'on en limitait l'analyse à l'ensemble de ces *conclusiones*. La dialectique du docteur super-subtil est trop souple et trop pénétrante pour se contenter d'une formulation directe et immédiate. Chaque *conclusio* est soumise à un contrôle méthodique qui exige l'examen des thèses différentes ou opposées. On ne saisit donc toutes les nuances de la pensée ripienne que si l'on analyse avec la même attention conclusions, objections et réponses. »

246

clusions that were seized upon by Mirecourt's inquisitors as dangerous. What it was that disturbed the inquisitors and, consequently, to what group or tradition they belonged can only be determined after examining the text of the *Lectura* [48]. The organization of *Sent.* I, q. 39 [49] on whether God is able to will or to make the world never to have been, differs slightly from the usual approach of Mirecourt. Instead of listing his conclusions together as a group in the first article, immediately following the *pro* and *con* arguments that introduce the question, the conclusions are spaced out across the question and the opposing arguments and replies are inserted after each conclusion. Moreover, at the beginning of the question, Mirecourt includes a long section in which he defines some of the terminology that will be used later on in the discussion, such as the various meanings of the terms *necessarium, facere,* and *agere* [50]. Finally, he indicates that his conclusions in this question are not proposed assertively [51]. Whether this disclaimer, occasionally used by Mirecourt, represents a device to protect him from heresy hunters or a careful statement of procedure should become evident as we

---

48. Of the manuscripts listed in footnote 3 that contain Book I, the following analysis is based on a collation of *Paris, Bibl. Nat. lat. 15882* (the principal text used by Michalski), *Lilienfeld 148* (a microfilm copy of which was gratiously loaned to the author by Damasus Trapp), *Bologna, Archiginnasio A 921* (gratiously loaned by Charles Ermatinger), and *Turin D IV 28* (the principal text used by Stegmüller). The Bologna manuscript is one of the earliest and, at least on this question, provides the most complete text. The manuscript from the Cistercian monastery of Lilienfeld, though grammatically incorrect at many points, follows the meaning of the Bologna text closely. The Paris and Turin manuscripts, though consistently better than the Lilienfeld, are not as complete as the Bologna manuscript. Although the wording of the manuscripts will occasionally differ, there are, for this question, no differences in meaning. For purposes of footnoting, therefore, I have chosen to reproduce the most complete and readable text, noting significant differences in the other texts where they occur.

49. The number of the questions of Mirecourt differs among the various manuscripts, due to the inclusion in Paris, Lilienfeld, Bologna, and others of one additional question. The traditional number of this question, as given in Stegmüller, is based on Birkenmajer. I have adopted the full and, I believe, the correct numbering.

50. This style of organization, not unique to this question nor, for that matter, unique to Mirecourt, was extensively used later by Pierre d'Ailly. About 25 % of Mirecourt's questions contain a section that discusses terminology, and many of the other questions refer back to earlier distinctions in usage.

51. JOHN OF MIRECOURT, *Lectura sententiarum,* L. I, q. 39 (henceforth referred to as *Sent.* I, q. 39) : « Pro ista quaestione pono breviter sine assertione aliqua conclusiones aliquas. » The wording is according to Lilienfeld, fol. 120va, but all texts examined have the phrase " sine assertione ".

follow his argument [52]. In any case, it stands here as a warning to the reader not to take the obvious verbal sense of each conclusion as being the definitive statement of Mirecourt.

The definitions of terms represent important prolegomena to Mirecourt's later discussion. He distinguishes two types of necessity : an absolute necessity according to which what always was, will always be ; and an accidental necessity according to which created things receive a relative necessity after creation. The whole question of the world's being or never having been falls within this second, accidental, type of necessity [53]. Secondly, the term "to make" can refer either to the creative power in itself (and that is the sense in which Mirecourt normally uses it) or it can refer to the creative power in relation to those things that are created [54]. Thirdly, action can be understood in the sense of creation or annihilation and, in a loose sense, even the failure to act is a form of action or creation if events or things result from that failure to act [55].

From these definitions Mirecourt extracts certain propositions, some of which are important to the structure of his argument. First, something that is necessary is able to be produced by another, namely by God. Although Mirecourt does not indicate which type of necessity he has in mind, it would seem to be the absolute type (that which always was and always shall be) since he uses as an example the Son of God who, although necessary, is produced by the Father [56]. Second,

---

52. What " sine assertione " means in this question does not indicate how it, or the similar term " probabiliter ", are used elsewhere in Mirecourt. It does, however, provide a beginning point for solving that issue. On a hurried count, I discovered the phrase " sine assertione " or its equivalent as a precautionary phrase introducing the conclusions in only five of the first thirty-nine questions of book I. Moreover, I noted that the only two questions in book IV are not qualified in this manner.

53. *Sent.* I, q. 39 (*B* 52ᵛ, *L* 120ᵛ, *P* 155ᵛ, *R* 101ᵛ) : « Primo sciendum quod dupliciter dicitur aliquid ' necessarium '. Uno modo simpliciter, quod semper fuit necessarium, semper erit. Alio modo per accidens, quod non semper fuit necessarium, sed est necessarium per accidens. sicut mundum numquam fuisse. »

54. *Ibid.* : « Secundo sciendum quod ' facere ' potest capi generaliter pro quolibet producere vel agere, et sic volo uti. Secundo generaliter pro agere extra se. »

55. *Ibid.* : « Tertio sciendum quod dupliciter potest dici aliqua res ' agere '. Uno modo positive ; alio modo privative. Positive dupliciter : uno modo ponendo aliquid in esse ; alio modo aliquid destruendo privative, sicut dicimus quod nauta per suam absentiam est causa perditionis navis, quia ipse non custodit navem quam custoditurus erat. Et isto modo dupliciter : uno modo aliquid destruendo aut impediendo ; alio modo aliquid construendo. » Cf. ARISTOTLE, *Physica* II, 3 (195a13-14) ; *Metaphysica* V, 2 (1013b11-15).

56. *Ibid.* : « Primum est quod aliquid quod est necessarium esse potest ab aliquo, scilicet a Deo, produci. Patet, quia filium Dei necessarium est esse, et tamen potest a Deo produci per productionem filii a patre. »

some things are necessarily true, and it lies outside the power of God to confer or remove such necessity. The rules of logic fall within the category of things that are absolutely necessary[57]. Third, God cannot cause his own non-existence[58]. Fourth, everything that is contingent, and is thus able to be or able not to be, is (or was) subject to the creative power of God[59].

When these distinctions and propositions are read in light of the distinctions Mirecourt makes in his later apology, one distinction is notably lacking, namely the distinction between the power to make *before* the act of making and the power to remake or unmake *after* that act has been accomplished. To some degree this distinction is implicit in his comment on *facere*, which distinguishes between the creative power *per se* and the creative power *ad extra*. But the major distinction employed in this early section of the *Lectura* question is between necessity and contingency.

With these distinctions in mind, Mirecourt begins his conclusions. His first conclusion is that it is not evident to the *viator*, nor has it been evidently proved, nor does it follow from faith that God is able to will the world never to have been[60]. Although the first part of this statement is placed in the negative — and thus we are not sure whether the reverse is any more evident or deduced from faith (namely, that God is not able to will the world never to have been) — as it stands this conclusion is anything but radical. Since he does not here qualify the term " to make " it would appear that he is speaking about God's ability to undo or alter the past, and he is stating that God's ability to do this cannot be established by any of the normal methods of proof available to man in his present state. Even if one were to read the conclusion to apply to God's creative power *before* creation, Mirecourt would be saying nothing more than that the non-necessity of creation is not self-evident nor deduced from faith, a point that he makes repeatedly in his apology.

---

57. *Ibid.* : « Secundum, aliqualiter potest esse et aliqualiter est, et nihil facit sic esse, et generaliter qualitercumque necessarium est esse simpliciter extra Deum. Patet, quia ita est quod si homo est, animal est, et Deus non facit sic esse. »

58. *Ibid.* : « Tertium, si impossibile sit simpliciter Deum non esse, Deus non potest facere Deum non esse. »

59. *Ibid.* : « Quartum, qualitercumque contingens est esse vel non esse, dicendo contingens contra necessarium, taliter potest Deus facere esse vel non esse. »

60. *Ibid.* (B 52ᵛ, L 120ᵛ, P 156ʳ, R 102ʳ) : « Non est evidens viatori, nec evidenter probatum, nec ex fide sequens quod Deus possit velle mundum numquam fuisse. Probatur sic, quia nec per experientiam, nec per aliquid per se notum, nec per demonstrationem. Patet, quia alias ego non possem dubitare vel non dubitare, et tamen est mihi dubium ; igitur, etc. »

When one turns to the discussion that follows this conclusion, one finds that Mirecourt's position is being attacked on both issues by an opposing argument that holds as evident God's total freedom to act or not to act, a freedom that is not diminished or compromised by a temporal sequence in which the " past " as such possesses some special characteristic that places it outside or beyond the power of God [61]. If the past possessed such a special characteristic according to which it could not be an object of the divine will, this could result only from a defect either in God's will or in the object, neither of which seems possible [62]. Moreover, according to the opposing argument, necessity and contingency are mutually exclusive. Either all things are subjected to the divine will, which remains free in spite of its own decisions, or God's will is subjected to necessity [63].

In reply Mirecourt affirms that neither God's freedom not to act nor his freedom to undo what he has done is demonstrably evident. In the tradition of Anselm Mirecourt rejects any necessity that binds

---

61. *Ibid.* : « Secundo, Deus quandoque potuit libere velle mundum numquam fuisse, immo de facto voluit libere, et nunc non potest libere velle mundum numquam fuisse ; ergo nunc est necessitata et deminuta potentia Dei et libertas [Dei. Absit ! Ergo]. »

62. *Ibid.* : « Tertio, quia si Deus non posset de isto velle mundum vel aliquid praeteritum numquam fuisse, vel hoc est quia illud quod praeteritum est non potest esse obiectum divinae voluntatis, ita quod defectus sit ex parte obiecti, vel hoc est quia voluntas divina non potest illud velle, ita quod sit defectus ex parte divinae voluntatis. Non secundo modo, quia tunc voluntas divina non foret omnipotens. Si dicatur quod hoc sit primo modo, quia illud quod praeteritum est non esse praeteritum non potest esse obiectum divinae voluntatis, ita quod defectus sit ex parte obiecti, contra : aliquid est praeteritum quod non esse praeteritum est bene et rationaliter in casu obiectum creatae voluntatis, igitur praeteritum potest esse obiectum divinae voluntatis, igitur non est defectus ex parte obiecti cum eodem modo se habeat nunc et prius. »

63. *Ibid.* (B 52ᵛ, L 121ʳ, P 156ʳ, R 102ʳ) : « Quarto, si Deus non potest velle mundum numquam fuisse, sequitur quod necessario vult mundum fuisse, quod est falsum, quia omnia quae Deus vult ad extra vult libere libertate indifferentiae. » *Ibid.* : « Quinto si Deus quandoque potuit velle mundum numquam fuisse et non potest modo mundum velle numquam fuisse, et ita necessarium est Deum sic velle; ergo voluntati Dei nunc accidit nova necessitas, huius necessitatis aliqua est causa, et non nisi praeteritio mundi; ergo praeteritio mundi necessitaret voluntatem Dei. Consequens est falsum, igitur falsitas consequentis. Probatur primo, quia si praeteritio rei necessitaret voluntatem Dei, voluntas Dei foret minus libera quam [voluntas] nostra, quia voluntatem nostram non potest necessitare praeteritio rei. » *Ibid.* : « Sexto, quia si Deus non posset velle mundum numquam fuisse, eadem ratione nec posset Deus nunc velle mundum prius fuisse quam fuit vel quod illud quod nunc primo est factum fuisset heri factum. Consequens videtur inconveniens, quia si Deus non posset velle mundum prius fuisse quam fuit, sequitur quod Deus non potuit ab aeterno produxisse mundum, [quod est falsum, ergo]. »

God from without but accepts a necessity that God creates by his actions or imposes on himself because of the consistency of his will [64]. This type of necessity was discussed among the distinctions at the beginning of the question. Mirecourt also utilizes the common distinction between the *voluntas Dei signi* (which is not always fulfilled) and the *voluntas Dei beneplaciti* (which is always fulfilled) to affirm that not everything that we ascribe to the will of God will necessarily take place, so that the necessity/contingency dilemma posed by the counter-argument is considerably more complex, and an either/or response is undesirable as well as unnecessary [65]. It is a false problem or an inappropriate way of speaking, suggests Mirecourt, to view the irrevocability of the past as a new necessity or limitation on the will of God. Just as God's knowledge is not augmented by things coming into existence, so his power is not diminished by things having happened [66]. But this is not to suggest that God is able to undo the past. The special character of the past seems more akin to the necessity of the rules of logic and therefore should not be considered a defect either in God's will or in the past event [67].

Before turning to the second conclusion, it might be well to note the context in which the first suspect proposition of Mirecourt occurs in the *Lectura*. In order to support the thesis that the non-necessity of

---

64. *Ibid.* (*B* 53ʳ, *L* 121ᵛ, *P* 156ᵛ, *R* 102ᵛ) : « Ad quintum dico quod voluntati divinae non accidit nova necessitas, sed Deus necessario vult mundum fuisse, et dico quod non prius vel non semper necessario voluit mundum fuisse. Dico etiam quod nulla est ibi causa nisi Deus, qui posuit [velle] mundum in esse quem non semper posuerat in esse, et ideo quia posuit [velle] mundum in esse, et voluit ponere mundum in esse voluntate beneplaciti, ideo necessarium est ipsum posuisse mundum in esse et sic voluisse et sic fuisse. »

65. *Ibid.* (*B* 53ʳ, *L* 121ʳ⁻ᵛ, *P* 156ᵛ, *R* 102ᵛ) : « Quia tamen in argumento probatur quod praeteritum non fuisse est bene et rationaliter in casu obiectum creatae voluntatis, immo debet sibi displicere quod illud numquam fuit, ergo et divinae voluntatis, potest dici quod Deum velle aliquid potest intelligi dupliciter. Uno modo voluntate signi ; alio modo voluntate beneplaciti. Et tunc dico quod Sortem non peccasse potest Deus velle voluntate signi, sed non voluntate beneplaciti, et ideo concedo consequentiam illam, quod est ' rationaliter obiectum creatae voluntatis, ergo et divinae, ' verum est voluntate signi, sed non oportet voluntate beneplaciti, quia impossibile non potest Deus velle voluntate beneplaciti. »

66. *Ibid.* (*B* 53ʳ, *L* 121ʳ, *P* 156ᵛ, *R* 102ᵛ) : « Ad secundum, nego consequentiam utriusque formae, sicut et istam : Deus scit quicquid ipse scivit, et scit quod Sortes est, quod numquam prius scivit, ergo scientia Dei est augmentata, nec sequitur Deus quandoque potuit facere Sortem primo esse, et modo non potest facere Sortem primo esse, ergo potentia Dei est deminuta ».

67. *Ibid.* « Ad tertium dico quod nullus est defectus nec ex parte praeteriti nec ex parte Dei, sed quia Deus alias produxit illud non est possibile quod non produxit illud, et per consequens quin velit se illud produxisse... »

creation as well as God's ability to undo the past is evident or deduced from faith, the opposing argument maintains that the same thing cannot be necessary and contingent. Therefore, since the antichrist is a future contingent and since Christ willed the antichrist, what Christ willed (and by implication what God wills) must either happen necessarily, in which case the antichrist would not be contingent (a determinism that binds God and man), or possibly not happen, in which case the future (and by implication the past) need not conform to an eternal divine will, either because God is not omnipotent (which seems unlikely) or because the divine will is not fixed and necessarily consistent. Mirecourt's answer parallels his discussion in the first apology and shows how the created will of Christ can will something of necessity which nevertheless remains a future contingent. It is part of Mirecourt's attempt to reject the simple and absolute alternatives of necessity and contingency[68].

---

68. *Ibid.* (B 52ᵛ, L 120ᵛ, P 156ʳ, R 102ʳ) : « Aliquis homo potest velle aliquid, et possibile est quod ipse numquam voluerit illud ; ergo cum hoc, quod deus voluerit aliquid, potest esse quod ipse numquam voluerit illud, et per consequens potest velle mundum numquam fuisse. Prima consequentia patet, quia non minus apparet possibile de Deo quam de homine. Secunda consequentia patet, quia non minus de isto volito quam de alio. Sed antecedens probo de Christo homine. Christus voluit antichristum fore, et non potest esse quod Christus numquam voluit antichristum fore, igitur necessario Christus voluit antichristum fore. Consequens falsum, quia si necesse est quod Christus voluit antichristum fore, et possibile est quod antichristus non erit, igitur possibile est quod Christus voluit aliquid fieri quod nec factum est nec fiet, et eadem ratione quod Deus aliquid voluit aliquid fieri, etc. » (B 53ʳ, L 121ʳ, P 156ᵛ, R 102ʳ) : « Ad primum, supponendo quod nulla creatura velle possit per volitionem increatam, sicut alias tenui, respondeo : concedo primam consequentiam et nego aliam, videlicet ' aliquid voluit Deus, et potest esse quod ipse numquam voluerit illud, ergo potest velle mundum numquam fuisse '. Et nego etiam antecedens primae consequentiae. Ad probationem, cum dicitur quod ' non minus de isto volito quam de alio ', nego istud, nam dico quod aliquid est volitum a Deo contingenter, et de tali volito non est possibile quod Deus numquam voluerit illud aliquod necessario, sicut quod ipse sit Deus, et quod mundus fuerit, et huiusmodi, et de tali volito non est possibile quod Deus numquam voluerit illud. Ad probationem antecedentis, cum dicitur Christus voluit antichristum fore, dico quod vel intelligitur de voluntate increata — et de illa dico quod quantumcumque voluerit antichristum fore adhuc est possibile quod ipse numquam sic voluerit — vel de volitione creata, et de ista dico quantumcumque voluerit antichristum fore, non est possibile ipsum numquam sic voluisse, et dico etiam quod satis erat possibile quod per volitionem creatam Christus aliquid voluerit et numquam sic voluit evenire, et sic haec copulativa est possibilis : Christus voluit ' a ' volitione creata, et ' a ' non erit, quia anima eius sic potuit voluisse et per communicationem idiomatum Christus ; tamen etiam ista copulativa non est vera de potentia Dei ordinata, nec de potentia absoluta sic quod cum hoc illa volitio creata esset conformis volitioni vel voluntati Dei increatae ; tamen cum

252

The second conclusion of Mirecourt seems to be a variation on the first, and it states that : " It is not evident to me, nor has it been evidently proved to me, that it is possible for the world not to have been [69]. " Again, the opposing argument rejects any special characteristic of the past that, in contrast to the present and future, places it outside the power of God [70]. In reply, Mirecourt rejects any attempt to place the past and the future on the same level in relation to the power of God [71]. The past possesses a special characteristic that, once past, makes it no longer contingent. Contingency and necessity are not qualities possessed by things eternally. Before things happen they are unnecessary and contingent ; after things happen they are not contingent and, in the relative sense described above, necessary [72].

The position of Mirecourt which, in his discussion of the first and second conclusions, rejected the possibility of God's undoing the past, is given more forceful prominence as the subject of the third conclusion, now phrased in a positive, direct manner : " It is evident to me that God is not able to make the world not to have been, taking ' make ' positively either, in the sense of creation or in the sense of destruction. It is obvious, because it implies a contradiction that he would make the world not to have been by placing the world in non-being or by destroying the world [73]. " On the basis of this conclu-

---

illa necessaria : Christus voluit ' a ', stat illa contingens ' a ', et vel ' a ' non erit vel ' a ' erit. »

69. *Ibid.* (*B* 53ʳ, *L* 121ᵛ, *P* 157ʳ, *R* 102ᵛ) : « Non est mihi evidens nec evidenter mihi probatum, quod possibile sit mundum non fuisse. »

70. *Ibid.* « Deus potest facere mundum non fuisse, ergo est possibile mundum non fuisse. Consequentia patet, sed antecedens probo, quia nisi Deus posset facere illud quod futurum est non esse et non fuisse futurum, non foret omnipotens ; ergo a simili, si Deus non potest facere et velle illud quod praeteritum est non esse praeteritum, non erit omnipotens. Secundo sic : praeteritum non esse praeteritum est imaginabile et ab intellectu nostro conceptabile, ergo Deo est possibile. » (*B* 53ʳ, *L* 122ʳ, *P* 157ʳ, *R* 103ʳ) : « Septimo : apud Deum nihil praeterit. Ergo, si potest facere apud eum quod nihil praeteriit, ergo potest facere apud creaturam quod nihil praeteriit. » *Ibid.* : « Octavo : mundum numquam fuisse formaliter non includit contradictionem ; igitur mundum numquam fuisse est simpliciter et per se possibile. »

71. *Ibid.* (*B* 53ʳ, *L* 122ʳ, *P* 157ʳ, *R* 103ʳ) : « Ad primum... nego consequentiam, quia non est simile de praeterito et de futuro, sicut nec de necessario nec de contingenti. »

72. *Ibid.* (*B* 53ʳ, *L* 122ʳ, *P* 157ᵛ, *R* 103ʳ) : « Ad quintum, dico quod mundus non necessario fuit, sed contingenter, et quod quandoque contingens fuit ipsum fuisse, sed modo non est contingens. »   •

73. *Ibid.* « Evidens est mihi quod Deus non potest facere mundum non fuisse, capiendo ' facere ' positive, vel pro positione vel destructione. Patet, quia implicat contradictionem quod faciat [faceret P] mundum non fuisse, mundum onendo inesse vel destruendo mundum. »

sion and his earlier argumentation one can see why Mirecourt was so insistent that he had disallowed the possibility of God's undoing the past.

With the fourth conclusion, which follows immediately upon the third, Mirecourt alters the structure of his *quaestio*. In order to show that the opposing position cannot, in one sense, be shown to be self-contradictory or unorthodox, Mirecourt changes roles and proposes two conclusion (four and five) *against* his own position. The fourth conclusion states : " It is not evident to me that it is impossible for some past thing never to have been, for neither through experience nor through reasons [is it evident], since these demonstrate nothing, as shall be seen " [74]. The fifth conclusion reads : " It is not evident to me, nor has it been evidently proved, nor does it follow from faith, that it is impossible that God could make the world never to have been, taking ' to make ' as before. It is proved entirely as the preceding conclusion [proves] " [75]. Mirecourt presents arguments against these conclusions and then shows how the arguments do not demonstrably destroy these two conclusions, or theological theorems, of the *adversarius*. In the sense that these conclusions suggest that God can undo the past, they can be shown to be evidently false, but in the sense that they suggest that God could have acted otherwise than he acted, or willed otherwise than he willed, they cannot be demonstrated to be false. Therefore, Mirecourt felt compelled to admit that the falsity of these two conclusions, as theorems, was not evident.

The arguments put forward against the fourth conclusion describe seemingly absurd and contradictory situations that could arise if God had the power to make the past never to have been, such as Christ's being born or crucified yesterday [76], an innocent person being a sinner [77], someone existing without father or mother [78], father and

---

74. *Ibid.* « Non est mihi evidens etiam quod impossibile sit praeteritum aliquod numquam fuisse, non enim per experientiam nec per rationes, quia nihil demonstrant, ut videtur ; igitur. »

75. *Ibid.* (B 53ᵛ, L 122ᵛ, P 158ʳ, R 103ᵛ) : « Non est mihi evidens, nec evidenter probatum, nec ex fide sequens, quod impossibile sit, quod Deus faciat mundum numquam fuisse, capiendo ' facere ' ut prius. Probatur omnino sicut praecedens conclusio [praecedentes conclusiones P]. »

76. *Ibid.* (B 53ʳ, L 122ʳ, P 157ᵛ, R 103ʳ) : « ... si sic, sequitur quod haec modo sit possibilis : Christus heri fuit crucifixus, heri natus, et a sua matre, negatus sicut a Petro. Patet consequentia, quia si de isto quod fuit potest fieri quod non fuit, ergo eadem ratione de illo quod fuit potest esse quod fuit. »

77. *Ibid.* (B 53ᵛ, L 122ʳ, P 157ᵛ, R 103ʳ) : « ... si de illo qui peccavit potest esse quod numquam peccavit, ergo eadem ratione econverso, et sic innocens necessitari posset ad peccandum. »

78. *Ibid.* (B 53ᵛ, L 122ʳ ᵛ, P 157ᵛ, R 103ʳ) : « ... si sic, igitur patrem tuum, te remanente, potest facere numquam fuisse, et sic istam verificare : Natus es de virgine, et similiter potest facere quod nullam matrem habuisti. »

son being the same age [79], and the world having existed for only one day [80]. Some of these situations, Mirecourt replies, imply a contradiction and are therefore impossible. It is possible for one who was innocent to become a sinner, but it is impossible for one to be innocent and a sinner simultaneously [81]. Similarly, it is impossible for father and son to be the same age, for the words imply a priority of one to the other in time based on procreation [82]. It is also impossible for one to be a father without ever having had offspring or for one to be a son without ever having had parents, for the terms imply this. None of the other examples, however, possess that type of contradiction. For Christ to have been born when he was rather than yesterday is not based on some universal law of necessity, but on the will of God. It is also a result of God's free choice that the world has lasted more than one day; consequently, there would be no contradiction in its having lasted only one day. Moreover, for one to exist without a father cannot imply a contradiction, otherwise the birth of Christ could not have taken place as it did. The adversary's position, it would seem, cannot be demolished in this way.

The arguments against the fifth conclusion are, therefore, of a different variety. Most center around the ideas that (1) a creative power is not able to be the cause of non-being so that God cannot cause anything not to be [83]; and, (2) contradictories cannot be true at the same time, which would be the case if God could make the past not to have been [84]. But as Mirecourt points out, for things to have been arranged differently does not result in contradictions being true at the same time. Moreover, if one affirms the idea of creation in time, then one has to concede that God allowed the world's not-being until he created it, so that in an improper sense,

---

79. Ibid. (B 53ᵛ, L 122ᵛ, P 157ᵛ, R 103ʳ) : « ... si sic, igitur patrem tuum et te potest facere coaevos... »

80. Ibid. (B 53ᵛ, L 122ᵛ, P 157ᵛ, R 103ʳ) : « ... et eadem ratione facere quod mundus iste non duravit [duraverit P] nisi per unum diem. »

81. Ibid. (B 53ᵛ, L 122ᵛ, P 158ʳ, R 103ᵛ) : « Dico quod quantumcumque non sit possibile quod innocens peccet, tamen illum qui fuit innocens possibile est peccasse. »

82. Ibid. : « [Adversarius] diceret : ' concedo consequentiam, ' et tamen dico quod haec est impossibilis : ' Pater tuus et tu estis coaevi ' ».

83. Ibid. (B 53ᵛ, L 123ʳ, P 158ʳ, R 103ᵛ) : « ... pure non ens non potest esse per se obiectum potentiae factibile... Probatur, quod Deus non potest facere per se et immediate quod mundus non sit vel quod non erit. » Cf. Counterarguments four and five.

84. Ibid. (B 53ᵛ, L 123ʳ, P 158ʳ⁻ᵛ, R 103ᵛ) : « Ergo [Deus] potest esse causa quare contradictoria non sunt simul vera et esse causa quare sunt simul vera, et ita contradictoria possent esse simul vera. »

as stated at the beginning of the question, it is possible to *facere privative* [85].

Six of the seven suspect propositions extracted from this question of Mirecourt were extracted from the responses to conclusions four and five. In most cases it seems that Mirecourt's inquisitors were aware that these conclusions did not represent the thought of Mirecourt but were the position of a real or imaginary *adversarius*. Most of their objections seem to stem from the conviction that Mirecourt should have been able to demolish the arguments of the *adversarius* better than he did. When reading the discussions which follow conclusions four and five, one can imagine that the commission might have felt that Mirecourt was not as precise or as complete in his answers as he might have been. The distinction between God's power over events before they happen and God's power over events after they happen, although implicit throughout his earlier discussion and stated succinctly in his first apology, is nowhere mentioned directly or recalled at this crucial juncture, unless one reads the qualifying sentence attached to conclusion five as a reference to the creative power *per se* as opposed to *ad extra*. Once Mirecourt clarified his meaning, as he did in his first apology, the issue was dropped. His fault, at least in the eyes of the commission, seems to have been that Mirecourt's position was not reasserted at every turn and that the adversary's argument was not effectively silenced.

But one must also recognize the justice of Mirecourt's claim that he was frequently misquoted or misinterpreted, the truth of which can be seen even by comparing the extracted propositions with the brief quotations from the text of the *Lectura* that Stegmüller already provided in the footnotes to his edition of the first apology.

Two further conclusions complete Mirecourt's treatment of this question, and both conclusions are his rather than the adversary's. In the sixth conclusion Mirecourt states that in the strict sense there is no cause of the non-being of the world before creation [86]. In the seventh and last conclusion, Mirecourt states that it seems truer to him and more probable that God is not able to make the world or any past thing never to have been [87]. In support of that position, he

---

85. *Ibid.* (B 53ᵛ, L 123ʳ, P 158ᵛ, R 104ʳ) : « Ita potest dici et fuit dictum in principio quaestionis quod ' facere ' potest dici dupliciter. Uno modo secundum rem quod non est nisi quando res aliqua sit. Alio modo secundum formam loquendi quomodo dicimus quod aliquis facit ne res sit. »

86. *Ibid.* (B 54ʳ, L 123ᵛ, P 159ʳ, R 104ᵛ) : « Quod proprie loquendo, non esset concedendum quod aliquid esset vel esse posset causa alicuius talis privationis vel negationis, quamquam [quemcumque P] ipsam sit possibilis. »

87. *Ibid.* (B 54ʳ, L 124ʳ, P 159ᵛ, R 104ᵛ) : « Verisimilius est mihi et probabilius quod Deus non possit facere mundum vel aliquod praeteritum numquam fuisse

quotes extensively from various works of Augustine and other patristic authorities. He also enlists the support of Alexander of Hales, St. Thomas, Giles of Rome, Henry of Ghent, Bonaventure, Godfrey of Fontaines, and, strangely enough, William of Auxerre, who, as we shall see in a moment, held the opposite of Mirecourt's position.

The general impression left after reading Mirecourt's question, especially in light of the first apology, is that he was not only opposed to the idea that God could undo the past but was addressing himself, in part, to those who believed that undoing the past was possible for God, *de potentia absoluta*. Those who drew up the list of suspect propositions shared the view of Mirecourt but felt that the adversary's two propositions were evidently false and that Mirecourt should have been able to have demonstrated their falsity. Mirecourt was caught between his adversaries, who believed it evident that God could undo the past, and his examiners, who believed that such propositions were evidently false.

If Mirecourt did not maintain the view ascribed to him by his inquisitors and later historians, who did ? Was the idea of God's undoing the past, associated with the name of Peter Damian, revived in the fourteenth century ? Moreover, now that we know something of the position of Mirecourt's inquisitors, can we identify any of them ?

Madison, University of Wisconsin.
(to be continued).

---

quam oppositum. » This last conclusion should not be viewed as a weakening of Mirecourt's conviction that God cannot undo the past. Bonaventure, who also believed that God was unable to undo the past, was equally dubious about devising an irrefutable demonstration. Cf. *Sent.* I, d. 42, q. 3 (*Opera omnia*, Quaracchi, I, 753-754).

John of Mirecourt
and Gregory of Rimini
on Whether God Can Undo the Past *

BRADWARDINE AND BUCKINGHAM

When we examine the writings of Mirecourt's contemporaries, we find that the question of God's power to undo the past was already a subject of debate among masters of theology in the ten years preceding Mirecourt's reading of the *Sentences*, that it may have had its revival at Oxford and that it may have been introduced at Paris by Thomas Buckingham.**

Sources for the issue lay much closer at hand than the seldom read treatise of Peter Damian on divine omnipotence. The elements of the problem were present in two widely read authors, Boethius [88] and Anselm [89], and the affirmative position, namely that God can undo

---

* Cf. the first part, *Rech. Théol. anc. méd.* 39 (1972) 224-256. — After the first part of this article was set in type, the author became aware of a general article on Mirecourt by the late Georges Tessier, privately circulated and eventually to appear in volume 40 of *Histoire littéraire de la France*. A copy of this work was gratiously supplied by Madame Ducos-Fonfrede of the Académie des Inscriptions et Belles-Lettres. At the same time Dr. Gilbert Ouy sent the author a microfilm copy of his thesis referred to in footnote 5. Both of these works represent valuable contributions. While independent in judgment, Tessier incorporated much of the important textual research of Ouy. Through a re-examination of the evidence similar to my own, Tessier also arrived at the date of 1344-45 for Mirecourt's lectures on the *Sentences*. Moreover, Tessier recognized the cautious tone of much of Mirecourt's *lectura*, but he fell back into the familiar trap of basing his assessment primarily on the lists of suspect and condemned propositions. Neither Ouy's nor Tessier's study invites changes in the present article, both because they are of a more general nature and because they are wedded to some presuppositions about Ockhamism and fourteenth-century thought no longer so easily accepted.

88. BOETHIUS, *De trinitate*, c. 4 (PL 64, 1252-53) ; cf. *Consolatio philosophiae*, L. IV (PL 63, 786-830).

89. ANSELM, *De concordia praescientiae et praedestinationis et gratia dei cum libero arbitrio* in *Opera omnia* (ed. F. S. SCHMITT, Edinburgh 1946, Vol. II, pp. 245-288) ; *Cur Deus Homo*, II, 17.

** See additional note on p. 174A

148

the past, *de potentia absoluta*, was upheld by Gilbert de la Porrée in his Commentary on Boethius' *De Trinitate* [90] and reaffirmed by William of Auxerre in his *Summa Aurea* [91]. The question was treated by the major theologians of the thirteenth century [92] who either, like Thomas, devoted an entire question to the problem, or who, like Bonaventure, considered the issue as one difficulty within a broader question. Although I have not been able to find any theologian between 1230 and 1330 who subscribed to the view of Gilbert, few of those who rejected his position found it easy to refute. Most of the elements of the problem, therefore, including *pro* and *con* arguments, were accessible to the fourteenth century through sources readily available in almost any scholastic library.

The importance of the question of God's power to undo the past declined sharply after 1300, if we are to judge by the sparse attention paid to it from then until 1335. The question re-entered the scholastic literature in the wake of renewed interest over the problem of future contingents, the importance of which increased steadily after 1320, becoming a major issue in the theological faculties of the fourteenth and fifteenth centuries [93]. In particular, the question of God's power to undo the past re-emerged and was given its fourteenth-century

90. GILBERT DE LA PORRÉE, *In Boethium de trinitate*, ch. 4 (PL 64, 1287B-1289A ; ed. N. HÄRING, in *Nine Medieval Thinkers*, Toronto 1955, pp. 69-75). Cf. M. E. WILLIAMS, *The Teaching of Gilbert Porreta on the Trinity as Found in His Commentaries on Boethius*, Rome 1951 ; M. A. SCHMIDT, *Gottheit und Trinität nach dem Kommentar des Gilbert Porreta zu Boethius, De Trinitate*, Basel 1956, pp. 126-127 ; H. C. VAN ELSWIJK, *Gilbert Porreta : sa vie, son œuvre, sa pensée*, Louvain 1966, pp. 307-310.

91. WILLIAM OF AUXERRE, *Summa aurea*, L. I, c. 11, q. 5-6, Paris, s.a., fol. 27ʳ-27ᵛ.

92. ALEXANDER OF HALES, *Summa theologica*, Pt. I, q. 21, m. 5, a. 2-4 (Quaracchi 1924, I, 233-238) ; ALBERTUS MAGNUS, *Sent.* I, d. 42, a. 6 (Paris 1893, XXVI, 362-366) ; BONAVENTURE, *Sent.* I, d. 42, art. un., q. 3 (*Opera omnia*, Quaracchi 1883, I, 753-755) ; THOMAS AQUINAS, *Sent.* I, d. 42, q. 2, a. 2 (Parma 1856, VI, 344-345) ; *Sent.* I, d. 44, q. un., a. 4 (Parma 1856, VI, 356) ; *De potentia Dei*, q. 1, a. 5 ; *Summa theologiae* I, q. 25, a. 3-4 (Ottawa 1941, I, 173a-175b) ; GERARD OF ABBEVILLE, *Quodl.* VII, q. 17 (*Paris, Nat. lat. 16405*, fol. 67) ; PETER OF TARANTASIA, *Sent.* I, d. 42, q. 2, a. 3 (Toulouse 1652, I, 350-352) ; GILES OF ROME, *Sent.* I, d. 42, prin. 2, q. 2 (Venice 1521, fol. 221ʳ) ; GILES OF ROME, *Sent.* I, d. 44, q. 4 (Venice 1521, fols. 227ʳ-227ᵛ) ; RICHARD OF MIDDLETON, *Sent.* I, d. 42, q. 4-6 (Brixen 1591, I, 374-377) ; HENRY OF GHENT, *Quodl.* I, q. 7 & 8 (Paris 1518, fols. 4ʳ-6ʳ) ; GODFREY OF FONTAINES, *Quodl.* VI, q. 2 (*Les quodlibets cinq, six et sept de Godefroid de Fontaines*, in *Les philosophes belges*, III ; Louvain 1914, 110-112) ; JOHN DUNS SCOTUS, *Report. Par.* I, d. 42, q. 2 (Lyons 1639, XI, 1, 225-227).

93. For a brief survey of the development of this problem and some of its fifteenth-century repercussions, see L. BAUDRY, *La querelle des futurs contingents (Louvain 1465-1475)*, (*Études de philosophie médiévale*, 38), Paris 1950.

form as a result of the controversy between Thomas Bradwardine and Thomas Buckingham on the interrelation of divine and human volition.

Bradwardine completed his *De causa Dei* in 1344, but the ideas contained in it had been in circulation for some time inasmuch as the work was based on lectures he gave as a *baccalarius sententiarum* of Merton College at Oxford around 1333 [94]. In order to counteract what he felt to be the Pelagian views of several of his contemporaries, Bradwardine reasserted divine omnipotence, omniscience, and to some degree, divine omnivolence. In his defense of the prerogatives and freedom of God, however, several of his contemporaries felt they discerned a theological determinism that restricted or even denied human free will.

The position of Bradwardine on the issue of God's power to undo the past resembles the argument of the *adversarius* in Mirecourt's question and therefore resembles the position under attack in the first part of the suspect propositions mistakenly charged against Mirecourt [95]. Bradwardine vehemently opposes the position of those who hold that the past is not able not to have been and that God is not able to make it not to have been [96]. Against that position he sides with Gilbert de la Porrée and William of Auxerre [97]. When a future contingent passes into the past, the divine will does not, for Bradwardine, cease to be free in regard to it, nor is some necessity added to it that binds God [98]. Moreover, it does not imply a contradiction for a past event to be altered [99]. In regard to future contingents, Bradwardine

---

94. Cf. H. A. OBERMAN, *Archbishop Thomas Bradwardine · A Fourteenth Century Augustinian*, Utrecht 1958, pp. 16-20.

95. THOMAS BRADWARDINE, *De causa Dei*, L. III, c. 52 (London 1618, 834-836, 844-845, 850, 856-864) ; L. III, c. 53 (875-876).

96. *Ibid.*, 857 : "Tertio dicitur a quibusdam, quod praeteritum non potest non fuisse, nec Deus potest hoc facere, quia utrumque contradictionem includit".

97. *Ibid.*, 859. Bradwardine' extensive and exact quotations from William of Auxerre betrays a first-hand knowledge of that source.

98. *Ibid.*, 857 : "Imo volutionem Dei oppositam, scilicet ' A ' non fuisse, est possibile simpliciter nunc esse, sicut fuit ante praeteritionem ' A '..." *Ibid.*, 875 : "Quod cum futura contingentia fiant praesentia, aut in praeteritum dilabuntur, voluntas divina respectu illorum non desinit esse libera aliqua libertate, seu aliquo modo libertatis intrinsecus, qua vel quo prius fuerat libera, nec incipit esse necessaria aliqua necessitate opposita respectu ipsorum."

99. *Ibid.*, 857 : "Respondebitur forsitan, quod ex praeteritione rei praeteritae oritur quaedam relatio, qua necesse est simpliciter illam fuisse, quare impossibile est simpliciter illam non fuisse. Sed hoc reprobatum est prius, quando monstrabatur ' A ' non fuisse, nullam contradictionem formaliter implicare. Illam etiam relationem, non est necesse simpliciter esse vel fuisse ; aliquando enim non fuit ; quare nec repugnaret formaliter eam nunc non esse ; ergo nihil facit necessarium

150

argues that they must happen as God foresees them, but that necessity depends ultimately on the divine will, on which the divine foreknowledge is based. In much the same way, statements about the past are true not because of some special quality that differentiates past events from future contingents but because they were so ordained by God and remained subject to his will [100].

If, on this issue, Bradwardine seems far closer to the position under attack in 1347 than does Mirecourt, Bradwardine at least holds an opinion concerning Christ's knowledge of future contingents that differs from the view of Mirecourt that was condemned in the first proposition in the final list [101].

Bradwardine's major opponent at Oxford and later at Paris was Thomas Buckingham,* also a fellow of Merton College, who lectured on the *Sentences* there between 1333 and 1338 [102]. The final version of Bradwardine's *De causa Dei* may contain, in part, a critique of ideas Buckingham put forward in his *Sentences*. Shortly after 1340, Buckingham seems to have gone to Paris, where he may have held a chair of theology until 1346 and where he engaged in a publicized debate *in aula* attacking the position of Bradwardine [103]. It may well have been at Paris that he wrote his *Quaestiones* in order to show that there was a middle position between the Pelagian emphasis on human freedom and Bradwardine's emphasis on divine determinism [104].

The *Sentences* Commentary of Buckingham concentrates on a small number of questions and explores these at length. The first article of

---

simpliciter. Illa quoque relatio vel est ad Deum seu ad voluntatem divinam, vel rem aliquam naturalem seu res aliquas naturales. Primum erat destructum per 30ᵘᵐ huius ; secundum stare non potest. "

100. *Ibid.*, 875.

101. *Ibid.*, 875-876 : " Quod si Christus secundum naturam suam humanam per actus naturales humanos distincte scivit, credidit, voluit, et asseruit, et iuravit de aliquo futuro contingenti quod hoc erit, illo adhuc manente futuro contingenti, necessarium est Christum ita fecisse, et ita necessarium tunc sicut erit quando illud erit praesens in praeteritumve transmissum."

102. MICHALSKI, *Le problème de la volonté...*, 250 ; A. B. EMDEN, *A Biographical Register of the University of Oxford to A. D. 1500*, Vol. I, Oxford 1957, 298-299. Cf. W. A. PANTIN, *The English Church in the Fourteenth Century*, London 1955, 113-115, 263-266 ; OBERMAN, 188-194.

103. THOMAS OF KRAKOW, ... *Paris, Bibl. Nat. lat. 16409*, fol. 23ᵛ.

104. *Oxford, New College 134*, fol. 324ʳ: " Quaestiones tractatae per Thomas Bukyngham, nuper ecclesiae Exoniensis cancellarium, ostendentes inter errores Pelagii, Chicheronis et Scoti, Catholicum medium invenire ac praedestinationem, praeordinationem, praevolutionem aeternam concursumque Dei stare cum libera voluntate et merito creaturae... " M.-D. CHENU, *Les Quaestiones de Thomas Buckingham*, in *Studia medievalia in honorem... R. J. Martin*, Bruges 1949, 229-241. Cf. F. M. POWICKE, *The Medieval Books of Merton College*, Oxford 1931, 113.

* See additional note on p. 174A

question three is entirely devoted to the issue of whether God is able to wish the world never to have been. Buckingham's discussion of this question is the longest and most thorough before 1340 that I have seen. In it he defends the position that God cannot undo the past and that God cannot make the world never to have been [105]. This he believes is evident and can be demonstrated. In response to Bradwardine, Buckingham believes that there is a special characteristic that differentiates the past from the future. The future is truly contingent upon divine and human will and is therefore not predetermined. If man is to be free in regard to future moral action, the foreknowledge of God cannot remove or negate the contingency of future events. The past, however, because it is no longer future, is no longer contingent, and it cannot be altered by man or God. Thus, propositions about the future are neither true nor false ; propositions about the past are necessarily true or false [106].

In support of his thesis Buckingham first argues from authority, and he marshalls an impressive list of quotations with full and accurate references from the fathers and doctors of the Church : Augustine's *Contra Faustum*, XXVI, 3 ; Jerome's letter to Eustochium ; Anselm's *Cur Deus Homo*, II, 17 ; Lombard's *Sentences*, I, d. 44,4 ; Aristotle's *Ethics*, VI, 2 ; Anselm's *De concordia*, 4 ; Aristotle's *Physics*, I ; Alexander, Thomas, Scotus, Giles of Rome, Albertus Magnus, Bonaventure, William of Auxerre, Richard Middleton, and Henry of Ghent — all with extensive quotations and a discussion of their position [107]. The extent of his zeal to bury his opponent under the weight of patristic and scholastic opinion is reflected in his use of only part of William of Auxerre's discussion, namely William's second response to the quotation from Jerome, not mentioning that William eventually rejected that position in favor of Gilbert's solution.

When one compares this list of authorities with the list given by Mirecourt in the discussion that follows his seventh conclusion in the

---

105. *Paris, Bibl. Nat. lat. 16400*, fol. 36ᵛ-46ʳ ; fol. 39ᵛ : "Ad idem arguo, per rationes probo quod Deus non potest velle de praeterito aliquo ipsum numquam fuisse" ; fol. 40ᵛ-41ʳ : "Ad articulum istum, utrum Deus potest velle mundum numquam fuisse, teneo quod non, et me movet quod non est ita quod mundus numquam fuit, nec potest esse Deus causa illius non-entis, nec facere quod mundus numquam fuit ; igitur non potest Deus velle mundum numquam fuisse. "

106. Cf. *Quaestiones*, concl. 13 (*Oxford, New College 134*, fol. 347ʳ : "Voluntas divina respectu futurorum contingentium quamdiu sunt futura, est libera libertate contradictionis ; sed cum fuerint praesentia in praeteritumve labuntur desinit esse libera huiusmodi libertate et incipit esse necessaria necessitate opposita respectu eorum, sine mutatione in Deo posita vel ponenda. "

107. *Sent.*, q. 3, a. 1 (*Paris, Bibl. Nat. lat. 16400*, fols. 38ʳ-39ᵛ).

Lectura question, one reaches some surprising results. The order of authorities in Mirecourt is almost identical to Buckingham's, although it has been reduced. Scotus, Albert, and Richard have been dropped and Godfrey of Fontaines added. Moreover, the words introducing the authorities are often identical, indicating either that Mirecourt had a copy of Buckingham in front of him when he prepared his *Lectura* or was using someone who had. Because of the precision with which Buckingham reproduced his authorities, especially someone as old and as comparatively rare as William of Auxerre, one suspects a first-hand knowledge of these sources which, when it misrepresented an authority — as it did in the case of William — did so by intention. That such is the case is revealed through a contemporary who shared that same love for exact quotations from past authority and caught Buckingham at his own game [108]. Not so with Mirecourt ! The latter slavishly copied Buckingham's list and supplied originality only by dropping a few sources and adding one. Although there is every reason to believe that Mirecourt was sufficiently familiar with the major scholastics, almost all of his authorities in this question were borrowed, and he was so confident that William of Auxerre supported his opinion that he listed him without noting that Buckingham had cautiously referred only to the second response of William, allowing his reader to assume (incorrectly) that this was William's final position.

It is not only the list of authorities that Mirecourt took from Buckingham. Many of the arguments put forward against the position of the *adversarius* in the discussions following conclusion four and, more especially, conclusion five are arguments used by Buckingham, e.g., the idea that nonbeing is not able to be the object of a factible power [109], or that God's power to undo the past would result in contradictories being true at the same time [110]. The discussion that follows conclusion six is also heavily indebted to Buckingham [111]. Moreover, Buckingham is identified by name as the author of these arguments in one of the Mirecourt manuscripts [112].

One should not surmise from this, however, that Mirecourt has simply copied the ideas of Buckingham, for this is far from the truth. While Mirecourt shares Buckingham's viewpoint and thus feels safe in using his authorities and several of his arguments, Mirecourt does not, as we have already seen, believe that Buckingham's position is

---

108. GREGORY OF RIMINI, *Sent.* I, d. 42-44, q. 1, a. 2 (Venice 1522, fol. 163r).
109. *Sent.*, q. 3, a. 1 (*Paris, Bibl. Nat. lat. 16400*, fol. 39v, 41r).
110. *Ibid.* (fols. 40r-40v).
111. *Ibid.* (fols. 41r-41v).
112. *Krakow, Bibl. Jag. 1184*, fols. 96r, 96v, 97r.

fully demonstrative. Mirecourt is saying that the position of the *adversarius*, which resembles the position of Bradwardine, cannot be demolished as easily as Buckingham thought, for Buckingham's arguments do not convincingly and evidently disprove the adversary's position. In order to uphold the truth of propositions about the past and in order to prove that the proposition " God can make the past never to have been " was in all cases and interpretations false, Buckingham gave to past events a necessity so strong that these events could never have happened otherwise, thus excluding what Mirecourt called the improper use of " facere " and implying that creation, because it is now past, was necessary [113]. But this excessive restriction of divine liberty in regard to past events was not evident to Mirecourt, and thus the proposition " God can make the past never to have been " cannot be disproved in all its possible interpretations.

If Mirecourt denied the final validity of Buckingham's reasoning about the necessity of past events, he seems to have shared Buckingham's indeterminism regarding future contingents. Mirecourt's statement on Christ's knowledge of future events, retained in the final list of condemned propositions, was taken almost *verbatim* from Buckingham and can be found in his *Quaestiones* [114] as well as his Commentary on the *Sentences* [115]. In support of his statement Buckingham specifically refers to the passage in Anselm reproduced in footnote 37 of the present article. Although Mirecourt had Anselm's argument in mind and believed that if his statement were properly inspected its harmlessness would be evident, Mirecourt's defense inclines somewhat in Bradwardine's direction. To what degree the

---

113. *Ibid.* (fols. 39ᵛ-40ᵛ) ; *Quaestiones*, concl. 11 (fol. 344ᵛ) : " De re lapsa in praeteritum est dicendum quod prius naturaliter est necesse illam rem fuisse, quam est necesse Deum velle illam rem fuisse. "

114. *Quaestiones*, concl. 15 (fol. 347ʳ) : " Sed Christus secundum naturam humanam scivit, voluit, asseruit et iuravit de aliquo contingenter futuro quod ipsum erit quamdiu ipsum contingens manet futurum contingens ; contingens est et liberum secundum contradictionem non necessariam Christum hoc sic scivisse, voluisse, asseruisse atque iurasse, sed potest esse quod hoc dixit, asseruit et iuravit ad aliud intellectum et non ad illum. "

115. *Sent.* (*Paris, Bibl. Nat. lat. 16400*, fol. 42ʳ) : " ... et dicitur ipse satis possibile [est] quod Christus voluit aliquid fieri, et tamen non factum est nec fiet. Similiter, quod Christus fuit ignorans, errans, desceptus. Similiter, est possibile quod Christus iuravit aliquid fieri quod nec factum est nec fiet, et eodem modo de [pro] missione et etiam quod Christus iuravit aliquid esse verum quod pro tunc scivit esse falsum ad intellectum ad quem iuravit id esse verum. " Abridged version, *Paris, Bibl. Nat. lat 14576*, fol. 262ᵛ : " ... quod est possibile, quod Christus fieri voluit aliquid quod tamen non est factum nec fiet, et de promissione etiam quod Christus iuravit aliquid esse verum quod tamen scivit esse falsum ad intellectum ad quem iuravit illud esse verum. "

154

Bradwardine-Buckingham controversy dominates the early propositions of Mirecourt in both the suspect and condemned lists will be discussed later in reference to the condemnation of 1347. It is already evident, however, that the condemnation was reaching out through Mirecourt to other theologians with whom he was not in entire agreement.

When viewed against the background of the Bradwardine-Buckingham controversy, it appears that Mirecourt was trying, very cautiously, to establish a middle position between the extremes of Bradwardine and Buckingham. He shared with Buckingham the view that God cannot undo the past, but he believed with Bradwardine that God was initially free to have acted otherwise, if he had so chosen. Because of the ambiguity of the wording of the proposition, Mirecourt did not believe that Buckingham's attack on Bradwardine's position on this issue was conclusive. He shared that belief with a contemporary who, although senior to Mirecourt in years and reputation, had lectured on the *Sentences* at Paris only two years earlier and who had already pointed to the weaknesses in Buckingham's argumentation on this issue. This contemporary was Gregory of Rimini.

GREGORY OF RIMINI*

On the basis of the theory of Damasus Trapp, referred to earlier [116], we might expect to gain some insight into the significance of the issue as well as Mirecourt's position from Gregory of Rimini, since it was supposedly he who, along with Robert de Bardis, chancellor of the University of Paris, drew up the lists of suspect propositions and encouraged the condemnation of Mirecourt. Trapp's theory was put forward in several articles, beginning in 1956, that helped to alter our image of Gregory [117]. In the older literature, Gregory was called the standard-bearer of the Nominalists and was considered to be a close disciple of Ockham. The thrust of Trapp's revision was to depict Gregory as a strong Augustinian (one of the strongest of the fourteenth century) and the standard-bearer against the Nominalists.

Trapp's view of Gregory of Rimini is part of a larger theory of the development of fourteenth-century thought. According to Trapp, the school conflicts of the late thirteenth century among Thomists, Scotists, and Augustinians led, in the fourteenth century, to a highly

---

116. Part I, 233.
117. Cf. footnote 20.
* See additional note on p. 174A

beneficial, critical movement that sought to establish more firmly the evidence behind philosophical and theological inquiry. One branch of this movement, termed the " historico-critical " approach, concentrated on reading and quoting the patristic sources with a greater fidelity for text and reference than was practiced by earlier generations. Most of the theologians of the Augustinian Hermits, according to Trapp, represent this approach. The second branch, termed the " logico-critical " approach, concentrated on empirical, logical, and mathematical evidence to insure a firmer foundation for philosophy. Within this approach might be placed Ockham and his immediate followers, although Trapp does not speculate on this. Regardless of which approach seems to be dominant in a particular fourteenth-century theologian, all are *moderni*, a neutral term, as used by Trapp, describing all those in the fourteenth century who shared this critical approach. The terms " modernist " and " nominalist " are reserved by Trapp for the radical, revolutionary, extremist wing of the logico-critical approach, who are best exemplified at Paris by Autrecourt and Mirecourt and at Oxford by Nicholas Aston and Uthred of Boldon.

The type of speculation found in Autrecourt, Mirecourt, and others, according to Trapp, turned away from the sources, from *evidentia*, in favor of an extreme application of the *potentia Dei absoluta* that lost " sight of all perspective and of all horizons. On an ever-increasing scale allowances are made for a possible divine intervention liable to suspend the created order ; ingenious but very doubtful ' cases ' are invented and uncritically adduced to invalidate the general rule " [118]. The main issue of 1347, the main characteristic of these radicals, was *subtilitas*, which Trapp defines as the " neglect of the Fathers and a logico-theological abuse of the doctrine of possible divine intervention. From the abuse of this premise flow all the errors of 1347, errors in Christology, errors in the doctrine of grace, errors about causality and about evidence " [119].

The curtailment of these aberrations, as Trapp calls them, that culminated in the condemnations of 1347 was achieved not by the *antiqui*, who " were nowhere in sight to defend the cause of evidence of any kind " [120], but by some *moderni*, principally those of the historico-critical approach, in particular, Gregory of Rimini. The evidence on which Trapp based his picture of Gregory as anti-nominalist, or anti-modernist, is varied and was accumulated across years of study in the Gregory texts. The Augustinianism of Gregory has

---

118. D. Trapp, *Augustinian Theology...*, 149.
119. *Ibid.*, 151.
120. *Ibid.*, 190.

long been appreciated, especially in his understanding of grace and predestination. To that picture of the Augustinian Gregory Trapp added a new appreciation for the number and quality of Gregory's quotations from Augustine and the precision in his references. In addition, Trapp noted the large number of times Gregory opposed Ockham and the number of times (usually on different issues) Gregory opposed theses frequently associated with the term " nominalism ". The single most important piece of evidence, however, on which Trapp based his view was his discovery of some references in the *Sentences* Commentary of the Cistercian, Peter of Ceffons, that seemed to point to Gregory of Rimini as the moving force behind the condemnation of Mirecourt. The evidence was based on the decipherment of several cryptic remarks or allusions by which Ceffons referred to those responsible for the condemnation of his friend and teacher, Mirecourt. Of the three " foreign old witches " to whom Ceffons alludes, Trapp feels he has identified two Italians : Gregory of Rimini and Robert de Bardis [121].

The juxtaposition of the extremist, radical, modernist Mirecourt and the conservative, Augustinian, historico-critical Rimini has important repercussions for the history of fourteenth-century thought. If Rimini was essentially an Ockhamist, then we have some significant evidence that would further separate Ockham and his followers from the so-called radical philosophical and theological tendencies of the fourteenth century. If Rimini was not an Ockhamist and if his brand of Augustinianism was opposed to the more energetic expressions of the logico-critical approach, then we are confronted with a conflict between Augustinianism and a philosophical/theological radicalism that may have had some of its origins in the thought of Ockham. Understanding the movements and conflicts of fourteenth-century thought concerns not only our description of the development of medieval thought but also our understanding of " nominalism " and Augustinianism in the generations that led up to the Protestant Reformation.

Given the limited state of our knowledge of fourteenth-century thought, the two alternative theories suggested above in no sense exhaust the possibilities. They are simply the alternatives that seem most plausible at the present time, and a solution can be found only through an examination and comparison of the sources, so abundantly available. Before we proceed in that direction, however, we must make certain that the Rimini-Mirecourt contrast has indeed been established. The only way to do this, it seems to me, would be

---

121. *Ibid.*, 188 ; D. Trapp, *Peter Ceffons...*, 147-154 ; *Gregory of Rimini Manuscripts...*, 428-429.

to compare each of the suspect and condemned propositions of 1347 with the thought of Rimini. If Rimini is the author or moving spirit behind the condemnation of Mirecourt, one should expect to find in every instance where he treats the same issue that he holds the opposite opinion or stated his position in language considerably more cautious and pious than that used by Mirecourt. Having now isolated one issue that concerned those who drew up the list of suspect propositions from the *Lectura* of Mirecourt and having described the positions of Mirecourt and his inquisitors, we should expect to find Rimini rejecting propositions that imply God's power to undo the past. But it is exactly this that we do not find. On the contrary, it is Gregory himself who maintains the thesis of God's power to undo the past, *de potentia absoluta*. Therefore, unless one believes that Gregory was so devious that he tried to convict Mirecourt for an opinion that he, himself, held and Mirecourt did not, or that Gregory entered the *affaire* Mirecourt only at the final stage, when the suspect list was being revised for condemnation, we must conclude that Gregory could not have been responsible for the 1347 condemnation of Mirecourt. Before reviewing the evidence behind Trapp's thesis and suggesting some alternate views, let us examine Rimini's position on God's power to undo the past.

When, after an absence of twelve years, Gregory returned to Paris in 1341 to proceed to the *baccalareatus* and ultimately the *magisterium*, he was already a seasoned theologian with broad and varied experience, having taught at Bologna, Padua, and Perugia [122]. Whether Gregory "read the *Sentences*" in 1342-43, as Trapp has argued [123], or in 1343-44, as was previously supposed, he had completed his Commentary on the *Sentences*, at least in its initial form, before Mirecourt began reading in 1344.

In most questions in Rimini's Commentary there are "additions" that appear to have been written between 1344 and 1356 in the margin and on the *pecia* ends of Gregory's personal copy. These additions either expanded or substituted for sections of the original Commentary, and occasionally they altered the thrust of the question or article in which they were inserted. The section with which we are concerned contains additions that show a development in Gregory's thinking, a development away from neutrality on the issue of God's power over the past toward the position of Bradwardine. Since this shift took place in the years immediately before or after 1347, we should examine both versions.

Gregory introduces the problem of God's power to undo the past in his first question on distinctions 42-45 of his *Primum Sententiarum*,

---

122. *CUP* II, 557, No. 1097.
123. D. TRAPP, *Gregory of Rimini Manuscripts...*, 425-428.

158

in which he asks whether God is able to do by his absolute power everything that can possibly be done [124]. The first article provides definitions of terms and some general conclusions. In the second article he infers two conclusions out of article one. The first of these conclusions is that God is able to make true any enuncible which, although not true, would not result in contradictories being true at the same time if it were true, using " facere " commonly in the first or second way indicated above (i.e., both in the sense of effecting or conserving and in the sense of not prohibiting or not making its opposite) [125]. The second is that every entity that God is able to produce or effect through the agency of secondary causality he is able to effect directly without that secondary cause [126]. In support of this second conclusion Rimini refers to the 63rd article condemned at Paris in 1277, which denied to God any such direct causality [127]. While the discussion and defense of the second conclusion centers around the ,, hatred of God " issue, which does not concern us here, the fourth counter-argument to his first conclusion argues that God cannot undo the past, even though it would imply no contradiction for God to do so. Therefore, there are some things which do not violate the principle of contradiction but which are, nevertheless, impossible for God [128].

In reply to the arguments against his first conclusion, Gregory begins with a long and, among all the theologians of the thirteenth and fourteenth centuries, perhaps the clearest definition of the distinction between the *potentia Dei absoluta* and the *potentia Dei ordinata* [129].

---

124. GREGORY OF RIMINI, *Super primum et secundum sententiarum* (Venice, 1522 ; reprint 1955, I, fol. 161ᵛ-165ᵛ).

125. *Ibid.* (162ʳC-D) : " Primum est quod omne enuntiabile non verum ad quod esse verum non sequitur contradictoria esse simul vera, seu primum principium non esse verum, Deus potest facere esse verum, loquendo de ' facere' communiter ad primum et ad secundum modum ; seu expeditius loquendo: omne tale potest per divinam potentiam esse verum. "

126. *Ibid.* (162ʳD) : " Secunda conclusio est quod omnem entitatem quam Deus (coagente secunda causa) potest producere vel efficere, potest per se illa non coagente. "

127. *Ibid.* (162ʳD-E) : " Ad hoc est articulus Parisiensis 63, dicens quod Deus non potest in effectum causae secundariae sine causa secundaria, error. " Cf. *CUP*, I, 547.

128. *Ibid.* (162ᵛN) : " Quarto, quia ad aliquid praeteritum non fuisse non sequitur primum principium non esse verum, et tamen nullum praeteritum potest Deus facere non fuisse, ergo non omne ad quod non sequitur primum principium non esse verum potest Deus facere esse•verum. "

129. *Ibid.* (162ᵛP-163ʳA) : " ... Deum posse hoc vel illud facere potest intelligi dupliciter : uno modo secundum potentiam ordinatam, et alio modo secundum potentiam absolutam. Non quod in Deo sint duae potentiae, una ordinata et alia absoluta, nec hoc volunt significare doctores, sed illud dicitur

The wording of the early part owes much to Ockham [130], and the fact that Gregory felt obliged to spell out the distinction in further detail is probably an indication that not everyone (Nicholas of Autrecourt ?) in the fourteenth century fully grasped its meaning. It is the fourth counter-argument, the issue of God's power to undo the past, that calls forth the longest response from Gregory [131]. Against the argument he states that some ancient doctors, Gilbert de la Porrée and William of Auxerre, held that the past, through divine power, is able not to have been. In answer to those, like Buckingham, who used the William of Auxerre passage to support the view that God cannot undo the past, Gregory points out that in the remainder of the passage William holds the opposite of that position, and he quotes it *verbatim* [132]. Without committing himself on the issue, Gregory adds that some contemporary doctors of an English university (meaning Oxford) hold that for the past not to have been

---

Deus ad intellectum recte intelligentium posse de potentia ordinata quod potest stante sua ordinatione et lege aeterna quae non est aliud quam eius voluntas qua aeternaliter voluit haec vel illa et tale vel tale esse futurum. Illud autem dicitur posse de potentia absoluta quod simpliciter et absolute potest. Econtra, illud non dicitur posse de potentia ordinata quod non potest stante lege et ordinatione sua quae nunc est ; illud vero non posse de potentia absoluta quod simpliciter et absolute non potest. Patet autem quod simpliciter et absolute sine suppositione contradictionis Deus multa potest quae non potest stante eius lege et voluntate qua voluit sic se facturum. Et hoc ideo, quia illa etsi sint simpliciter possibilia, sunt tamen incompossibilia ordinationi divinae. ... Quamvis autem ista sunt incompossibilia, quia tamen illa ordinatio non est necessaria, id est, non est necessarium Deum sic ordinasse, quinimmo possibile est ipsum ordinasse et voluisse oppositum ; ideo illud quod solum est impossibile ex suppositione ordinationis, utpote ei incompossibile non est absolute impossibile sed possibile, et simpliciter loquendo illud Deus potest facere. Huic distinctioni satis concordat alia antiqua, qua dictum est quod quaedam Deus non potest de iustitia quae potest de potentia. ... Illud ergo dicitur Deus non posse de iustitia quod est incompossibile suae ordinationi et voluntati, quae est prima iustitia. Illud autem est omne cuius oppositum Deus vult quamquam ipsum sit secundum se possibile simpliciter. "

130. WILLIAM OF OCKHAM, *Quodlibeta Septem* VI, 1 : " Quaedam Deus potest facere de potentia ordinata et quaedam de potentia absoluta. Haec distinctio non est sic intelligenda quod in Deo realiter sint duae potentiae, quarum una sit ordinata, alia absoluta, quia unica est potentia in Deo ad extra, quae omnimodo est ipse Deus. Nec sic est intelligenda quod aliqua potest Deus ordinate facere et alia potest absolute et non ordinate, quia Deus nihil potest facere inordinate. Sed est sic intelligenda quod ' posse [facere] aliquid ' aliquando accipitur secundum leges ordinatas et institutas a Deo et illa Deus dicitur posse facere de potentia ordinata. Aliter accipitur ' posse ' pro posse facere omne illud quod non includit contradictionem fieri, sive Deus ordinavit se hoc facturum sive non, quia Deus multa potest facere quae non vult facere. "

131. GREGORY OF RIMINI, *Super primum*... (163ʳB-165ʳB).

132. *Ibid.* (163ʳC-D).

does not imply a contradiction and, moreover, that such is possible for God [133].

That position, which we have come to know as the opinion of Bradwardine (to whom Gregory may possibly have been referring), is examined at length by Gregory, who gives *pro* and *con* arguments in the form of a running debate [134]. The arguments and authorities cited by Bradwardine are reproduced in a highly persuasive manner. But Gregory feels that the opposite position, namely that God cannot make a past thing not to have been, has more support among the doctors [135]. In detailing this second view Gregory relies on Buckingham, who, in the margin, is credited with the arguments [136].

Had Gregory ended there, one would have been left with the impression that he agreed with Buckingham, although Buckingham's position received only half as much space as the affirmative position. However, Gregory goes on to say that those maintaining that God can make a past thing not to have been can easily answer the arguments of Buckingham, and Gregory proceeds to do so in a section even longer than the first exposition of Bradwardine's position [137]. After a brief retort from the Buckingham side [138], Gregory informs his reader (as if it needed saying) that he has put forward the proofs and defenses of both sides of the question, and he leaves the task of choosing the preferable opinion to the judgment of the doctors [139].

Whatever caution or indecision lay behind Gregory's treatment of this issue before 1344, he abandoned neutrality in the next few years in favor of Bradwardine's position, to which, although he knew it to be a minority view, he had already given prominence in the original version of his Commentary. Gregory's first addition to this question adds a third conclusion to article two, namely that God is able to make any past thing not to have been [140]. It does not imply a contradiction for a past thing not to have been, and therefore the possibi-

---

133. *Ibid.* (163ʳD) : " Hoc etiam adhuc aliqui viventes doctores universitatis anglicanae tenent, non videntes aliquam contradictionem implicari vel sequi ex eo quod aliqua res quae praeterita est. "

134. *Ibid.* (163ʳD-163ᵛM).

135. *Ibid.* (163ᵛM) : " Oppositam vero partem multo plures et maioris auctoritatis doctores tenuerunt et tenent quod certe satis est ponderandum ".

136. *Ibid.* (163ᵛO-Q).

137. *Ibid.* (164ʳA-164ᵛQ ; 164ʳA) : " Qui primam partem vellet sustinere, satis bene posset ad ea quae pro parte secunda inducta sunt respondere. "

138. *Ibid.* (164ᵛQ) : " Qui vero tenent negativam possent ad rationes pro opposita parte adductas etiam respondere. "

139. *Ibid.* (165ʳB) : " Ecce posui utriusque partis probationes et defensiones, quarum quae cui praeferenda sit doctorum iudicio relinquo. "

140. *Ibid.* (162ʳE) : " Tertia conclusio est quod quamlibet rem praeteritam potest Deus facere non fuisse. "

lity of such lies within the power of God considered absolutely [141]. Inasmuch as God retains the theoretical power to do things he does not wish to do and consequently will not do, he also retains the power not to have done the things he willed to do and did do. Gregory is saying more than simply that the past could have been different, that things could have happened otherwise had God so chosen (which is the position of Mirecourt). God dwells in eternity, and therefore the power (whether exercised or not) that God possesses over events is not restricted to what for us is called the future. Everything that God was able to wish from all eternity he is now able to have wished from all eternity, and everything that God was able not to wish from all eternity he is now able not to have wished from all eternity [142].

Gregory admits, as he did earlier, that this position is not commonly held by his contemporaries, but he claims the support of the ancient doctors, Gilbert and William (as did Bradwardine) [143]. Throughout his discussion Gregory seems more intent on affirming that the past could have happened otherwise than on affirming that God can now undo the past. His enemies are those contemporaries who hold as evident the proposition that every affirmative statement about the past, if true, is necessary [144]. For Gregory, only God is necessary. Past events, therefore, are contingent upon the divine will, which could have chosen otherwise.

Following his usual form, Gregory raises counter-arguments against his new conclusion [145]. This second addition is brief, listing only a few authorities and reasons. There is no final section giving Gregory's refutation of these counter-arguments. He may have assumed that his position was sufficiently established, or the addition which he wrote failed to be inserted in the revised copy of the Commentary.

Gregory was known to have held the affirmative side of the question before the condemnations of 1347. In fact, he seems to have joined the camp of Bradwardine on this issue by the time Mirecourt was lecturing on the *Sentences* in 1344-45. A fellow Augustinian, Alphonsus

---

141. *Ibid.* : " Quamlibet rem praeteritam non fuisse non implicat contradictionem ; igitur quamlibet praeteritam rem potest Deus facere non fuisse. "

142. *Ibid.* : " Omne quod Deus potuit ab aeterno velle, potest nunc ab aeterno voluisse, et quod potuit non velle, potest [nunc] non voluisse. "

143. *Ibid.* (162ʳG) : " Hanc conclusionem, quamvis ipsa communiter non teneatur a modernis, venerabiles tamen doctores antiqui tenuerunt, sicut magister Gilbertus Porretanus... Item ille venerabilis doctor Altissiodorensis... "

144. *Ibid.* (162ᵛI) : " Ex hac autem conclusione sequitur falsum esse quod multi moderni dicunt et quasi pro maxima et principio multorum suorum dictorum utuntur, scilicet quod omnis propositio affirmativa de praeterito, si est vera, est necessaria. "

145. *Ibid.* (162ᵛN-P).

162

Vargas of Toledo, who was lecturing on the *Sentences* at Paris the same year as Mirecourt, pointed to Gregory and the Franciscan, Rodulphus de Cornaco, as major defenders of the idea that God is able to make a past thing not to have been [146]. By contrast, Alphonsus maintained that God cannot make a past thing never to have been [147] and, similarly, that it is impossible for God not to have revealed what he revealed [148].

A later fourteenth-century witness to this debate, Pierre d'Ailly, apparently knowing only the original version of Gregory, thought that the latter believed both positions on this question defensible [149]. According to d'Ailly, the leading representative of the position that God cannot undo the past was William of Ockham [150]. Although d'Ailly admits that that is the majority opinion, he sides with Bradwardine, whom he mentions by name [151].

---

146. ALPHONSUS VARGAS, *In primum sententiarum*, dist. 42-44 (Venice, 1490 ; reprint, 1952, cols. 631-635, 639-641).

147. *Ibid.* (col. 631) : " Quod tanta necessitate praeteritum est praeteritum, quod Deus non potest facere praeteritum non fuisse. "

148. *Ibid.* (col. 635) : " Quod revelatio qua Deus revelavit antichristum fore vel aliquid huiusmodi non potest per aliquam potentiam non fuisse revelatio, vel quod idem est : tantum necessitate revelatum est revelatum, quod Deus non potest numquam revelasse quod revelavit. "

149. PIERRE D'AILLY, *Quaestiones super libros sententiarum*, L. I, q. 11, H (Strassburg 1490) : " Nam quidam antiqui doctores concesserunt quod praeteritum per divinam potentiam potest non fuisse, sicut Gilbertus Poritanus... et similiter Guillermus Altissiodorensis... Aliqui etiam moderni doctores idem tenent... Aliqui autem ad utramque partem adducunt rationes et nullam audent asserere, sed utramque relinquunt tanquam disputabilem, sicut magister Gregorius. "

150. *Ibid.* : " Aliqui autem, sicut Ockham et plures alii, tenent partem negativam, et ista communiter tenetur. " It should be noted that Ockham rejected the determinism expressed in the Aristotelian proposition (*Perihermenias*, 19a, 23-32) : " Omne quod est, quando est, necesse est esse. " In his *Commentary on Perihermenias* Ockham remarked concerning this proposition : " sciendum est, quod ista propositio : Omne quod est quando est necesse est esse, de virtute sermonis est simpliciter falsa. " However, Ockham believed that past events are fixed and, once past, are outside the power of God ; thus propositions concerning past events are necessarily true or false. OCKHAM, *Sent.* I, dist. 38, q. 1 : " Hoc est communiter concessum a philosophis et theologis, quod Deus non potest facere de praeterito non praeteritum, quin semper sit postea verum dicere, quod fuit praeteritum. " Cf. *Summa logicae*, P. III, c. 30 ; *The Tractatus de praedestinatione et de praescientia Dei et de futuris contingentibus*, ed. Ph. BOEHNER (*Franciscan Institute Publications, Philos. Ser.*, 2), St. Bonaventure 1945.

151. D'Ailly believes that with the supposition of the past, the proposition is false, but without that supposition it can be conceded. PIERRE D'AILLY, *Quaestiones...*, I : " De virtute sermonis haec est falsa : Deus potest facere rem quae fuit non fuisse. Et eodem modo ista : Deus potest facere rem quae erit

Since we know that those who drew up the list of suspect propositions against Mirecourt were opposed to granting any validity to the proposition that God can make a past thing not to have been, and since we know that Gregory believed that proposition was defensible and eventually affirmed it, it seems highly unlikely that Gregory was responsible for drawing up that list. Moreover, given the number of times the inquisitors misinterpreted the thought and intention of Mirecourt, it seems unlikely they would have among their number anyone so critical and gifted as Gregory. In fact, if, as Trapp has insisted [152], the condemnations of 1347 were not definitive or exhaustive but were meant to be examples of the type of teaching that was not to be permitted at Paris, then Gregory had every reason to feel as uncomfortable as Mirecourt, if not more so. As far as I know, there is no evidence to suggest that Gregory remained in Paris in the years after 1345, and the condemnations of 1347 may have made his departure for Italy expedient. If Gregory had any reason to attack Mirecourt on this issue, it would have been for limiting rather than expanding divine omnipotence, and that is not the approach taken by those responsible for the condemnation. Admittedly, Mirecourt's argument is subtle, and certain statements taken at face value might be considered " *male sonant* ", but Gregory's treatment is no less subtle, and he does assert the position for which Mirecourt was eventually and wrongly accused.

But what of the evidence we have from Peter Ceffons who, according to Trapp, identified Gregory as the promoter of the condemnation of Mirecourt ? Would not Ceffons, a Cistercian lecturing on the *Sentences* at Paris within a few years of the condemnation, be in a position to know ? Ceffons' preoccupation with the events of 1347 suggests that he was aware of the names of those responsible for the condemnation of his master and friend. But nowhere does he explicitly name Gregory as the one responsible for that event, nor does he name anyone else [153]. The text of Ceffons from which Trapp extracted the

---

non fore, quia ista est impossibilis propter implicationem Deus facit rem quae fuit non fuisse, et sic ista : Deus facit rem quae erit non fore ; et sic istae sunt falsae : Deus potest facere mundum qui fuit non fuisse ; Deus potest facere antichristum qui erit non fore. Et ita posset dici de istis : Deus potest facere praeteritum non fuisse, vel Deus potest facere futurum non fore, etc. Tertio dico quod tales propositiones in sensu diviso probabiliter possunt concedi : rem quae fuit vel rem praeteritam Deus potest facere non fuisse... Et similiter iste in sensu composito : Deus potest facere mundum vel Adam non fuisse... ''

152. D. TRAPP, *Augustinian Theology...*, 223-224.

153. The allusions to Gregory that Trapp felt he had found in Ceffons are less than convincing, D. TRAPP, *Peter Ceffons...*, 149 : '' In the *Sermo in Capitulo Generali* the name of Robertus de *Bardis* may be hidden under an allusion

idea that "three foreign old witches" were responsible for Mirecourt's condemnation may be interpreted differently. Ceffons' hope is that "these three shriveled-up old women might be speedily driven out of the kingdom of France"[154]. If this is a reference to those principally responsible for Mirecourt's condemnation, it suggests to me that his accusers were probably old, which Rimini certainly was not, and not necessarily foreign. Ceffons thinks they should be forced to leave France ; he is not saying they are not French.

Nor was Robert de Bardis necessarily among the instigators of the condemnation of Mirecourt. As chancellor of the university he was required to preside over the condemnation and authorize the decision of the theological faculty, but that is not identical with being the promoter of the condemnation.

Ceffons sometimes refers to Gregory in company with Adam Wodeham, Walter Chatton, and Thomas Buckingham, a group that Trapp terms the "'paladins of orthodoxy' whom Ceffons cordially hates", supposedly because Ceffons and his master, Mirecourt, belong to the unorthodox radicals[155]. All that these "paladins" have in common, however, is that they are well-known fourteenth-century theologians. Chatton and Wodeham were enemies on a large number of issues, and Gregory and Buckingham differed on the question we are presently treating. It is indeed strange to see Trapp depicting Adam Wodeham, who is usually placed within the leadership of the radical English School of Ockhamism, as a conservative, orthodox theologian opposed to the type of radicalism under attack in 1347. But Ceffons does not hate these distinguished *moderni* with whom he will, on occasion, disagree. He is contrasting the intellectual atmosphere that prevailed before 1347 with the limited horizons, the suspicion and caution, that characterized the University of Paris in 1350. In the only passage from Ceffons in which the name of Gregory appears in close proximity to a discussion of the condemnation, a contrast is being made, not a

---

(*Musca Gravissima*, French 'bourdon' = Bardis ?). Here in the *Epistula* the *Musca* occurs again (148) followed by a passage (148) where the words *tortuose*, *distorto* are given prominence although the harmonious flow of the phrase is somewhat impaired. I see in *tortuose*, *distorto* — words which in the Commentary occur under similar circumstances — a possible allusion to the name of Gregory of Rimini, of the family *Tortorici*. The reader may raise his eye-brows but, as a matter of fact, these allusions or mystifications are rather common practice in the 14th century." The only explicit reference in Ceffons that, according to Trapp, links Gregory and the condemnations is reproduced in footnote 156.

154. *Ibid.* 138 : "Et utinam hae tres Vetulae Rugosae festinanter a regno Franciae proscriptione solemni totaliter abigantur..."

155. *Ibid.* 152 ; *Augustinian Theology...*, 225-226.

connection [156]. Ceffons' point is that Gregory and Buckingham, who is also mentioned (and from what we know a far more likely candidate for the promoter of the condemnation of Mirecourt), both noted theologians, debated questions and maintained positions before 1345 that are now, after 1347, dangerous, a development that Ceffons regrets.

THE NECESSITY OF THE PAST

The question of whether God has the power to make a past thing never to have been was considered by most theologians in the thirteenth and fourteenth centuries to be an eminently debatable and fruitful topic. It was a sub-question under the problem of future contingents, and it had some fascinating ramifications. In logic it concerned the necessity of statements about the past. In theology, like the problem of future contingents, it raised the issue of freedom vs. necessity in God and added to it the dimension of the necessity or non-necessity of creation. If God's foreknowledge of the future is such that it cannot happen in any way other than the way God foresees it, then the future becomes necessary and determined, a necessity that is as binding for God as it is for us. If, on the other hand, the future is open and undetermined, contingent upon God's freedom and our freedom, then God cannot know any more about it than we do. Moreover, if the a-temporality of God, the concept of eternity, is taken seriously, then the determinist and indeterminist solutions apply to the past just as much as to the future. If God cannot now alter future events, then he could not alter past events even before they happened, and thus creation becomes necessary. If God retains the power to alter future events, then does he not have that same power over past events after they have happened ?

---

156. *Peter Ceffons...*, 149-150 : " Item sint haec omnia dicta argumentative ut videatur quomodo solvantur per illos qui tenent opinionem *Gregorii et Bokinkam*. Item solvant [= Hugolinus de Urbeveteri, O.E.S.A.] mihi hoc argumentum : Deus vult aliquod antecedens et vult consequentiam esse bonam, ideo facit colligationem et connexionem inter antecedens et consequens. Declaretur quomodo ipse non velit consequens... Item dicunt quod Deus est auctor omnis paenae et omnis boni, et tamen dicunt quod peccatum est paena sub ratione qua est peccatum. Solvant hoc ! Et advertatur quod multum sobrie loquor quia revera non volo errare. Et etiam quia homines sunt invidissimi et truculentissimi. Aliquibus si hoc daretur ad examinandum multum tristarentur si non invenirent aliquid in quod mordere possent cum etiam in veritatem libenter mordeant carpantque nefande. Multi alii scripserunt patenter quod Deus vult peccatum ; non volo ita dicere quia etiam hoc diebus nostris revocatum fuit... O quam libenter et alacriter insurgerent plures dicendo : Hic blasphemat ! "

This dilemma was one of the central problems of fourteenth-century thought and, if understood as the problem of how to make the omnipotence and omniscience of God compatible with human freedom, it might be considered *the* central question of the fourteenth century. Many different solutions were proposed, which need not detain us here. Some, in order to stress the immutability and omniscience of God, tolerated a certain degree of necessity and determinism, both divine and human, to a point that bordered on divine omnivolence. Others, in order to stress the omnipotence and freedom of God, advanced an indeterminism and divine freedom that applied to events before and after they have happened. It should be noted that both positions tried to recognize and do justice to the transcendence and power of God, that both inherited something from the Augustinian revival that shaped theology in the generations following 1277, and that both were speaking *de potentia absoluta*, not *ordinata*. Working from theologically accepted premises and applying a rigorous consistency to their views, neither position could be viewed as denying the faith or being logically impossible. Even those upholding the necessity of creation were not affirming the eternity of the world, nor even the eternity of creation, two things that St. Thomas felt could be proved false by faith, although not by reason. They were only affirming that God's knowledge of his own unchanging will prohibits his acting in any other way, and in that sense God acts of necessity, a conclusion that seemed false and impious to many, including Mirecourt.

No one that I have examined on the question of God's power to make a past thing never to have been ever envisaged God's wishing to change the past. That is excluded from the realm of real possibility because of the ordained order and the consistency of divine action. Nor could God, even *de potentia absoluta*, alter the past with the supposition of the past, for that implied a contradiction. Within the bounds of acceptable opinion Bradwardine and Rimini believed that God, *de potentia absoluta*, retained the power to make a past thing never to have been, and on the other side Buckingham and Vargas believed that God could not, even *de potentia absoluta*. Mirecourt maintained a middle position, that before a fact happened God could have prevented it ; afterwards, it could not be changed.

Toward a Re-evaluation of John of Mirecourt

The traditional, cautious stance taken by Mirecourt on the question of God's power over the past conflicts with his radical image, as presented in the earlier literature, but coincides with some recent studies that are also based on the text of the *Lectura*. Although these " soundings " into Mirecourt are far too few to permit an integrated description of his thought, they do, when taken together, begin to suggest a different personality.

The first work in this group is Werner Dettloff's *Die Entwicklung der Akzeptations- und Verdienstlehre von Duns Scotus bis Luther*, in which along with other theologians he treats John of Mirecourt [157]. Dettloff starts from the premise that Mirecourt was an extreme nominalist. As with most fourteenth-century authors he treats, Dettloff takes the conclusions of Mirecourt as a direct and clear expression of his thought — a questionable and risky procedure, as we have seen, if the full discussion is not read. Even so, the thought which these conclusions express does not appear radical at all. Many conclusions parallel the thought of Gregory of Rimini. Mirecourt believes that the Holy Spirit and the habit of grace are mutually dependent and always given together. Like so many of his contemporaries, Mirecourt rejects Peter Aureol's view on the absolute necessity of the *acceptatio caritatis*. Standing within the tradition of Scotus and Ockham, Mirecourt maintains that *de potentia absoluta* one may love God or be accepted by God without the habit of grace. However, within the order that God has established and which he will maintain, no one can be accepted by God without the habit of grace. In his evaluation of human nature apart from grace Mirecourt stands within the Franciscan tradition and is not so pessimistic as the Augustinian Gregory. Mirecourt's understanding of the relationship of grace and merit lies fully within the Scotistic tradition. Moreover, he rejects *meritum de condigno* which played such an important part in the semi-Pelagian soteriology of the nominalists. In conclusion Dettloff remarks that he found no extreme, negative *potentia Dei absoluta* speculation in Mirecourt and that he did not appear to be a radical thinker [158]. Rather than question the common assumptions about Mirecourt, however, Dettloff suggests that the extremism must lie in some other area, probably moral theology.

---

157. (*Beiträge zur Geschichte der Philosophie und Theologie des Mittelalters* 40.2), Münster i.W. 1963, pp. 325-328. Dettloff based his study on two manuscripts of the original, long edition, *Vat. Pal. lat. 340* and *Naples, Bibl. Naz. VII C 28*, and one manuscript of the shorter redaction, *Paris, Bibl. Nat. lat. 14570*. Interestingly, he found no difference between the two redactions in the sections he examined that would reflect two separate versions, and that judgment is borne out in the sections I have examined

158. *Ibid.*, 328 : " Hevorheben möchten wir lediglich, dass wir innerhalb der von uns untersuchten Quaestionen auf keine extrem negative *potentia-dei-absoluta*-Spekulation gestossen sind und auch sonst Johannes von Mirecourt eigentlich nicht als auffallend extremen Denker kennen gelernt haben. "

A doctoral dissertation at the University of Wisconsin by Roy Van Neste has examined the epistemology of Mirecourt on the basis of the manuscripts and thus gives us an insight into another area of Mirecourt's thought [159]. In epistemology Mirecourt seems to have no connection with Autrecourt ; instead he follows the basic outlines of the Ockhamist epistemology, as did most thinkers of his generation, including Rimini. But here again Mirecourt shows himself to be more conservative than many of his respected contemporaries. Mirecourt rejected intuitive cognition of a non-existent, thus departing from the Ockhamist position, which Mirecourt says is in the majority [160]. Here, as in the sections we have examined earlier, Mirecourt seems to be limiting rather than expanding divine omnipotence and *potentia absoluta* argumentation.

Another sampling of Mirecourt's thought was made by myself on the problem of sacramental causality, the full results of which will be appearing separately [161]. To state the conclusions of that study briefly, Mirecourt affirmed dispositive causality, a position Thomas Aquinas took in his *Sentences* Commentary and one that was maintained in the fourteenth century almost exclusively by the Thomists [162]. Mirecourt did not adopt any form of covenantal causality, which was one of the most distinguishing trade-marks of the Ockhamist tradition [163].

The view of Mirecourt that emerges from these recent studies runs contrary to the " established " version found in the textbooks. Mirecourt, who uses the distinction between *potentia absoluta* and *potentia ordinata* with precision, who presupposes the validity of the causal principle, who limits rather than expands the possibilities of divine intervention, and who had a strong regard for evidence, had little in common with Autrecourt. In general he stands closer to Ockham, but Mirecourt is more conservative or traditional than Ockham on a series of important points touched on above. Nor can one agree with

---

159. Roy VAN NESTE, *The Epistemology of John of Mirecourt in Relation to Fourteenth Century Thought* (Dissertation, University of Wisconsin, 1972).

160. *Lectura*, I, q. 2. See A. FRANZINELLI, *Questioni inedite di Giovanni di Mirecourt sulla conoscenza*, in *Rivista critica di storia della filosofia* 13 (1958) 329-330.

161. The section in Mirecourt is the first question of book four.

162. For the early development of this tradition see : W. J. COURTENAY, *The King and the Leaden Coin : The Economic Background of ' Sine Qua Non ' Causality*, in *Traditio* 28 (1972) 185-209.

163. On the significance of covenantal causality for the Ockhamist tradition, in addition to the article cited in the previous footnote, see : W. J. COURTENAY, *Covenant and Causality in Pierre d'Ailly*, in *Speculum* 46 (1971) 94-119 ; *The Critique on Natural Causality in the Mutakallimun and Nominalism*, in *Harvard Theological Review* 66 (1973) 77-94.

Trapp, that Mirecourt has abandoned the Bible and the Fathers. In the sections I have examined, where such authorities could be introduced, I have found extensive biblical and patristic citations, especially from St. Augustine who was favored by Mirecourt on a number of points [164].

Although certain aspects of the older view of Mirecourt must now be rejected, it is too early to integrate the new information into a consistent and reliable picture. The major area that must be examined is the area with which most of the suspect and condemned propositions were concerned, namely the interrelation of divine and human will. On the basis of what has already turned up by looking into the *Lectura* of Mirecourt, the results of further investigation should be equally surprising and rewarding.

' POTENTIA ABSOLUTA ' AND THE CONDEMNATIONS OF 1347

In the traditional view, the Parisian condemnations of Autrecourt and Mirecourt in 1347 are seen as the counterpart to those at Paris and Oxford in 1277, and both were turning points in the history of medieval thought. If the Parisian articles of 1277 rejected the Averroistic limitations on divine omnipotence and freedom, reasserted the contingency of the world, and opened the way for more speculations on the possibilities that were open to God, the articles of 1347 were an attempt to curb the more extreme results of *potentia absoluta* speculation, which had far exceeded proper bounds. 1347 thus closed a chapter in intellectual history that began in 1277.

Michalski and Trapp have contributed the most to our present understanding of the condemnation of Mirecourt. According to Michalski the condemnations attacked a *type* of speculation that was considered dangerous, and it was not so much particular propositions that were being condemned but an intellectual tendency or approach that had become increasingly prevalent within the schools, particularly Paris and Oxford, in the first half of the fourteenth century [165]. That tendency, generally described as skepticism in regard to the basic tenets of metaphysics and natural theology (as these had been established in the thirteenth century) and as extremism in regard to the unbridled use of *potentia absoluta* speculation, was finally checked in 1347. The condemned propositions were in the area of theodicy and moral theology, particularly the relation of the divine and human

---

164. COPLESTON also points to Augustinian precedents for the thought of Mirecourt ; *History of Philosophy*, III, 129.

165. This view is best represented in one of MICHALSKI's last articles, *La volonté...*

wills, and the theological determinism of Bradwardine and the psychological determinism of Holcot were among the issues proscribed.

Trapp, as we have seen, accepted and expanded upon the views of Michalski. In Trapp's version the extremists, modernists, or nominalists of 1347 belonged to the logico-critical branch of fourteenth-century thought and used *subtilitas* and extreme *potentia absoluta* speculation to undermine the teaching of the Church [166]. Scripture and the Fathers were being neglected in favor of speculation on all possible types of divine intervention. The radicals of 1347, especially Mirecourt, were rejecting most of the kinds of *evidentia* that had been generally accepted and were replacing that with fideism.

The first issue that needs to be answered in regard to the condemnations of 1347 is how many separate condemnations were there, and what is the relationship among them ? We know that there were at least two, and there may possibly have been more. We possess the *cedulae* containing the propositions of Autrecourt that were condemned at Avignon in 1346 and retracted at Paris in 1347. Through the second apology of Mirecourt we know those of his propositions that were finally condemned in 1347. We also know several " Parisian " articles that do not appear in any of the earlier lists but which are referred to as early as 1364 [167].

Hugolino of Orvieto, at the time of the founding of the theological faculty at the University of Bologna in 1364, was familiar with three lists of prohibited articles contained in the acts of the Parisian faculty of theology [168]. Stegmüller conjectured that the first list was probably the articles taken from the writings of Autrecourt, but I am inclined to think that Hugolino was referring to the articles of 1277 [169]. Hugolino, who helped draw up the statutes of the theological faculty at Bologna and who appended a list of prohibited articles " lest they corrupt our University of Bologna ", did not attach the first list of condemned theses because they were well known, a statement that would more accurately describe the articles of 1277 than those of Autrecourt [170]. Before 1347, references to the " Parisian articles ',

---

166. TRAPP's view is best reflected in *Augustinian Theology...*
167. See Hugolino of Orvieto's list, reproduced by DENIFLE, *CUP* II, 610-613.
168. F. EHRLE, *I più antichi statuti della Facoltà teologica dell' Università di Bologna*, Bologna 1932, pp. 60-73.
169. STEGMÜLLER, 45 : " Die erste Verurteilung, die nach Hugolin Sätze betraf deren Gefährlichkeit leichter offen zutage trat, ist vielleicht die Verurteilung von Nicolaus von Autrecourt. "
170. EHRLE, *I più antichi...*, 68 : " Verum quia posteriores articuli secunda et tertia vice... sunt magis latentes, ego fr. Ugolinus de Urbe Veteri... ipsos articulos utique noxios, ne nostram Bononiae universitatem inficiant, hic inferius annotavi. "

invariably meant those of 1277 [171]. After 1347, although there are many references to " new " or " subsequent " Parisian articles, I know of only two references to the condemned propositions of Autrecourt [172]. Inasmuch as Autrecourt was condemned by a papal commission at Avignon, not the Parisian faculty of theology, his propositions may not have been included within the Parisian statutes. By contrast, we are certain of the content and arrangement of the second Parisian list, which Hugolino reproduced in its entirety in the Bolognese statutes, although in a rearranged sequence. Originally this list contained 41 propositions, but sometime between 1348 and 1364 the wording of certain propositions was altered or lengthened, and the list was reduced to 40 prohibited articles either by combining articles 16 and 17 or, more likely, by dropping article 23 [173]. Conrad of Ebrach, a student of Hugolino and one of the first bachelors of theology at Bologna (1368-69), was familiar with Hugolino's topical rearrangement of the prohibited articles, but his references to Mirecourt's articles coincide with the numbering of the second Parisian list in its post-1348 form [174]. We probably know only a portion of the articles contained in the third Parisian list, drawn up some time between 1348 and 1364. From this list Hugolino drew twelve propositions [175]. From other sources we know of additional condemned articles probably contained in this third list [176].

---

171. As, for example, in GREGORY OF RIMINI, *Sent.* I, dist. 42-44, q. 1, a. 2 (I, 162 D).

172. *Paris, Bibl. Nat. lat. 16409,* fol. 132ᵛ ; PIERRE D'AILLY, *Conceptus et insolubilia* (Paris, s.a., fol. 15ᵛ).

173. This change had to have taken place after 1348, because Hugolino, commenting on the *Sentences* in that year, refers to the condemned articles in their original order ; e.g., *Sent.* I, dist. 1, q. 5 *(Paris, Bibl. Nat. lat. 15840,* fol. 37ᵛᵃ). In Hugolino's 1364 list the number of Mirecourt propositions is reduced to 38 by combining numbers 16 and 17, 31 and 34, and by dropping number 23. Conrad of Ebrach *(Krakow, Bibl. Jag. 1249),* who quotes the condemned propositions of Mirecourt according to the numbering of the second Parisian list, refers to proposition 30 as 29, thus revealing that the reduction of articles from 41 to 40 has taken place before article 29.

174. CONRAD OF EBRACH, *Sent.* I, dist. 40-41, q. 1 *(Krakow 1249,* fol. 55ʳᵃ) ; *Sent.* II, dist. 1, q. 1 (fol. 68ʳᵃ-68ʳᵇ) ; *Sent.* II, dist. 28-29, q. 1 (fol. 93ᵛᵇ) ; *Sent.* II, dist. 34, q. 3 (fol. 114ʳᵃ).

175. Nos. 4, 6, 7, 8, 30, 32, 39, 40, 41, 42, 44, and 49 in Denifle's list; *CUP* II, 610-613.

176. E.g., ANDREW OF NEUFCHÂTEAU, O.F.M., *In libros sententiarum,* L. I, dist. 45, q. 6 (Paris, s.a., fol. 216ʳ) : " Item in posterioribus articulis Parisiensibus sic dicitur : ' quod Deus potest facere omnem rem praeteritam non fuisse ut quod potest facere Magdalenam non peccasse. Error ! ' " Andrew, who supports the articles of Paris, seems to have had Averroistic leanings and advocated a

172

It is my conjecture that the phrase *posteriores articuli*, used by Hugolino to designate the second and third lists in contrast to the first, was also a phrase commonly used to distinguish the articles condemned in 1347 and shortly thereafter from those of 1277 [177]. By 1368 the articles of 1277 were referred to as the *articuli antiqui*, or *inter antiquos* [178]. The second Parisian list was referred to as the *articuli novelli, articuli dici novelli, articuli in ordine novellorum, inter novos,* or *inter novellos Parisius condempnatos*, and they were cited according to the order of the second Parisian list, even by those at Bologna [179]. The articles that Hugolino included within the Bolognese statutes that were not taken from the second Parisian list were referred to as the *articuli Bononiensis,* or *inter novos Bononienses* [180].

There does not seem to have been any attempt in the fourteenth century to combine or even associate the condemned articles of Autrecourt with those of Mirecourt. Given the differences between Autrecourt and Mirecourt noted above, it might be wise to consider these condemnations separately until we have some hard evidence that would bind them together. If we restrict our evaluation of the condemnations of 1347 to the articles of Mirecourt and, in particular, the one issue from the condemned articles that we have traced back through the apologies to the *Lectura*, we are able to gain some insight into the mentality and viewpoint of the commission that examined Mirecourt's work.

We know first of all that the inquisitors supported the view that the proposition " God can make the world or some past thing never to have been " was evidently false or, at the very least, " ill-sounding ". To that degree they favored the position of Buckingham and Vargas and rejected the position of Bradwardine and Rimini. But, given the similarity between the first condemned proposition and the wording of a similar proposition in Buckingham, it is unlikely that he was

---

determinism in regard to the past that limited divine action before events took place ; cf. fol. 215ᵛ-216ᵛ.

· 177. The phrase is used by Hugolino and Andrew of Neufchâteau.

178. CONRAD OF EBRACH, *Sent.* II, dist. 1, q. 1 (fol. 68ᵛᵃ) ; *Sent.* II, dist. 6, q. 1 (*Bordeaux, Bibl. mun. 159*, fol. 77ᵛᵇ) ; *Sent.* II, dist. 16-18, q.1 (*Bordeaux,* fol. 85ᵛᵇ).

179. This designation occurs as early as 1348 ; cf. HUGOLINO OF ORVIETO, *Sent.* I, dist. 38, q. 4 (*Paris, Bibl. Nat. lat. 15840*, fol. 77ʳ) : '' Patet per articulos condempnatos, primum, secundum, et duodecimum de novellis... '' CONRAD OF EBRACH, *Sent.* I, dist. 40-41, q. 1 (*Krakow 1249*, fol. 55ʳᵃ) ; *Sent.* II, dist. 1, q. 1 (fol. 68ʳᵇ) ; *Sent.* II, dist. 28-29, q. 1 (fol. 93ᵛᵇ) ; and *Sent.* II, dist. 34, q. 3 (fol. 114ʳᵃ).

180. CONRAD OF EBRACH, *Sent.* II, dist. 1, q. 1 (*Krakow 1249*, fol. 68ʳᵇ); *Sent.* II, dist. 34, q. 3 (fol. 114ʳᵃ).

among the inquisitors or that they particularly favored his stand in the controversy with Bradwardine.

The comments Peter Ceffons makes about the commission that examined Mirecourt, although undoubtedly biased, do not seem so extreme when compared with the results of our investigation into Mirecourt's texts. Ceffons claimed that propositions were pulled out of context without regard to original meaning [181]. The examining theologians were neither intelligent nor well-trained, and they did not know how to read or write a *quaestio* [182]. They believed that more theological doctrines were evidently demonstrable than did Mirecourt. They viewed *subtilitas* as the principal evil and demanded instead a return to the Fathers and the Bible [183]. D'Ailly's famous remark has a similar flavor, namely that many things were condemned by reason of ill-will which, nevertheless, were afterwards taught [184].

On the basis of what has been examined to date, the central issue of 1347 was not extreme speculation, *de potentia Dei absoluta*. If anything, Mirecourt limited the power of God more than was customary for the fourteenth century. If the commission was attacking an overuse of *potentia absoluta* argumentation, they had the wrong man in Mirecourt, and he said so in no uncertain terms. Nor does the issue seem to have been skepticism or fideism, neither of which can be found in the sections of Mirecourt that I or others have examined. If we assume that the examining commission knew what they were about (which has yet to be established), then we must seek a solution elsewhere.

It is more likely that Mirecourt was being attacked not for *potentia absoluta* speculation, not for skepticism or fideism, but for his use of *aporia* and *subtilitas*, the later understood as careful argumentation and refined distinctions [185]. The commission that investigated Mirecourt, possibly made up of conservative, older theologians, perhaps predominantly seculars, who may have been in a numerical majority in the theological faculty but whose reputations did not survive as

---

181. TRAPP, *Augustinian Theology...*, 224.

182. TRAPP, *Peter Ceffons...*, 148, 152. Trapp admits that this charge makes it difficult to see Gregory as the promoter of the condemnation of Mirecourt.

183. TRAPP, *Augustinian Theology...*, 187.

184. PIERRE D'AILLY, *Conceptus et insolubilia* (Paris, s.a., fol. 15ᵛ) : " Multa fuerunt condemnata contra eum [Nicholas of Autrecourt] causa invidiae, quae tamen postea in scholis publice sunt concessa. "

185. *Subtilitas* was a favorable description. Only in the mind of Mirecourt's accusers was it a pejorative term that was to be contrasted with reliance upon Scripture and the Fathers.

174

well as those they attacked [186], wanted to put an end to the heated debates over future contingents and the relation of human and divine will that had distinguished the writings of Bradwardine and Buckingham and were dominating the *Sentences* Commentaries of those who were reading in the 1340's. Mirecourt was singled out not as the chief offender but as a typical example. Unlike those theologians in the mendicant orders or those who came from England or Italy, the French Cistercian Mirecourt could be censured successfully without arousing retaliatory action from significant educational forces outside Paris. There was no backlash, but it is also true that Mirecourt was grossly misrepresented in order to fit the scheme.

If those responsible for the condemnation of Mirecourt were not representative of the most respected intellectual traditions of that day, then we need not and should not place as much importance on Mirecourt's condemnation as has been done. The same may be true of Autrecourt as well, although that condemnation seems to have had more ecclesiastical significance. We are far from having an adequate picture of the events of 1347, but that can be reconstructed only after more investigations have been made into the relationship between the suspect and condemned propositions of Mirecourt and the text of his *Lectura*.

Madison, University of Wisconsin.

---

186. Those theologians in the thirteenth and fourteenth centuries who distinguished themselves through their thought and writings were always in the minority. Although there were numerous chairs in theology for seculars at Paris in the period under discussion, few of them were significant enough to be remembered.

CORRIGENDA

Subsequent to the publication of "John of Mirecourt and Gregory of Rimini on Whether God Can Undo the Past," two discoveries were made that lead me to revise some points in my argument.

First, the statement on pages 147 and 150 that Thomas Bradwardine and Thomas. Buckingham debated at Paris, while almost a commonplace in the secondary literature, is without foundation in the documents of the period. For the truth of the matter and for the history of this mistaken notion see Zenon Kaluza, "La prétendue discussion parisienne de Thomas Bradwardine avec Thomas de Buckingham. Témoignage de Thomas de Cracovie," _Recherches de Théologie ancienne et médié-vale_, 43 (1976), 219-36.

Second, in the section beginning on page 154, I discussed the differences between the position adopted by Gregory of Rimini in what was then thought to be the original text of his _Sentences_ commentary and the position espoused in the later _additiones_. If the _additiones_ were written later, then Gregory moved from a neutral position to one that was being or recently had been condemned -- a rather daring and psychologically curious move that I found difficult to accept. The editors of the critical edition of Gregory's _Lectura super primum et secundum sententiarum_, vol. IV (Berlin: De Gruyter, 1974), xxxiv-xxxix, have opened the way to a more convincing solution. On the basis of careful textual analysis, it now appears that some of the _additiones_ represent earlier versions of the arguments presented in the main body of the text, not later revisions. It seems more likely to me, therefore, that the more extreme position that appears in the _additiones_ is the position Gregory initially held, before the investigation and condemnation of Mirecourt, and that he modified his position in light of subsequent events at Paris. The more probable order is that Gregory initially agreed with Bradwardine and later revised his argument so as to leave the question open.

COVENANT AND CAUSALITY IN PIERRE D'AILLY

FEW problems are as central to the philosophy and theology of the late Middle Ages as the problem of causality. The acceptance of a causal connection between certain phenomena, where the presence of one follows immediately and invariably upon the presence of another, lies at the heart of the mediaeval understanding of physics and metaphysics, salvation and sacrament. Whether the cause was considered external, according to the Aristotelian principle that *omne quod movetur ab alio movetur*, or was thought to be internal in the sense of self-motion, it was assumed that every movement from non-being to being, from potency to act, required a cause which could, with varying degrees of accuracy, be ascertained. Without such a causal connection it seemed impossible to talk about physical laws which regulated the universe upon which man depended, impossible to describe how man comes to know external reality, impossible to construct proofs for the existence of God, and impossible to teach that merit brings reward or that the sacraments produce grace. Both the economy of the natural universe and the economy of salvation depended for their normal explanation on the idea of cause and effect.

It is because of the fundamental importance of the principle of causality in mediaeval thought that fourteenth-century discussions of causality, which appeared to alter or abolish efficient causation, seemed so devastating and irresponsible to historians of mediaeval thought. Nominalism in general and William of Ockham and Nicholas of Autrecourt in particular have been credited with an attack on the principle of causality, similar to that later undertaken by Hume, which defined it as nothing more than habit-formed expectation. In spite of some notable scholarly opinion to the contrary, this evaluation has remained and is one of the major judgments according to which Nominalism is considered skeptical and fideistic.[1]

The history of the critique on causality in the fourteenth century is an enormous topic that has yet to be adequately investigated and is, in any case, far beyond the bounds of a single article.[2] The inquiry here will limit itself to one

[1] For a more balanced and scholarly view of Nominalism see: Ph. Boehner, *Collected Articles on Ockham*, ed. E. M. Buytaert (Franciscan Institute Publications: Philosophy Series, XII; St. Bonaventure, N.Y., 1958); E. A. Moody, "Ockham, Buridan and Nicholas of Autrecourt: The Parisian Statutes of 1339 and 1340," *Franciscan Studies*, VII (1947), 113–146; E. A. Moody, "Ockham and Aegidius of Rome," *Franciscan Studies*, IX (1949), 417–442; E. A. Moody, "Empiricism and Metaphysics in Medieval Philosophy," *Philosophical Review*, LXVII (1958), 145–163; E. Hochstetter, *Studien zur Metaphysik und Erkenntnislehre Wilhelms von Ockham*, (Berlin, 1927); E. Hochstetter, "Nominalismus?" *Franciscan Studies*, IX (1949), 370–403; H. A. Oberman, "Some Notes on the Theology of Nominalism with attention to its Relation to the Renaissance," *Harvard Theological Review*, LIII (1960), 47–76; H. A. Oberman, *The Harvest of Medieval Theology* (Cambridge, Mass., 1963).

[2] For a general treatment of causality and motion, especially in the natural order see: J. R. Weinberg, *Nicolaus of Autrecourt: A Study in 14th Century Thought* (Princeton, N.J., 1948); H. Shapiro,

aspect of that question, namely causality within the economy of salvation, and attempt to ascertain the operation and implications of such causality in the thought of a leading Nominalist thinker at the end of the fourteenth century.

Pierre d'Ailly has for many years been one of the focal points for the discussion of the Nominalist view of causality. In the older literature,[3] especially because of the presumed connection between d'Ailly and Luther, d'Ailly was used as a key example for the supposedly Nominalist teaching on double truth and the radical use of God's *potentia absoluta* to undermine causation in both the natural and spiritual orders. This judgment was based in part on a misunderstanding of the distinction between *potentia absoluta* and *potentia ordinata*[4] and in part on a failure, where the distinction was understood, to note carefully in which category the writer intended a particular statement to be read. D'Ailly was at times assessed as a forerunner of Luther, especially in the supposedly radical emphasis on God's omnipotence, which denied validity or significance to the normal channels of justification and sanctification, and in d'Ailly's preference, at least on the level of natural reason, for the theory that the substance of bread remained on the altar after consecration. At other times he was seen as a thoroughgoing skeptic in the tradition of Autrecourt, thus helping to prepare the way for the radical critique of David Hume.

D'Ailly has received somewhat better treatment in the last generation, although we still lack an over-all analysis and evaluation of his thought based on the revised view of Ockham and Nominalism.[5] Recent areas of inquiry have been

---

Motion, Time and Place According to William Ockham (Franciscan Institute Publications: Philosophy Series, xiii; St. Bonaventure, N.Y., 1957); R. R. Effler, *John Duns Scotus and the Principle: "Omne Quod Movetur Ab Alio Movetur"* (Franciscan Institute Publications: Philosophy Series, xv; St. Bonaventure, N.Y., 1962).

[3] Most of the older literature labors under misconceptions that have been clarified in the last few decades in a way that has met with acceptance by most scholars working in this area. For the older view of Nominalism as reflected in d'Ailly see: P. Tschackert, *Peter von Ailly* (Gotha, 1877); H. Denifle, *Luther und Luthertum* (Mainz, 1904), ii, 501, 571, 589; G. M. Manser, "Drei Zweifler auf dem Kausalitätsprinzip im XIV Jahrhundert," *Jahrbuch für Philosophie und spekulative Theologie*, xxvii (1912), 291–305; E. Gilson, "La doctrine de la double vérité," *Etudes de philosophie médiévale* (Strasbourg, 1921); F. Ehrle, *Der Sentenzenkommentar Peters von Candia, des Pisaner Papstes Alexanders V* (Franziskanische Studien, ix; Münster i.W., 1925).

[4] The distinction (used by many theologians outside Nominalism) means that according to absolute power God, inasmuch as he is omnipotent, retains the *ability* to do many things which he does not *will* to do, has never done, nor ever will do. One should ascribe to God the capacity to do anything that does not involve a contradiction, but such a recognition of the magnitude of divine power never implies that God would or in any practical sense could act in a way contrary to his revealed nature and will. What God wills to do is equivalent with what he has ordained (whether revealed yet or not), and events and circumstances can never be such that God would act otherwise. Even miracles are not incursions of God's absolute power, since, although they suspend the ordained laws of nature and seem to be contradictions from the human point of view, they were foreseen and foreordained by God. They are reminders to man of the contingency of the natural order and the benevolence of God, and they do not, for the Nominalists, inspire distrust in the orderliness of God's universe nor in the reasonableness of divine action.

[5] A more critical and balanced presentation of d'Ailly's thought begins with the article of M. Patronnier de Gandillac, "De l'usage et de la valeur des arguments probables dans les questions du

d'Ailly's political thought[6] and his understanding of the dialectic of the two powers. Francis Oakley[7] has attacked George Lindbeck's[8] interpretation of Nominalism, rightly spurning the dichotomy between d'Ailly's Nominalist philosophy and his moral theology but incorrectly claiming the support of Heiko Oberman[9] and others[10] for his thesis that Nominalism is principally and almost exclusively a "theology of divine omnipotence."

When one approaches these questions from the standpoint of causality, it becomes apparent that the "principal thesis" of Nominalism in general and d'Ailly in particular is neither the omnipotence of God nor his ordained power but the combination or dialectic of the two powers. Far deeper and more basic to Nominalist thought is the concept of covenant, which in turn gives rise to the dialectic of ordained and absolute power. The idea of covenant can perhaps be most clearly seen in the discussion of causality, already touched on in part by

---

cardinal Pierre d'Ailly sur le *Livre des Sentences,*" *Archives d'historie doctrinale et littéraire du moyen âge,* VIII (1933), 43–91. This article is still the best survey, in spite of its anachronistic attempt to read d'Ailly through Cartesian categories. For a more recent evaluation of d'Ailly, little affected by changes in Nominalist scholarship, see: B. Meller, *Studien zur Erkenntnislehre des Peter von Ailly* (Freiburger Theologische Studien, LXVII; Freiburg i.B., 1954). Another recent — and almost the briefest — treatment of d'Ailly is given by W. Dettloff, *Die Entwicklung der Akzeptations- und Verdienstlehre von Duns Scotus bis Luther* (Beiträge zur Geschichte der Philosophie und Theologie des Mittelalters, XL, 2; Münster i.W., 1963), 332–334.

[6] Francis Oakley, *The Political Thought of Pierre d'Ailly: The Voluntarist Tradition* (Yale Historical Publications: Miscellany, LXXXI; New Haven, 1964).

[7] F. Oakley, "Pierre d'Ailly and the Absolute Power of God: Another Note on the Theology of Nominalism," *Harvard Theological Review,* LVI (1963), 59–73.

[8] G. Lindbeck, "Nominalism and the Problem of Meaning as Illustrated by Pierre d'Ailly on Predestination and Justification," *Harvard Theological Review,* LII (1959), 43–60.

[9] Oberman, *Harvard Theological Review,* LIII, 47–76. Oberman's concentration on the *potentia absoluta* in this article, although never as strong as Oakley indicates, is clarified and balanced in relation to the *potentia ordinata* in his later treatment, *Harvest of Medieval Theology,* pp. 30–47.

[10] While it is true that Léon Baudry and Paul Vignaux have tended to place the greatest importance on the *potentia absoluta,* the position of Philotheus Boehner is far more balanced than Oakley would suggest. It is misleading to suggest, as does Oakley, that recent historians of Nominalism can be divided into two groups on the basis of the relation of the movement to the condemnations of 1277, the understanding of God's *potentia absoluta,* and the relative importance of philosophy and theology for the Nominalists. The major difference between groups of historians on this subject regrettably remains the degree to which Nominalism is considered a positive movement, strongly theological, continuing certain constructive and orthodox tendencies of the thirteenth century. It is indeed surprising to find Oakley placing within the category of an enlightened approach to Nominalism such names as Gilson and Lagarde, while at the same time excluding E. A. Moody, who supposedly holds "a very different approach" from Boehner and Oberman, similar to that of Lindbeck. The problem is perhaps that Oakley, at least before 1964, was only partially aware of the nature of the revision in Nominalist studies. It is certainly to confuse fourteenth-century Nominalism with twelfth-century Nominalism to suggest that the former group rejected the universal completely and maintained that "the world is a collection of singular existents 'isolated in the absoluteness of their existence'," Oakley, *Political Thought,* p. 21. This was convincingly rejected by Boehner, 161–163 and Damasus Trapp, "Augustinian Theology of the 14th Century," *Augustiniana,* VI (1956), 147–148. Moreover, Boehner, Trapp, and Oberman would certainly not place such exclusive emphasis on volitionalism (or, as Oakley would say, voluntarism) in Nominalism. Oakley himself admits that for the Nominalists there is no distinction, not even formal, between God's intellect and will. God always acts wisely.

most of those who have written on d'Ailly, including Lindbeck and Oakley. It is hoped that certain aspects of the problem of causality, especially the relation between *sine qua non* causation and occasionalism, between sacramental causation and the teaching on merit and grace, will become clearer. If, as is generally maintained, d'Ailly stands as a major figure among the faithful disciples of Ockham,[11] then an examination of d'Ailly's thought on these questions should indicate not only d'Ailly's position in late mediaeval thought vis-à-vis Ockham and Autrecourt, but should also shed some light on the Nominalist understanding of causality.

I. CAUSALITY

It is necessary at the beginning to distinguish clearly between natural causality in the physical universe and what might be called theological causality. Natural causality was operative in the created universe and could be studied under the disciplines of physics and metaphysics. Theological causality refers to the rules of cause and effect that were felt to apply in the economy of salvation within the Christian Church on the basis of the new covenant or testament and was used to explain the operation of redemption, justification and sanctification. One might, for purposes of a more balanced contrast, call this second type "supernatural" causality, except that this term would be misleading for the Nominalists, who felt that theological causality worked according to a revealed law that could be relied upon, and therefore did not represent supernatural action in the sense of a miracle.[12]

Theological causality concerned several areas of mediaeval theology. It explained the way in which Christ's death on the cross effected redemption; the way in which the words of consecration in the eucharist effected the presence of the body of Christ; the way in which the sacraments were the cause of grace; the way in which good actions merited grace; and, the way in which good actions done in a state of grace merited eternal life. In short, the major issues defining the process of salvation were frequently discussed within the problem of causation, as indeed the problem of causation, even for the natural order, was often discussed within the problem of salvation. Moreover, the continuing mediaeval argument between the Augustinian and Pelagian extremes as to what role man played in his salvation often took the form of a discussion on causality, so that under the rubric of causation a fundamental theological orientation might be revealed.

Although theologians of the thirteenth and fourteenth centuries, especially those of the Franciscan tradition, frequently related these different areas of theological causality by explaining their operation in the same way, the most extensive discussion of causality in the economy of salvation occurred within the

---

[11] That d'Ailly shared the Ockhamistic approach has never been doubted, although we lack a study that compares the positions of the two men on a wide variety of philosophical and theological topics. In future articles I intend to examine other areas of d'Ailly's thought that relate to the question of his Ockhamism.

[12] Oakley sometimes terms this type of causality "supernatural." Cf. *Political Thought*, p. 28.

98   *Covenant and Causality in Pierre d'Ailly*

question of sacramental causality. While all affirmed some causal connection between the sacraments and grace — this much was clearly the doctrine of the Church as it was clarified during the Albigensian crisis — all were equally unwilling to confer on the sacraments as creatures the power to create grace *ex nihilo*. Thus various definitions or explanations of such causality were suggested. For example, Thomas Aquinas affirmed an instrumental, physical causality in which God, as prime cause, passed on to certain material agencies the power to effect grace and redemption. Such efficient causality was not physical in the strict sense of natural·causation, nor did it imply that the creature had the power to create *ex natura rei*. It did, however, affirm that the sacraments possessed a supernatural virtue given them by God that enabled them to effect grace in the recipient.[13]

A second, less direct type of causality, also associated with Thomas[14] but appearing in many forms in the late Middle Ages, was termed dispositive. According to dispositive causality there are two stages in the creation of grace. The creature directly, physically and immediately creates only a disposition which, in turn, requires the presence of grace. Dispositive causality, while having an interesting history in the fourteenth century among Thomists,

---

[13] Thomas Aquinas, *Summa theologica*, III, q. 62. The degree to which Thomas taught physical causality in the sacraments has been debated by scholars, especially in light of the change or development in Thomas' position or at least in his terminology between the *Commentary on the Sentences* and the *Summa*. Among those supporting the physical causality or perfective causality interpretation of Thomas are: Edouard Hugon, O.P., *La causalité instrumentale en théologie* (Paris, 1907); Gennaro Bucceroni, *Commentarius de sacramentorum causalitate* (Paris, 1884); B. Lavaud, "Saint Thomas et la causalité physique instrumentale de la sainte humanité et des sacrements," *Revue thomiste*, XXXII (1927), 292–316; B. Lavaud, "La thèse thomiste de la causalité physique de la sainte humanité et des sacrements se heurte-t-elle à d'insurmontables difficultés?" *Revue thomiste*, XXXII (1927), 405–422; A. Teixidor, "De causalitate sacramentorum," *Gregorianum*, VIII (1927), 76–100; H. D. Simonin and S. Meersseman, *De sacramentorum efficientia apud theologos ord. praed.*, I: *1229–1276* (Rome, 1936). Supporting the moral causality interpretation of the thought of Thomas are: H. Bouessé, "La causalité efficiente instrumentale de l'humanité du Christ et des sacrements chrétiens," *Revue thomiste*, XXXIX (1934), 370–393; M. Gierens, "Zur Lehre des hl. Thomas über die Kausalität der Sakramente," *Scholastik*, IX (1934), 321–345. Supporting the dispositive, intentional causality interpretation of the thought of Thomas made popular by Louis Billot are: Van Noort, *Tractatus de Sacramentis*, (4th ed., Hilversum, 1927), pp. 42–53; Bellevue, *La grâce sacramentelle* (Paris, 1900), pp. 66 ff.; Manzoni, *Compendium theologiae dogmaticae* (Turin, 1912), IV, n. 42; A. de Smet, *De sacramentis in genere*, (2nd ed., Bruges, 1925), pp. 13–62; P. Richard, "La causalité instrumentale: physique, morale, intentionnelle," *Revue néo-scholastique*, XVI (1909), 1–31; H. Merkelbach, "De sacramentis sub conditione: 'si es dispositus' non ministrandis," *Revue ecclésiastique de Liége*, V (1909–1910), 145–160; A. Van Hove, *La doctrine du miracle chez saint Thomas* (Wetteren, 1927), pp. 148–159.

[14] Thomas Aquinas, *Commentum in quatuor libros sententiarum*, IV, d. 1, q. 1, a. 4. On the development in Thomas from dispositive to physical causality see: T. M. Pègues, "De la causalité des sacrements d'apres le R. P. Billot," *Revue thomiste*, XI (1903), 689–708; T. M. Pègues, "Si les sacrements sont causes perfectives de la grace?" *Revue thomiste*, XII (1904), 339–356; E. Neveu, "De causalitate sacramentorum iuxta D. Thomam et quemdam recentem theologum," *Divus Thomas* (Piacenza), V (1904), 9–36; A. Unterleidner, "La causalité des sacrements," *Revue augustinienne*, VI (1905), 353–368, 465–488; A. Unterleidner, "L'effet immédiat des sacrements," *Revue augustinienne*, XII (1908), 186–194; A. Unterleidner, "La causalité des sacrements," *Revue augustinienne*, XVI (1910), 409–440; XVII (1910), 25–57; A. Michel, "Sacrements," *Dictionnaire de théologie catholique*. XIV (1939), 584–586.

Scotists, and Cistercians, does not concern us here, since it figures neither in d'Ailly nor in Nominalist teaching. A third type of causality within the economy of salvation has been termed juridical[15] or volitional[16] but might better be called covenantal. According to this interpretation, one thing does not instrumentally and physically cause another on the basis of its own nature but only on the basis of an agreement which is more or less legally binding. To give a modern illustration, the buying power or negotiability of paper currency does not depend on the inherent value of the paper but rather on the value ascribed to it by the issuing agency and accepted by those who use it, whether that value is based on the gold standard or the economic stability of the country.[17] The typical mediaeval example of this type of causality is similar. In its usual form, a king declares himself willing to pay on demand a large sum of money to whomever has in his possession a lead coin. The lead coin does not "cause" the reward on the basis of its own nature but only because the king ascribes such value to it.[18] While the name juridical has often been applied to this type of causality, that term places too much emphasis upon the legally binding nature of the agreement. The mediaeval example points more to the decision of the king who has the power and freedom to make such agreements. It is nowhere stated that the king could not go back on his word. It is only assumed that the king does not act in such an arbitrary way. Most of the other mediaeval illustrations of this type of causality are biblical, explaining it by reference to God's relationship with his "chosen people" of the Old and New Testaments. Therefore, the term "covenant" better describes this causal relationship, not only because it places this type of causality in a religious and biblical context, but because it stresses the partners of the agreement, namely the king and his subjects or God and man, rather than the legal enforcement of the agreement. It was this type of theological causality that was primary for the Franciscan tradition in general and Nominalist theology in particular.

This third type of causality, based as it is on the will of the king or God and operative according to a pact or covenant, has frequently been described, mis-

---

[15] Cf. R. M. Huber, "The Doctrine of Ven. John Duns Scotus concerning the causality of the sacraments," *Franciscan Studies*, IV (1926), 9–10.

[16] This term might be appropriate for d'Ailly inasmuch as he repeatedly describes this type of causality as dependent on the will of God, and it is in this sense that Oakley probably means the term "voluntaristic." This last term, however, is somewhat misleading in that it implies the concept of voluntary association or Tönnies' *Gesellschaft*, a concept quite foreign to Nominalism in which the voluntary aspect is entirely on the side of God.

[17] A similar example is given by Huber, 9.

[18] Ockham, *Sent.* IV, q. 1 C: " . . . sicut si rex ordinaret quod quicumque acciperet denarium plumbeum haberet certum donum, et tunc denarius plumbeus esset causa sine qua non respectu illius doni, et sic esset in proposito de sacramento respectu gratiae. . . . " Cf. also Gabriel Biel, *Collectorium* IV, d. 1, q. 1. The development of the analogy of the king and the leaden coin and its significance for mediaeval thought has been explored by me in an article that will appear in the 1972 issue of *Traditio* under the title: "The King and the Leaden Coin: The Economic Background of *Sine Qua Non* Causality."

leadingly, as moral causality.[19] This term, however, better describes a fourth type of causality, one which is based not on a *pactio divina* but rather on the moral nature of God. Illustrative of this type would be the way in which a beggar's pleading "causes" the alms he receives or the way in which man's cry for salvation "causes" the gift of grace. Such causality is not *ex pacto* but *ex misericordia Dei.* In such a definition, not only would the petition not cause the effect directly or instrumentally, but man would have no claim on God whatsoever, unless of course one considers God "morally bound" to relieve man's need. Contrary to much modern discussion of this type of causality, it seems far less effective than juridical or covenantal causality.

A fifth type of causality can best be described as occasional or accidental. Here there is no relationship between cause and effect except that one thing happens to be present at the time of the appearance of another. Cause and effect are not related physically, juridically, or morally, but only happen to coincide by chance. In modern discussions this type of causality is frequently described as *sine qua non* causality, in spite of the fact that this term seldom conveyed such a meaning in the thirteenth or fourteenth centuries.[20] The definition of *sine qua non* causation given by William of Ockham expressly rejects any overtones of accidental or occasional causality and makes *sine qua non* identical with juridical or covenantal causality.[21] Ockham's definition, in turn, became the only meaning of *sine qua non* causality for the Nominalists, although certain fourteenth-century figures rejected *sine qua non* causality by adopting Thomas' interpretation, which did not differentiate *sine qua non* from accidental causality.[22]

Occasional causality brings us face to face with one of the major innovations in Western thought in the fourteenth century: the critique of the principle of

[19] The term "moral causality" is generally applied in modern Catholic theology to the position of Melchior Cano (d. 1560) and others, who placed causality in the moral worth of the sacraments rather than in an infused virtue or a divine covenant. However, it has sometimes been used to describe "juridical" or "intentional" causality, so there is no uniformity on the usage. Compare, e.g., Michel, 614–617, and Huber, 9. For purposes of clarity the term "moral causality" has been restricted to causality *ex misericordia Dei*, in spite of other usage.

[20] The tendency to define *sine qua non* causality as occasionalism, a tendency almost universal in modern Catholic scholarship, is based primarily on Thomas Aquinas' fusion or confusion of these terms. Thomas classifies as *sine qua non* causality such diverse examples as the way in which the lead *denarius* effects the reward of the king and the way in which the whiteness of an architect or builder effects the constructed house. This last example was understood as accidental or occasional causality, while the former example, *sine qua non* proper, was understood as juridical or covenantal causality. For the fusion see: Thomas Aquinas, *Commentum in quatuor libros sententiarum*, L. IV, d. 1, q. 1, a. 4, qu. 1. For the distinction of these terms see: Bonaventura, *Sent.* IV, d. 1, p. 1, a. un, q. 4; Durand de St. Pourçain, *Sent.* IV, d. 1, q. 4, n. 26.

[21] Ockham, *Sent.* IV, q. 1, E: "Prima non, quia causa sine qua non aliquid plus dicit quam causa per accidens secundum eundem. Sed meritum non est nisi causa sine qua non respectu praemii et gratiae, quia nec est principalis nec instrumentalis, sicut etiam modo passio Christi est causa sine qua non respectu gratiae, et tamen neutrum est causa per accidens respectu gratiae. Praeterea causa per accidens est illa quae amota nihilominus ponitur effectus. Exemplum de albo quod est causa per accidens respectu actus aedificandi, sed amotis sacramentis non sequitur aliquid in anima, nec confertur gratia; igitur etc."

[22] E.g., Peter of Palude, *Sent.* IV, d. 1, q. 1.

causality by Nicholas of Autrecourt.[23] While the intention of Autrecourt's critique is not altogether certain,[24] its meaning and implications are clear. Beginning with the type of miraculous action in which no contradiction of nature is apparent to the beholder, such as the presence of the body of Christ under the accidents of bread and wine, Autrecourt asserted that one can never with absolute certainty infer from accidents the existence of a particular substance. Similarly, using the idea of covenantal causality as applied by the Franciscans in the theological order, Autrecourt argued that one can never be certain that a particular effect is the direct result of the secondary cause that precedes it or accompanies it. Since we can never know where God is acting through secondary causes and where he is acting directly (for even when "a" is present God may intervene to cause "b"), we cannot say with certainty that "a" causes "b." There is, therefore, no necessary connection between cause and effect but only the appearance of such based on repeated observation, and, consequently, the principle of causality cannot be established as necessary and true.

These conclusions were never made nor intended by Ockham or his followers. In fact, several Ockhamists contemporary with Autrecourt took an active part in his condemnation, and the latter's position was based on several un-Ockhamistic conceptions or procedures.[25] In the first place, Autrecourt seems to have thought that covenantal causality operated miraculously by the direct intervention of God rather than quasi-legally on the basis of the pact.[26] Secondly,

---

[23] For the primary sources on Autrecourt's critique on causality see the condemned propositions in *Chartularium universitatis Parisiensis*, ed. Denifle and Chatelain, II (Paris, 1891), 576–587, Nr. 1124, and the letters edited by J. Lappe, *Nicolaus von Autrecourt: Sein Leben, seine Philosophie, seine Schriften* (Beiträge zur Geschichte der Philosophie des Mittelalters, VII, 2; Münster i. W., 1908), pp. 2*–14*. For secondary literature see: Weinberg, pp. 31–77; Moody, *Franciscan Studies*, VII, 113–146. Among several contemporary references to Autrecourt's theory of causality one of the most interesting is a remark of John of Mirecourt (Bibliothèque nationale, Ms lat. 16408, fol. 83ʳ, and Ms lat. 16409, fol. 134ᵛ): " . . . quod nulla demonstratio seu inquisitio de effectibus quibuscumque, unde proveniunt vel causis naturalibus, quos vel quales effectus producunt vel producent, est aliquo modo evidens sive certa: hoc satis deducit Autricort et oppositum diceret esset divinae libertati contradicere."

[24] It has been suggested that Autrecourt's basic motivation was not radical but a conservative anti-Aristotelianism which hoped to support the validity of theological arguments by attacking the validity of philosophical arguments. Cf. J. R. O'Donnell, "The Philosophy of Nicholas of Autrecourt and his Appraisal of Aristotle," *Medieval Studies*, IV (1942), 97–125; Weinberg, pp. 8, 226–230.

[25] It would appear that the Ockhamists were among the key opponents of both Autrecourt and Mirecourt and were responsible for their condemnations. Cf. Moody, *Franciscan Studies*, VII, 113–146; D. Trapp, "Peter Ceffons of Clairvaux," *Recherches de Théologie ancienne et médiévale*, XXIV (1957), 101–154.

[26] *Chartularium universitatis Parisiensis*, II, 577: "Item, dixi epistola predicta quod nescimus evidenter, quod ali[a a Deo possint] esse causa alicujus effectus. — *Falsam et revocandam.* Item, dixi epistola predicta quod nescimus evidenter, quod aliqua causa causet efficienter que non sit Deus. — *Falsam et revocandam.* Item, dixi epistola predicta quod nescimus evidenter, quod aliqua causa efficiens naturalis sit vel esse possit. — *Falsam et revocandam.* Item, dixi epistola predicta quod nescimus evidenter, utrum aliquis effectus sit vel esse possit naturaliter productus. — *Falsam et revocandam.*" The understanding of *ex pacto* causation as direct divine intervention, suggested at one point by Bonaventura (*Sent.* IV, d. 1, p. 1, a. un, q. 4) found fuller treatment with Henry of Ghent (*Quodlibeta* IV, q.

102   *Covenant and Causality in Pierre d'Ailly*

Autrecourt denied or at least ignored the distinction between *potentia absoluta* and *potentia ordinata* by allowing the Ockhamistic affirmation of divine omnipotence — that God retains the capacity to act in ways other than those he has chosen — to become the skeptical and un-Ockhamistic suggestion that God might and perhaps does act in ways other than those revealed.[27] Thirdly, Autrecourt did not feel obliged to add that God would not alter the reality beneath appearances without doing so for a specific purpose that would inevitably be revealed to man. Finally, Autrecourt did not maintain a clear distinction between the theological and natural orders but assumed that what happened in the former might also be happening in the latter.[28]

All of these definitions of theological causality, save Autrecourt's, assume some causal relationship between religious acts and divine gifts; they are all based on what was conceived to be a valid law of cause and effect. It is clear that Ockham did not reject this law, although he sharply qualified the discussion of motion.[29] Did d'Ailly, however, coming after Autrecourt and sharing his thought as some scholars have suggested, reject or limit the law of causality in nature and the Church? Which of the various definitions of theological causality fits the thought of d'Ailly?

In the following sections we will treat the two major areas of theological causality as they occur in the *Sentence Commentary* of d'Ailly: in what way can man be said to merit grace and eternal life, and in what way can the sacraments be said to be the cause of grace.[30] Although the various types of causality mentioned above might apply to either the natural or theological orders, our concern is primarily with causality in the economy of salvation and only secondarily with causality in the natural order. Moreover, it will be necessary to keep firmly in mind the distinction between what God *theoretically* could do on the basis of his omnipotence, *de potentia absoluta*, and what he *in fact* does do and will do on the basis of his revealed will, *de potentia ordinata*.

II. MERIT AND GRACE

D'Ailly attempts to answer the question of the relation of merit to grace and eternal life in the second article of the ninth question of the first book of the

---

ult.). Such an understanding was rejected by Scotus (*Oxon.* IV, d. 1, q. 4–5) and Ockham (*Sent.* IV, q. 1).

[27] Lappe, p. 3*; Moody, *Franciscan Studies*, VII, 120–122.

[28] Cf. John Buridan's remark on Autrecourt's position, *In metaphysicam Aristotelis Quaestiones*, II, q. 1; Moody, *Franciscan Studies*, VII, 138–142.

[29] Ockham, *Philosophia Naturalis* (Rome, 1637), IV, 16; *Tractatus de Successivis*, ed. P. Boehner (Franciscan Institute Publications: Philosophy Series, I; St. Bonaventure, N.Y., 1944), p. 99; *Sent.* II, q. 12 O-P. Cf. E. Hochstetter, *Studien zur Metaphysik und Erkenntnislehre Wilhelms von Ockham* (Berlin and Leipzig, 1927).

[30] The type of causality operating in particular sacraments is discussed by d'Ailly within the question of general sacramental causality. D'Ailly does not treat the causal relation of Christ's death to our redemption. In fact, d'Ailly reduces the entire third book of the *Sentences* to one question on the relation of the two natures in Christ.

Sentences.[31] In this *quaestio*, which covers distinctions fourteen through eighteen of Lombard's *Sentences*, d'Ailly investigates the problems of the gift of uncreated grace and its relation to created grace (art. 1); the habit of grace and its relation to eternal reward (art. 2); and, the increase or decrease of grace (art. 3). It is in this second article that d'Ailly raises the problem of causality.

D'Ailly opens the question, according to his normal procedure, with some conclusions which he explains and defends in the remainder of the article. These conclusions are typically Nominalist and can be found in almost identical form in Ockham,[32] Gregory of Rimini,[33] and Gabriel Biel.[34] According to the first conclusion, no one is able to be a friend of God, *de lege ordinata*, who does not have in himself some infused quality which is charity or grace.[35] Secondly, someone is able to be a friend of God, *de potentia absoluta*, who does not have some infused quality which is charity or grace.[36] Thirdly, someone is able not to be a friend of God, *de potentia absoluta*, who has some infused quality which is charity or grace.[37] None of these conclusions can be proven by natural reason alone, apart from revelation.[38] Rather they rest on authority or on the nature of God's omnipotence.

In good Nominalist fashion, d'Ailly carefully defines the terms used in these conclusions. The infused habit of grace, a created grace given to man at baptism and augmented at various points in his life, was such an accepted term that it needed no definition. The same is true for the technical terms *de lege ordinata* (another version of *de potentia ordinata*) and *de potentia absoluta*. The term "friend of God" or related terms such as "dear to God" or "acceptable to God" refer specifically to the person either (a) elected to eternal life, *secundum voluntatem beneplaciti*, or (b) given grace, *secundum praesentem iustitiam*, in such a way that if he died immediately, he would receive eternal life.[39] The gift of grace

---

[31] *Quaestiones . . . super primum, tertium et quartum sententiarum* (Paris, n.d.), fols. 137ᵛ–143ʳ. All references to the *Sentence Commentary* of d'Ailly will be to this edition and will be abbreviated as: *Sent.* I, *Sent.* III, and *Sent.* IV.

[32] William of Ockham, *Sent.* I, d. 17, q. 1–3.

[33] Gregory of Rimini, *Sent.* I, d. 17, q. 1, a. 1–2.

[34] Gabriel Biel, *Sent.* I, d. 17; *Sent.* II, d. 27, q. 1.

[35] Pierre d'Ailly, *Sent.* I, q. 9, a. 2 (fol. 137ᵛF): "Nullus potest esse amicus Dei de lege ordinata non habendo in se aliquam qualitatem infusam quae sit charitas vel gratia."

[36] *Ibid.*: "Aliquis potest esse amicus Dei de potentia absoluta non habendo aliquam qualitatem infusam quae sit charitas vel gratia."

[37] *Ibid.*: "Aliquis potest esse non amicus Dei de potentia absoluta habendo aliquam qualitatem infusam quae sit charitas vel gratia."

[38] *Ibid.*

[39] *Ibid.*, fol. 138ᵛE: "Ad cuius probationem et declarationem ac etiam praecedentis conclusionis distinguendum est quod esse amicum Dei, sive Deo carum, aut acceptum ad vitam aeternam potest dupliciter intelligi. Uno modo idem est quod esse a Deo ordinatum ad vitam aeternam finaliter obtinendam, et sic quilibet electorum in quocumque statu sit gratiae vel culpae est Deo carus, et acceptus, et Dei amicus, et nullus reproborum, licet sit in statu gratiae est Dei amicus. Et isto modo non intelligitur prima conclusio, quia sic esset falsa, etc. Alio modo idem est quod esse in statu vel dispositione in qua si perseveraverit Deus dabit sibi vitam aeternam, et sic non quilibet electus est Deo gratus vel acceptus, nec Dei amicus, sicut ille qui est in statu culpae mortalis, et aliquis reprobus est Deo carus et Dei amicus, sicut ille qui est in statu gratiae etc. Simili modo Magister, tertio sententiarum, dist. 31, dicit

and election to eternal life are not identical or coterminous, even *de potentia
ordinata*. To take an example that d'Ailly might have used, but did not, Judas
was in a state of grace and was a "friend of God" until he betrayed Jesus; he
was never one of the elect. Paul, on the other hand, was an "enemy of God" while
he was persecuting the Church and became a "friend of God" only at his conversion and baptism. But even while an "enemy of God" Paul was elect. The
term "friend of God" can therefore refer to the elect alone or to those who are in a
state of grace at an earlier time in their life, regardless of their final destiny,
and it is in this last sense that d'Ailly uses the term in his conclusions.[40] D'Ailly
is willing to admit that to restrict the phrase "meriting eternal life" to the elect,
thus excluding the damned from any merit or grace, would make better verbal
sense, but such a usage would go against observed fact or would seem too harsh a
doctrine to many.[41] Used in this way, the term "friend of God" includes both
the *praedestinati* and the *reprobati* or *praesciti*. D'Ailly also intends the phrase
"habit of grace" to be taken according to present justice.[42]

With these qualifications in mind, the conclusions would be: *De potentia ordinata*, no one is acceptable for eternal life according to present justice, who does
not also possess the infused habit of grace at that same moment. Secondly, *de
potentia absoluta*, someone is able to be acceptable for eternal life, according to
present justice, who does not have the infused habit of grace at that same
moment. Thirdly, *de potentia absoluta*, someone is able not to be acceptable for
eternal life, according to present justice, who does have the infused habit of
grace at that same moment. These conclusions would be true for d'Ailly or any
Nominalist if both terms in each conclusion were read according to ultimate disposition rather than present justice.

While the first conclusion is supported by various quotations from the New
Testament and Augustine, the second and third conclusions are based on the
concept of God's omnipotence and on an analysis of the relation between the
habit of grace and God's acceptation. In the course of a long defense, punctuated
with objections, replies, propositions, and corollaries, d'Ailly supports his last
two conclusions with six interrelated arguments, most of them driving a wedge
between acceptation and infused habit.

---

quod aliquem esse scriptum in libro vitae potest intelligi dupliciter, scilicet secundum aeternam praescientiam vel secundum praesentem iustitiam, et multi sunt scripti primo modo et non secundo modo,
et econverso. Sic in proposito potest dici quod aliquem esse amicum Dei potest intelligi dupliciter, vel
secundum aeternam Dei dilectionem vel secundum praesentem dispositionem, et aliquis potest esse
amicus Dei primo modo et non secundo modo, et econverso."

[40] *Ibid.*: "In ista ergo quaestione intendo istis terminis 'carus,' 'gratus acceptus Deo,' 'amicus Dei,'
'dignus vita aeterna' et huiusmodi secundo modo uti et non primo modo."

[41] *Ibid.*, fol. 139ᵛG: "Aliqui tamen secundum aliam assignationem huius quod est mereri vitam aeternam aliquando dixerunt quod nullus reproborum meretur, vel umquam meruit vitam aeternam
quia si mereretur ipsam aliquando haberet ipsam, cum mereri dicatur respectu praemii. Et iste modus
dicendi videretur mihi valde probabilis, nisi quia non bene sonat in auribus multorum. Ideo melius est
dare assignationem per quam possit sustineri quod uterque, scilicet tam reprobus quam electus, aliquando meretur vitam aeternam, licet multum sit difficile hoc assignare de virtute sermonis. . . . "

[42] Otherwise the first conclusion would be false in any theological system, and the second and
third conculusions would not need to be *de potentia absoluta*.

D'Ailly's first argument plays on the distinction between created and un-created grace.[43] If, as he maintained in his first article, the Holy Spirit, or un-created grace, could be given, *de potentia absoluta*, to someone without the ac-companying gift of the habit of grace or created grace, then it implies no con-tradiction for God to accept someone without the habit of grace, since the gift of the Holy Spirit would alone suffice. D'Ailly returns time and time again to this distinction between the Holy Spirit and the infused habit, placing the greater importance on the former.

The second argument is based strictly on God's omnipotence and is the most common form of such an *absoluta* argument.[44] God could have, *de potentia absoluta*, created another system in which the habit of grace would not have been necessary, for the presently ordained system is not a necessary one but rather one chosen freely by God.

D'Ailly's third argument returns to the distinction between habit and grace or between grace and election.[45] Even *de potentia ordinata* grace and election

[43] D'Ailly, *Sent.* I, q. 9, a. 2, fol. 139ʳA: "Spiritus Sanctus potest dari alicui absolute loquendo sine charitate creata aut alio eius dono, sicut patet ex primo articulo. Sed ipse solus sine alio dono creato potest tantum dignificare creaturam respectu praemii beatifici aut alterius boni quantum ipse cum alio dono, quia alias ipsa charitas creata ex natura sua aliquam dignitatem respectu vitae aeternae tribueret ipsi creaturae, quam dignitatem nullo modo posset sibi Spiritus Sanctus per seipsum tribuere, quod est absurdum." *Ibid.*, fol. 141ᵛD: "Prima est quod possibile est transire de contradictorio ad contra-dictorium, sive contradictoria successive verificari, absque motu locali aut positione novae rei vel destructione praeexistentis cuius verificationis lapsus temporis non sit in causa, quamvis sine lapsu temporis actuali vel potentialiter contingere non possit, alias enim contradictoria simul essent vera. Patet quia possibile est quod aliquis, non habens Spiritum Sanctum illo modo speciali de quo dictum est in primo articulo, habeat postea Spiritum Sanctum eo non mutato localiter, nec aliqua alia re nova facta, vel aliqua destructa, ut patet ex dictis ibidem. Et constat quod mutatio non est in Spiritu Sancto, nec oportet quod sit in alio, nec lapsus temporis ad hoc facit, etc." *Ibid.*, fol. 141ᵛF: "Tertia propositio est quod esto quod sine mutatione in tali re non contingeret talia contradictoria verificari, adhuc non sequitur quod per mutationem acquisitam. Et iterum esto quod per acquisitionem, etiam non sequi-tur quod per acquisitionem charitatis aut gratiae, vel habitus alicuius supernaturalis." *Ibid.*, fol. 142ʳB: "Tertia propositio est quod licet non sit possibile quod ab aliquo tollatur carentia charitatis vel gratiae infusae absque hoc quod infundatur sibi talis iustitia, tamen possibile est quod ab eo tol-latur carentia charitatis vel gratiae debitae inesse absque hoc quod infundatur sibi charitas vel gratia. Patet si tollatur debitum habendi eam, etc."

[44] *Ibid.*, fol. 139ʳA: "Secundo probatur, quia esse carum Deo, vel gratum, vel amicum, vel vita aeterna dignum, secundo modo, nihil est aliud proprie loquendo quam esse in aliquo statu in quo si quis decederet haberet vitam aeternam secundum Dei ordinationem. Sed nullam contradictionem im-plicat quod Deus ordinaret eam dare alicui sine charitate aut alio dono creato, etc. Tertio sic, quia nullam contradictionem implicat quod Deus ordinaret talem quod quicumque decederet sine chari-tate vel gratia tali lege stante esset amicus Dei et dignus vita aeterna illo modo dicto supra. Consequen-tia est clara et antecedens patet, quia Dei voluntas sufficit acceptare aliquem ad vitam aeternam sine quocumque dono creato, et per consequens sola Dei voluntas acceptans sufficit facere aliquem sibi carum, gratum, et amicum, et vita aeterna dignum, seu dignificare ipsum." *Ibid.*, fol. 139ᵛE: "Quarto sequitur quod de potentia absoluta est possibile creaturam rationalem diligere Deum meritorie sine habitu infuso charitatis vel gratiae. Patet ex secunda conclusione et similiter quia actus dilectionis est meritorius ex divinae voluntatis acceptatione modo ipsa potest talem actum acceptare ita bene si non fiat in gratia sive in puris naturalibus, sicut si fiat in gratia, ut patet ex dictis, etc."

[45] *Ibid.*, fol. 139ʳB: "Tertia conclusio probatur, quia absolute possibile est Deum dare alicui chari-tatem et numquam velle dare illi beatitudinem, igitur, etc. Consequentia patet ex dictis et antecedens,

106   _Covenant and Causality in Pierre d'Ailly_

are not identical and coterminous. D'Ailly uses the example of Esau, whom it is reported God hated, although he must have been in a state of grace at the time of his circumcision. D'Ailly frequently observes that while the elect were always elect, they were not always in a state of grace. This is not only true for the classic figure of Paul, but for the life of any saint. Final acceptance, from the human point of view, is dependent on whether one dies in a state of grace. It is this obvious and common discrepancy between the sometime possession of grace and the eternal election to eternal life that provides d'Ailly with an historical example, _de potentia ordinata_, to show the possibility of a separation between grace and election, _de potentia absoluta_.

Moreover, God can and does give charity or the habit of grace to some that he knows will not persevere and receive eternal life. Therefore, the gifts of grace and election are separate in God, one not really depending on the other, at least not absolutely. There is the general love of God that allows some to be in a state of grace whom God knows will not persevere. Then, there is a special love of God that has elected some to eternal life, for whom the habit of grace and final acceptance will be coterminous at death. If this were not the case, Judas and Esau would never have been in a state of grace, which seems absurd.

---

licet posset multipliciter probari, tamen ex hoc patet quod illud nullo modo implicat contradictionem et per consequens est Deo possibile." _Ibid._: "Tertio, quia carenti charitate et gratia Deus non est debitor illius sed illam gratis donat, sed propter hoc quod Deus gratis donat aliquod munus non fit alterius muneris debitor. Ergo ei cui dedit charitatem vel gratiam potest non dare vitam aeternam. Et breviter istae duae conclusiones possent multipliciter probari, sed videntur mihi adeo clare quod non egent ampliori declaratione, etc." _Ibid._, fol. 140ʳA: "Prima est quod aliquis est dignus vita aeterna et meretur ipsam qui tamen numquam habebit eam. Patet de reprobo qui, licet quandoque mereatur, sit dignus vita aeterna, quia est in gratia, tamen numquam habebit vitam aeternam eo quod indignificabit se postea et non revertetur ad talem dignitatem, ideo damnabitur, etc." _Ibid._, fol. 141ʳB: "Tertio distinguendum est quod illo modo ultimo adhuc aliquis potest dici 'amicus Dei' dupliciter. Uno modo, quia Deus vult illum pro tunc habere aliquod magnum donum quod non est vita aeterna, sicut est charitas, vel gratia, vel originalis iustitia; sive velit quod semper permaneat in tali bono sive non, et hoc voluntate beneplaciti. Et hoc vocamus 'diligere secundum praesentem iustitiam,' et sic Deus diligit solum rationales creaturas quae sunt in gratia gratum faciente, sive sint electe sive reprobate. Alio modo, quia Deus vult illum non pro illo tunc tamen aliquando habere, vel habiturum esse illud speciale donum quod est vita aeterna. Et sic Deus diligit solum rationales creaturas, non tamen omnes illas quae sunt in gratia gratum faciente, sed solum illas quae sunt electe et non reprobe, sive sint in gratia sive in mortali culpa. Et hoc voco 'dilectionem secundum aeternam praescientiam' de qua ad·Rom. 9: 'Jacob dilexi, Esau autem odio habui.' Et ista potest vocari 'dilectio simpliciter prima' aut 'dilectio secundum quid,' quia in scriptura simpliciter loquendo dicitur: 'Esau autem odio habui,' licet forte et sine forte Esau quandoque habuerit charitatem, saltem quando fuit noviter circumcisus. Et ita de quolibet reprobo potest dici simpliciter quod Deus odit ipsum, licet secundum quid scilicet secundum praesentem iustitiam diligat ipsum quando habet charitatem vel gratiam, etc." _Ibid._, 141ʳC: "Prima quod loquendo _de dilectione generali_ omnis entitas est a Deo diligibilis ex natura rei. Patet ex dictis. Secunda est quod loquendo illo modo nulla entitas est Deo odibilis ex natura rei. Patet, quia nulla talis est secundum se mala sed simpliciter bona. Tertia est quod loquendo _de dilectione speciali_ ultimo modo dicta nulla entitas est a Deo diligibilis ex natura rei sive ex sui natura. Patet, quia quod aliqua res sit accepta Deo ad vitam aeternam solum est ex ordinatione voluntaria et gratuita voluntate divina, etc. Quarta est quod loquendo isto modo nec odium Dei, nec alius quicumque actus culpabilis est Deo odibilis ex natura rei sive ex sui natura. Patet, nullus talis actus deacceptatur ad vitam aeternam, vel imputatur ad poenam aeternam, nisi ex mera voluntate divina, cte." The italics are mine.

Fourthly, the gift of eternal life is always *gratis*, even *de potentia ordinata*, and therefore, as such, is not absolutely founded on the habit of grace.[46]

Fifthly, grace and charity as terms do not always or necessarily refer to an infused habit within the mind.[47] The words themselves do not signify this, but only have this denotation by common usage. Charity and grace might, for instance, refer to the Holy Spirit. Therefore, when it is said that grace and charity are necessary in order to merit eternal life, this does not necessarily imply that the infused habit of grace is necessary.

Finally, even *de potentia ordinata*, someone can love God meritoriously for some temporal good and do so without grace.[48] It is a little difficult to know what case d'Ailly has in mind here, but the most likely example would be that man, *ex puris naturalibus et faciens quod in se est*, might merit the first gift of grace.

Certain aspects of d'Ailly's discussion are clear and familiar to anyone acquainted with the Nominalist understanding of grace.[49] Within the framework of *absoluta* argumentation d'Ailly sharply attacks the whole concept of an infused habit, which the Nominalists felt was a supernatural mechanism that limited both the freedom of God and the natural powers of man. Secondly, the dialectic of the two powers allows this attack on infused habit while, at the same time, strictly upholds the *de facto* necessity of the habit of grace.[50] The distinction

[46] *Ibid.*, fol. 139ʳB: "Secundo, quia animam charitatem habentem Deus pure gratis acceptat ad beatitudinem, igitur absolute possibile est, etc. Consequentia patet et antecedens apparet per illud Rom. 6: 'Stipendia peccati, mors; gratia autem Dei, vita aeterna.' Item, Rom. 8: 'Non sunt condignae passiones huius temporis ad futuram gloriam.' Item, Luc. 17: 'Cum feceritis omnia quae praecepta sunt vobis, dicite: Servi inutiles sumus.' "

[47] *Ibid.*, fol. 139ʳC-139ᵛD: "Ex praedictis sequuntur aliqua correlaria. Primum est responsivum ad articulum, scilicet quod charitas vel gratia est quaedam qualitas infusa. Unde in duabus praedictis conclusionibus usus sum istis terminis 'charitas' et 'gratia' ut supponunt absolute pro tali qualitate, ut sit sensus quod sine tali qualitate aliquis potest absolute amicus Dei esse, et cum tali qualitate non esse amicus Dei. Tamen utendo illis terminis, scilicet 'charitas' et 'gratia,' secundum suam connotationem de virtute sermonis, istae propositiones essent concedendae. Aliquis habet charitatem vel gratiam, vel est amicus Dei, ergo est Deo carus et gratus et ad vitam aeternam acceptus, et ea dignus, quia illi termini hoc connotant. Et hoc non esset, igitur conclusio vera, etc. Secundo, sequitur quod nulla qualitas infusa est vel esse potest formaliter et intrinsece charitas vel gratia. Patet, quia quaelibet talis existens vel possibilis absolute potest esse et non facere aliquem carum vel gratum, igitur quaelibet talis absolute potest esse et non esse charitas vel gratia. Consequentia patet ex connotatis istorum terminorum, etc., et antecedens apparet ex dictis, et per consequens sequitur quod nulla talis qualitas potest esse formaliter et intrinsece charitas, quia nihil est formaliter et intrinsece tale quod potest esse et non esse tale, etc."

[48] *Ibid.*, F: "Unde, cum meritum dicatur in respectu ad praemium et praemium sit duplex, scilicet aeternum et temporale, satis constat quod etiam de lege ordinata aliquis possit ipsum Deum diligere meritorie ad aliquod bonum temporale sine habitu charitatis vel gratiae, et non ad vitam aeternam."

[49] Cf. Paul Vignaux, *Justification et prédestination au XIVe siècle: Duns Scot, Pierre d'Auriole, Guillaume d'Occam, Grégoire de Rimini* (Paris, 1934).

[50] D'Ailly, *Sent.* I, q. 9, a. 2, fol. 140ʳC: ". . . licet de lege ordinata ad istam dignitatem sive ad meritum vitae aeternae concurrant cum causalitate et acceptatione divina ipsa voluntas creata et charitas sive gratia, tamen absolute staret ista non concurrere, et tamen istam dignitatem esse meritum vitae aeternae. Et per consequens non ab aliis sed a sola divina acceptatione consurgit ista dignitas vitae aeternae, pro quo facit istud dictum scripturae, Hester 6: 'Hoc honore dignus est quem rex voluerit honorare.' Unde patet quod licet voluntas causet actum meritorium, ex hac tamen causalitate non convenit tali actui esse meritorium vel vita aeterna dignum."

is used only to stress that this habit of grace is not the only way God could have chosen to save men, but rather is operative only because he freely chose it. It stresses the absolute contingency as well as the practical dependability of the present order. Thirdly, although d'Ailly does not treat the problem of the relation between human and divine effort in the process of salvation, there are good indications that he holds the Ockhamistic approach. In one place he states that man can, *de potentia ordinata*, achieve some temporal good without grace, and this probably refers to meriting first grace *ex puris naturalibus*.[51] Furthermore, while he excludes condign merit, *de potentia absoluta*, in the achievement of eternal life, he leaves the way open and, indeed, his very formulation suggests that condign merit would be possible *de potentia ordinata*.[52]

There are other aspects of his discussion, however, that have not been developed by past scholars and which lend to d'Ailly's treatment its own unique quality. For example, d'Ailly never uses the *de potentia absoluta* argument in its strongest form, namely that God is able on the basis of his omnipotence, without any contradiction, to accept the total sinner who has no grace or merit whatsoever. Although his second conclusion would seem to suggest this, his defense of that conclusion leads us away from this interpretation. What d'Ailly wishes to exclude, *de potentia absoluta*, is not all grace but only the infused habit of grace. This is suggested by the fact that the grace which is unnecessary, *de potentia absoluta*, is always the habit of grace, never grace in the form of another gift, such as the Holy Spirit. Moreover, d'Ailly goes to great lengths to show that this infused habit is not the only definition of the word "grace" and that he means to exclude in his second and third conclusions only this infused habit. Finally, he indicates that the Holy Spirit or uncreated grace can be given apart from the infused habit of grace, suggesting that this is indeed the principal "other gift" that is necessary for acceptation, even *de potentia absoluta*. But unlike the infused habit of grace, the gift of the Holy Spirit does not change man or reform his nature. It does, however, make him acceptable to God.

This interpretation is strengthened by certain analogies d'Ailly draws. In all of these analogies the emphasis is on the unchanged nature of man and on the passage of time essential in distinguishing the unrighteous period in a man's life from the righteous period. This change from unrighteousness to righteousness is like the change of the accidents of bread from inhering in the substance of bread to being present with the body of Christ, without inhering in it.[53] D'Ailly's main point is that nothing happens to the accidents of bread. However, does he mean to carry the analogy further in order to suggest that man and his sinful

---

[51] *Ibid.*, fol. 139ᵛF.

[52] *Ibid.*, fol. 140ʳC: "Unde sequitur ulterius quod licet aliquis sit dignus vita aeterna in sensu prius dicto, nullus tamen eam mereri potest de condigno, et hoc intelligendo in sensu immediate tacto [that is the distinction between *de lege ordinata* and *de potentia absoluta*]. Cf. *Ibid.*, fol. 142ᵛF.

[53] *Ibid.*, fol. 141ᵛD: "Patet, quia hoc non minus est possibile quam quod accidentia sacramentalia sint aeque praesentia corpori Christi sicut erant substantiae panis, et tamen non informant ipsum, etc."

state are bound together like accidents and substance and that man and his righteousness do not inhere in one another but are simply placed together without any unity or union? Similarly vague is the analogy d'Ailly draws between the effect of acceptation on man's nature and the way in which God might, *de potentia absoluta*, conserve the light from a candle after it has been snuffed.[54] Again, his point is that the light has remained unchanged. This ambiguity is solved in part by later examples. In a third analogy d'Ailly compares the change to a Jewish slave who, according to the Law, after six years of bondage, was to be freed.[55] No change takes place in the slave, but only in his situation, in the name and restrictions placed upon him or removed. Finally, d'Ailly uses the example of the king who might decide to punish a certain group of people found in the treasury on Monday and reward those found in the treasury on Tuesday.[56]

In all of these analogies d'Ailly wishes to stress that no real, material or essential change takes place in the person, nor is there a loss or acquisition of any habit. There is only a change in his status, effected through a change in time.[57] This, however, does not exclude the possibility that this very change from one category to another can be and is occasioned by the gift of the Holy Spirit which, while not changing the man, makes him acceptable to God. In fact, the eucharistic analogy suggests that the new state in which man is acceptable is that state in which he has righteousness in the form of the gift of the Holy Spirit.

However, in spite of the gift of the Holy Spirit, is not such an acceptation, which does not change man the sinner in any way, only a forensic justification, imputed rather than imparted or earned by man?[58] Indeed, it would seem so, al-

---

[54] *Ibid.*: "Item, absolute Deus posset se solo conservare lumen quod causat candela quiescens in aere, nulla mutatione locali facta ad hoc, aut aliqua re noviter creata vel destructa, etc."

[55] *Ibid.*, fol. 141ᵛE: "Similiter in casu sufficit ad talem verificationem lapsus temporis, et hoc quando determinatio temporis cadit sub statuto, sicut apud Hebraeos lex erat ut quilibet servus, completo sexto anno servitutis, rediret ad libertatem; ideo absque ulla ipsius mutatione, solo temporis lapsu, fiebat de servo non servus et de non libero liber, et ita posset esse in proposito, etc."

[56] *Ibid.*, fol. 140ʳB: "Tertia est quod aliquis non dignus vita aeterna potest fieri dignus ea de potentia absoluta absque aliqua mutatione in ipso aut in quolibet alio facta, praeter solam transitionem temporis existentis vel possibilis. Patet, quia sicut rex posset statuere inventos in camera die lune debere puniri et inventos die martis debere praemiari, sic nulla est contradictio quod Deus statueret existentes sub 'a' mensura esse habituros beatitudinem et non ante vel post, etc."

[57] Cf. *Ibid.*, fol. 140ʳA–B; fol. 141ʳ–141ᵛ.

[58] *Ibid.*, fol. 140ᵛE: "Unde ad primam et pro dictis et dicendis distinguendum est quod aliquem esse Deo gratum et carum vel Dei amicum potest dupliciter dici. Uno modo denominatione intrinseca ab habitu vel actu charitatis vel gratiae animam ipsius informante. Alio modo denominatione extrinseca ab ipsa divina voluntate acceptante. Vel magis proprie loquendo aliquis potest dici amicus Dei dupliciter, vel quia diligit Deum vel quia diligitur a Deo. Primo modo potest aliquis esse carus et gratus sine aliqua qualitate supernaturali infusa quae sit charitas vel gratia, non tamen sine aliqua qualitate creata quae sit dilectio et quae potest dici charitas vel gratia, etc. Secundo modo potest aliquis esse carus et gratus sine aliqua qualitate informante, nec est simile de esse album et albedine sicut hic, etc." *Ibid.*, fol. 142ʳA: "Secunda propositio est quod carentia charitatis, licet sit peccatum, tamen potest esse vel non esse peccatum. Patet, quia non est peccatum nisi in eo qui debet et tenetur habere eam, et quia Deus posset hominem absolvere a tali debito habendi, esto quod non daret sibi charitatem, sequitur quod possibile est talem carere charitate absque peccato."

though one would have to know more about what effect, for d'Ailly, the gift of the Holy Spirit has on man. In any case, this possibility of acceptation without the habit of grace is not really a possibility at all. It is what God might have done or still theoretically could do, if he had not finally committed himself to save man through a system of infused, created grace.

Throughout this discussion, in large part because d'Ailly concerns himself with *absoluta* possibilities, little has been said about how man, *de facto*, merits grace and eternal life beyond the simple assurance that it is through an infused habit of grace or charity.[59] On the absolute level there is no necessary connection between merit and grace, so that none of the various types of causation about which we spoke are operative here. Moreover, there is only the briefest discussion of the *de facto* relationship, so that there is no direct statement of the type of causation operative on the level of *ordinata*. However, the very distinction being made between the two orders does indicate the type of causality d'Ailly has in mind as operative *de potentia ordinata*. The fact that the prevailing system is not a necessary one, but only one chosen freely by God, points away from any kind of connection between merit and grace based on a natural power of a good act to be meritorious in and of itself. Moreover, d'Ailly's treatment would not suggest a causality based on the moral nature of God, which supposedly corresponds with our moral sense.[60] Rather d'Ailly hints at a chosen system within which merit does effect the gift of grace. How this system works, what kind of causality is operative, becomes clearer when we turn to d'Ailly's discussion of sacramental causality.

III. SACRAMENTAL CAUSALITY

The fullest treatment given by d'Ailly to the problem of theological causation is provided in the first article of the first question of book four on the *Sentences*.[61] Here d'Ailly asks whether the sacraments of the new law have efficient causality in respect to grace. His response to this question is, typically, to posit three conclusions and to defend them against opposing arguments. These three conclusions, two negative and one positive, are all *de potentia ordinata*. First of all, the sacraments of the new law are not the efficient causes of grace in the sense that they cause grace directly through some physical, instrumental causality, as if they possessed some special virtue.[62] Secondly, the sacraments of the new law are not the efficient causes of grace in the sense that they occasion God's direct

---

[59] The discussion of d'Ailly might appear more balanced if we possessed his second book of the *Sentences* where, in the twenty-seventh distinction, the *de facto* relationship of merit and reward is normally discussed.

[60] *Ibid.*, fol. 142ᵛE: "Nec aliqua qualitas est ex natura rei iustitia sed ex mera acceptatione divina, nec Deus iustus est quia iustitiam diligit sed potius econtra aliqua res est iustitia quia Deus eam diligit, id est acceptat, etc."

[61] D'Ailly, *Sent.* IV, q. 1, a. 1, fols. 224ʳ-226ᵛC.

[62] *Ibid.*, fol. 224ᵛB: "Nullum sacramentum debet propter hoc dici causa effectiva gratiae, quia in ipso sit aliqua virtus spiritualis quae sit ei principium agendi inquantum est instrumentum divinae misericordiae et per quam ispum sit causa characteris vel ornatus, aut cuiuscumque alterius dispositionis in anima ad gratiam praevie."

action.[63] Thirdly, the sacraments of the new law are the efficient or effective causes of grace in the sense that they are *sine qua non* causes.[64] The meaning of *sine qua non* causality for d'Ailly becomes apparent in his defense of these three conclusions.

The first conclusion was directed against the position of Thomas Aquinas which gave to the sacraments, as was indicated above, a physical, instrumental causality that enabled them to effect grace directly. Such instrumental causality operates not out of any natural virtue in itself but rather out of a special power or virtue granted to the sacraments by God. Such causality is, for Thomas, far more than *sine qua non* causality which he identifies with accidental causality.

D'Ailly feels that this position of Thomas was sufficiently and cogently rejected by Scotus and Ockham, and d'Ailly refers the reader to their lengthy discussions.[65] D'Ailly contents himself with one argument against Thomas taken from natural reason, that is, from philosophical argumentation apart from revelation. Since, according to Aristotle, nature works in the shortest and fastest possible way, there is no reason or need to place some special supernatural virtue in the baptismal water or the words of the eucharist or to place in the soul some prevenient disposition for grace which is character or ornament, because one can save appearances without positing such pluralities.[66]

The second conclusion was directed against Henry of Ghent, who suggested that God directly assisted in the sacraments to cause their effect. Henry wished in this way to retain the sacraments as causes but deny them any direct action in regard to the effect.[67] Again, d'Ailly relies upon the previous refutation of Henry's position made by Scotus, according to which it is asserted that God is present not directly, but only according to his will.[68] If, d'Ailly says, Henry

---

[63] *Ibid.*, fol. 225ʳB: "Nullum sacramentum debet propter hoc dici causa effectiva gratiae, quas Deus in sacramento assistat per modum specialis praesentiae."

[64] *Ibid.*, fol. 225ᵛE: "Sacramenta legis novae primo modo non sunt causae effectivae gratiae sed bene secundo modo et improprie," that is, as *causae sine quibus non.*

[65] *Ibid.*, fol. 225ʳ: "Hanc autem opinionem quoad singula eius puncta reprobat multipliciter et diffuse Johannes Scotus, lib. IV, ad quartam quaestionem et ad quintam unica ratione probando, et similiter post eum Ockham in prima quaestione quarti."

[66] *Ibid.*, A: "Sed quia nolo hic insistere, arguo contra eam unica ratione probando conclusionem praedictam, quia illa positio est irrationabilis quae ponit pluralitatem sine necessitate. Nam hoc est contra doctrinam philosophorum, ut patet primo Physicorum de opinione Mellissi et Anaxagorae, et 3 de Anima et 7 Physicorum. Quia enim natura nihil facit frustra, semper ubi paucitas sufficit ad salvandum apparentias magis est ponenda. Et sicut sequendo rationem naturalem nihil est ponendum nisi quod ratio naturalis concludit, ita sequendo fidem nihil est ponendum nisi quod veritas fidei convincit. Sed praedicta opinio nec ex ratione naturali nec ex veritate fidei cogitur ponere sacramenta legis novae esse causas effectivas gratiae modo superius declarato, ut in sequentibus patebit. Nec est aliqua necessitas immo omnino fictio et superfluitas ponere universaliter in sacramentis talem virtutem supernaturalem, sicut in aqua vel in verbis prolatis, aut ponere in anima aliquam dispositionem praeviam gratiae quae sit character vel ornatus, quia sine tali pluralitate possunt omnia salvari, ut inferius apparebit. Igitur praedicta opinio est irrationalis et per consequens conclusio vera."

[67] *Ibid.*, B: "Ista conclusio est contra Henricum de Gandavo, quarto quodlibet, quest. 3, ubi tenet quod Deus assistit specialiter sacramentis et per hoc vult salvare quod sacramenta sunt causae gratiae."

[68] *Ibid.*

means to say that God acts directly and personally in the sacrament to cause its effect, then his opinion is to be rejected. But, if Henry holds rather that this "special assistance of God" works in the sense that God has ordained that a certain effect will take place, an ordination that takes the form of a free promise that binds God to his Church, then this is the position of Scotus and, we may assume, also of d'Ailly, since he is satisfied with this refutation.[69]

D'Ailly prefaces his third conclusion with a discussion of two possible interpretations of the term "efficient causality". In one sense it can mean that the existence of one thing follows directly out of the existence of another, such as fire being the cause of heat. This direct, physical causality, *ex natura rei*, is the proper meaning of efficient causality.[70] In a second way, loosely or improperly, efficient causality can refer to the situation in which the existence of one thing follows out of the existence of another, not by its own virtue, *ex natura rei*, but rather out of the will of another. This second type of efficient causality is termed *sine qua non* causation, although it is not really a cause in the strict sense of *ex natura rei* causation.[71] D'Ailly here distinguishes clearly between causality in the natural order and causality in the order of salvation. He clearly restricts *sine qua non* causation to the order of salvation by asserting that in nature the effect always follows from the cause *ex natura rei*, never *ex voluntate Dei*.[72]

On the basis of this distinction d'Ailly defends his third conclusion that the sacraments of the new law are causes *sine quibus non* of grace. This d'Ailly feels is established by the fact that grace does not follow from the sacraments by their own virtue but only by virtue of another, namely God. This conclusion agrees with the teaching of the Fathers and Doctors of the Church, according to d'Ailly. Moreover, its defense is best maintained by Ockham with whom d'Ailly is in complete agreement on this question.[73]

[69] *Ibid.*, fol. 225ʳB: "Et per consequens vel opinio illa falsum praesupponit (scilicet Deum aliter assistere sacramentis quam dictum est) vel ipsa habet concedere quod propter specialem assistentiam Dei sacramenta non sunt causae gratiae nisi ad istum sensum improprium quod Deus in sacramentis ordinavit sic agere, non quod ipsa sacramenta sic agant, et de tali ordinatione et libera promissione ipse certificavit ecclesiam." *Certificare*, literally "to certify or guarantee," is a technical term used to seal or validate legally binding contracts. Cf. C. DuCange, *Glossarium mediae et infimae latinitatis* (Paris, 1840–50), II, 294, and J. F. Niermeyer, *Mediae latinitatis lexicon minus* (Leiden, 1954ff.), II, p. 172.

[70] This definition would make even Aquinas' instrumental causality an improper use of the term "causare." Therefore to assume, as has been done, that d'Ailly teaches occasionalism because he refuses to make the sacraments causes in the proper sense of the term would mean that Aquinas also taught occasionalism, which is absurd.

[71] D'Ailly, *Sent.* IV, q. 1, a. 1, fol. 225ᵛC–D: "Uno modo proprie, quando ad praesentiam esse unius, virtute eius et ex natura rei, sequitur esse alterius, et sic ignis est causa caloris. Alio modo improprie, quando ad praesentiam esse unius sequitur esse alterius, non tamen virtute eius nec ex natura rei sed ex sola voluntate alterius, et sic actus meritorius dicitur causa respectu praemii. Sic etiam causa sine qua non dicitur causa. Ex quo sequitur primo quod causa sine qua non, non debet absolute et simpliciter dici causa, quia proprie non est causa."

[72] *Ibid.*: "Secundo, sequitur quod in naturalibus non reperitur aliqua causa sine qua non respectu alicuius effectus, sed in voluntariis bene reperitur talis causa, quia in naturalibus semper ex natura rei sequitur effectus, sed non in voluntariis."

[73] *Ibid.*, E–F: "Ad praesentiam sacramentorum ex virtute ipsorum non sequitur gratia sed solum ex virtute alterius, scilicet Dei sic agentis, nec talis sequela est ex natura rei sed solum ex voluntate

At this point in the discussion d'Ailly raises a possible objection to his position, an objection that tries to defend the physical, direct causality of the sacraments by comparing their operation to physical causality in the natural order while, at the same time, reducing natural causation to the level of accidental causality or direct divine intervention. Although no name is attached to this objection, the argumentation is surprisingly close to that of Autrecourt. The existence of the cause can no more logically be inferred from the effect than the existence of the effect could be inferred from the supposed cause. One cannot infer the existence of one thing from the existence of another. We normally say that fire is the cause of heat, but this is not necessarily the case; instead, it is contingent upon our observation that heat follows fire. The case of the three children in the fiery furnace indicates that there is no necessary connection between fire and heat. If God can prevent heat from being present with fire, does he not also effect heat at other times when fire is present? God might, by himself alone, cause heat, thus suspending the action of the fire. Therefore, when we say that something is properly the cause of another, we mean only that when "a" is present, "b" usually follows, but not necessarily as a result of "a". In this same way the sacraments are indeed the proper and efficient cause of grace.[74]

That d'Ailly had Autrecourt or some of his followers in mind by this argument is clear from certain distinctive features.[75] The dialectic of the two powers does not appear, as it always did when Ockham used the example of the children in

---

libera Dei; igitur conclusio vera. Consequentia tenet ex terminis et antecedens patet quia solum ex eo sequitur gratia ad praesentiam sacramentorum, quia Deus sic instituit quod non conferatur gratia nisi positis sacramentis et ipsis positis conferatur. Et si oppositum instituisset, effectus oppositus sequeretur. Ex hac distinctione sequuntur duo correlaria contra sanctum Thomam. Primum est quod quodlibet novae legis sacramentum solum est causa gratiae sine qua non, et ita possunt intelligi omnia dicta vel auctoritates sanctorum aut doctorum quae videntur sonare quod sacramenta legis novae sunt causae gratiae. Unde quando Magister et sancti dicunt quod sacramenta novae legis efficiunt quod figurant non est intelligendum quod proprie efficiant gratiam sed quod Deus efficit eam ad eorum praesentiam, et hoc sufficit magistris et aliis ad ponendum differentiam inter nova et antiqua sacramenta. Secundo, sequitur quod nullum sacramentum legis novae sive per virtutem propriam sive per virtutem ei collatam est proprie causa efficiens alicuius dispositionis in anima ad gratiam praevie. Patet quia talis ratio potest fieri de tali dispositione, sicut facta est de gratia; hoc etiam diffuse probat Ockham in solutione primae quaestionis quarti libri."

[74] *Ibid.*, fols. 225ᵛG–226ʳ: "Contra istud correlarium et secundam partem conclusionis arguo sic et probo quod sacramentum sit proprie causa gratiae et etiam dispositionis ad eam praevie quia videtur quod omne illud quo posito ponitur aliud sit proprie causa illius. Nam de ratione causae proprie dictae non est quod ad ipsam necessario sequatur effectus aut quod non possit poni sine ipsa, quia ignis est proprie causa caloris, et tamen non necessario sed mere contingenter ad ignem sequitur calor, sicut patuit de igne trium puerorum in fornace; similiter calor etiam igne praesente potest produci igni nihil causante, sicut patet si Deus de se solo produceret calorem suspendendo actionem ignis praesentis. Igitur ad hoc quod aliquid sit proprie causa alterius sufficit quod ipso posito ponatur illud et ipso non posito non ponatur, sed sic est de sacramentis respectu gratiae, etc., igitur etc. Et confirmatur, quia sicut ad praesentiam sacramentorum sequitur gratia solum ex voluntate alterius, scilicet Dei, sic volentis ita ad praesentiam ignis sequitur calor solum ex voluntate Dei, quia ipso sic volente sequitur calor, et ipso sic non volente non sequitur. Igitur ita proprie sacramenta sunt causae gratiae sicut ignis est causa caloris, cuius oppositum dictum est."

[75] Cf. the references to Autrecourt's position given in footnotes 23–28. D'Ailly was no more universally opposed to Autrecourt than he was in total agreement with Ockham; cf. d'Ailly's attack on Ockham's concept of quantity, *Sent.* IV, q. 1, a. 2 and d'Ailly's support of some of Autrecourt's

the fiery furnace. There is no suggestion of the difference between what God could do and what in fact does happen. Secondly, no distinction is being made between the natural order and the economy of salvation, but we move freely from one to the other with no apparent difference. Thirdly, the whole argument that the principle of causality is nothing more than habit-formed expectation points to Autrecourt. In other words, in order to give causal validity to sacramental causation the author of this argument dissolves the law of causality in nature.[76]

The refutation of this objection takes the form of a series of propositions that, on the one hand, uphold the law of causality in nature and, on the other, reject divine intervention in theological causality. While d'Ailly seems to feel that Autrecourt's argument is logically convincing, he is not prepared to admit its validity.

D'Ailly begins his refutation by asserting that whenever God creates some effect by way of secondary causes, he makes that secondary cause the direct cause of the effect. Moreover, although God could effect such action directly, he does not work in that way but, rather, regularly operates through secondary causes.[77] It is true, d'Ailly admits, that the law of cause and effect cannot be established beyond a contingent relationship between the existence of one thing and the existence of another;[78] however, he rejects the idea of God's direct intervention as well as *sine qua non* causation in the physical order. In spite of the seeming validity of Autrecourt's argument, d'Ailly maintains that some efficient secondary cause can properly be a cause in that it produces the effect by its own proper virtue. While nothing happens without the consent and will of God — and all mediaeval theologians admitted that God was the prime cause — causes act, and principally so, by their own proper virtue, *ex natura rei*.[79]

---

positions, *Conceptus et insolubilia* (Paris, s.d.), fol. 15ᵛ: "Omnes propositiones proprie dictae ad invicem contradictoriae significant idem aut eadem omnino, licet alio et alio modo. Si vero obiiciatur contra has conclusiones quod inter articulos Parisiis condemnatos contra magistrum Nicolaum de Alticuria unus est iste: 'dicere hae propositiones: "Deus est," "Deus non est," idem significant licet alio et alio modo est error,' respondeo quod multa fuerunt condemnata contra eum causa invidiae quae tamen postea in scholis publice sunt concessa. Tamen propter reverentiam articuli dico," etc.

[76] Oakley incorrectly believes this argument to be the position of d'Ailly, presumably because it is introduced with the phrase "arguo et probo." However, it is an attack on d'Ailly's three conclusions and d'Ailly goes on to refute it. Cf. Oakley, *Harvard Theological Review*, LVI, 65.

[77] D'Ailly, *Sent.* IV, q. 1, a. 1, fol. 226ʳA: "Pro solutione huius dubii pono aliquas propositiones. Prima est quod quandocumque Deus facit aliquem effectum mediante causa secunda, ipse non solum facit illum effectum sed etiam facit causam secundam esse causam illius effectus. Probatur, quia Deus facit omne positivum, causam autem secundam causare effectum suum est quid positivum, igitur, etc. Secunda propositio sequens ex praedicta est quod Deus nihil facit fieri per aliud quin illud idem facit per seipsum, immo prius natura et principalius facit illud. Tertia: Plus facit Deus faciendo aliquem effectum mediante causa secunda quam si faceret eundem effectum se solo, quia in prima factione sunt plures termini divinae actionis quam in secunda factione, ut patet ex prima propositione."

[78] *Ibid.*, fol. 226ʳB: "Quarta propositio est quod nulla causa secunda sic est proprie causa alicuius effectus nec aliquis effectus sic ex natura rei sequitur ex aliqua causa secunda quod causa necessario inferat effectum vel quod effectus necessario praesupponat illam causam, immo effectus pure contingenter sequitur ex secunda, et secunda causa pure contingenter antecedit effectum suum."

[79] *Ibid.*: "Quinta propositio quod non obstantibus praedictis aliqua causa efficiens secunda sic est

D'Ailly finds it difficult to refute Autrecourt directly. Autrecourt's attack on causation seems very convincing, but d'Ailly is unwilling to reduce all causation to either *ex pacto* causality or divine intervention. Therefore, he hedges, saying that causation in the physical universe is a product both of a natural virtue within the thing and of the will of God. He could have, like Ockham before him, defended natural causation as physical, direct causation without recourse to Autrecourt's argument. On the other hand, d'Ailly follows the intention of Ockham in differentiating between natural and theological causation and upholds the natural operation of the physical universe. D'Ailly was a man caught between the rigorous logic of the "mediaeval Hume" and the necessity of upholding a predictable, reliable, secure universe. The problem was real and his solution significant.

D'Ailly therefore concedes in his fourth proposition the first part of Autrecourt's doubt, namely that what appears to be causation cannot be *proven* to be anything more than habit-formed expectation. But d'Ailly rejects the second part, namely that there is then no difference between natural and theological causation. He argues that in natural causation the effect springs from a virtue in the cause as well as from the will of God, because when fire produces heat, such heat follows principally (as prime cause) out of the divine will and secondarily out of the natural virtue of the fire.[80]

It is clear from this discussion that d'Ailly rejects the main intention of Autrecourt's argument and, while admitting the logic of his critique on the law of causality, upholds physical causation in the natural order. Biblical examples such as the three children in the fiery furnace are good illustrations of the fact that God could have and in the past has acted directly to cause what he normally

---

proprie causa quod ipsa agit effectum virtute propria, dico autem virtute propria non quidem propria per exclusionem virtutis extraneae vel alienae sed virtute propria, id est virtute quae est in ipsa vel quae est ipsamet et non sibi aliena. Sic enim ignis agit calorem virtute propria, scilicet aliqua virtute quae non est sibi aliena. Nec tamen excludo quin agat virtute Dei quae est sibi virtus aliena et a sua propria virtute distincta. Sexta propositio est: Aliqua est causa efficiens secunda ad cuius positionem sequitur effectus non solum ex voluntate Dei sed ex natura rei, et sola talis causa secunda est causa proprie dicta. Ista patet ex praecedente, quia effectus qui sequitur ad positionem causae et hoc ex virtute propria ipsius causae non solum sequitur ex voluntate Dei sed ex natura rei."

[80] *Ibid.*, fol. 226ʳC-226ᵛ: "Concedo antecedens quia facit pro quarta propositione posita, sed nego consequentiam, quia nec primum requiritur, nec secundum sufficit ad hoc quod causa secunda sit causa proprie dicta, sed requiritur et sufficit quod posita ipsa ponatur effectus, scilicet ex virtute ipsius causae et non solum ex voluntate Dei; sic autem non est de sacramentis, etc. Ad confirmationem autem quando dicitur quod ad praesentiam ignis sequitur calor sequitur ex voluntate Dei, nego istud, quia quando ignis producit calorem talis calor sequitur ex voluntate Dei principaliter, sed tamen inus cum hoc virtute ignis. Et quando probatur oppositum quia Deo sic volente sequitur calor etc., dico quod hoc est verum, sed non est ideo verum quod ille calor sequatur solum ex voluntate Dei, sed quia cessante voluntate Dei cessant singula ex quibus ille calor sequitur seu ponitur in esse, ideo, etc. Unde concedo istam septimam propositionem quod licet ad praesentiam causae secundae proprie dictae sequatur effectus non solum ex voluntate Dei sed ex virtute ipsius causae et ex natura rei, tamen quod ad praesentiam alicuius causae secundae sequatur aliquis effectus virtute ipsius causae seu ex natura rei solum est ex voluntate Dei, nam hoc solum est quia Deus vult talem causam assumere ad cooperandum sibi talem effectum quem, si vellet, posset sine ea producere. Ex qua sequitur octava propositio quod licet omnis causa secunda proprie dicta causet effectum ex natura rei, tamen quod ipsa sit causa proprie dicta non est ex natura rei quia solum ex voluntate Dei."

causes mediately through secondary causes. But these are only occasional miracles that affirm the contingency, the created nature of our world and in no way undermine our confidence in the dependability of that world. If anything, the dependability of the natural order is increased by realizing that it was created and is maintained by a loving God.

Even if d'Ailly upholds natural, physical causation and clearly differentiates the orders of nature and salvation, does he not reduce sacramental causation to *sine qua non* without separating it ·clearly from accidental causation? Does he not maintain that the sacraments are not real causes in the proper sense but depend rather on the will of God? And since he indicates that merits effect grace in the same way that the sacraments effect grace, does that not dissolve the relation between merit and grace to the arbitrary and inscrutable acceptation of God's will?

The answer to these questions appears when the position of d'Ailly is looked at more carefully. When d'Ailly indicates that *sine qua non* causation is not proper causation, he means, as the context clearly indicates, that it is not causative in the strict sense of *ex natura rei.* He in no sense rules out covenantal or moral causality. Moreover, d'Ailly depends continually on the argumentation of Scotus and Ockham, referring his reader to their discussions. It seems natural, therefore, that he would define *sine qua non* as they would, namely as juridical or covenantal causality. Furthermore, by his rejection of Autrecourt's position as well as Henry of Ghent's, d'Ailly makes it clear he does not define *sine qua non* causality as direct divine intervention. Rather his acceptance of Ockham's definition is made clear when, against Henry, he states that the sacraments act out of the ordination and promise of God on the basis of a contract or agreement with the Church.[81]

Why, however, does d'Ailly reject the infused habit of grace only *de potentia absoluta* and reject the physical causality of the sacraments *de potentia ordinata?* Would not his position have been more forceful and unified if he had rejected both, *de potentia ordinata?* The answer to this question lies in the concept of the covenant which forms the key to the dialectic of the two powers,· to the relationship of nature and grace, and to the relationship among the various aspects of causality within the economy of salvation. It is to the concept of the covenant that we now must turn.

IV. COVENANT AND CAUSATION

The contract or covenant between God and man, although touched on only sparingly by d'Ailly, is the major assumption which combines his conclusions into one unified system. At the center of this concept of covenant is the biblical concept of God, strikingly reaffirmed once more in the Nominalist system, divested of the rationalistic limitations of the Aristotelian as well as Anselmian systems. Once more the God of Abraham, Isaac, and Jacob has appeared in all his awesome terror, establishing the natural and moral orders on the basis of his own free will. This will of God, upon which everything depends and in relation

[81] Cf. above, footnote 67.

to which everything is contingent, is not moved from without nor is it ever really comprehensible to man. God does not act according to some absolute, established norm of justice and right but instead creates justice and right by his action, because whatever God does is *ipso facto* right. Just as God created this world out of the infinite possibilities he might have chosen, so he established certain norms of justice by his action, norms that are not absolute but grow directly out of God's action.

This does not mean, however, that for the Nominalists God's action is arbitrary or likely to be reversed simply because it depends upon his will. *God always acts wisely*, not because his actions accord with some previously established norm but rather because he possesses an inward sense of justice, consistent with his nature, which will always be unknowable by man. For the Nominalists, there is no distinction in God between will and intellect. Accordingly, God's action, although completely voluntary, is internally consistent and, when revealed to man, is absolutely dependable.

The contingency and dependability of God's acts are, for the Nominalists, always understood from the point of view of covenant. There are, in fact, two covenants rather than one. One covenant is with the world in general, a covenant which God has made with all mankind, begun at creation and assured through promises made to Adam and Noah. The second covenant is with the Church, understood in the broad, Augustinian sense of all those belonging to the City of God either for a time or for all eternity. As such, it includes the saints before Christ's coming as well as after and is the covenant through which God's plan for redemption is effected, a covenant assured as far back as the promises to Abraham and to his descendants (understood in the Pauline sense of those who have faith). According to the first covenant, God commits himself to uphold his created universe and the laws that govern it, in spite of their contingent nature or the sinfulness of man. This is the area of natural causality. According to the second covenant, God commits himself to a process of salvation which, in spite of its contingent nature or the basic unacceptability of man, he will uphold. This is the area of theological causality. Therefore, both the order of nature and the order of salvation are covenants which apply to different situations and persons. All mankind stands under the covenant of creation; only those in the Church, that is, in a state of grace, stand under the covenant of salvation. These covenants, by their very nature, affirm that God's will, and consequently God's action, are bound by nothing except his own decision to act in particular ways. They also affirm, however, that the very nature of God as revealed to man, a nature consistent and dependable, commits God, in fact, restricts God, to act in limited, defined ways.

To give an analogy, God's pacts with man, especially the covenant with the Church, operate like the relationship between an affectionate parent and a child. The child knows the parent has unlimited power over it, but it does not, because of that knowledge, live in a state of continual fear. The belief in the parent's love, based on past experience, permits the child to predict future parental behavior. If the child acts against the parent's stated wishes, the child fears a punishment that might be quite severe, and that fear may grow more intense until the two are reconciled.

Such is, I think, the essence of the Nominalist concept of divine covenant. *De potentia absoluta*, the parent *could* act in any way whatsoever toward the child. *De potentia ordinata*, the parent *will* act in certain established ways. The power of the parent is not restricted by any law other than his own nature as revealed to the child. The child fears only when it has acted contrary to the known demands of the parent, just as does the sinner who has stepped out of the covenant of salvation by committing mortal sin. Penance is the reconciliation which readmits one to that covenant relationship and translates the possibility of absolute wrath into the promise of ordained forgiveness. Viewed in this way, the Nominalist speculations, *de potentia absoluta*, besides the "scientific" opportunity they provide to consider a variety of possibilities, are in theology a reprimand to the child in man not to take the given order for granted. The orders of nature and salvation originate in divine freedom, not necessity.

Although never used by fourteenth century theologians, I feel this analogy best expresses the Nominalist understanding of the relation between the two powers. Unlike other examples, it immediately clarifies how the Nominalists can speak of God's omnipotence in such strong terms without fearing the arbitrariness of God's action. Such Nominalists as Gabriel Biel repeatedly taught that the one who does what is in him can trust God's promises, indicating that when one stands inside the covenant one need not fear.[82] This is simply another way of saying that the child who obeys the parent has nothing to fear. That the fourteenth century did not hit upon this analogy does not detract from its applicability but rather indicates a world in which the examples of master and slave, king and subject came more readily to mind.

This concept of covenant or pact should not be equated with that early form of social contract theory found in Marsilius of Padua. Both of these Nominalist covenants are instituted by God *from above*. While they were made as an act of kindness toward man, they were in no sense made by man as an equal or participating partner. In every illustration of the covenant it is the will of the king or master that creates and sustains the relationship, that gives to it whatever validity it possesses. But, with the same psychology by which the ancient Hebrews continually interpreted the covenant in their favor, seeing God as committed to support Israel regardless of Israel's ultimate worth, the Nominalists often interpreted the covenant of salvation in the sense that God was a debtor, committed to reward with grace and, eventually, with eternal life the man who did what was in him.[83]

The dialectic of the two powers operating within the motif of covenant allows a Nominalist such as d'Ailly to do justice seemingly to both partners, God and

---

[82] Cf. Oberman, *Harvest of Medieval Theology*, pp. 131–145, 217–235.

[83] A similar shift in emphasis took place in the feudal contract from the ninth to the twelfth century. The initial importance of the vassal's loyalty, the beneficence of the lord, and the obligation of service gave way in favor of the rights of the vassal and his heirs to the lands held in fief, even to the detriment of the lord.

man. God's omnipotence is protected in the natural order by the fact that it is a contingent order, dependent upon his will. The reliability of the natural order is assured because God has obliged himself to support his creation. *De potentia absoluta*, none of the natural laws are necessary, not even the law of causality. *De potentia ordinata*, God works through these laws and secondary causation. The occasional miracle, recorded in the Bible, by which God suspends the natural order, is rare and always for a specific purpose, to remind us of the ultimate contingency of the universe.

In the same way, God's omnipotence is protected in the order of salvation, in spite of the fact that he has obliged himself to work in a specified way. *De potentia absoluta*, the sacraments do not produce grace nor do good acts done in a state of grace merit eternal life. *De potentia ordinata*, the sacraments do effect grace and man can merit eternal life.

The covenant forms the link which unites the *absoluta* arguments of d'Ailly on merit and grace with the *ordinata* arguments on sacramental causation. In both instances d'Ailly, the Nominalist, expressed a certain dislike for supernatural mechanisms such as the infused habit of grace and the infused virtue of the sacraments, mechanisms that limit God's omnipotence and man's freedom. But while d'Ailly rejected such a sacramental virtue *de potentia ordinata*, he rejected the infused habit of grace only *de potentia absoluta*. This was probably because the infused habit of grace was far more firmly established than the special virtue of the sacraments. The real consistency of d'Ailly's position, however, is indicated by the fact that the infused habit of grace is the cause, and is therefore equivalent to the sacraments and not to instrumental causality, which is a means, not a cause. Both conclusions stress the fact that there is no necessary relationship *de potentia absoluta*. Neither the habit of grace nor the sacraments themselves are absolutely necessary. God could have devised another system of salvation just as he could have created another universe. But, *de potentia ordinata*, the habit of grace effects acceptation and the sacraments effect grace *ex pacto*, that is, they operate within and because of God's ordained system, his covenant with the Church.

To summarize, then, no causal connection is necessary in nature or the Church, absolutely. All such connections are contingent upon the will of God; they all assume a covenant for their validity and are, *de potentia ordinata*, *ex pacto*. Natural causation, *de potentia ordinata*, is not just *ex pacto*, it is also — and more importantly—*ex natura rei*. Theological causation, *de potentia ordinata*, is, on the other hand, exclusively *ex pacto* or *sine qua non*, not in the sense of accidental causality or direct divine intervention, but in the sense that man's merit or the sacraments are signs or tokens that will unfailingly and directly produce their effect because God has committed himself to accord such a value to them.

THE UNIVERSITY OF WISCONSIN

CRANMER AS A NOMINALIST
Sed contra

In the last issue of the Harvard Theological Review,[1] Mr. Eugene McGee has rendered the service of repeating the old caricature of Nominalist Eucharistic theology (this time pinning the donkey's tail on the English reformer Cranmer) and extending this line of argument in such a way that it can be clearly faced and perhaps finally silenced. For, contrary to Mr. McGee's claim,[2] he is not the first to "discover" the Nominalism of Cranmer. Throughout the forties and fifties of this century there raged a controversy over whether Cranmer could be called a Zwinglian and, if so, to what degree. Into this controversy were drawn Dom Gregory Dix,[3] G. B. Timms,[4] E. C. Ratcliff,[5] C. C. Richardson,[6] and G. W. Bromiley.[7] In the course of their arguments both Dix and Richardson referred to the Nominalism of Zwingli and Cranmer, who, Dix and Richardson felt, shared essentially the same position. "Cranmer," Dix said,[8] "was a man of the high Renaissance period, with all its deliberate 'subjectivism,' which sought so intently to segregate what was present in the forefront of consciousness as *words* as the only significant element in human life." Richardson expanded on this charge. "The philosophic presuppositions of Zwingli's thought on the Eucharist," he said,[9] "are derived from Nominalism and humanism. Like most of the Reformers Zwingli attacks transubstantiation from a Nominalist

---

[1] Eugene K. McGee, "Cranmer and Nominalism," HTR 57 (1964), 189–216.
[2] McGee, op. cit., 189.
[3] The Shape of the Liturgy (Westminster, 1945), pp. 613–734; "Dixit Cranmer et non timuit," Church Quarterly Review 145 (1948), 145–76; 146 (1948), 44–60.
[4] Dixit Cranmer (London, 1946); reprinted as "Dixit Cranmer," Church Quarterly Review 143 (1947), 217–34; 144 (1947), 33–51.
[5] The Book of Common Prayer in the Church of England; its Making and Revisions, 1549–1661 (London, 1949).
[6] Zwingli and Cranmer on the Eucharist (Cranmer dixit et contradixit) (Evanston, 1949).
[7] Thomas Cranmer, Theologian (London, 1956).
[8] "Dixit Cranmer et non timuit," Church Quarterly Review 145 (1948), 174.
[9] Zwingli and Cranmer on the Eucharist (Cranmer dixit et contradixit) (Evanston, 1949), pp. 8–9.

point of view." McGee's exposition bears a striking resemblance to Richardson's development of this thesis, and is to be regarded as its "re-presentation." When we now review the more serious charges made by Mr. McGee against Nominalism, we will, for the purposes of exposition, do Mr. McGee the favor of systematizing his position.

I. On TRANSUBSTANTIATION Cranmer was a Nominalist because:

a) of the various explanations of transubstantiation he favored annihilation.[10]

b) he held that transubstantiation was unreasonable because accidents must inhere in something.[11]

c) he held that consubstantiation was more reasonable than transubstantiation.[12]

Furthermore:

d) Scotus, Durand of St. Pourçain, Ockham, and Biel accepted transubstantiation, not on the grounds of reason or revelation, but only on the authority of the pope.[13]

II. On CHRIST'S PRESENCE Cranmer was a Nominalist because:

a) he held that the physical dimensions of the body of Christ could not be reduced to the dimensions of a piece of bread.[14]

b) he believed that Christ's physical body could not be in heaven *and* on the altar, that is, it could not be in two places at the same time.[15]

---

[10] McGee, op. cit., 206–07.   [11] McGee, op. cit., 200.

[12] "Here Cranmer was obviously equating philosophy and Nominalist philosophy, for it was only Nominalist philosophy which held that Consubstantiation was more reasonable than Transubstantiation." McGee, op. cit., 201.

[13] "Even though Durandus, Duns Scotus, and Gabriel Biel all accepted Transubstantiation, Cranmer cited with approval the fact that all did so on the authority of the Church, that is, the bishop of Rome. He quoted Scotus, the subtilest of the school authors, as saying of the words of Scripture that they 'might be expounded more easily and more plainly without transubstantiation,' but Rome chose otherwise. Gabriel Biel was quoted in the same sense. Thus, Cranmer concluded that transubstantiation was held because of the authority of Rome. . . ." McGee, op. cit., 195; contrast my footnote 18.

[14] McGee, op. cit., 200.

[15] McGee, op. cit., 200; cf. also 212.

III. On the REMAINING ACCIDENTS Cranmer was a Nominalist because:

a) he believed that substance was made up of its accidents and that any change of substance would necessitate a change of accidents.[16]

IV. More generally Cranmer was a Nominalist because:

a) he held the plurality of substantial forms in man.[17]

b) he held that the only doctrines contrary to reason that can be accepted are those in Scripture. All others must conform to reason.[18]

c) he divorced faith and reason.[19]

d) he believed that God's will triumphs over his reason.[20]

e) he had an atomistic approach toward the universe, toward doctrine, and toward the Church.[21]

[16] McGee, op. cit., 193.

[17] "Although Cranmer did not say that by philosophy he meant Nominalism, yet the position which he takes here as the true teaching is a Nominalist one. A non-Nominalist, like St. Thomas, held that the body and soul were one substance, not two." McGee, op. cit., 209.

[18] "Nonetheless, his [Cranmer's] Nominalist position on the power of God's will had something to do [sic!] with his reverence for Scripture alone as the source of truth." — "Those things which were 'discrepant from reason' were nonetheless to be believed as the omnipotent God's 'pleasure and will,' if, and only if, 'we find these things written in scripture.' " — ". . . and so for Cranmer Scripture as opposed to man's vain imagination was the only adequate basis for truth." McGee, op. cit., 202; cf. also 195; cf. my footnote 13.

[19] "He [Gardiner] charged Cranmer with trying to dispense with 'mystery or marvel,' and trying to use 'reason without faith,' 'blind reason,' a reason that had 'no participation with faith,' in order to find a 'jolly easy way' like the Sabellians and the Arians. He did all but coin the term 'rationalism' to describe Cranmer's method." McGee, op. cit., 199; "Furthermore, it was also a Nominalist characteristic to separate philosophy and theology, or reason and faith." McGee, op. cit., 202; cf. also 201–02.

[20] "He [Cranmer] did not put reason before faith; he did not make reason the rule of faith. Rather he subordinated reason to faith by use of the Nominalist principle that God's will was superior to his reason." McGee, op. cit., 201; cf. 202, 210.

[21] "Another example that could be taken would be the idea of the Church. A Realist would hold that the universal Church as the mystical body of Christ really existed as a whole, and that individual churches or Christians were members of it, and were subordinate to its authority." — "A Nominalist, on the other hand, would see the individual churches and Christians as the real units, and the Church would be a collective name for Christians." — "Late medieval conciliarism was Nominalist in origin and concept, and Cranmer was a conciliarist." McGee, op. cit., 204. "The Nominalists had rejected universal ideas and the Neoplatonic notion of divine ideas in the mind of God, for ideas seemed to come between the omnipotent creator and the creature so as to govern the divine mind. Similarly,

f) he, along with Luther and the Nominalists, affirmed only imputed righteousness.[22]

Assuming that these statements do justice to Cranmer's position (a problem which, for lack of space, we cannot treat here), we must ask ourselves whether they are the typical and uniquely Nominalist positions McGee claims them to be. It is to this problem that we will direct ourselves, treating the statements and issues in the order raised.

I. TRANSUBSTANTIATION

To summarize the five points made under this heading, Mr. McGee feels that the Nominalists (notably Ockham and Biel) gave little more than lip service to the doctrine of transubstantiation and, while opting for the interpretation based on the annihilation of the substance of bread and wine, were really in favor of "consubstantiation" or "remanentism." They avoided heresy only by blindly submitting themselves to ecclesiastical authority.[23] In support of this it is first claimed that Cranmer, following the Nominalists and opposing the orthodox and common tradition, favored annihilation. The interpretation of transubstantiation as the annihilation of the substance of bread and wine followed by the succession of the body of Christ has a longer history. As Ockham describes [24] it, there are three possible interpretations of transubstantiation: production, i.e., the body of Christ is produced out of the substance of bread and wine; succession, i.e., the substance of bread and wine cease to be present, only the accidents remaining, and under these accidents the body and blood of Christ begin to be; and remanentism, i.e., the body of Christ exists alongside the substance of bread and wine under the accidents of the latter. Annihilation is only one of the various explanations of succession. For purposes of theological harmony and for his own support Ockham places Thomas among those holding succession and claims that it is the common opinion.

Nominalists abolished real relations, for if a relationship were real, it would exist outside the mind as a third thing." McGee, op. cit., 210.

[22] McGee, op. cit., 206. [23] McGee, op. cit., 195.

[24] De corpore christi, c.5 (The "De Sacramento Altaris" of William of Ockham, ed. T. B. Birch [Burlington, Iowa, 1930], pp. 182–86, hereafter referred to as Birch).

Although Thomas taught production [25] (a fact which has led many, including Mr. McGee, to think Ockham ill-informed),[26] there are grounds for asserting that succession was the "common opinion." It was favored by Lombard,[27] Innocent III himself,[28] William of Auvergne,[29] Alexander of Hales,[30] the author of the Glossa Ordinaria on Gratian's Decretum,[31] Hostiensis,[32] Scotus,[33] Durand of St. Pourçain,[34] Francis Mayronnes,[35] and many others. Of these, William of Auvergne, Scotus, and Durand held annihilation; and although Scotus in his later years rejected [36] annihilation and went over to the "production" theory of Thomas, his disciples continued to affirm annihilation, and it became the common property of the entire Scotistic tradition, not just of the Nominalists. It was often, as in the case of Durand,[37] affirmed side by side with a Thomistic understanding of quantity. Furthermore, it should be remembered that annihilation was only one of many interpretations of the 1215 decision [38] which were debated in the thirteenth to fifteenth centuries and which, since no decision had yet been reached by the Church on the proper interpretation, were all theologically defendable and arguable.

[25] Summa theologica, P.III, q.75, a.2–3 (Summa Theologica, Institutus Studiorum Medievalium Ottaviensis [Ottawa, 1945–1955], IV, 2940a–42a, hereafter referred to as Ot) and In Scripto Sententiarum, L.IV, d.xi, q.1, a.1–2 (In Scripto Sententiarum, ed. A. Moos [Rome, 1947], IV, 433–42, hereafter referred to as Moos).

[26] McGee, op. cit., 207.

[27] Liber Sententiarum, L.IV, d.xi (Patrologiae Cursus Completus, series Latina, ed. J. P. Migne [Paris, 1880], vol. 192, coll. 862–63, henceforth referred to as PL; and Libri IV Sententiarum [Quaracchi, 1916], pp. 803–05, henceforth referred to as QR).

[28] De sacro altaris mysterio, L.IV, c.20 (PL 217, 870 A–871 D); c.1, X (1,1) (Corpus juris canonici, ed. Friedberg [Leipzig, 1922], II, 5–6, referred to hereafter as RF); c.6, X (3,41) (RF II, 636–39).

[29] De sacramento eucharistiae, c.1 (Opera Omnia [Paris, 1674], I, 434a–34b).

[30] Summa theologica, P.IV, q.38, m.2 (Summa Theologica [Lyon, 1516], IV, fol. 175ʳ–175ᵛ).

[31] Glossa ordinaria Decreti Gratiani, col. 1873 (Decretum D. Gratiani, totius propemodum juris canonici compendium, una cum Glossis [Lyon, 1560]).

[32] Summa super Titulis Decretalium Compilata (Lyon, 1542), fol. 185ʳ.

[33] Sent., L.IV, d.x, q.1 (Opera Omnia [Paris, 1891–95], XVII, 152–86); Sent., L.IV, d.xi, q.1 (XVII, 319); Sent., L.IV, d.xi, q.3 (XVII, 388–90).

[34] Sent., L.IV, d.xi, q.1 (In Sententias Commentariorum Libri Quatuor [Lyon, 1562, (1549)], foll. 275ᵛ–76ʳ).

[35] Sent., L.IV, d.xi, q.20 (In Libros Sententiarum [Venice, 1507], IV, fol. 18ʳ).

[36] Quodlibeta, q.10 (XXV, 403 ff.).

[37] Loc. cit.; Sent., L.IV, d.xii, q.1 (277ᵛ–78ʳ).

[38] C.1, X (1,1) (RF II, 5–6); c.6, X (3,41) (RF II, 636–39).

372

We may conclude from this that McGee is wrong in restricting annihilation to the Nominalists and in viewing it as theologically suspect. Hostiensis, possibly the greatest canon lawyer of the thirteenth century, judged both annihilation and remanentism orthodox and of the three interpretations of transubstantiation found production the least likely.[39]

Secondly, McGee maintains that it is Nominalist to hold, as Cranmer held, that transubstantiation was unreasonable because accidents must inhere in something. This position was held in several different versions in the eleventh, twelfth, and thirteenth centuries by various groups, e.g., the disciples of Berengarius whom Guitmundus called *Impanatores*,[40] the Petrobrusians,[41] and Rupert of Deutz.[42] In contrast, it was the common opinion of the thirteenth-century doctors that the accidents after conversion did not inhere in either the substance of bread or the substance of the body of Christ, but, in as much as they believed quantity could be separated from substance, the accidents inhered in the *quantum* of the bread and wine as in a subject.[43] Thomas implies [44] that accidents without a subject become a problem only for those who lack theological imagination. Because of the metaphysical implications of the idea of accidents without a subject it was necessary for the thirteenth-century theologian to assert that they inhered in the *quantum* of the substance of bread and wine as in a subject.[45] It was Ockham's discovery [46] that quantity, like quality and duration, could not be separated from substance. These categories were the way in which substance existed. Because of this realization Ockham [47] affirmed that in transubstantiation the accidents are upheld by the power of God

[39] Loc. cit.

[40] De corpore et sanguine christi, L.I (PL 149, 1430); L.III (PL 149, 1480).

[41] Petri Venerabilis Tractatus contra Petrobrusianos (PL 189, 787–819).

[42] De divinis officiis, L.II, c.2 (PL 170, 35); cf. L.II, c.5 (PL 70, 38); L.II, c.9 (PL 170, 40); De Trinitate, L.VI, c.32 (PL 167, 431).

[43] G. N. Buescher, The Eucharistic Teaching of William Ockham (Washington, 1950), pp. 65–93; E. A. Moody, "Ockham, Buridan, and Nicholas of Autrecourt," Franciscan Studies 7 (1947), 138–42.

[44] Summa theol., P.III, q.75, a.6 (Ot IV, 2944b–45a).

[45] Moody, op. cit., 138–40.

[46] De corp. christi, cc.17–41 (Birch, pp. 246–500); cf. Buescher, op. cit., pp. 67–86.

[47] De corp. christi, c. 16 (Birch, 240–44); cc. 23–24 (Birch, 284–88).

and inhere in nothing. Three avenues are open to the theologian once Ockham's position has been accepted: 1) to reject transubstantiation as irrational; 2) to reject the concept of substance, since accidents can exist without it; 3) to accept transubstantiation as a miracle which cannot be comprehended, being a daily reminder in our midst that we live in a created, not a necessary order. The first course was taken by Wyclif and, so McGee feels,[48] by Cranmer. The second course was that adopted by Nicholas of Autrecourt, which earned for him the title of the "medieval Hume." [49] The third course was that taken by Ockham and Biel, leading away from both heresy and scepticism. Nominalism could not be further away from the position Mr. McGee describes.

Thirdly, Mr. McGee says that Cranmer along with the Nominalists held that consubstantiation was more reasonable than transubstantiation. If one replaces the anachronistic and heavily charged term "consubstantiation" with the simpler term "remanentism" [50] (i.e., that the substance of bread remains alongside the body of Christ after consecration, thus giving the accidents a subject in which to inhere) the statement is true. But here again this is not the difference between Nominalism and orthodoxy, but between the Thomistic and Scotistic schools. While Thomas rejected [51] "remanentism" as being unreasonable and involving a contradiction, Scotus maintained [52] that it was quite logical and the more probable solution, but that it was not a live option for the theologian after 1215.[53]

The realization here that Ockham's position is not so much a tenet of the Nominalists as much as of the whole Scotistic tradi-

---

[48] McGee, op. cit., 200.

[49] Moody, op. cit., 139.

[50] As the key words in describing succession are *desinit esse*, so the key word in describing this theory is *remanet* or *manente*.

[51] Sent., L.IV, d.xi, q.1, a.1, qu.3, sol.1 (Opera Omnia [Parma, 1852–69], VII, 631; Moos IV, 436–37).

[52] Sent., L.IV, d.x, q.1, n.5–8 (XVII, 172–74).

[53] It is interesting to note that although John Teutonicus and Hostiensis considered remanentism to be a valid interpretation of the 1215 decision, Scotus and Ockham considered it excluded, thus anticipating the thirteenth session of the Council of Trent, which, for the first time, unambiguously excluded remanentism; cf. H. Denzinger, Enchiridion Symbolorum Definitionum et Declarationum (Rome, 1963 [1854]), 1642 (877).

tion may not bother Mr. McGee, since he generally seems to feel that Scotus was also a Nominalist.[54] He does not, however, find this in Copleston's work [55] upon which he relies so heavily, and it would be considered untenable by most Scotus scholars. Being open, however, to the suggestion that Scotus was a Nominalist before Ockham, we would ask Mr. McGee whether he is referring here to epistemology, predestination, penance, or transubstantiation.

This leads us into the last point under this heading, the charge of ecclesiastical positivism against Scotus, Durand, Ockham and Biel in their understanding of transubstantiation.[56] Blind acceptance of ecclesiastical authority is not the lone alternative to reason or demonstrable proof, and belief in the logical validity of "remanentism" does not exclude the belief that such logical validity is *de facto* wrong. Thomas held that the eternity of the world was logically valid and could not be disproved by rational demonstration; yet, he says, [57] we know through Scripture that the world was created. Scotus [58] and Ockham [59] held that "remanentism" was logically valid; yet, they said, we know through the Church that transubstantiation is true. These cases, identical in all respects save in the means of revelation, stress the Christian distinction between what would be true if the human mind were all we had to deal with and what in fact is true, known through revelation. For both Ockham and Thomas the respective doctrines under consideration are not true because Scripture or the Church has said they were true; on the contrary, Scripture and the Church are simply witnesses to what was always true.

II. Christ's Presence

To summarize Mr. McGee's view, the Nominalist understanding of Christ's presence is a materialistic and rationalistic [60] ap-

---

[54] McGee, op. cit., 194–95.

[55] A History of Philosophy, II (London, 1959) ; III (London, 1960).

[56] A very strange position, since elsewhere (McGee, op. cit., 202) the Nominalists were supposed to have made Scripture the only exception to rational proof.

[57] Summa theol., P.I, q.46, a.2 (Ot I, 294a–94b).

[58] Sent., L.IV, d.x, q.1, n.5–8 (XVII, 172–74).

[59] Sent., L.IV, q.6 D; De corp. christi, c.5 (Birch, 182–86).

[60] McGee, op. cit., 199.

proach in which Christ's physical body retains its historic shape
and size and must be localized in one place, preferably in heaven
on the right hand of the Father. In such a view the two assertions
to which Mr. McGee refers would be true, viz., that Christ's body
could not be reduced to the dimensions of a piece of bread and
that it could not be in heaven *and* on the altar at the same time.
Such, however, is not Ockham's position. Ockham held with
Thomas that the body of Christ is whole in every part, no matter
how small, without confusion.[61] Secondly, it was Thomas who
had maintained that for a body to be circumscriptively present [62]
in two places at once involved a contradiction and therefore could
not happen even *de potentia absoluta*.[63] On the other hand, it
was the common opinion of Richard Middleton,[64] Scotus,[65] Ockham [66] and Biel [67] that although the body of Christ was not circumscriptively present in heaven *and* on the altar, such presence
involved no contradiction and was possible *de potentia absoluta*.
In fact, Ockham maintained,[68] two bodies have existed simultaneously in the same place, as, for example, when Christ was born
without removing the virginity of Mary and the post-Resurrection
appearances of Christ when he came to his disciples through
closed doors. *De potentia ordinata*, however, the body of Christ
is present only definitively, i.e., without its proper dimensions,[69]
a position which agrees with Thomas.[70] The truth is therefore the
exact opposite of what Mr. McGee maintains. Ockham accepted
definitive presence. The circumscriptive presence of Christ's

[61] Ockham, De corp. christi, c. 6 (Birch, 188–96); Quodl. IV, q.24; Quodl. IV, q. 36; Biel, Expositio canonis misse, lect. 43 *per totum* (Gabrielis Biel Canonis Misse Expositio, ed. H. A. Oberman and W. J. Courtenay, II [Wiesbaden, 1964], 110–36); Thomas, Summa theol., P.III, q.76, a.3 (Ot IV, 2951b–52b).

[62] A body is circumscriptively present when it occupies space, each part of the body occupying a different place within that space, neither confused within nor found outside that space, e.g., as a person occupies a chair. It is usually contrasted with definitive presence, in which the whole occupies every single part, e.g., as the soul occupies the body.

[63] Thomas, Summa theol., P.III, q.76, a.5 (Ot IV, 2954a–54b); cf. q.75, a.2 (Ot IV, 2940a–40b).

[64] Richard, Sent., L.IV, d.x, a.2, q.2.

[65] Scotus, Sent., L.IV, d.x, q.3 (XVII, 222–25); d.xi, q.3 (XVII, 375–76).

[66] Ockham, De corp. christi, c.6 (Birch 192–96); cf. c.29 (Birch, 336–52).

[67] Biel, Expos. can. misse, lect. 43 *per totum*.

[68] Ockham, De corp. christi, c.6 (Birch, 192); cf. also Quodl. IV, q.36.

[69] Ibid.

[70] Thomas, Summa theol., P.III, q.76, a.5 (Ot IV, 2954a–54b).

body on the altar, i.e., in its proper dimensions, had never been maintained, and while it was not a contradiction for Scotus or Ockham, it did not in fact take place.

III. Remaining Accidents

To some degree we have already dealt with this problem. Mr. McGee maintains that Cranmer and the Nominalists believed that substance was made up of its accidents and that any change of substance would necessitate a change of accidents. Ockham would have accepted the first part of this statement. For any Aristotelian, accidents are the way in which substance exists. The last part, however, was rejected as much by the Nominalists as it was by Thomas. The point for Ockham was that quantity could not be separated from substance. Because of this realization Ockham affirmed that in transubstantiation the accidents are upheld by the power of God rather than inhering in the *quantum* of the substance of bread. Cranmer, as we have said, went in the opposite direction and rejected transubstantiation entirely.

IV. General Nominalist Positions

Behind these individual statements about the Eucharist, which Mr. McGee calls Nominalist, lies the unstated assumption that Nominalism is nothing more nor less than rationalistic humanism. The only qualification to this, for McGee, is that when reason and Scripture conflict, the Nominalist will follow Scripture. This brings us to the more important, non-Eucharistic, charges of Cranmer's Nominalism. Out of many such charges we will choose only the six which seem to us to be the most important and decisive:

1) Anthropology
2) Rationalism tempered with the *sola Scriptura* principle
3) Divorce of faith and reason
4) God's will over his reason
5) Atomistic approach
6) Forensic justification

McGee states that Cranmer held the Nominalist principle that body and soul are two substances, not one.[71] He gives Copleston as his source for this.[72] We assume that he is referring to what Copleston discussed in the place cited, namely, that Ockham held the plurality of forms in man in contrast to Thomas, who affirmed the oneness. Had McGee studied further, he would have discovered that the plurality of forms in man was also affirmed by Alexander of Hales,[73] Bonaventura,[74] John Peckham,[75] Robert Kilwardby,[76] Henry of Ghent,[77] and Scotus,[78] while Gregory of Rimini [79] and Gabriel Biel,[80] both usually considered Nominalists, affirmed the oneness of forms in man, alongside Thomas. Scotus and Ockham both opted for the plurality of forms for theological reasons, viz., that it facilitates the explanation of the simultaneous presence of Christ on the altar and in heaven, and the separation of Christ's body and soul during the three days between his death and resurrection. Clearly, the Nominalists were as much divided on this question as were the thirteenth-century doctors.

The second charge is one that sets Cranmer and the other Reformers off from Nominalism. None of the Nominalists held that only doctrines found in Scripture were to be accepted apart from the laws of rational, demonstrable proof. Ockham,[81] Gerson,[82] d'Ailly,[83] and Biel [84] all accepted the validity of certain doctrines

---

[71] McGee, op. cit., 209.

[72] Frederick Copleston, A History of Philosophy, III (London, 1960), 97.

[73] Summa theol., P.II, q.63, m.4 (Summa Theologica, II [Quaracchi, 1930], 421–22).

[74] Sent., L.II, d.xii, a.1, q.3 (Opera Omnia, II [Quaracchi, 1882], 299–301); d.xiii, a.2, q.2 (II, 319–22); cf. d.xvii, a.2, q.2, ad 6um (II, 423).

[75] Registrum Epistolarum Johannis Pecham Archiepiscopi Cantuariensis, III, ed. C. P. Martin (London, 1885 [1882–85]), 840, 852, 862, 864, 870, 896.

[76] Letters edited by Ehrle, "Der Augustinismus und der Aristotelismus in der Scholastik," Archiv für Literatur- und Kirchengeschichte des M.A. 5 (1889), 614–32.

[77] Quodl. II, qq.2–5 (Quodlibeta, 1518, 1961, vol. I, 29ʳ–31ᵛ); Quodl. IV, qq.13–14 (I, 104ᵛ–23ᵛ).

[78] Sent., L.IV, d.xi, q.3, a.2 (XVII, 411–38).

[79] Sent., L.II, d.xvi–xvii, q.3, a.1 (Super Primum et Secundum Sententiarum, II [Venice, 1522], fol. 86 E–F).

[80] Sent., L.II, d.xvi, q.1, a.1, nota 1 C.

[81] Dialogus, P.I, lib. 2, c.12 in Monarchia romani imperii, ed. Goldast, II, 419–20.

[82] Contra haeresim de communione laicorum (Opera Omnia, I [Antwerp, 1706], 458 C); ibid. (Opera I, 463 A).

[83] Collectio Judiciorum, ed. C. Duplessis d'Argentre (Paris, 1728), I, 77; cf. de Vooght, Les sources de la Doctrine Chrétienne (Paris, 1954), p. 237; Apologia, in Gerson, Opera I, 715 C–D; cf. ibid., 710 C–D.

[84] Sent., L.III, d.xxxvii, q.1, a.1 C.

which they admitted were not found in Scripture but which nevertheless stemmed from Apostolic tradition, e.g., the Immaculate Conception.[85]

Surprisingly enough McGee can affirm, as above, that the Nominalists were thoroughgoing rationalists[86] and thoroughgoing Biblicists,[87] and that they were also sceptics who in the face of doubt professed blind acceptance of ecclesiastical authority.[88] This brings us to the third charge, that of a divorce between faith and reason, which, like the charges of rationalism and Biblicism, is based on a superficial reading of the sources, both Nominalist and Reformation. Even as Mr. McGee cites it,[89] it is only a charge against Cranmer made by Gardiner which, as is so often the case, McGee reads as conclusive proof. Prof. Oberman has shown[90] that Biel's position on faith and reason is not far removed from that of Thomas. Nominalism can no longer be charged with fideism, scepticism, or ecclesiastical positivism. While the number of doctrines attainable through reason may have been reduced, Christian truth has not become a calculated risk which, in place of reasonable arguments, is protected and comforted under the skirts of Mother Church. The theological task has remained the same, that is, to give reason and logic to that which is already believed.

This brings us to the fourth point, the supposed complete voluntarism of Nominalism which is founded in the arbitrary will of God. It has generally been assumed that Nominalism took the voluntarism of Scotus to a destructive extreme, a misinterpretation which forgets that the Nominalists made no formal distinction, much less a real distinction, between God's will and his intellect. For the Nominalist, God never acts apart from his reason; he always acts wisely.[91]

The fifth point for McGee is that Cranmer shares the Nominalist atomistic approach to reality in general and theological questions in particular. This view is based on the assumption

---

[85] Cf. H. A. Oberman, The Harvest of Medieval Theology (Cambridge, 1963), pp. 361–412.

[86] McGee, op. cit., 199, 202.　　　　[87] McGee, op. cit., 202–03.

[88] McGee, op. cit., 195.　　　　[89] McGee, op. cit., 199.

[90] Op. cit., pp. 88–89.

[91] Biel, Sent., L.I, d.vii, q.1, a.2, concl. 3 and 5; cf. Oberman, op. cit., pp. 98–99; 50–68.

that Nominalist logic and epistemology (which Boehner [92] has shown to have been a simple and positive outgrowth of the thirteenth century) pervaded and determined their theological conclusions. Such, however, was not the case. To take McGee's example of conciliarism, E. F. Jacob [93] has shown that the original suggestion for a general council was advanced before the actual inception of the Great Schism and came not from the universities and Nominalists, but from three Italian cardinals, James Orsini, Peter Corsini, and Simon de Borsano. Tierney [94] has pointed to the strong conciliar tradition in the canon lawyers of the twelfth and thirteenth centuries, notably in Gratian, Huguccio, and Hostiensis. The conciliarism of Gerson and d'Ailly grew out of their very concern for the Church universal, for the unity of the body of Christ.

This brings us to the sixth and last point, that Cranmer, along with Luther and the Nominalists, taught imputed righteousness. While the Nominalists did affirm that our acts are without merit until God accepts them as meritorious, that the sole criterion for "good" is the will of God, this was a way of affirming the omnipotence of God, which was more than counterbalanced by their insistent affirmation that God has committed himself to always reward with grace and ultimately with eternal life him who *facit quod in se est*. To the one who does what is in him, that is, does the best he can, God will grant his grace (*gratia gratum faciens*), which enables the *viator* to increase in righteousness. For Ockham and Biel, as for Thomas and Bonaventura, there is always a gap between the merit of man's actions and the gift of eternal life. God always rewards *ultra condignum*. Justification for Ockham and Biel is the result of both inherent, created grace and the inhabitation of the Holy Spirit within the *viator*. For the Nominalists there is no distinction between justification and sanctification.[95]

With Luther, at least the Luther of 1519, the terminology is

[92] Collected Articles on Ockham (St. Bonaventure, N.Y., 1958); cf. D. Trapp, "Augustinian Theology of the Fourteenth Century," Augustiniana 6 (1956), 147–48.

[93] E. F. Jacob, Essays in the Conciliar Epoch (Manchester, 1952); cf. Ph. Boehner, "Ockham's Political Ideas," The Review of Politics 3 (1943), 462–87, reprinted in Collected Articles on Ockham, pp. 442–68.

[94] Brian Tierney, Foundations of the Conciliar Theory (Cambridge, 1958).

[95] Cf. Oberman, op. cit., pp. 353 ff.

different, yet the acquittal is no less decisive. There is, on the one hand, the alien righteousness or righteousness of Christ, which is compared with original sin, since it is given to us "from without," like original sin. There is also our own proper righteousness (compared with our own actual sin), which we effect in ourselves by working with that alien righteousness in us. Righteousness, therefore, for the young Luther, is not only imputed; it is imparted. In the first instance it is given from without; in the second, it effects a change from within.[96]

In conclusion we must point out that the Nominalism which Mr. McGee describes and with which he charges Cranmer cannot be found in Ockham, Gerson, d'Ailly or Biel, those four men whose thought has been the norm for the definition of Nominalism. To whom, then, we may ask, is Mr. McGee referring when he uses this term? It is our feeling, supported by the fact that his footnotes for Nominalism are all from secondary sources, that he is not referring to anyone with whom he is directly familiar.

It is time that the recent advances made in our understanding of Nominalism affected related fields, especially that of Reformation studies. The question of Cranmer's Nominalism still remains open and can be solved only when it is examined on the basis of the fourteenth- and fifteenth-century sources themselves.

[96] "Secunda iusticia est nostra et propria, non quod nos soli operemur eam, sed quod cooperemur illi primae et alienae. Haec nunc est illa conversatio bona in operibus bonis, Primo in mortificatione carnis et crucifixione concupiscentiarum erga seipsum . . . , Secundo et in charitate erga proximum, Tercio et in humilitate ac timore erga deum, . . ." Sermo de duplici iustitia. 1519 (WA, II [1884], 146–47); cf. also Sermo de triplici iustitia. 1518 (ibid., 43–47).

XI

NOMINALISM AND LATE MEDIEVAL RELIGION

Nominalism has long been considered a major intellectual movement within late medieval society. The altered form which it supposedly gave to late scholasticism, the dominant role it played in the universities of northern Europe, the personalities that contributed to its formation and dissemination have attracted the attention of those interested in the philosophy, theology, political thought, literature, and art not only of the late Middle Ages but of the Renaissance and Reformation as well. It is natural to expect that nominalism should provide some insight into the spirit and mood of the age, and many parallels have been drawn between nominalism and other developments contemporary with it. As necessary and fruitful as this enterprise is, however, it has become difficult to realize. During the last forty years a revision has taken place in the traditional understanding of the nature and implications of nominalism. Although a new consensus has been reached on the thought of certain figures within the nominalist movement, the interpretation of the majority of figures and issues is still controversial.

It is obvious that when the interpretation of nominalism is significantly altered, the theories that relate nominalism to other late medieval developments must also be revised. It is the intent of this paper to describe briefly the changing assessment of late medieval nominalism and, for purposes of discussion, to make some tentative suggestions about how the most recent views might relate to other aspects of late medieval society, especially late medieval religion.

1. The Traditional Assessment of Nominalism

Scholars of late medieval thought writing before 1930 had the comforting assurance that they knew what nominalism was and who the nominalists were. Nominalism was the view in logic that defined universals as concepts created by the mind without real, or extramental, referents, and thus without meaning as a description of external reality. Building upon the atomism implicit in this epistemological and ontological premise derived from such twelfth-century thinkers as Roscelin and Peter Abelard, the late medieval nominalists, principally William of Ockham, Gregory of Rimini, Pierre d'Ailly, Marsilius of Inghen, and Gabriel Biel, attacked metaphysics, ethics, and even scientific methodology, thus undermining and destroying the major achievements of high scholasticism. The pervasive influence in the late Middle Ages of this philosophical trend with its devastating theological implications was an established fact that did not need to be questioned or re-examined. As far back as Werner,[1] Denifle,[2] and DeWulf[3] the meaning and influence of nominalism was a "given" to which other evidence and insights had to conform.

This picture of nominalism had been fashioned over several centuries and was a composite based more on the late medieval nominalists than upon their twelfth-century counterparts.[4] A particular body of ideas, all interrelated and mutually reinforced, contributed to the definition of nominalism. These recurrent ideas or themes that together compose the traditional view of nominalism are : (1) atomism, particularism, or individualism; (2) excessive stress on the omnipotence of God; (3) voluntarism; (4) skepticism; and (5) fideism. These themes reappeared in different ways and in different groupings as the various areas of nominalist thought were explained.

---

[1] Karl Werner, *Die Scholastik des späteren Mittelalters*, vols. 1-4 (Vienna, 1881-1887).

[2] Heinrich Denifle, *Luther und Luthertum* (Mainz, 1904-1909).

[3] Maurice de Wulf, *Histoire de la philosophie médiévale* (Paris, 1900).

[4] The basic elements in the traditional view of nominalism can be found in Constantine Michalski, "Les courants philosophiques à Oxford et à Paris pendant le XIVe siècle," *Bulletin international de l'Academie Polonaise des Sciences et des Lettres*, classe d'histoire et de philosophie, 1919-1920 (Cracow, 1922), 59-88; "Les sources du criticisme et du scepticism dans la philosophie du XIVe siècle," *International Congress of Historical Sciences* (La Pologne au Ve Congrès international des Sciences Historiques) (Bruxelles, 1923-24), 241-268; "Le criticisme et le scepticisme dans la philosophie du XIVe siècle," *BIAPSL*, CHP (Cracow, 1927), 41-122; "Les courants critiques et sceptiques dans la philosophie du XIVe siècle," *BIAPSL*, CHP (Cracow, 1927), 192-242; "Le problème de la volonté à Oxford et à Paris au XIVe siècle," *Studia Philosophica : Commentarii Societatis Philosophicae Polonorum*, vol. II (Lvov, 1937), 233-367; Franz Ehrle, *Der Sentenzenkommentar Peters von Candia* (Münster i.W., 1925). More recent versions of this assessment can be found in Gordon Leff, *Medieval Thought from Saint Augustine to Ockham* (St. Albans, 1958); Armand A. Maurer, *Medieval Philosophy* (New York, 1962); and David Knowles, *The Evolution of Medieval Thought* (London, 1962).

The beginning point for nominalism, the basic view that shaped the rest of the system, has traditionally been discovered in the area of logic and, closely related to that, epistemology. It has been thought that the nominalists believed that only the individual was real and that common nature was a figment of the imagination. Moreover, logic concerned the interrelation of mental concepts, not external reality, and thus logic was the study of terms and signs rather than things.

One of the results of this nominalist, or terminist, logic was epistemological skepticism, for which several explanations have been given. In some versions the stress on signs and the rejection of universals was construed to mean that there was an unbridgeable gap between the object and the knowing mind. Moreover, the primacy and autonomy of the individual, combined with the denial of the validity, or at least the demonstrability, of the principle of causality, dissolved the cause-effect relationship of object and mind. In other versions nominalism was thoroughly empirical, ascribing truth only to those propositions that were self-evident and could be known analytically or whose content was derived directly from sense experience. In both cases, in order to be true the contrary of the proposition could not be asserted without involving a contradiction. Viewed in this way, it was not external reality but metaphysical truth that could not be known by man in this life.

The traditional evaluation of the relation of nominalism to the development of science depended upon a certain understanding of the operation and implications of the nominalist epistemology. If one believed that nominalism severed the tie between the knowing mind and external reality, then scientific inquiry became impossible. Even if one accepted the view that nominalism was empirical, its scientific value could still be questioned. Was not a proper scientific method impossible where universals were rejected in favor of an atomistic view of the physical universe and the composition of matter and where the idea of relation and the principle of causality were regarded as unknowable or indemonstrable? Moreover, the nominalist view of divine activity envisaged the possibility of divine intervention and direct divine causality within the natural order, so that God might deceive man by producing an intuitive cognition of a non-existent.

Perhaps the most disturbing aspect of nominalist thought in the traditional interpretation was the effect nominalism purportedly had upon metaphysics. If truth were limited to those propositions that were self-evident or based directly on sense experience, then one could not validly speculate on form and matter nor on substance and relation. In addition, the principle of causality upon which so much metaphysical speculation was based, could not be demonstrated. Furthermore, one could not demonstrate the existence of God and other issues in natural theology that were so important for thirteenth-century metaphysics. The rejection of metaphysics as a proper scientific area of human inquiry brought about a separation of faith and reason that could only be bridged by fideism, a blind trust in the authority of the church.

Closely related to the destruction of natural theology and metaphysics was the rejection of the ethical system based on natural law and its replacement by a system of moral positivism. This developed from the nominalist stress on divine omnipotence and the primacy of the divine will, attributes of God which could not be analyzed, predicted, or judged. The order that prevails, be it the order of the physical universe or the moral order, is in no sense necessary. God could have established and still could establish a different moral order in which murder and adultery would be virtuous acts. God could even cause a man to hate him and accept such action as meritorious. The moral order which presently pertains, therefore, is dependent solely on the arbitrary will of God and can be altered.

Finally, the traditional assessment of the nominalist view of the nature of the church and society again stressed individuality and atomism. Both institutions were supposedly composed solely of autonomous individuals. Thus nominalism favored representative forms of government. The church universal and the political commonwealth were mental creations superimposed on Christendom.

It was conceded that the system thus described was accurate only as a description of late medieval nominalism. The principle of God's absolute power, of the possibility of divine intervention, was not a developed part of twelfth-century nominalism. Further, it was admitted that the system was a composite, derived from an examination of the thought of various fourteenth- and fifteenth-century thinkers, principally Ockham, d'Ailly, and Biel. The description, however, purported to be an accurate picture of the full implications of the nominalist system that was developed in the early fourteenth century and continued as a major intellectual force into the sixteenth century.

Nominalism was not, in the traditional interpretation, simply a system of thought. It was a school that had its own peculiar historical development. John Duns Scotus, Durand of St. Pourçain, and Peter Aureol were the precursors of the movement that was brought to fruition by William of Ockham around 1320. The destructive tendency of Ockham's thought, both in philosophy and theology, was recognized by his contemporaries, and he was summoned to Avignon in 1324 to stand trial. He avoided condemnation only by fleeing Avignon before the completion of the process against him. The forces unleashed by him continued to flourish unchecked in England (through the teaching of Robert Holcot, O. P., Adam Wodham, O. F. M., and Richard of Billingham) and at Paris (through the teaching of Nicholas of Autrecourt, John of Mirecourt, O. Cist., and Pierre de Guichart.).

Opposition to Ockhamism was slow to crystalize in an effective manner. Walter Chatton's critique of Ockham and Wodham produced no censures of nominalism in England during the 1330's. By the end of that decade, however, the Arts Faculty at Paris had become sufficiently concerned over Ockhamism to begin proscribing nominalist teaching. In September, 1339, the Parisian Arts Faculty censured Ockhamism and, fourteen months later, Nicholas of Autrecourt and others were summoned to Avignon to answer charges of teaching things contrary to the faith. In the next month the Arts Faculty at Paris followed that papal action by condemning a series of nominalist propositions.

The effectiveness of the prohibitions of 1339-1340 was momentary. The investigation of the teaching of Nicholas of Autrecourt dragged on, due to a change in popes and the desire of the curial commission to give Nicholas an opportunity for an adequate defense. Finally, however, action was taken by papacy and university alike. Autrecourt was condemned in 1346, and in the following year he burned his books and made a public retraction at Paris. Moreover, in that same year (1347) the Faculty of Theology condemned John of Mirecourt, and a long series of propositions, taken largely from his writings but including statements from Arnold of Villanova and Adam Wodham, were prohibited. Although no corresponding condemnation took place at Oxford (as had happened in 1277), the teaching at both universities seems to have become more cautious and conservative.

At the end of the fourteenth century nominalism (in a form less radical than Autrecourt) captured the arts and theological faculties of the newly founded German universities and dominated them in the fifteenth century as it had dominated Paris and Oxford in the fourteenth. Many of the best known theologians of this period have been placed within the nominalist school : Pierre d'Ailly, John Gerson, Marsilius of Inghen, Henry of Langenstein, and Henry Totting of Oyta. Although constantly at war with the *via antiqua* in the fifteenth century, nominalism lived on in Germany, especially through the teaching of Gabriel Biel and his disciples, to contribute, both negatively and positively, to the Protestant Reformation.

The traditional analysis of nominalism and the picture of its historical development were already undergoing modification before 1930. However, a surprisingly large portion of the traditional view has lived on to dominate even the most recent textbooks on the history of medieval thought. When parallels or contrasts are made between late scholasticism and art, literature, and religion in the late Middle Ages, it is frequently the older view of nominalism that forms the basis for comparison. For example, those familiar with Erwin Panofsky's *Gothic Architecture and Scholasticism* will immediately recognize in his description of the relation of late gothic architecture to late medieval thought the traditional description of nominalism, where the fragmentation of design and structure into meaningless and unrelated ornamentation or austere simplicity is paralleled by the critical Ockhamist movement that destroyed the synthesis of high scholasticism, with its balance, harmony, and universality.[1] The late medieval mood of pessimism, despair, and decay that Huizinga describes in his *Waning of the Middle Ages*, based largely on literary evidence, also owes something to the traditional assessment of nominalism, as his chapter on "Symbolism in its Decline" reveals.[2] The flowering of late medieval piety and mysticism is often attributed to the fideism and skepticism that followed the break-up of the thirteenth-century synthesis. Numerous theories on the origin and meaning of the Protestant Reformation, not the least of which is the view of Luther taken by Joseph Lortz, have been based on a negative assessment of late medieval nominalism, whose decadence not only required some type of theological reform but obscured the issues so that reform could not recapture the purity of pre-fourteenth century Catholic theology but rather led to a fragmentation of Christianity.[3]

---

[1] Erwin Panofsky, *Gothic Architecture and Scholasticism* (Archabbey, Pa., 1951).

[2] Johan Huizinga, *The Waning of the Middle Ages* (London, 1924).

[3] Joseph Lortz, *Die Reformation in Deutschland*, (Freiburg, 1940, 1949).

2. Revisions in the Understanding of Late Medieval Thought

The changing evaluation of nominalism and late medieval thought that has been taking place since about 1930 has not made the impact it deserves. There are several reasons for this. First of all, the statements upon which the earlier view was based can, for the most part, be found in the writings of Ockham and/or others in the fourteenth and fifteenth centuries traditionally associated with him. The question is, therefore, one of interpretation, and many of the points at issue between the old and newer views depend upon the interpretation of the nominalist use of the distinction between the absolute and ordained powers of God. Secondly, the difficulties of working in a field where there are very few printed sources has discouraged many from checking the texts on which the old and new views are based, and consequently, the number of participating scholars is relatively small. Thirdly, those who have done research in the late medieval field since 1930 have (unlike earlier scholars such as Michalski and De Wulf) generally concentrated their efforts on only one aspect of the thought of that period (for example, logic, science, theology, or political thought). Consequently, there are few recent works that treat Ockhamism or nominalism in general. Finally, vested interests (both Protestant and Catholic) committed to the earlier assessment have prolonged the life of the traditional approach in spite of the weakening evidence in support of it. Some Catholic intellectual historians of a Thomist persuasion, possibly believing that a more positive evaluation of late medieval thought would diminish the significance of Thomas and the validity of Neo-Thomist metaphysics, have ignored or rejected the revision without listening to its case and without re-examining the texts. Protestant historians have been equally committed to the view of the decline and corruption of late medieval thought. which could be viewed as one of the great justifying causes of the Reformation.

Most of those whose research has contributed to the revised understanding of nominalism and late medieval thought have utilized one of two basic approaches. There are those, first of all, who have accepted the traditional view or definition of nominalism and, upon discovering that a theologian traditionally regarded as a nominalist (for example, Ockham or Gregory of Rimini) does not maintain that system or the particular aspect of it under consideration, have removed that theologian from the ranks of the nominalists. In some cases this research was conducted by historians with no visible confessional or parochial interest, and the results of their research (perhaps quite different from what they expected) left the general understanding of late medieval thought and nominalism intact. Albert Lang's study of Henry Totting of Oyta [1] and Gerhard Ritter's work on Marsilius of Inghen [2] fall within this category. Other historians using this approach belonged to religious orders and have concentrated their research on a figure or figures within their own order. This has led some to question the motives of these scholars and to cast doubt, unjustly I think, on the disinterestedness and validity of the conclusions of their research. Philotheus Boehner and his students and followers at St. Bonaventure's fall within this category.[3] Among the non-Franciscans who have adopted this approach is the Augustinian, Damasus Trapp.[4]

On the other hand, there are those who initially take the term 'nominalism' as a neutral term that simply describes the thought of William of Ockham and his followers. Upon discovering that Ockham and other 'nominalists' did not maintain the positions once attributed to them, they proceeded to redefine the term 'nominalism' along the lines of a more accurate description of the thought of Ockham or Biel. Within this approach may be placed the contributions of Paul Vignaux (for example, his articles in the *DTC* on Ockham and nominalism as well as his later study of nominalism) [5] and Heiko Oberman (both his

---

[1] Albert Lang, *Heinrich Totting von Oyta* (Beiträge zur Geschichte der Philosophie und Theologie des Mittelalters, XXXIII, 4/5; Münster i.W., 1937).

[2] Gerhard Ritter, *Studien zur Spätscholastik*, vol. I : *Marsilius von Inghen und die okkamistische Schule in Deutschland* (Sitzungsberichte der Heidelberger Akademie der Wissenschaften, Philosophische-historische Klasse; Heidelberg, 1921).

[3] Philotheus Boehner, *Collected Articles on Ockham* (Franciscan Institute Publications, Philosophy Series, No. 12; St. Bonaventure, N.Y., 1958); Oswald Fuchs, *The Psychology of Habit According to William Ockham* (FIP, Phil. Ser., No. 8; St. Bonaventure, 1952); Matthew C. Menges, *The Concept of Univocity Regarding the Predication of God and Creature According to William Ockham* (FIP, Phil. Ser., No. 9; St. Bonaventure, 1952); Damascene Webering, *Theory of Demonstration According to William Ockham* (FIP, Phil. Ser., No. 10; St. Bonaventure, 1953); and Herman Shapiro, *Motion, Time and Place According to William Ockham* (FIP, Phil. Ser., No. 13; St. Bonaventure, 1957).

[4] Damasus Trapp, "Augustinian Theology of the 14th Century," *Augustiniana*, VI (1956), 146-274; "Peter Ceffons of Clairvaux," *Recherches de théologie ancienne et médiévale*, XXIV (1957), 101-154; "Clm 27034 : Unchristened Nominalism and Wycliffite Realism at Prague in 1381," *RTAM*, XXIV (1957), 320-360.

[5] Paul Vignaux, "Nominalisme," in *Dictionnaire de théologie catholique*, XI.1 (Paris, 1930), cols. 717-784; 'Occam," in *DTC*, XI.1 (Paris, 1930), cols. 876-889; *Nominalisme au XIVe siècle* (Paris, 1948).

early article on nominalism and his subsequent study of Gabriel Biel).[1]

The first approach concludes that a given figure was not a nominalist if his thought is more in keeping with the method and moderation of the thirteenth century. This approach has the advantage that the content of the term 'nominalism' remains intact and everyone knows what it means. The difficulty, however, may be that as more and more figures are examined and found not to conform with the traditional understanding of nominalism, we may end up with an important late medieval school of thought in which we cannot place any important late medieval thinker. The second approach takes a similarly positive attitude toward figures traditionally associated with nominalism but, believing that the term 'nominalism' is only a descriptive term for the thought of these men, also gives the term 'nominalism' a positive connotation. In this second approach the term 'nominalism' loses its specific, traditional content, and runs the risk of being redefined with every new study.

Regardless of approach, the end result of the research of these historians has been to construct a three-school, or three-movement, theory of late scholasticism.[2] There was first of all the conservative, Augustinian branch of late medieval thought (including such figures as Thomas Bradwardine, Gregory of Rimini, and Hugolino Malbranche of Orvieto), designated by the terms "right-wing nominalism"[3] or "historico-critical group".[4] Second, there was the moderate, central, or middle branch of late medieval thought (including such figures as Ockham, Pierre d'Ailly, and Gabriel Biel), to which were ascribed the terms 'moderate nominalism', 'Ockhamism', or the less radical

---

[1] Heiko A. Oberman, "Some Notes on the Theology of Nominalism with attention to its Relation to the Renaissance," *Harvard Theological Review*, LIII (1960), 47-76; *The Harvest of Medieval Theology* (Cambridge, Mass., 1963).

[2] Oberman actually designated four branches of late medieval nominalism : a conservative "right wing," a radical "left wing," an Ockhamistic, moderate, middle-of-the-road position, and a syncretistic school that combined Ockhamism and Scotism. This fourth "school," in which Oberman placed John of Ripa and Peter of Candia, was ignored in *The Harvest of Medieval Theology*, and the recent studies of Paul Vignaux make it doubtful whether Ripa and Candia should be connected with nominalism at all. Trapp seems to have a "two-school" theory, but he implies a distinction within what he calls the "logico-critical" school between moderates and extremists.

[3] "Right wing" and 'left wing" are terms used by Oberman, "Some Notes on the Theology of Nominalism ..."

[4] "Historico-critical," "logico-critical," and "modernist" are terms used by Trapp, "Augustinian Theology ..."

branch of the "logico-critical group". Finally there was the radical branch of late medieval thought (those that supposedly resembled the traditional view of nominalism, for instance, Robert Holcot, Adam Wodham, Nicholas of Autrecourt, and John of Mirecourt), described as "left-wing nominalism", "modernism", or the radical branch of the "critico-logical group". I will have more to say about the suitability of these categorizations and approaches after examining the major aspects of the revised understanding of late medieval thought as constructed in the period from 1930 to 1965.

It is inappropriate to dismiss the revision, as is sometimes done, with the suggestion that it is the product of a misguided Franciscan chauvinism. This view suggests that the Franciscans originated the revision and encouraged it in order to remove certain Franscicans, in particular William of Ockham, from the ranks of the nominalists and thus to absolve the Franciscans from contributing to the late medieval decay of philosophy and theology and, inadvertently, to the Reformation.[1] When one examines the stages in the revised understanding of late scholasticism, the absurdity of this view becomes apparent. The two earliest scholars upon whose work the revision is founded, Erich Hochstetter [2] and Paul Vignaux, were not even in religious orders. If anything, they came from backgrounds that were sympathetic to Thomas. Two other scholars whose contribution has been equally important are also "secular" in background, E. A. Moody [3]

---

[1] This charge has been made against Boehner. It more properly applies, however, to the research of Ludger Meier in his attempt to dissassociate the Erfurt Franciscans from Ockhamism. In particular, see : "De schola franciscana erfordiensi saeculi XV," *Antonianum*, V (1930), 57-94, 157-202. 333-362, 443-474; "Ein neutrales Zeugnis für den Gegensatz von Skotismus und Ockhamismus im spätmittelalterlichen Erfurt," *Franziskanische Studien*, XXVI (1939), 167-182, 258-287; "Research that Has Been Made and Is Yet to Be Made on the Ockhamism of Martin Luther at Erfurt," *Archivum Franciscanum Historicum*, XLIII (1950), 56-67; and *Die Barfüsserschule zu Erfurt* (Münster i.W., 1958).

[2] Erich Hochstetter, *Studien zur Metaphysik und Erkenntnislehre Wilhelms von Ockham* (Berlin and Leipzig, 1927); "Nominalismus?" *Franciscan Studies*, IX (1949), 370-403; "Viator mundi : Einige Bemerkungen zur Situation des Menschen bei Wilhelm von Ockham," *Franziskanische Studien*, XXXII (1950), 1-20.

[3] E. A. Moody, *The Logic of William of Ockham* (New York, 1935); "Ockham, Buridan, and Nicholas of Autrecourt," *Franciscan Studies*, VII (1947), 113-146; "Ockham and Aegidius of Rome," *Franciscan Studies*, IX (1949), 417-442; *Truth and Consequence in Medieval Logic* (Amsterdam, 1953); "Empiricism and Metaphysics in Medieval Philosophy," *Philosophical Review*, LXVII (1958), 145-163; "Buridan and a Dilemma of Nominalism," *Harry Austryn Wolfson Jubilee Volume*, vol. II (Jerusalem, 1965),

and Heiko Oberman. In fact, the only Franciscan among the major contributors to the revision is Philotheus Boehner.

A new assessment of Ockhamism or, if you like, moderate nominalism, has emerged during the last forty years through the efforts of Hochstetter, Vignaux, Boehner, Moody, and Oberman. The following description is a composite made up from their research into the thought of Ockham and Biel, and it contrasts sharply with the traditional overview presented above.

a) *Universals and the Relation of Logic to External Reality*

No one disputes the fact that Ockham gave primacy to the singular and rejected the idea that there existed a "common nature," which inhered in things that "look alike" and which produced their resemblance. For Ockham, resemblance among things of the same species exists in external reality and is experienced by man. This however, is not the result of a common nature inhering in things of the same species. One need not pursue resemblance into "an intelligible order of abstract essences and necessary relations ontologically prior to particular things."[1] Similarity among things of the same species has a genetic origin, and it is based on what each individual has in himself, not on any shared nature or essence. Socrates resembles Plato more than a donkey because Socrates has a rational soul and Plato has a rational soul; they do not, however, have a rational soul "in common."[2]

The first stage by which a natural resemblance becomes a universal concept is the natural sign. A natural sign is a concept applicable to many particulars that resemble one another before an individual mind has expressed that concept in language. When a concept is expressed in language, whether it remains a thought (mental concept) or is spoken or written, it becomes a conventional sign, or term. The concept, whether as a natural or conventional sign, is the act of understanding and is predicable of many individual things that resemble one another.

577-596; "Ockhamism," in *Encyclopedia of Philosophy*, vol. V (New York, 1968), 533-534; and "William of Ockham," in *Encyclopedia of Philosophy*, vol. VIII (New York, 1968), 306-317.

[1] Moody, "William of Ockham," 307.

[2] Ockham, *Summa Logicae*, Pt. I, ch. 17 (Boehner edition, St. Bonaventure, 1957), 53. Cf. Hochstetter, *Studien zur Metaphysik* ..., 78-117; Vignaux, "Nominalisme," 736-742; Boehner, "The Realistic Conceptualism of William Ockham," in *Collected Articles* ..., 156-174; Moody, "William of Ockham," 307-312.

Logic concerns the correct manipulation of natural and conventional signs within propositions and syllogisms. Moreover, truth or falsity is applicable only to propositions and syllogisms, not objects in external reality. For example, there is nothing true or false about the terms 'God' or 'man'. There is something true or false about the propositions 'God exists' or 'Socrates existed'. Propositional knowledge, although it is a mental creation concerned with universality rather than particularity, is directly related to and dependent upon external reality through sense experience. This is the reason why Ockham's thought is considered empirical. But before we examine Ockham's epistemology and the principle of cause and effect on which it was based, it may be helpful to examine Ockham's understanding of divine power and will which supposedly, along with the principle of singularity or particularity, destroyed the medieval philosophical system.

b) *The Dialectic of the Two Powers of God*

Because of the importance of this distinction for nominalist thought and because its meaning has been frequently misunderstood, the dialectic of the two powers deserves a fuller treatment than the other areas of nominalism. The distinction between the absolute and ordained powers of God had its origin in the late eleventh century and was the common property of the schools from the twelfth century on.[1] Simply put, the distinction meant that according to absolute power God, inasmuch as he is omnipotent, has the *ability* to do many things that he does not *will* to do, has never done, nor ever will do. By viewing God's intellect and will from the temporal standpoint and by attributing to God a distinction between the ability to act and the desire to act, theologians acknowledged an area of initial possibility for divine action, limited only by the principle of contradiction, out of which the things God did do or is going to do were chosen.

The distinction was theological, and its major function in the thirteenth century, as the discussion of the distinction in Thomas

---

[1] On the origin of the distinction see : W. J. Courtenay, "Necessity and Freedom in Anselm's Conception of God," *Wirkungsgeschichte Anselms von Canterbury* (Proceedings of the International Anselm Congress, Bad Wimpfen, Germany, 13-16 September, 1970.) to be published in 1974; R. P. Desharnais, *The History of the Distinction between God's Absolute and Ordained Power and Its Influence on Martin Luther* (Unpublished dissertation, Catholic University of America, Washington, 1966); A. Lang, *Die Wege der Glaubensbegründung bei den Scholastikern des 14. Jahrhunderts* (Beiträge zur Geschichte der Philosophie des Mittelalters, XXX.1/2; Münster i.W., 1930).

illustrates, was to affirm that God did not act of necessity; he could have done things other than those he chose to do.[1] Thus the present order, the order that God has established, is not identical with his

---

[1] Thomas Aquinas, *On the Power of God* (*Quaestiones disputatae de potentia Dei*), q. 1, a. 5 (Westminster, Maryland, 1952), 29-31 : "I reply that the error of those who say that God cannot do otherwise than, he does is connected with two schools of thought. Certain philosophers maintained that God acts from natural necessity : in which case since nature is confined to one effect, the divine power could not extend to other things besides what it actually does. Then there have been certain theologians who maintained that God cannot act beside the order of divine justice and wisdom according to which he works, and thus they came to say that God cannot do otherwise than he does. ... Accordingly we conclude that a thing which acts from natural necessity cannot be a principle of action, since its end is determined by another. Hence it is impossible that God act from natural necessity, and so the foundation of the first opinion is false.

"It remains for us to examine the second opinion. Observe then that there are two senses in which one is said to be unable to do a thing. First, absolutely : when, namely, one of the principles necessary for an action does not extend to that action; thus if his foot be fractured a man cannot walk. Secondly, by supposition, for if we suppose the opposite of an action, that action cannot be done, thus so long as I sit I cannot walk. ... For even as the divine goodness is made manifest through these things that are and through this order of things, so could it be made manifest through other creatures and another order : wherefore God's will without prejudice to his goodness, justice and wisdom, can extend to other things besides those which he has made. And this is where they erred : for they thought that the created order was commensurate and necessary to the divine goodness. It is clear then that God absolutely can do otherwise than he has done. Since, however, he cannot make contradictories to be true at the same time, it can be said *ex hypothesi* that God cannot make other things besides those he has made : for if we suppose that he does not wish to do otherwise, or that he foresaw that he would not do otherwise, as long as the supposition stands, he cannot do otherwise, though apart from that supposition he can." *Summa theologiae*, Pt. I, q. 25, a. 5 : "Some laid it down that God acts from natural necessity ... But we showed above that God does not act from natural necessity, but that His will is the cause of all things ... Others, however, said that the divine power is restricted to this present scheme of things be-cause of the order of the divine wisdom and justice, without which God does nothing. ... However, the order established in creation by divine wisdom ... is not so equal to the divine wisdom that the divine wisdom should be restricted to it. ... Therefore, the divine wisdom is not so restricted to any particular order that no other scheme of things could proceed from it. Hence we must say absolutely that God can do other things than those He has done. In ourselves ... something can reside in our power which cannot reside in a just will or in a wise intellect. But in God, power, essence, will, intellect, wisdom and justice are one and the same. ... what is attributed to His power considered in itself God is said to be able to do in accordance with His absolute power. ... what is attri-buted to the divine power, according as it carries into execution the command of a just will, God is said to be able to do by His ordained power. In this manner, we must say that by His absolute power God can do other things than those He has foreknown and pre-ordained to do. But it could not happen that He should do anything which

goodness, justice, and wisdom, because they could have found expression in another system. The distinction is deceptive for the modern reader because it seems to be talking about possibilities and avenues for divine action when in fact it is making a statement about the non-necessity of the created order. Both parts of the dialectic, which must be taken together to be meaningful, face in the direction of creation, not God. Together they declare the contingent, non-necessary, covenantal character of our created world.

Potentia absoluta and *potentia ordinata* are not, therefore, two ways in which God can act or might act, normally and with the concurrence of nature in the case of the latter and extraordinarily, supernaturally, and miraculously in the case of the former.[1] *Potentia absoluta* referred to the total possibilities *initially* open to God, some of which were realized by creating the established order; the unrealized possibilities are now only hypothetically possible. Viewed another way, the *potentia absoluta* is God's power considered absolutely, that is, without taking into account the order established by God.[2] *Potentia ordinata*, on the other hand, is the total ordained will of God, the complete plan of God for his creation. The ordained power is not identical with the particular ordinances that God has willed, for those ordinances are only the most common way through which the ordained will of God is expressed.

Before considering Ockham, several aspects of the thirteenth-century understanding of this distinction should be noted. First, the distinction was not so extensively used in the thirteenth century as in the later period. It is not one that appears repeatedly in Alexander, Bonaventure, Albert, and Thomas. Second, the area of things that God cannot do because they imply contradictions is larger in the thirteenth century than in the fourteenth. Stated another way, a

---

He has not foreknown and not pre-ordained that He would do. For His doing is subject to His foreknowledge and preordination, though His power, which is His nature, is not." Cf. *Summa contra Gentiles*, L. II, ch. 23-30.

[1] Ockham, *Quodlibeta*, VI, q. 1 : "Haec distinctio non est sic intelligenda quod in Deo realiter sint duae potentiae quarum una sit ordinata, alia absoluta, quia unica est potentia in Deo ad extra quae omni modo est ipse Deus. Nec sic est intelligenda quod aliqua potest Deus ordinate facere, et alia potest absolute et non ordinate, quia Deus nihil potest facere inordinate." Similar statements can be found in Rimini, d'Ailly, and Biel : see below, 40, n. 1.

[2] This is the reason why the term *absoluta* is used. It does not imply that God acts or could act imperiously.

larger number of aspects of the created order are absolutely necessary for Thomas than for Ockham. Third, there is no basis in the thirteenth century for equating *potentia absoluta* with the ability of God to transcend the present order, to interrupt it by miraculous activity. Nor did the thirteenth century equate *potentia ordinata* with the particular laws by which the established order normally operated. The antinomy of miracle vs. the common course of nature was treated separately from the distinction of *potentia absoluta* and *potentia ordinata*. The latter distinction was not an antinomy, since what God ordained was chosen from the possibilities open to him and therefore they are not mutually exclusive. Furthermore, miracles were not contradictions of God's ordained will, although they contradicted particular principles that normally operated within God's ordained order.

Ockham's understanding and use of the distinction of the two powers of God did not markedly depart from previous usage, although there were some differences.[1] Ockham shared with other theologians

---

[1] Ockham, *Quodlibeta*, VI, q. 1 : "Quaedam Deus potest facere de potentia ordinata et quaedam de potentia absoluta. Haec distinctio non est sic intelligenda quod in Deo realiter sint duae potentiae quarum una sit ordinata, alia absoluta, quia unica est potentia in Deo ad extra, quae omnimodo est ipse Deus. Nec sic est intelligenda quod aliqua potest Deus ordinate facere et alia potest absolute et non ordinate, quia Deus nihil potest facere inordinate. Sed est sic intelligenda quod 'posse [facere] aliquid' aliquando accipitur secundum leges ordinatas et institutas a Deo et illa Deus dicitur posse facere de potentia ordinata. Aliter accipitur 'posse' pro posse facere omne illud quod non includit contradictionem fieri, sive Deus ordinavit se hoc facturum sive non, quia Deus multa potest facere quae non vult facere." Gregory of Rimini, *Super primum et secundum sententiarum*, L. I, dist. 42-44, q. 1, a. 2 (Venice, 1522; reprint 1955), I, fol. 162ᵛP-163ʳA :
"... Deum posse hoc vel illud facere potest intelligi dupliciter : uno modo secundum potentiam ordinatam, et alio modo secundum potentiam absolutam. Non quod in Deo sint duae potentiae, una ordinata et alia absoluta, nec hoc volunt significare doctores, sed illud dicitur Deus ad intellectum recte intelligentium posse de potentia ordinata quod potest stante sua ordinatione et lege aeterna quae non est aliud quam eius voluntas qua aeternaliter voluit haec vel illa et tale vel tale esse futurum. Illud autem dicitur posse de potentia absoluta quod simpliciter et absolute potest. Econtra, illud non dicitur posse de potentia ordinata quod non potest stante lege et ordinatione sua quae nunc est; illud vero non posse de potentia absoluta quod simpliciter et absoluta potest. Patet autem quod simpliciter et absolute sine suppositione contradictionis Deus multa potest quae non potest stante eius lege et voluntate qua voluit sic se facturum. Et hoc ideo, quia illa etsi sint simpliciter possibilia, sunt tamen incompossibilia ordinationi divinae. ... Quamvis autem ista sunt incompossibilia, quia tamen illa ordinatio non est necessaria, id est, non est necessarium Deum sic ordinasse, quinimmo possibile est ipsum ordinasse et voluisse oppositum; ideo illud quod solum est impossibile ex suppositione ordinationis, utpote ei incompossibile non est absolute impossibile sed possibile,

in the late thirteenth and early fourteenth centuries an appreciation
for the usefulness of the distinction in combating Greco-Arabian
necessitarianism, and he made extensive use of the distinction to

et simpliciter loquendo illud Deus potest facere. Huic distinctioni satis concordat alia
antiqua, qua dictum est quod quaedam Deus non potest de iustitia quae potest de
potentia. ... Illud ergo dicitur Deus non posse de iustitia quod est incompossibile suae
ordinationi et voluntati, quae est prima iustitia. Illud autem est omne cuius oppositum
Deus vult quamquam ipsum sit secundum se possibile simpliciter." Pierre d'Ailly,
Quaestiones super libros sententiarum cum quibusdam in fine adjunctis, L. I, q. 13, a. 1
(Strasbourg, 1490; reprint 1968), D : "Unde Deum posse aliquid facere solet dupliciter
intelligi : uno modo secundum potentiam absolutam; alio modo secundum potentiam
ordinatam. Non quod in Deo sint duae potentiae, una absoluta et alia ordinata, sed
Deus dicitur illud posse de potentia absoluta quod simpliciter et absolute potest. Et
sic intelligitur Deus omnipotens, et de tali potentia semper loquar in praesenti articulo,
ut satis patet. Sed Deum aliquid posse de potentia ordinata potest dupliciter intelligi.
Uno modo stricte quod potest stante sua ordinatione qua aeternaliter voluit se sic vel
sic esse facturum, et sic solum potest illa quae ipse ordinavit se facturum, Alio modo
potest intelligi magis large, quod potest stante veritate legis seu scripturae divinae. Et
sic possibile ordinate potest dici illud quod est possibile et non obviat alicui veritati
legis ordinatae vel scripturae sacrae. Et utroque istorum modorum dicitur quod impossibile est de potentia ordinata ultimum iudicium non fore, quia licet sit simpliciter
et absolute possibile, tamen non stat cum aeterna Dei ordinatione et obviat scripturae.
Isti autem duo modi differunt, quia aliquid est impossibile de potentia ordinata primo
modo et non secundo modo, sicut si Sortes sit reprobatus, haec est impossibilis de potentia ordinata primo modo : 'Sortes salvabitur,' ut patet etc., et tamen non est impossibilis secundo modo, quia est absoluta possibilis, nec obviat sacrae scripturae, cum nec
hoc nec eius oppositum sit revelatum in scriptura. Similiter etiam aliquid est possibile
de potentia ordinata secundo modo et non primo modo, sed nunquam econverso, quia
quidquid obviat scripturae sacrae repugnat ordinationi divinae, sed non econverso. Et
ideo secundus modus est in plus quam primus, ut patet, quia quidquid est possibile
primo modo est possibile secundo modo, sed non econverso, ut dictum est. Secundus
autem modus videtur magis proprius quam primus, quia secundum primum modum
nihil est possibile de potentia ordinata nisi quod est vel erit. Similiter, isto modo cuius-
libet contradictionis de contingenti una pars est impossibilis de potentia ordinata, non
autem secundo modo, ut patet de istis : 'Sortes salvabitur', 'Sortes non salvabitur'
demonstrato aliquo viatore. Et istud faciliter patet, etc." Cf. d'Ailly, *Sent.* IV, q. 1,
a. 2 N : "Sicut dicitur quod Deus aliquid potest de potentia absoluta quod non potest
de potentia ordinata, ita dico de creatura. ... licet creatura de potentia naturali seu
naturaliter ordinata non possit creare vel annihilare, ut dictum est, tamen ista potest
de potentia simpliciter absoluta, scilicet supernaturaliter seu miraculose." Gabriel Biel,
Collectorium circa quattuor sententiarum libros, L. I, dist. 17, q. 1, a. 3 H, quotes the
passage from Ockham's *Quodlibeta*. However, in the following section, he seems to
equate *potentia ordinata* with particulars laws that can be changed from time to time
rather with the general ordained will of God (d'Ailly's first sense of *potentia ordinata*).
The same tendency noted in d'Ailly, *Sent.* IV, q. 1, a. 2, can be seen in Biel, *Sent.* IV,
dist. 1, q. 1, a. 3, dub. 2 M : "Et ideo notat hic Petrus de aliaco ... quod sicut dicitur

stress the non-necessity of divine action and thus the chosen quality of the created world. It was an important theological and philosophical tool for distinguishing relative and absolute necessity in things and events. Moreover, Ockham reduced the number of things God could not do because they implied contradictions. Specifically, he placed within the absolute power of God actions that *seemingly* contradicted God's goodness, justice, or wisdom. In this way he underscored the contingency of the present order by acknowledging other orders God *might have* established, had he so chosen. Ockham, however, did not believe these other orders were now possible.

Ockham's use of the distinction of the powers of God is a natural outgrowth of the thirteenth-century use, not a contradiction of it. Ockham was as aware as Thomas that the analogy between human and divine volition on which the distinction was based (namely, that God shares the human experience of feeling one has the physical power to do many things one does not desire to do and will never do) is basically inapplicable because of God's immutability and a-temporality, and because of the unity of God's wisdom, will, and essence. The distinction, therefore, was a statement about the created order, not the divine nature. Moreover, Ockham did not associate absolute power with miracle, nor did he identify the ordained will of God with particular willed ordinances. Confusion on this point has arisen because Ockham introduced miraculous examples into *potentia absoluta* discussions. These supernatural events were not, for Ockham, examples of divine action, *de potentia absoluta*, but were examples of historical incidents (for instance, the three children in the fiery furnace or the burning of Elijah's offering on Mount Carmel), proving that the principles involved (in this case the causal principles that fire always burns and water always quenches fire) were contingent and not abso-

---

quod Deus aliquid potest de potentia absoluta quod non potest de potentia ordinata, sic etiam creatura potest aliquid de potentia ordinata quae videlicet potest secundum ordinem a Deo nunc institutum. Potest etiam aliquid de potentia absoluta sive obedientiali secundum quam potest quicquid mediante ipsa Deus potest producere non solum secundum ordinem nunc institutum sed secundum ordinem institui possibilem. Et ita natura aliqua potest in effectus contrarios effectibus quos modo potest. Sicut de cataplasmate ficuum apposito vulneri regis Ezechiae per Esaiam prophetam quo sanatus est, ut habetur IV Reg. 20. Dicunt expositores quod ficus, secundum naturam propriam, erant contrariae sanationi ulceris, tamen ex speciali miraculo et ordinatione divina speciali induxerunt effectum contrarium." Obediential power specifically implies a contradiction of nature; cf. Bonaventure, *Sent.* I, dist. 42, a. un., q. 3 (Quaracchi edition, vol. I, 755)

lutely necessary. Miracles for Ockham, whether past or future. were always expressions of divine benevolence and compatible with the revealed nature of God. *Potentia absoluta* speculations, on the other hand, such as whether God could have become incarnate in an irrational animal, were not concerned with the appropriateness or likelihood of the postulated situation. Rather, as Vignaux points out, "the invocation of divine omnipotence—*potentia Dei absoluta*—allows the dialectical proof that separates the accidental from the essential in the object of an investigation."[1]

The distinction between the two powers of God in Ockham, therefore, is not a description of divine action, a distinction between the way God *normally* acts *(de potentia ordinata)* and the way he *occasionally* acts *(de potentia absoluta,* or miraculously). If, as Francis Oakley has argued,[2] this is the meaning of the distinction for d'Ailly (and there is some evidence that points in that direction, not only for d'Ailly but for Gregory of Rimini as well)[3], it represents a change from Ockham's usage, which is far closer to the thirteenth century. Even in the later "nominalists" the distinction excludes the idea of a capricious, arbitrary God who might change his mind and reverse the established laws that obtain in the orders of nature and salvation. God has committed himself to maintain the order that he has created, and when he occasionally acts contrary to certain principles or laws that normally operate within that order, it is for reasons that are in keeping with the broader design of his established will.

c) *Epistemology*

Working on the foundations laid by Duns Scotus and others, Ockham rejected the thirteenth-century Aristotelian epistemology of active

---

[1] Paul Vignaux, *Philosophy in the Middle Ages* (New York, 1959), 173.

[2] Francis Oakley, "Medieval Theories of Natural Law : William of Ockham and the Significance of the Voluntarist Tradition," *Natural Law Forum*, VI (1961), 65-83; "Christian Theology and the Newtonian Science : The Rise of the Concept of the Laws of Nature," *Church History*, XXX (1961), 433-457; "Pierre d'Ailly and the Absolute Power of God : Another Note on the Theology of Nominalism," *Harvard Theological Review*, LVI (1963), 59-73; *The Political Thought of Pierre d'Ailly* (New Haven, 1964), 163-197; "From Constance to 1688 Revisited," *Journal of the History of Ideas*, XXVII (1966), 429-432; "Jacobean Political Theology : The Absolute and Ordinary Powers of the King," *Journal of the History of Ideas*, XXIX (1968), 323-346.

[3] The crucial passage in d'Ailly (*Sent.* IV, q. 1, a. 2) is reproduced above, 40, n. 1. Although Rimini's usage is closer to Ockham, he occasionally opposes *naturaliter* with *absoluta*, e.g. Sent. I, dist. 42-44, q. 1, a. 2 (I, 165 F).

44

object informing a passive mind through the agency of sensible species, intelligible species and the agent intellect. In place of the process of extracting or abstracting the universal from the particular, Ockham asserted that the mind intuited the particular and knew it directly and immediately. Intuitive cognition for Ockham, upon which all knowledge is ultimately based, is the knowledge according to which one judges a thing to be present and existing. Nothing can deceive the mind and force it to judge that something exists or is experienced when it is not.[1]

The distinction of God's powers was examined before Ockham's epistemology because the more recent versions of the traditional affirmation of Ockham's epistemological skepticism and the non-empirical, non-scientific import of his system have centered around Ockham's assertion that God can cause, de potentia absoluta, the intuitive cognition of a non-existent.[2] Although Ockham made this assertion (it seemed to follow naturally from the theological principle, accepted by Thomas[3] and reaffirmed in the Parisian articles of 1277,[4] that God can cause directly whatever he causes through secondary means), he placed several safeguards that, regardless of their philosophic or scientific validity, seemed to him sufficient to protect the empiricism of his epistemology. First, the possibility is only de potentia absoluta, and God does not in fact act that way. Second, even if we imagine such a thing happening, one would only perceive the object to exist; one would not judge it to exist.[5]

---

[1] Ockham, Ordinatio (Sent. I), prol., q. 1; Boehner, "The Notitia Intuitiva of Non-Existents According to William Ockham," in Collected Articles, 268-300; Sebastian J. Day, Intuitive Cognition : A Key to the Significance of the Later Scholastics (FIP, Phil. Ser., No. 4; St. Bonaventure, 1947).

[2] Anton Pegis, "Concerning William of Ockham," Traditio, II (1944), 465-480.

[3] Thomas Aquinas, Summa contra Gentiles, L. III, ch. 70 : "Patet etiam quod, si res naturalis producat proprium effectum, non est superfluum quod Deus illum producat. Quia res naturalis non producit ipsum, nisi in virtute divina. Neque est superfluum, si Deus per seipsum potest omnes effectus naturales producere, quod per quasdam alias causas producantur. Non enim hoc est ex insufficientia divinae virtutis, sed ex immensitate bonitatis ..."

[4] Art. 63 (CUP I, 547).

[5] The philosophical and scientific validity of Ockham's reasoning has recently been questioned by T. K. Scott, "Ockham on Evidence, Necessity, and Intuition," Journal of the History of Philosophy, VII (1969), 27-49; "Nicholas of Autrecourt, Buridan and Ockhamism," Journal of the History of Philosophy, IX (1971), 15-41.

d) *The Relation of Nominalism to Science*

On the basis of the empiricism of Ockham's epistemology and his adherence to a highly sophisticated terminist logic, the contribution of Ockham and his followers to the development of medieval science seems firmly established. Many of those viewed as followers of Ockham are also important names in fourteenth-century science : John Buridan, Nicholas of Oresme, Albert of Saxony, Pierre d'Ailly, Henry of Langenstein, and Marsilius of Inghen. Moreover, Ockham upheld the validity of the principle of causality. Although God could do directly what he normally does through secondary causes, secondary causality does obtain in the natural order and Ockham specifically excludes *sine qua non* causality *in naturalibus*.[1]

It is interesting along this line to note that the defenders of atomism in the fourteenth century—and there were some—were not the Ockhamists but the anti-Ockhamists. Adam Wodham, a disciple of Ockham, energetically attacked the atomism of Walter Chatton, who was one of the earliest critics of the thought of Ockham.[2]

e) *Metaphysics and Natural Theology*

In this area there is some disagreement among those who have contributed to the revision. It was the belief of Boehner and those influenced by him that Ockham altered metaphysics and natural theology only in two respects. First, he concentrated on existing individuals rather than abstract essences, but he believed in and continued to use the concepts of essence and existence, form and matter, substance and accidents, causality, and relation. Ockham still affirmed that there was such a thing as metaphysics and that its purpose was to study being *qua* being. Although he never wrote a work specifically on metaphysics, it was his expressed intention to do so. Second, he reduced the number of things in theology that could be demonstrated apart from relevation, but he maintained the importance of probable

---

[1] Ockham, *Sent.* IV, q. 1, G-H; *Sent.* II, q. 4 & 5. For a discussion of Ockham's position on natural causality see : Hochstetter, *Studien zur Metaphysik* ..., 144-173; Webering, *Theory of Demonstration* ..., 143-165; Courtenay, "The Critique on Natural Causality in the Mutakallimun and Nominalism," *Harvard Theological Review*, LXVI (1973).

[2] J. E. Murdoch and E. A. Synan, "Two Questions on the Continuum : Walter Chatton (?), O. F. M. and Adam Wodeham, O. F. M.," *Franciscan Studies*, XXVI (1966), 212-288.

arguments and even felt that the existence of God could be demonstrated. The thrust of Boehner's argumentation is that Ockham did have a metaphysics and a natural theology, although they were greatly simplified and to a large extent reduced.[1]

Moody, on the other hand, believes that Ockham radically altered metaphysics. By adopting a strict definition of demonstration and by using an empiricist criterion for the evidence used in demonstration, the so-called demonstrations generally used in metaphysics and natural theology became un-scientific and only probable. Thus natural theology was eliminated in favor of a positive theology based on revelation and faith rather than reason. Moody admits that Ockham allows "that a descriptive concept of God can be formed from the concept of 'being' or 'thing'," and Moody admits that Ockham has an argument for the existence of a sustaining cause of the universe, but Ockham does not believe that the existence of one sustaining cause can be rationally demonstrated, although it may indeed be highly probable.[2]

Whether one accepts Boehner's or Moody's version of Ockham's metaphysics, the limitations on natural theology are apparent. One can no longer accept, however, the thesis that Ockham engaged in the wholesale destruction of metaphysics and disallowed natural theology in principle.

f) *Ethics*

The newer view of the ethical system of Ockham or of Biel is altered considerably by a better understanding of the distinction between *potentia absoluta* and *potentia ordinata*. The ethical system that prevails is not a necessary system, which God was forced to adopt, but a chosen system, one of several God might have chosen to institute, had he so desired. Having chosen this one, however, it is binding and God will not arbitrarily or capriciously interrupt the present order to institute a new morality. Moreover, there is a close relationship between the eternal law of God, natural law, and the positive law that obtains in the church. Man, therefore, can and should act according to the dictates of right reason within him, as supported by the customs of the church and the statements of Scripture. An ethical system does not become totally positivistic just because God was not

---

[1] Boehner, "The Metaphysics of William Ockham," in *Collected Articles* ..., 373-399.
[2] Moody, "William of Ockham," 307-308, 313-315.

forced to choose it. It is the belief of both Ockham and Biel that the ethical system reflects the wisdom and intellect of God as well as his will (these being one and the same), and the voluntary nature of the present moral order (voluntary only for God, not for man) does not prevent God from having his own reasons for choosing the present order, even if man cannot know them.[1]

g) *Soteriology*

The nominalist position on grace and salvation, although seldom a major part of the traditional exposition of nominalism (at least not in expositions of Ockham's thought), has received considerable attention lately.[2] Again, the understanding of the two powers is the crucial issue by which the nominalist position is explained. For those who saw in the absolute power of God the possibility of divine intervention and who believed this concept represented the true thought of nominalism, God became omnipotent and arbitrary in such a way that the established system of salvation was violated and God accepted and rejected man according to his own inscrutable will—a position that some have seen as an extreme Augustinianism stemming from Duns Scotus. For those who saw in the ordained power of God the obligation of divine faithfulness and who believed this concept represented the true thought of nominalism, Ockham and his followers were semi-Pelagians who believed that God was obliged to reward with grace and eventually with eternal life any man who did what was in him.

The newer appreciation of the powers of God has stressed both aspects and has seen that the dialectic of the two powers is particularly useful in soteriology because it grants freedom and omnipotence to God without undermining the operation or predictability of the present order. If the newer research sees one aspect stressed more than another, it is the semi-Pelagian aspect.[3]

---

[1] Ockham, *Sent.* II, q. 4; *Sent.* II, q. 19; *Sent.* III, q. 8; *Quodl.* III, q. 13; *Sent.* I, dist. 45, q. 1; *Sent.* I, dist. 47, q. 1; *Sent.* I, dist. 48, q. 1; Oberman, *Harvest* ..., 90-93.

[2] The nominalist view of grace and justification has long been a part of Biel scholarship. It has only recently become a major issue in the literature on Ockham. Cf. Erwin Iserloh, *Gnade und Eucharistie in der philosophischen Theologie des Wilhelm von Ockham* (Wiesbaden, 1956); Dettloff, *Die Entwicklung der Akzeptations- und Verdienstlehre von Duns Scotus bis Luther* (Beiträge zur Geschichte der Phil. und Theol. des Mittelalters; Münster i.W., 1963), 253-290; Oberman, *Harvest* ..., 146-248,.

[3] Oberman, *Harvest* ..., 146-184.

48

h) *Sacramental Theology*

The second major area of nominalist theology that has been a subject of revision is the Ockhamist and post-Ockhamist view of the sacraments, in particular the eucharist. In earlier views this was the area in which Ockham supposedly had crossed over into heresy and for which he was called to account at Avignon. Recent evaluations have found little that is unique or particularly heretical in Ockham's eucharistic teaching.[1] Since he was never condemned on this issue, it may be that the theological commission examining his work was equally unable to find convincing evidence of heresy. Biel, the one follower of Ockham to dwell extensively on eucharistic theology, is now considered to be within the mainstream of catholic orthodoxy on this issue.[2]

i) *View of Society and the Church*

The Ockhamist view of the nature of society and the constitution of the church has attracted the attention of several recent historians, in particular Boehner,[3] Oberman,[4] Tierney,[5] and Oakley.[6] Although there is some disagreement among these scholars on the exact nature of the political thought of Ockham, d'Ailly, and Biel, there is a consensus that Ockham's views, especially as expressed in his more considered and thoughtful studies like the *Dialogus*, are more traditional than was once thought and heavily dependent on canonist teaching. Ockham was not the originator of conciliar theory, nor did he share the attitude toward papal power and the constitution of the church expressed in *Defensor pacis*. Moreover, his view of society and the church seems less atomistic and voluntaristic than it once did. If Ockham's political thought was one of the major sources for the

---

[1] Gabriel N. Buescher, *The Eucharistic Teaching of William Ockham* (Washington, 1950).

[2] P. Anatriello, *La dottrina di Gabriele Biel sull' Eucaristia* (Milan, 1936); Courtenay, "Cranmer as a Nominalist—*Sed Contra*," *Harvard Theological Review*, LVII (1964), 367-380; *The Eucharistic Thought of Gabriel Biel* (Doc. diss., Harvard Univ., 1967).

[3] Boehner, "Ockham's Political Ideas," in *Collected Articles ...*, 442-468.

[4] Oberman, *Harvest ...*, 361-422.

[5] Brian Tierney, "A Conciliar Theory of the Thirteenth Century," *Catholic Historical Review*, XXXVI (1951), 415-440; "Ockham, the Conciliar Theory and the Canonists," *Journal of the History of Ideas*, XV (1954), 40-70.

[6] Oakley, *The Political Thought ...*, 198-211.

political thought of d'Ailly and Biel (and this seems now to be generally accepted), then these later "nominalists" can also be seen as more conservative, especially Biel, the great defender of papal prerogatives.[1]

In addition to the more favorable and positive evaluation of the contribution of moderate nominalism, described above, the history of nominalism has also been revised. For example, the relation of Scotus, Durand, Aureol, and Ockham is now seen to be more complex and is not one continuous development. While recognizing the importance for Ockham's thought of the Scotistic idea of intuitive cognition, the limitations on theology as a science, the importance of God's omnipotence as expressed in predestination and divine acceptation, and the covenantal approach to theology that Scotus inherited from the Franciscan tradition, the differences between Scotus and Ockham, especially in the areas of logic and metaphysics, seem more significant. E. A. Moody has credited Ockham with the destruction of the muddy and confused philosophy and theology of the late thirteenth and early fourteenth centuries, particularly associated with Giles of Rome, Henry of Ghent, and John Duns Scotus, and has pointed to some surprising similarities between the thought of Ockham and Thomas Aquinas.[2] Boehner and Buescher have similarly pointed up important contrasts between Ockham on the one hand and Durand and Aureol on the other.[3] Consequently, no direct line of continuity runs from 1277 and the "second Augustinian school", through Scotus, Durand, and Aureol, to Ockham.

Similarly, the lines of development that stem from Ockham have been reinterpreted, in particular the relation of Ockham to radical nominalism. Moody has shown that the Parisian decree of 1339 was not a censure of Ockhamism but only a statement that Ockham should not be taught dogmatically to the exclusion of other points of view.[4] The nominalist theses condemned in the decree of 1340 were

---

[1] See the introduction to *Defensorium Obedientiae Apostolicae et Alia Documenta*, ed. by H. A. Oberman, D. E. Zerfoss, and W. J. Courtenay (Cambridge, Mass., 1968), 3-55.

[2] Moody, "Ockham and Aegidius of Rome."

[3] Boehner, "Realistic Conceptualism ...," in *Collected Articles* ..., 156-174; and "Ockham's Tractatus de Praedestinatione et de Praescientia Dei et de Futuris Contingentibus and its Main Problems," in *Collected Articles* ..., 420-441; Buescher, *Eucharistic Teaching* ..., Kenneth Plotnik; *Hervaeus Natalis O.P. and the Controversies over the Real Presence and Transubstantiation* (München, 1970).

[4] Moody, "Ockham, Buridan ..."

50

inconsistent with the thought of Ockham, although they paralleled the thought of Nicholas of Autrecourt, summoned to Avignon the month before and later condemned in 1346/47. Moreover, the two major opponents of Autrecourt, John Buridan and Bernard of Arezzo, were Ockhamists, leading one to the conclusion that Ockham and Autrecourt had little in common. In addition, both Boehner and Moody have detailed important differences between Ockham and Holcot,[1] and Damasus Trapp believes he has discovered in Gregory of Rimini the major opponent of John of Mirecourt.[2] Thus, in light of recent research, radical nominalism has become a movement that had only the most tenuous ties with Ockham and lasted only two decades until it was effectively silenced by the condemnations of 1347, conceived and implemented by the Ockhamists.

Changes in the interpretation of the subsequent history of nominalism are not as dramatic. D'Ailly and Biel are still seen as close followers of Ockham, although a "revised" Ockham has been paralleled by a "revised" d'Ailly [3] and a "revised" Biel.[4] More crucial for this later period is the relationship between nominalism (in either the old or new versions) and mysticism, especially as focused in the life and writings of John Gerson.[5]

The combined effect of the research of Hochstetter, Vignaux, Boehner, Moody, and Oberman has been to establish the orthodox, non-radical character of the thought of Ockham and Biel, and, by extension, d'Ailly. This more favorable and positive evaluation of these late medieval thinkers was achieved on two fronts : by a more careful and exhaustive analysis of the thought of each figure and by severing the ties that bound these moderate nominalists to the so-

---

[1] Boehner, "The Medieval Crisis of Logic and the Author of the Centiloquium Attributed to Ockham," in *Collected Articles* ..., 351-372; Moody, "A Quodlibetal Question of Robert Holkot, O. P. on the Problem of the Objects of Knowledge and of Belief," *Speculum*, XXXIX (1964), 53-74. For a corrected edition of this quodlibet see : Courtenay, "A Revised Text of Robert Holcot's Quodlibetal Dispute on Whether God is Able to Know More Than He Knows," *Archiv für Geschichte der Philosophie*, LIII (1971), 1-21.

[2] Damasus Trapp, "Augustinian Theology ...;" "Peter Ceffons ...;" and "Gregory of Rimini Manuscripts : Editions and Additions," *Augustiniana*, VIII (1958), 425-443.

[3] Courtenay, "Covenant and Causality in Pierre d'Ailly," *Speculum*, XLVI (1971), 94-119.

[4] Oberman, *Harvest* ...

[5] Steven Ozment, *Homo Spiritualis* (Leiden, 1969).

called radical nominalism of Holcot, Wodham, Autrecourt, and Mirecourt. Although it was recognized that the thought of Ockham,
d'Ailly, and Biel was not identical in all respects, it was felt they
had enough in common to permit them to be grouped together as if
they were a school. The principal ideas that were the source and
unifying elements of that movement were discovered to be more
theological than philosophical. It was not the atomistic metaphysics
of the individual (so long misunderstood) nor the epistemology of
intuitive cognition (Scotist in origin and adopted by almost everyone
in the late Middle Ages) that distinguished this movement, but rather
a conception of the centrality, efficacy, and dependability of verbal,
contractual agreements for all aspects of the relationship between
God and man. Each individual idea in this moderate nominalist system
(for example, the idea of the two powers of God, or the semi-Pelagian
soteriology, or the non-necessity of the Judeo-Christian ethical system,
or the idea of *sine qua non* causality in the sacraments) can probably
be found in earlier thinkers or in contemporaries to whom one would
never apply the terms nominalist or Ockhamist. The unique feature
of Ockhamist thought was that these ideas were all present and
grounded in the idea of pact, or covenant—willed verbal agreements
that are no less dependable and certain because they are in origin
voluntary.[1]

3. New Perspectives, 1965-1972

Certain details of the "revised" picture, particularly in regard to
the historical development of nominalism, are presently being questioned and altered. Inasmuch as these may lead to a different history
of late medieval thought in the near future, they should be treated
as a separate section.

a) *Terminology*

It is already becoming apparent that the term "nominalism," as a
description of the thought of Ockham, Buridan, Rimini, d'Ailly, Biel,

---

[1] I have treated aspects of this issue in the following articles : "Necessity and Freedom in Anselm ...;" "Sacrament, Symbol, and Causality in Bernard of Clairvaux,"
Bernard of Clairvaux : Studies presented to Jean Leclercq (Washington D.C., 1973), 111-22;
"The King and the Leaden Coin : The Economic Background of *Sine Qua Non* Causality," *Traditio*, XXVIII (1972), 185-209; "Covenant and Causality. ..."

and other late medieval thinkers, is no longer as appropriate as it once seemed. If Ockham did not reject generic similarity in nature or destroy metaphysics, and if the essential structure of his thought (and even more that of Biel) was theological rather than philosophical, then should not the term "nominalism" be dropped in favor of a more descriptive label? Has anything other than habit and familiarity prolonged the usage?

The case against using the term "nominalism" to designate a school or schools in the fourteenth and fifteenth centuries is strong. Even those contributors to the revision who, like Oberman, have continued to use the term, do not believe that Ockham or Biel were nominalists in the traditional sense. Even if one restricts the term "nominalism" to the area of logic and epistemology and acknowledges that Ockham did indeed reject "common nature" and stress knowledge of the particular, Ockham was not a thorough-going nominalist; nor are there valid grounds for assuming that Ockham's position on the question of universals is the key to his thought, from which all else follows.

It is not surprising, therefore, to learn that none of Ockham's contemporaries ever called him a nominalist. "Nominalist" was a twelfth-century term that described a particular position on the question of universals, and when *nominales* or *opinio nominalium* were used in the thirteenth century, they described the position of twelfth-century logicians.[1] By 1270 these labels had ceased to be used and were only reintroduced in the fifteenth century (possibly associated with the revival of Albertism and Thomism) to describe a position in logic or, more accurately, a way of teaching logic.[2] Similarly, the words *terministae* and *via moderna* are fifteenth century in origin and concern logic, not epistemology, metaphysics, or theology. When, in the fifteenth century, Ockham's name occurs in a list of *nominales*, the intent was to indicate that he shared with others a particular approach to logic, not that all those named in the list belonged to a school of which Ockham was the founder.[3] The only descriptive term

---

[1] Cf. Vignaux, "Nominalisme," 717-718; F. Pelster, "Nominales und reales in 13. Jahrhundert," *Sophia* (1946), 154-161.

[2] Ehrle, *Der Sentenzenkommentar* ...; Ritter, *Studien zur Spätscholastik*, vol. II : *Via antiqua und via moderna auf den deutschen Universitäten des XV. Jahrhunderts* (Sitzungsberichte der Heidelberger Akademie ..., 7. Abhandlung (Heidelberg, 1922; reprint 1963).

[3] C. E. Bulaeus, *Historia Universitatis Parisiensis*, vol. V (Paris, 1670), 708; Plessis d'Argentré, *Collectio judiciorum novis erroribus*, vol. I (Paris, 1728), 134, sp. 2; Stephen

in the fourteenth century was *moderni*, which simply meant any contemporary theologian or, in a pejorative sense, any opponent. Within this mass of confusing labels Moody has shown admirable caution. He has consistently refused to apply the term "nominalist" or even "Ockhamist" to an entire group of theologians in the fourteenth and fifteenth centuries as if they constituted a school. Nominalism was and is, for Moody, a philosophical position and a method. It was essentially the application of logical analysis to philosophical and theological problems in such a way that they became problems about "the meaning and reference of terms and the truth conditions of sentences."[1] Thus nominalism was a philosophy of language, and as a method it eventually came to be known as the *via moderna*. Moody has noted that no theologian in the fourteenth century designated himself as an Ockhamist, nor was that term used to describe anyone's thought save Ockham's.[2] Moody has, therefore, chosen to confine "nominalism" to its logical, epistemological, and metaphysical meaning and to confine "Ockhamism" to Ockham. Although he sees a consistency in Ockham's thought, he does not see that consistency as the result of one or two peculiarly nominalist principles, and although he is aware of the use later theologians made of Ockham and the parallel thinking to which one can point, he does not believe that constitutes a nominalist or Ockhamist school. "Partyism" or "Schoolism" seems to be a child of the fifteenth and sixteenth centuries that should not be read back into the fourteenth century.

How is one then to describe the unity of thought among Ockham, d'Ailly, and Biel to which various scholars have pointed ? "Ockhamism" seems to be the least undesirable term. "Nominalism" should perhaps be left to the realm of logic, where it was subscribed to by many *moderni* who otherwise have little in common. The best argument for retaining "nominalism" as the proper title for the thought described above seems to be the importance that Ockham, d'Ailly, and Biel gave to the ideas of assigned value and willed verbal covenants.

Baluzius, *Miscellanea novo ordine digesta*, vol. II (Lucca, 1761), 293-294; Ehrle, *Der Sentenzenkommentar* ..., 305-321.

[1] E. A. Moody, "Buridan and a Dilemma of Nominalism," in *H. A. Wolfson Jubilee Volume* (Jerusalem, 1965), II, 577. See also "A Quodlibetal Question of Robert Holkot, O. P., on the Problem of the Objects of Knowledge and of Belief," *Speculum*, 39 (1964), 53-74; "Ockhamism," in *Encyclopedia of Philosophy* (New York, 1968), V, 533-534; "William of Ockham," in *Encyclopedia of Philosophy* (New York, 1968), VIII, 306-317.

[2] Moody, "Ockhamism," 533.

54

b) *The "English School" of Nominalism*

The radicalism attributed to the thought of Holcot and Wodham is presently being questioned. As a side product of the re-evaluation of Ockham, the radicalism of Holcot had been accentuated in the period from 1940 to 1965. Boehner had passed the onus of authoring the radical *Centiloquium* from Ockham to Holcot in 1944.[1] Moody, in an article in 1964, pointed out some logical issues on which Holcot was more radical and nominalist than Ockham.[2]

Moody's evidence still seems solid and incontrovertible, but the association of Holcot and the *Centiloquium* now appears doubtful.[3] The evidence on which Boehner based his supposition was drawn from a hasty and inaccurate reading of the Holcot texts. The impression of skepticism and fideism that one gleans from the earlier statements on Holcot's thought has been considerably dispelled by Oberman's research into Holcot's views on faith and reason, predestination and grace.[4] The texts recently published by Paolo Molteni support Oberman's findings, although Molteni's interpretation is still wedded to the older viewpoint.[5] Most attention has been given to Holcot's logic and epistemology, and in the latter area Holcot adopted the general outlines of the Ockhamist theory of cognition but reintroduced species in a manner that seems to relate back to Thomas.[6] Recently, Heinrich Schepers has argued that radical nominalism at Oxford was specifically an anti-Ockhamist movement, and Holcot, far from being a radical nominalist, was a faithful disciple of Ockham and helped lead the counter-attack against the nominalists, whose leader was the Dominican, William of Crathorn.[7] The publication of the critical edition of Holcot's *Quodlibets* and *Sentence Commentary*, now underway,

---

[1] Boehner, "The Medieval Crisis ..."

[2] Moody, "A Quodlibetal Question ..."

[3] See the forthcoming doctoral dissertation of Hester Gelber, University of Wisconsin, 1974.

[4] Oberman, " 'Facientibus Quod In Se Est Deus Non Denegat Gratiam.' Robert Hoicot, O. P., and the Beginnings of Luther's Theology," *Harvard Theological Review*, LV (1962), 317-342; *Harvest* ..., 235-248.

[5] Paolo Molteni, *Roberto Holcot o.p. Dottrina della grazia e della giustificazione con due questioni quodlibetali inedite* (Pinerolo, 1968).

[6] See the forthcoming dissertations of Hester Gelber (University of Wisconsin, 1974) and Anne Brinkley (Harvard Univ., 1972).

[7] Heinrich Schepers, "Holkot contra dicta Crathorn," *Philosophisches Jahrbuch*, LXXVII (1970), 320-354, LXXIX (1972), 106-36.

should speed the process of determining the exact position of this important English theologian.[1] Adam Wodham, the other leading English nominalist, may undergo a similar transformation. Dettloff has found nothing unusual about the soteriology of Wodham, which seems to follow Ockham closely.[2] On the issues of quantity and continuum Wodham placed himself in opposition to Walter Chatton, one of Ockham's leading opponents.[3] A recent study has pointed to the more conservative tone of Wodham's defense of Ockham's eucharistic thought.[4] However, adequate texts of Wodham's thought are even more scarce than for Holcot, and it may be some time before a new picture of Wodham can be constructed.

Even on the basis of the studies that have been done to date, the history of Ockhamism and nominalism in England appears to be quite different from what was thought five or ten years ago. As a result, radical nominalism has moved one stage further away from Ockham.

c) *The "Parisian School" of Nominalism*

Of all the nominalists that appeared in the pages of the older literature, the appropriateness of "nominalism" as a designation for Autrecourt and Mirecourt seemed most certain. In addition to internal evidence from their writings, their status as arch-nominalists was confirmed by the condemnations of 1346 and 1347. The research of Damasus Trapp, only a little more than a decade ago, assured us that Gregory of Rimini, an Ockhamist, was the central figure behind the condemnation of Mirecourt in 1347.

That assessment, however, is now open to grave doubt. In examining the views of Mirecourt on grace and justification, Dettloff found nothing out of keeping with Ockham's thought, and he therefore concluded that Mirecourt's radicalism must lie in some other area.[5] Roy Van Neste, in a recent doctoral dissertation at the University of

---

[1] The critical edition of Holcot's *Quaestiones Quodlibetales*, edited by W. J. Courtenay, H. Gelber, and Anne Brinkley, will be published in three volumes, the first to appear in 1974. The publication of the *Sentence Commentary* will follow the *Quodlibets*.

[2] Dettloff, *Die Entwicklung* ..., 329-332.

[3] Murdoch and Synan, "Two Questions ..."

[4] Thomas Mitchell, *Medieval Discussions of Quantity and the Development of Eucharistic Thought with Special Concentration on the Ockhamist Tradition* (Master's thesis, University of Wisconsin, 1971).

[5] Dettloff, *Die Entwicklung* ..., 325-328.

Wisconsin, discovered that Mirecourt's epistemology had little in common with Autrecourt and instead followed the outline of Ockham's theory of knowledge.[1] Moreover, Mirecourt rejected intuitive cognition of a non-existent, thus increasing empirical certitude at the expense of possibly incurring the anger of the Ockhamists.[2] In my own examination of Mirecourt's position on sacramental causality I found him maintaining the Thomist position against the Ockhamists.[3] Finally, one of the positions of Mirecourt most often cited as indicative of his radicalism, namely the belief in God's power to make a past thing not to have been, was not maintained by Mirecourt at all. Among those who held this opinion was Gregory of Rimini. Since this was one of the issues in the process against Mirecourt, it seems unlikely that Rimini could have been the spirit behind the condemnation of 1347.[4]

The picture of Mirecourt that emerges from these recent studies is that of a cautious, non-radical, somewhat eclectic theologian who was misjudged on certain issues. It may be some consolation to the reader's sense of disorientation in the face of the rapid change in characterization undergone by the nominalists to discover that the reputation of the "prince of the nominalists," Nicholas of Autrecourt, has remained unchanged. This may in part be due to the paucity of his extant writings upon which to base any reconstruction. However, as we know more about the figures that surrounded Autrecourt, our understanding of his thought and intention is bound to change as well.

4. On Relating the "Revision" to Other Late Medieval Developments

On the basis of the foregoing analysis it is evident that the clichés about nominalism, such as atomism, skepticism, fideism, divorce of faith and reason, can no longer be used to show parallels or dissimilarities with other aspects of late medieval society. It is not clear how

---

[1] Roy J. Van Neste, *The Epistemology of John of Mirecourt in Relation to Fourteenth Century Thought* (Doctoral dissertation, University of Wisconsin, 1972).

[2] *Ibid.*

[3] The results of this research will appear as part of a longer study, "Sacramental Causality in 14th-Century Cistercian Thought : John of Mirecourt, James of Eltville, Gottschalk of Nepomuk, and Conrad of Ebrach."

[4] Courtenay, "John of Mirecourt and Gregory of Rimini on Whether God can Undo the Past," *Recherches de Théologie ancienne et médiévale*, XXXVIII (1972).

the newer views relate, although some work has already been done in this direction. The conclusions drawn here are, of course, speculative, and are intended only to provide a basis for discussion with scholars in other disciplines represented at this conference.

If the fragmentation of the medieval synthesis can no longer be used as the hallmark of nominalism around which to build a theory of the development of late gothic art, the increased importance given to empiricism in the nominalist system should have some implications for the development of the visual and plastic arts, if not architecture. Ockhamist epistemology is not simply empirical; it is based on visual experience, and it takes the eye as the primary sense organ around which to build a theory of knowledge. The rapidity with which the mind reaches out to know the object is particularly appropriate to (and in fact is based on and illustrated by) visual experience. "Knowing" in Ockhamism is primarily "seeing." Such an epistemology certainly parallels the emphasis in late medieval and early Renaissance art on rendering the visual world with increasing accuracy.

The themes of late medieval art are supported by the theology of Ockhamism. In particular, the dignity of man, a theme both in Renaissance art and literature, lies at the heart of the Ockhamist semi-Pelagian soteriology, as has been pointed out already by Oberman.[1] The chosen quality of the present order as well as its dependability give to the world around the *viator* an intensified meaning.

The close examination of life as it is lived and the stress on the dignity of man are themes of late medieval literature as well as art. If there is a pessimistic note to certain types of late medieval literature, it cannot be ascribed to Ockhamism, which was much more positive in its outlook. Perhaps the most obvious connection between Ockhamism and late medieval literature lies in the type of theological issues one finds reflected in the poetry. In particular one recalls Chaucer's discussion of the issue of determination and free will as associated with the controversy between Bradwardine and the "Pelagians".[2] The issue of grace and justification, central to the recent research in nominalism, is also found as a recurring theme in late medieval literature.[3]

---

[1] Oberman, "Some Notes on the Theology of Nominalism ..."

[2] Geoffrey Chaucer, *The Canterbury Tales*, "The Nun's Priest's Tale."

[3] See the recent dissertation by J. F. McNamara, *Responses to Ockhamist Theology in the Poetry of the "Pearl"-Poet, Langland, and Chaucer* (Louisiana State University, 1968).

The connections between Ockhamism, art and literature are, at best, the reflection of common interests. When we turn to late medieval religion, however, the connections are much closer and stronger. Central to the revised view of nominalism is the Biblical conception of God, who remains omnipotent and free, and who communicates directly with man through covenants. The stress on omnipotence and divine power, the stress on the covenantal nature of man's relation with God, the continual use of Biblical (especially Old Testament) examples in the writings of Ockham and Biel, all mark a re-emphasis on the Judeo-Christian conception of God in contrast with the more distant and more mechanistic deity of Latin Averroism as influenced by Aristotle's Prime Mover. Gilson has already pointed out that this trend back to a Biblical conception of God was stimulated by the condemnations of 1277 and represents a reaction to Greco-Arabian necessitarianism.[1] Ockhamism was only one part of that changing conception of God, although one of the more visible and important parts. The tendency to see God as the Biblical Yahweh rather than the Aristotelian Prime Mover remained strong as long as Averroism needed to be combatted, i.e., throughout most of the fourteenth and fifteenth centuries.

One aspect of this increase in Biblical theology and the Biblical conception of God that has not been sufficiently noted is that theology became less apologetic in the process. The apologetic focus of so much of thirteenth century theology—one thinks especially of Raymund Lull, Roger Bacon's *Opus majus*, Thomas' *Summa contra gentiles*, and Raymund Martin's *Pugio fidei*—was designed to convert the Jew and the Moslem and reconvert the heretic. The emergence of a scientific theology that could be rationally demonstrated, a theology that begins with the existence and nature of God, established a common ground for dialogue between Christian and non-Christian. All this began to change in 1277. With the attack on the scientific nature of theology and the limitation of the amount of knowledge of God that could be gained through the unaided reason, theology as a tool for defending the faith and converting others was replaced by a more internal and internally consistent theological system. Perhaps the Christo-centric approach of Luther is the culmination of a long process away from a "philosophic," natural theology that could serve apologetic

---

[1] Etienne Gilson, *History of Christian Philosophy in the Middle Ages* (New York, 1955), 402-410, 498-499.

ends. May not Holcot's idea that a knowledge of God will be granted to the one who does what is in him be a residue of thirteenth-century Dominican theology in Ockhamist garb ?

If Ockhamism reduced the common ground shared by Christian and non-Christian, it encouraged a more active religious life for the Christian by guaranteeing salvation to the one who did what was in him. Although the degree of an individual's love for God and the implementation of that love in works of charity could only be judged worthy by God, the requirements were revealed in Scripture and the teaching of the church, and one could, without fear, trust God to keep his covenants. The covenantal theme of Ockhamist theology is, perhaps, the key to that system, and it was as important for late medieval religion as it was later to be for the Reformation. [1]

---

[1] Cf. Oberman, "Wir sein pettler. Hoc est verum. Bund und Gnade in der Theologie des Mittelalters und der Reformation," *Zeitschrift für Kirchengeschichte*, LXXVIII (1967), 232-252; Martin Greschat, "Der Bundesgedanke in der Theologie des späten Mittelalters," *Zeitschrift für Kirchengeschichte*, LXXXI (1970), 44-63.

XII

NOMINALISM AND LATE MEDIEVAL THOUGHT:
A BIBLIOGRAPHICAL ESSAY

Research trends on the thought of the late Middle Ages have seldom been the subject of a bulletin article. Generally one has had to ferret out the important literature from the *Bulletin de théologie ancienne et médiévale* (which regrettably has run somewhat behind in its review of the secondary literature on medieval thought), the *Revue des sciences philosophiques et théologiques* (which briefly reviews the current periodical literature and maintains a sequential bulletin article on medieval doctrine), the bibliographies of individual authors which have appeared from time to time, or the various checklists available for medieval studies.[1] The only recent bibliographical survey that treats late medieval thought is Heiko Oberman, "Theologie des späten Mittelalters: Stand und Aufgaben der Forschung," *Theologische Literaturzeitung* 91 (1966) 401–16. Oberman's article concentrates on the themes of Scripture and tradition, ecclesiology and conciliarism, and Gabriel Biel. The difficulty in getting a synthetic overview of the research in this field has widened the gap, perhaps more than in any other area of medieval thought, between the standard view, as recorded in textbooks, and the discoveries and new interpretations that have marked the research of the last few decades. In a separate article I have compared the traditional interpretation with the newer assessments, and for a fuller treatment of the earlier literature and the revised view of William of

---

[1] The recent bulletin articles in the *Revue des sciences philosophiques et théologiques* (*RSPT*) that concern late medieval thought are: Louis-Jacques Bataillon, "Bulletin d'histoire des doctrines médiévales: VII: La fin du moyen âge," *RSPT* 47 (1963) 444–79; J. N. Walty, "Bulletin d'histoire des doctrines, XVᵉ–XVIᵉ siècles," *RSPT* 51 (1967) 461–81; Bataillon, "Bulletin d'histoire des doctrines médiévales: La période scholastique (XIIIᵉ–XVᵉ s.)," *RSPT* 53 (1969) 707-43. Bibliographies of late medieval authors, where these exist, will be treated in the appropriate place in the following bulletin. Other useful bibliographies that are either general or concern pre-fourteenth-century authors are: Ermenegildo Frascadore and Herwig Ooms, *Bibliografia delle bibliografie francescane* (Florence, 1964-65); Odulfus Schäfer, *Bibliographia de vita operibus et doctrina Iohannis Duns Scoti* (Rome, 1955). The most important checklists are: *Progress of Medieval and Renaissance Studies in the United States and Canada* (Boulder, Col.); *International Guide to Medieval Studies: A Quarterly Index to Periodical Literature* (Darien, Conn.); *Quarterly Check-List of Medievalia: An International Index of Current Books, Monographs, Brochures, and Separates* (Darien, Conn.); *International Medieval Bibliography* (Leeds, Eng.); *Répertoire bibliographique de la philosophie* (Louvain). Future issues of the *Archiv für Reformationsgeschichte* will, along with other topics, contain a checklist for late medieval thought. Future projects as well as completed ones are listed in *Bulletin de philosophie médiévale* (Louvain).

Ockham the reader is directed to that study.[2] The purpose of the present article is to survey in more detail the new approaches taken toward the theology and philosophy of the late medieval period. In order to stay within a manageable length, there are several important areas of late medieval thought that will receive little or no attention. Most of these deserve and have often received separate treatment, e.g., Renaissance thought, fourteenth-century science, conciliarism and late medieval political thought, mysticism, hermeneutics and preaching, Mariology, and heterodox movements. The works that will be discussed are, of course, selected and in no sense represent the total available literature.

NEW STIMULI FOR RESEARCH

Although the study of late medieval thought is as old as the field of medieval intellectual history, it has not received as much attention as earlier periods, and interest in it has frequently been distorted by the polemical concerns of both Protestants and Catholics.[3] In the last generation, however, the field has attracted the attention of historians of philosophy and science, and even those whose interests lie in the area of theology have shown more caution and care in analyzing and evaluating the sources.

There are many things that have stimulated this renewed and broadened interest in the late medieval period. The abundance of source materials, vastly greater than in earlier periods, now seems to excite rather than terrify the would-be student. The reading rooms of manuscript libraries have become more popular places, and the availability of microfilming has accelerated research and made it possible to bring to one location the combined resources of multiple European archives. Apart from what the individual scholar can collect for his own immediate needs, there have been large filming projects, such as the Vatican manuscripts at the Vatican Film Library of St. Louis University, the manuscripts of the Ambrosiana in Milan at the Medieval Institute of Notre Dame University, and the manuscripts of the Austrian monastic libraries at St. John's College in Collegeville, Minnesota. Moreover, the photographic reprint process has placed those works that were fortunate enough to be preserved in early printed editions on a library shelf near the working scholar. The Franciscan Institute at St. Bonaventure, N.Y.,

---

[2] William J. Courtenay, "Nominalism and Late Medieval Religion," to be published among the papers from the Conference on Late Medieval and Renaissance Religion (Ann Arbor, 1972) in *Studies in Medieval and Reformation Thought* (Tübingen), due to appear in 1973.

[3] This is even true of scholars, such as Francis Ehrle and Constantine Michalski, who had a firsthand knowledge of many of the manuscript sources. For the relevant work of Ehrle and Michalski, see the article referred to in the previous footnote.

took an early lead in this production, but they have subsequently been surpassed by the numerous offerings of Gregg Press in London and Minerva Press in Frankfurt.

Several institutes devoted to the study of particular aspects of late medieval thought have encouraged research and have published the results. Among these are the Franciscan Institute, which has maintained publication series for texts and studies in the philosophy and theology of the period; the Augustinian Historical Institute in New York, which has produced text editions and monographs under the series title *Cassiciacum*; and the Institut für Spätmittelalter und Reformation in Tübingen, which, under the direction of Heiko Oberman, has been publishing the series *Studies in Medieval and Reformation Thought*. The Société internationale pour l'étude de la philosophie médiévale (Louvain) has, through the international congresses it has convoked and through the publication of the *Bulletin de philosophie médiévale*, provided channels of communication for the scholars working in this field.

THE CHANGING MEANING OF NOMINALISM

Until the last generation the term "nominalism," when applied to late medieval thought, had a commonly accepted meaning. In the narrow sense it referred to the philosophical position that denied to universals any extramental existence and substituted for the idea of a common nature an atomistic world of particulars, or individuals. In the broader sense it referred to a system of thought, derived from this epistemological and ontological rejection of universals, that destroyed metaphysics and made the doctrines and moral principles of theology dependent solely on the omnipotent and arbitrary will of God. The leading nominalist of the period was William of Ockham, and since his followers dominated the universities of the fourteenth and fifteenth centuries, the scholastic thought of this period has often been termed nominalist.

The meaning and application of the term "nominalism" has today become a subject of debate that is far from being resolved. Part of the problem arises from the fact that "nominalist" has been a pejorative as well as a descriptive term, and the intensive research on late medieval thinkers conducted across the past few decades has found the value judgment unacceptable and the traditional description questionable for one reason or another.

Some historians have continued to believe that nominalists in the traditional sense did exist despite the fact that those whom they have studied do not conform to the older definition. Albert Lang, *Heinrich Totting von Oyta* (Münster, 1937), maintained that Oyta was only half a nominalist, because he followed Ockham in philosophy and Thomas in theology. Philotheus Boehner, who piloted a re-evaluation of Ockham, argued that Ockham was not a nominalist in either philosophy or theology. In a series of studies, posthumously republished as *Collected Articles on Ockham* (St. Bonaventure, 1958), he suggested that Ockham might better be considered a realistic conceptualist, since he believed that universal terms refer to concepts that exist apart from the language through which they are expressed, and that these concepts, in turn, refer to similarities among existing individuals that are real and experienced. In like manner, Boehner attempted to show the conservative and constructive nature of Ockham's ideas in theology and political thought. For Boehner, the radical nominalists were to be found among some of Ockham's disciples (for whom he was not responsible), such as Robert Holcot. More recently, Damasus Trapp has argued that another famous nominalist, Gregory of Rimini, was rather the standard-bearer against the nominalists.[4]

With the declining enrollment within the nominalist school, some historians have begun to question the appropriateness of the label "nominalist" when applied to Ockham or other fourteenth-century thinkers. Erich Hochstetter, "Nominalismus?" *Franciscan Studies* 9 (1949) 370–403, suggested that the term should be discarded, especially for Ockham. Both he and Trapp noted that the label was introduced later by the opponents of the followers of Ockham and may therefore be suspect. Trapp has preferred to use the terms *moderni* and "modernists" to distinguish the constructive and destructive elements within late medieval thought.[5]

A different approach to nominalism has been taken by other scholars. While still insisting that nominalism is an entire system, a particular approach to reality, they have taken it to be principally a name that identifies the thought of William of Ockham and his most prominent followers, Pierre d'Ailly and Gabriel Biel. When faced with the conflict between the traditional meaning of nominalism and the newer assessment of Ockham and others, these scholars have chosen to alter the definition of nominalism rather than suggest that the term is inappropri-

---

[4] Among Damasus Trapp's numerous articles, those that sketch out this thesis are: "Augustinian Theology of the 14th Century: Notes on Editions, Marginalia, Opinions and Book-Lore," *Augustiniana* 6 (1956) 146–274; "Peter Ceffons of Clairvaux," *Recherches de théologie ancienne et médiévale* 24 (1957) 101–54; "Gregory of Rimini Manuscripts: Editions and Additions," *Augustiniana* 8 (1958) 425–43; "Gregory de Rimini y el nominalismo," *Augustinianum* 4 (1964) 5–20.

[5] In particular see: "Augustinian Theology"; "Peter Ceffons"; "Clm 27034: Unchristened Nominalism and Wycliffite Realism at Prague in 1381," *Recherches de théologie ancienne et médiévale* 24 (1957) 320–60; "'Modern' and 'Modernists' in MS Fribourg Cordeliers 26," *Augustinianum* 5 (1965) 241–70.

720

ate to these figures. This approach now has a long and respectable history. One finds it in Paul Vignaux, "Nominalisme," *Dictionnaire de théologie catholique*, 11/1 (Paris, 1930) cols. 717–84; "Occam," *ibid.*, cols. 876–89; and *Nominalisme au XIVe siècle* (Montreal, 1948). It is also found in Heiko Oberman, "Some Notes on the Theology of Nominalism with Attention to its Relation to the Renaissance," *Harvard Theological Review* 53 (1960) 47–76, and *The Harvest of Medieval Theology* (Cambridge, Mass., 1963).

Among those responsible for the revision in the understanding of late medieval thought there are two scholars who, for different reasons, have retained the label "nominalist" in describing the thought of Ockham and others. For E. A. Moody, nominalism is essentially the application of logical analysis to philosophical and theological problems in such a way that they become problems about "the meaning and reference of terms and the truth conditions of sentences."[6] In metaphysics this resulted in the elimination of intensional entities that exist apart from concrete particulars. Ockham's repudiation of the idea of a "common nature" which inheres in things of the same species was a major result of this linguistic analysis. Thus nominalism was a philosophy of language, and as a method it came to be known as the *via moderna*. As used by Moody in this strict philosophical sense, nominalism was one of the more important aspects of Ockham's thought, but it does not explain or dictate Ockham's positions in theology and political thought. Nominalism was and is a philosophical position (in epistemology and metaphysics) and a method; it was not a "school." Moreover, one could be more or less nominalistic depending on how far one carried the rejection of common natures. Moody has suggested that Ockham's nominalism may have been "restricted to the first-order language of physical objects."[7]

Heiko Oberman has defended the position that nominalism was as much a theology as a philosophy, if not more so. Indeed, it was not so much the method of linguistic analysis that characterized nominalism as it was the dialectic of the two powers of God applied to a series of philosophical and theological problems, especially the atonement, justification and sanctification, natural law and ethics. One can therefore identify the nominalist as the one who applies this dialectic, with its twofold stress on the omnipotence of God and the stability and dependability of

---

[6] E. A. Moody, "Buridan and a Dilemma of Nominalism," in *H. A. Wolfson Jubilee Volume* 2 (Jerusalem, 1965) 577. See also "A Quodlibetal Question of Robert Holkot, O.P.,. on the Problem of the Objects of Knowledge and of Belief," *Speculum* 39 (1964) 53–74; "Ockhamism," *Encyclopedia of Philosophy* 5 (New York, 1968) 533–34; "William of Ockham," *ibid.* 8 (New York, 1968) 306–17.

[7] "A Quodlibetal Question," p. 74.

the created order, to various problems in theology and (to a lesser degree) philosophy.

Although not all scholars are willing to define nominalism in terms of the dialectic of the two powers, an increasing number share with Oberman his belief that the dialectic of the two powers and, behind it, a particular understanding of covenant and contingency is an important key to the thought of Ockham and many of his followers—perhaps ultimately more significant than the approach to language, although both aspects can certainly be found in Ockham, d'Ailly, and Biel. Recent discussions of the "covenantal" theme of late medieval thought include: Heiko Oberman, "Wir sein pettler. Hoc est verum: Bund und Gnade in der Theologie des Mittelalters und der Reformation," *Zeitschrift für Kirchengeschichte* 78 (1967) 232–52; Martin Greschat, "Der Bundesgedanke in der Theologie des späten Mittelalters," *ibid.* 81 (1970) 44–63; William J. Courtenay, "Covenant and Causality in Pierre d'Ailly," *Speculum* 46 (1971) 94–119; "The King and the Leaden Coin: The Economic Background of *Sine qua non* Causality," *Traditio* 28 (1972) 185–209; Steven Ozment, "Mysticism, Nominalism and Dissent," to be published among the papers from the Conference on Late Medieval and Renaissance Religion (Ann Arbor, 1972) in *Studies in Medieval and Reformation Thought* (Tübingen), due to appear in 1973.

Not all works that have recently appeared show the signs of the revision in late medieval studies. The traditional assessment can still be found, relatively undisturbed, in Ramón M. Torelló, "El Ockhamismo y la decadencia escolástica en el siglo XIV," *Pensamiento* 9 (1953) 199–228; 11 (1955) 171–88, 259–83; Juan Roig Gironella, "Para la historia del nominalismo y de la reacción antinominalista de Suárez," *ibid.* 17 (1961) 279–310; Karl Anton Sprengard, *Systematische-historische Untersuchungen zur philosophie des XIV. Jahrhunderts* (2 vols.; Bonn, 1967–68).

WILLIAM OF OCKHAM

In the history of philosophy Ockham is generally approached by way of his two most prominent "forerunners," Durand of St. Pourçain and Peter Aureol. Little that has altered our understanding of Durand and Aureol has appeared in recent years. The major interpretive studies still remain Johannes Koch, *Durandus de S. Porciano O.P.: Forschungen zum Streit um Thomas von Aquin zu Beginn des 14. Jahrhunderts* 1: *Literargeschichtliche Grundlegung* (Münster, 1927); R. Dreiling, *Der Konzeptualismus in der Universalienlehre des Franziskanerbischofs Petrus Aureoli* (Münster, 1913); Paul Vignaux, *Justification et prédestination au XIVe siècle: Duns Scot, Pierre d'Auriole et Grégoire de*

Rimini (Paris, 1934); and R. Schmücker, *Propositio per se nota, Gottes-beweis und ihr Verhältnis nach Petrus Aureoli* (Werl, 1941).

The picture of the relationship between these thinkers and Ockham has, however, undergone some revision. Philotheus Boehner has pointed to areas in which Ockham and Aureol were not in agreement: "The Text Tradition of Ockham's Ordinatio," *New Scholasticism* 16 (1942) 203-41. Recently Kenneth Plotnick, *Hervaeus Natalis OP and the Controversies over the Real Presence and Transubstantiation* (Munich, 1970), has suggested some areas of Eucharistic thought in which Ockham and Durand were in opposition. For further discussion see my review of Plotnik's work in *Journal of the American Academy of Religion* 40 (1972) 256-58. More changes may be forthcoming now that the texts of these two authors have become more accessible. The Franciscan Institute has published a critical edition of the first part of Aureol's Commentary on the *Sentences: Scriptum super primum Sententiarum* 1 & 2 (St. Bonaventure, 1953-56). The Vatican Film Library in St. Louis has made available, through its "Manuscripta" series, a microfilm copy of the entire *Sentences* Commentary of Aureol. In 1964 Gregg Press reprinted in photocopy the *Sentences* Commentary of Durand from the edition of Venice, 1571.

In contrast to Durand and Aureol, Ockham seems to be of perennial interest to a wide group of scholars, and the recent literature on him is abundant. The groundwork for the revision in Ockham studies, and thus the foundation for the more recent literature, can be found in the works of Erich Hochstetter, especially his *Studien zur Metaphysik und Erkenntnislehre Wilhelms von Ockham* (Berlin, 1927), and the articles of Paul Vignaux, Philotheus Boehner, and E. A. Moody referred to earlier. Occasionally, whole issues of journals have been given over to studies on Ockham, such as the 1950 issue of *Franziskanische Studien.* Similarly, Ockham was one of the main themes of the III Convegno dei lettori di filosofia italiani, meeting at the Apostolic Institute in Castel Fogliani in 1954, and those papers were published in *Studi francescani* 52 (1955) 169-215.

Several helpful bibliographies have made this literature more accessible: Valens Heynck, "Ockham-Literatur 1919-1949," *Franziskanische Studien* 32 (1950) 164-83; J. P. Reilly, "Ockham Bibliography: 1950-1967," *Franciscan Studies* 28 (1968) 197-214; and the annotated bibliography of Alessandro Ghisalberti, "Bibliografia su Guglielmo di Occam dal 1950-1968," *Rivista di filosofia neo-scolastica* 61 (1969) 273-84, 545-71.

The early stages of this literature and the revised picture of Ockham have been surveyed several times: Erich Hochstetter, "Ockham-

Forschung in Italien," *Zeitschrift für philosophische Forschung* 1 (1947) 559-78; Philotheus Boehner, "Ockham's Philosophy in the Light of Recent Research," *Proceedings of the Tenth International Congress of Philosophy* (Amsterdam, 1949) pp. 1113-16, and "Der Stand der Ockham-Forschung," *Franziskanische Studien* 34 (1952) 12-31, both reprinted in *Collected Articles*; Timotheus Barth, "Wilhelm Ockham im Lichte der neuesten Forschung," *Philosophisches Jahrbuch* 60 (1950) 464-67, and "Nuove interpretazioni della filosofia di Occam," *Studi francescani* 52 (1955) 187-204. Most of these studies have been surpassed by the thorough work of Helmar Junghans, *Ockham im Lichte der neueren Forschung* ("Arbeiten zur Geschichte und Theologie des Luthertums," no. 21; Berlin, 1968).

Given the abundance of recent literature on Ockham, one can mention only the most important trends and contributions. The first area that has attracted attention is the establishing of an accurate chronology of the life and writings of Ockham. Much of the early work on this was done by Boehner and can be found in his *Collected Articles*. Equally important in this regard is Léon Baudry, *Guillaume d'Occam, Sa vie, ses oeuvres, ses idées sociales et politiques* 1: *L'homme et les oeuvres* (Paris, 1950). This task now seems to be complete, thanks to the painstaking research of Charles K. Brampton.[8]

There have been several general works since 1949 that have further documented various aspects of the revised picture of Ockham: Gottfried Martin, *Wilhelm von Ockham: Untersuchungen zur Ontologie der Ordnungen* (Berlin, 1949); Damascene Webering, *Theory of Demonstration according to William Ockham* (St. Bonaventure, 1953), which covers much more than the title would suggest; Oswald Fuchs, *The Psychology of Habit according to William Ockham* (St. Bonaventure, 1952); and Jürgen Miethke, *Ockham Weg zur Sozialphilosophie* (Berlin, 1969).

Ockham's theory of knowledge and its relation to our knowledge of God has long been an important topic in Ockham studies. Two early but still important works on this subject were products of the Franciscan Institute: Sebastian J. Day, *Intuitive Cognition: A Key to the Significance of the Later Scholastics* (St. Bonaventure, 1947), and Matthew C. Menges, *The Concept of Univocity regarding the Predication of God and Creature according to William of Ockham* (St. Bonaventure, 1952). In recent years these topics have been reopened. The relation of the teaching on intuitive cognition in Duns Scotus and Ockham has been re-examined by Charles K. Brampton, "Scotus, Ockham and the Theory of Intuitive Cognition," *Antonianum* 40 (1965) 449-66. A further exami-

---

[8] The full list of Brampton's articles is given in the bibliographies of Reilly and Ghisalberti cited above.

nation of the sources and limitations on our knowledge of God according to Ockham has been provided by Léon Baudry, "Guillaume d'Occam: Critique des preuves scotistes de l'unicité de Dieu," *Archives d'histoire doctrinale et littéraire du moyen âge* 20 (1953) 99–112; "Les rapports de la raison et de la foi selon Guillaume d'Occam," *ibid.* 29 (1962) 33–92; Alessandro Ghisalberti, "Il Dio dei filosofi secondo Guglielmo di Occam; fede e ragione," *Rivista di filosofia neo-scolastica* 62 (1970) 272-90. Gordon Leff, a prolific writer on fourteenth-century topics, has given a foretaste of his forthcoming book on Ockham by treating this topic in his "Ockham, Knowledge and Its Relation to the Status of Theology," *Journal of Ecclesiastical History* 20 (1969) 7-17. On Ockham's ontology, Gustav Bergmann briefly engaged E. A. Moody over the proper interpretation; see Bergmann, "Some Remarks on the Ontology of Ockham," *Philosophical Review* 63 (1954) 560-71, and Moody's reply, "Comment: Some Remarks on the Ontology of Ockham," *ibid.*, pp. 572-76.

The controversy between Boehner and Anton Pegis over Ockham's theory of intuitive cognition of nonexistents, which seemingly had been resolved in Boehner's favor, has flared up again.[9] The problem has been independently pursued by R. C. Richards, "Ockham and Skepticism," *New Scholasticism* 42 (1968) 345-63; T. K. Scott, "Ockham on Evidence, Necessity, and Intuition," *Journal of the History of Philosophy* 7 (1969) 27-49; Marilyn M. Adams, "Intuitive Cognition, Certainty, and Skepticism in William Ockham," *Traditio* 26 (1970) 389-98. While all three scholars accept the general conclusions of Boehner, they also feel that Ockham's solution is not satisfactory from a philosophical point of view.

In a similar way the question of Ockham's theory of relation has been revived. Initially the problem was treated by P. Doncoeur, "Le nominalisme de Guillaume d'Occam: La théorie de la relation," *Revue néoscolastique de philosophie* 23 (1921) 5-25, and Léon Baudry, "A propos de la théorie occamiste de la relation," *Archives d'histoire doctrinale et littéraire du moyen âge* 9 (1934) 199-203. In contrast to Doncoeur, who argued that relation for Ockham was only a *res rationis*, an intellectual relation, Gottfried Martin, "Ist Ockhams Relationstheorie Nominalismus?" *Franziskanische Studien* 32 (1950) 31-49, maintained that Ockham made a distinction between two types of relation, one real and one intellectual, and that both were valid. Recently Hermann Greive, "Zur Relationslehre Wilhelms von Ockham," *Franziskanische Studien* 49 (1967) 248-58, has tried to show that these two theses are not incompatible.

[9] Philotheus Boehner, "The Notitia Intuitiva of Non-Existents according to William Ockham," *Traditio* 1 (1943) 223-75; Anton Pegis, "Concerning William of Ockham," *ibid.* 2 (1944) 465-80; Ph. Boehner, "In propria causa," *Franciscan Studies* 5 (1945) 37-54.

Ockham's view of nature and natural causality, touched on earlier in the works of Hochstetter and Webering, has received further discussion lately. Francesco Corvino, who has rendered noble service to the field by editing so many of Ockham's unpublished texts, has examined Ockham's use of the term *natura*, "Il significato del termine natura nelle opere filosofiche di Occam," in *La filosofia della natura nel medioevo* (Atti del terzo congresso internazionale di filosofia medioevale; Milan, 1966) pp. 605–15. Ockham's view of nature in relation to divine causality has been examined by William J. Courtenay, "The Critique on Natural Causality in the Mutakallimun and Nominalism," *Harvard Theological Review* 66 (1973).

The question of Ockham's understanding of divine omnipotence in relation to possibility and causality has been and will increasingly be an important area of Ockham's thought. Allan Wolter, "Ockham and the Textbooks: On the Origin of Possibility," *Franziskanische Studien* 32 (1950) 70–96, has argued that Ockham's teaching was sound and basically in conformity with the thought of Aquinas. Not surprisingly, Franz Pelster, "Die Lehre Ockhams von Grund der Möglichkeit der Possibilien," *Scholastik* 28 (1953) 405–7, remained unconvinced. An interesting contribution to the discussion has been given by Marie Anne Pernoud, "Innovation in William of Ockham's References to the 'Potentia Dei,'" *Antonianum* 45 (1970) 65–97.

The theology of Ockham has by no means been ignored. In addition to the works cited above that have theological implication, the most rewarding perspectives have been opened up by Erich Hochstetter, "Viator Mundi: Einige Bemerkungen zur Situation des Menschen bei Wilhelm von Ockham," *Franziskanische Studien* 32 (1950) 1–20, and Wilhelm Kölmel, "Die Freiheit des Menschen bei Wilhelm Ockham," *Beilage zur Festschrift der Lessingschule* (Mannheim, 1952); "Wilhelm Ockham: Der Mensch zwischen Ordnung und Freiheit," *Beiträge zum Berufsbewusstsein des mittelalterlichen Menschen* (Miscellanea medievalia, no. 3; Berlin, 1964) pp. 204–24.

In the continuation to his study of Duns Scotus' doctrine of *acceptatio divina*, Werner Dettloff, *Die Entwicklung der Akzeptations- und Verdienstlehre von Duns Scotus bis Luther mit besonderer Berücksichtigung der Franziskanertheologen* (Münster, 1963), has treated Ockham's doctrine of justification. A related theme has been examined by Giuseppe Barbaglio, *Fede acquisita e fede infusa secondo Duns Scoto, Occam et Biel* (Brescia, 1968). Ockham's views on justification were also the subject of Erwin Iserloh's *Gnade und Eucharistie in der philosophischen Theologie des Wilhelm von Ockham: Ihre Bedeutung für die Ursachen der Reformation* (Wiesbaden, 1956), which, unlike Dettloff's later work, finds Ockham's doctrine subversive. Earlier, the Eucharistic

726

thought of Ockham had been defended by Gabriel N. Buescher, *The Eucharistic Teaching of William of Ockham* (St. Bonaventure, 1950).

As with so many other areas of late medieval thought, the research on Ockham has been facilitated and improved by the greater accessibility of the sources. Most of the works of Ockham are now available either in photographic reprint or in modern critical edition. Particularly noteworthy in this regard is the appearance of the critical edition of Ockham's Commentary on the *Sentences, Opera philosophica et theologica. Opera theologica: Scriptum in librum primum Sententiarum ordinatio* (St. Bonaventure, 1967 ff.)

OCKHAMISM

One of the most heated areas of scholarly debate in the late medieval field is in the description of the development of post-Ockhamist thought—in particular, Ockham's relation to the so-called radical nominalists, Nicholas of Autrecourt and John of Mirecourt. The debate on this issue begins with the immediate disciples and critics of Ockham.

We know considerably more today about some of the earliest critics of Ockham: John Lutterell, John of Reading, Walter Chatton, and Walter Burley. The important texts along with an interpretive study of Lutterell have been published by Fritz Hoffmann, *Die Schriften des Oxforder Kanzlers Iohannes Lutterell: Texte zur Theologie des vierzehnten Jahrhunderts* (Leipzig, 1959). The only study of John of Reading remains that of E. Longpré, "Jean de Reading et le Bx Jean Duns Scot: L'école franciscaine d'Oxford au début du XIV⁰ siècle," *La France franciscaine* 7 (1924) 99–109. Recently, however, a number of important texts have been published that cast considerable light on the relationship of Reading and Ockham: Stephen Brown, "Sources for Ockham's Prologue to the *Sentences*," *Franciscan Studies* 26 (1966) 36–51; Gideon Gál, "Quaestio Ioannis de Reading De necessitate specierum intelligibilium: Defensio doctrinae Scoti," *Franciscan Studies* 29 (1969) 66–156; and Stephen Brown and Gideon Gál, in the introduction to William of Ockham, *Opera philosophica et theologica: Opera theologica* 2 (St. Bonaventure, 1970).

Of these two critiques on Ockham, that of Lutterell seems to be highly conservative and possibly motivated by personal hostility; that of Reading is a more reasoned defense of Scotistic thought, which had come under attack by Ockham. Walter Chatton, the third critic, seems to have been more gifted than the first two, and his arguments are rapidly becoming available to us through the publication of his texts. The first two questions of the prologue of his *Sentences Commentary* have

now been published: Maria Elena Reina, "La prima questione del prologo del 'Commento alle Sentenze' di Walter Catton," *Rivista critica di
storia della filosofia* 25 (1970), 48–74, 290–314; Jeremiah O'Callaghan,
"The Second Question of the Prologue to Walter Catton's Commentary
on the Sentences: On Intuitive and Abstractive Knowledge," in J. R.
O'Donnell, ed., *Nine Mediaeval Thinkers* (Toronto, 1955). In addition,
Gideon Gál has published the second question of the third distinction
of Chatton's *Reportatio I*, "Gualteri de Chatton et Guillelmi de Ockham
Controversia de natura conceptus universalis," *Franciscan Studies* 27
(1967) 191–212.[10] The important studies on Chatton are: E. Longpré,
"Gualterio di Chatton: Un maestro francescano d'Oxford," *Studi fran-
cescani* 9 (1923) 101–14; Léon Baudry, "Gauthier de Chatton et son
Commentaire des Sentences," *Archives d'histoire doctrinale et litté-
raire du moyen âge* 14 (1943–45) 337–69; Johann Auer, "Die 'skotisti-
sche' Lehre von der Heilsgewissheit: Walter von Chatton, der erste
"Skotist,'" *Wissenschaft und Weisheit* 15 (1952) 1–19; Charles K.
Brampton, "Gauthier de Chatton et la provenance des mss. lat. Paris
Bibl. Nat. 15886 et 15887," *Etudes franciscaines* 13 (1963) 200–205;
E. A. Moody, "A Quodlibetal Question of Robert Holkot, O.P., on the
Problem of the Objects of Knowledge and of Belief," *Speculum* 39 (1964)
53–74. The only work on Burley's critique of Ockham remains Léon
Baudry, "Les rapports de Guillaume d'Occam et de Walter Burleigh,"
Archives d'histoire doctrinale et littéraire du moyen âge 9 (1934) 155–73.

There were several issues on which Chatton placed himself at odds
with Ockham and his followers, and these issues have been examined in
part in the literature cited: the object of knowledge and belief (Moody);
the problem of quantity and continuum (Murdoch and Synan); the nature of universals (Gál); and the Eucharist (Brampton). In most of these
cases, the defenders of the Ockhamist position against Chatton were
Adam Wodham and Robert Holcot. Much of the literature on Chatton,
therefore, concerns Wodham and Holcot as well.

Only three issues in Wodham have received study recently. Dettloff,
in his work on the development of the *acceptatio divina*, examined
Wodham and found that his view of justification closely paralleled
Ockham's. Murdoch has shown, in the work cited above, that Wodham
was attacking the atomism of Chatton. Thomas Mitchell, *Medieval Discussions of Quantity and the Development of Eucharistic Thought with
Special Concentration on the Ockhamist Tradition* (unpublished mas-

[10] See also the texts published by John Murdoch and Edward Synan, "Two Questions
on the Continuum: Walter Chatton (?), O.F.M., and Adam Wodeham, O.F.M.," *Franciscan Studies* 26 (1966) 212–88.

ter's thesis, University of Wisconsin, 1971), has pointed to the more conservative tone of Wodham's defense of Ockham's Eucharistic thought.

Robert Holcot, the second of the two "disciples" of Ockham, has been seen as a critic of the Scotist Chatton and of the nominalist Crathorn. Once considered a close disciple of Ockham, Holcot was cast as an extreme nominalist in the scholarly literature of the period from 1944 to 1964. As Ockham came to be considered more traditional, Holcot was thought to be more radical and was credited with the authorship of the infamous *Centiloquium* by Philotheus Boehner, "The Medieval Crisis of Logic and the Author of the Centiloquium Attributed to Ockham," *Franciscan Studies* 4 (1944) 151–70. This view was shared by Erich Hochstetter, "Nominalismus?" *Franciscan Studies* 9 (1949) 370–403, and Beryl Smalley, "Robert Holcot, OP," *Archivum Fratrum praedicatorum* 26 (1956) 5–97. E. A. Moody, "A Quodlibetal Question of Robert Holcot, O.P., on the Problem of the Objects of Knowledge and of Belief," *Speculum* 39 (1964) 53–74, not only contrasted the positions of Holcot and Chatton, but also suggested that Holcot was a more thoroughgoing nominalist than was Ockham.

In the more recent literature Holcot seems less extreme. The charges of skepticism and fideism made in the earlier literature have been considerably dispelled by Oberman, "Facientibus quod in se est Deus non denegat gratiam: Robert Holcot, O.P., and the Beginnings of Luther's Theology," *Harvard Theological Review* 55 (1962) 317–42. Paolo Molteni, *Roberto Holcot O.P. dottrina della grazia e della giustificazione con due questioni quodlibetali inedite* (Pinerolo, 1968), supports Oberman's findings, although Molteni's interpretation of Holcot's views outside the area of justification and grace are still wedded to the older viewpoint.

Most of the attention in Holcot research today, however, is given over to the problems of logic, epistemology, and metaphysics, as the article by Moody already suggests. Within this context, Holcot is seen in battle against both Chatton and Crathorn. The important contributions to this discussion are: Mario Dal Pra, "Linguaggio e conoscenza assertiva nel pensiero di Robert Holkot," *Rivista critica di storia della filosofia* 9 (1956) 15–40; Fritz Hoffmann, "Robert Holcot: Die Logik in der Theologie," in *Die Metaphysik im Mittelalter* (Acts of the 2nd International Congress of Medieval Philosophy; Berlin, 1963) pp. 624–39; "Der Satz als Zeichen der theologischen Aussage bei Holcot, Crathorn und Gregor von Rimini," in *Der Begriff der Repraesentatio im Mittelalter: Stellvertretung, Symbol, Zeichen, Bild* (Miscellanea mediaevalia 8; Berlin, 1971) pp. 296–313; Henrich Schepers, "Holkot contra dicta Crathorn,"

Philosophisches Jahrbuch 77 (1970) 320–54; 79 (1972) 106–36. For an evaluation of another recent contribution to the Holcot-Crathorn debate, Karl Anton Sprengard, *Systematische-historische Untersuchungen zur Philosophie des XIV. Jahrhunderts* (2 vols.; Bonn, 1967–68), see H. Schepers's review, *Philosophisches Jahrbuch* 76 (1969) 395–400.

If the extremist appellations that were once applied to Wodham and Holcot are now being modified, their Parisian counterparts, Nicholas of Autrecourt and John of Mirecourt, have only in the last two years begun to be re-examined in light of our newer knowledge. From 1947 until 1970 the best evidence seemed to suggest that there was little relation between the moderate and orthodox theologian Ockham and the radical Autrecourt. E. A. Moody, "Ockham, Buridan, and Nicholas of Autrecourt," *Franciscan Studies* 7 (1947) 113–46, argued that the positions of Ockham and Autrecourt were opposed. The Parisian decree of 1339 did not condemn Ockham but only prevented his being taught to the exclusion of other writers. The decree of 1340, by contrast, was directed against Autrecourt. Moody supported this thesis by contrasting in detail the thought of the two men and by pointing out that Bernard of Arezzo and John Buridan, the two leading opponents of Autrecourt, were faithful disciples of Ockham. Erich Hochstetter, "Nominalismus," accepted that thesis, and from 1950 on it seemed to meet with general approval.

Recently, however, Moody's argument has been attacked with the intent of showing a closer tie between the thought of Ockham and Autrecourt. T. K. Scott, "Nicholas of Autrecourt, Buridan, and Ockhamism," *Journal of the History of Philosophy* 9 (1971) 15–41, has attempted to show that the seeds of Autrecourt's position were already in Ockham. Similarly, the Ockhamism of Buridan has been questioned by Scott.[11] An exhaustive analysis of the 1340 document by Ruprecht Paqué, *Das Pariser Nominalistenstatut zur Entstehung des Realitätsbegriffs der neuzeitlichen Naturwissenschaft (Occam, Buridan und Petrus Hispanus, Nikolaus von Autrecourt und Gregor von Rimini)* (Berlin, 1970), purports to show that Ockham, not Autrecourt, was the object of the condemnation of 1340.[12]

[11] For a discussion of Buridan's nominalism, see: T. K. Scott, "John Buridan on the Objects of Demonstrative Science," *Speculum* 40 (1965) 654–73; J. J. Walsh, "Nominalism and the *Ethics*: Some Remarks about Buridan's *Commentary*," *Journal of the History of Philosophy* 4 (1966) 1–13; T. K. Scott, "Nicholas of Autrecourt, Buridan and Ockhamism," *ibid.* 9 (1971) 15–41. Also significant are: M. E. Reina, "Il problema del linguaggio in Buridano," *Rivista critica di storia della filosofia* 14 (1959) 367–417; 15 (1960) 141–65, 238–64; L. Kuksewicz, "Deux 'Quaestiones de universali' de Jean Buridan," *Bulletin société internationale pour l'étude de la philosophie médiévale* 4 (1962) 126–29.

[12] Important additions to the understanding of Autrecourt's thought by Mario Dal Pra, "La fondazione dell'empirismo e le sue apone nel pensiero di Nicola di Autrecourt,"

Our view of the other Parisian nominalist, John of Mirecourt, may soon be modified to a considerable extent. Dettloff, *Die Entwicklung* ..., in examining the views of Mirecourt on grace and justification, found nothing out of keeping with Ockham's thought, and he therefore concluded that Mirecourt's radicalism must lie in some other area. Roy Van Neste, *The Epistemology of John of Mirecourt in Relation to Fourteenth Century Thought* (unpublished doctoral dissertation, University of Wisconsin, 1972), discovered that Mirecourt's epistemology had little in common with Autrecourt and instead followed the outline of Ockham's theory of knowledge. Moreover, Mirecourt rejected intuitive cognition of a nonexistent, thus increasing empirical certitude at the expense of possibly incurring the anger of the Ockhamists. In my "John of Mirecourt and Gregory of Rimini on Whether God Can Undo the Past," *Recherches de théologie ancienne et médiévale* 39 (1972), I argue that Mirecourt was far more conservative on the issue of divine omnipotence than the condemnation of 1347 would lead us to believe.

AUGUSTINIANS AND CISTERCIANS

One of the most expanding research areas on late medieval thought concerns the theologians of the Augustinian order and the Cistercians who seem to have been intellectually related to them. Much work has been done on the educational background of these theologians. Of special note are the works of Eelcko Ypma, *La formation des professeurs chez les Ermites de saint-Augustin de 1256 à 1354* (Paris, 1956); "Notice sur le 'Studium' de Paris au cours de la deuxième moitie du XIVe siècle," *Augustiniana* 17 (1967) 14–36; "Notice sur le 'Studium' de Paris au début du schisme d'Occident," *Augustiniana* 18 (1968) 82–99; Adolar Zumkeller, "Die Augustinerschule des Mittelalters: Vertreter und philosophisch-theologische Lehre," *Analecta Augustiniana* 27 (1964) 167–262; *Manuskripte von Werken der Autoren des Augustiner-Eremitenordens in mitteleuropäischen Bibliotheken* (Würzburg, 1966).

Among those who have contributed to our better understanding of fourteenth-century Augustinianism, the most important contributions have been those of Damasus Trapp and Adolar Zumkeller. Trapp's extensive study of the theologians in the Augustinian order, "Augustinian Theology of the 14th Century: Notes on Editions, Marginalia, Opinions and Book-Lore," *Augustiniana* 6 (1956) 146–274, has surveyed the field

---

Rivista critica di storia della filosofia 7 (1952) 389–402, and Piotr Chojnacki, "Les facteurs et les limites de la connaissance humaine d'après la critique d'Occam et de Nicolas d'Autrecourt," in *L'homme et son destin d'après les penseurs du moyen âge* (Actes du premier Congrès international de philosophie médiévale; Louvain, 1960) pp. 680–87.

and marked out the nature of the work to be done. In a series of additional articles Trapp has concentrated on individual authors: "Hiltalinger's Augustinian Quotations," *Augustiniana* 4 (1954) 412–49; "Gregory of Rimini Manuscripts: Editions and Additions," *Augustiniana* 8 (1958) 425–43; "New Approaches to Gregory of Rimini," *Augustinianum* 2 (1962) 115–30; "Gregorio de Rimini y el nominalismo," *ibid.* 4 (1964) 5–20; "Notes on John Klenkok, OSA (d. 1374)," *ibid.*, pp. 358–404. Trapp's position on nominalism, already referred to earlier and contained in the above articles, has recently been expanded in "Modern' and 'Modernists' in MS Fribourg Cordeliers 26," *Augustinianum* 5 (1965) 241–70.

A thesis that runs through many of Trapp's articles is that Gregory of Rimini, far from being a nominalist, was the standard-bearer against the nominalists because he played an important role in the condemnation of John of Mirecourt. I have recently questioned the validity of that thesis in the article on John of Mirecourt and Gregory of Rimini referred to above.

The second historian who has made a major contribution to our knowledge of fourteenth-century Augustinian theologians is Adolar Zumkeller. In particular, Zumkeller has provided a series of studies on Hugolino Malbranche of Orvieto, one of the most conservative Augustinians of the period: *Hugolin von Orvieto und seine theologische Erkenntnislehre* (Würzburg, 1941); "Hugolin von Orvieto (d. 1373) über Urstand und Erbsünde," *Augustiniana* 3 (1953) 35–62, 165–93; 4 (1954) 25–46; "Hugolin von Orvieto über Prädestination, Rechtfertigung und Verdienst," *ibid.* 4 (1954) 109–56; 5 (1955) 5–51.

Both Trapp and Zumkeller have pointed to contacts and similarities between Augustinian and Cistercian theologians in the fourteenth century. One of the more striking proofs of this affinity lies in the number of times theologians of these two religious orders based their Commentaries on the *Sentences* on the structure and content of a Commentary from the other order. Gottschalk of Nepomuk, a Cistercian, read according to Gregory of Rimini. The Commentary of Hugolino Malbranche of Orvieto formed the basis for the Commentary of Conrad of Ebrach, a Cistercian, who was in turn read by Dionysius of Montina, an Augustinian. James of Eltville, a Cistercian, read according to John Hiltalingen of Basel, an Augustinian, and James was later read to his own monks by Henry of Langenstein.

Of these Cistercian theologians, few have yet been studied. The groundwork, however, has been established by Zumkeller, *Dionysius de Montina* (Würzburg, 1948), and Kassian Lauterer, *Konrad von Ebrach S.O.Cist. (d. 1399): Lebenslauf und Schrifttum* (Rome, 1962).

LATE FOURTEENTH-CENTURY THINKERS

Because of interest in the questions of nominalism, conciliarism, and political thought, Pierre d'Ailly is one of the most studied writers in this period. Pursuing the important issue of epistemology, Bernhard Meller has contributed *Studien zur Erkenntnislehre des Peter von Ailly* (Freiburg, 1954), several aspects of which have been criticized by other scholars. The problem of divine omnipotence in relation to human volition has received the most concentration. Various aspects of this issue have been considered by George Lindbeck, "Nominalism and the Problem of Meaning as Illustrated by Pierre d'Ailly on Predestination and Justification," *Harvard Theological Review* 52 (1959) 43–60; Francis Oakley, "Pierre d'Ailly and the Absolute Power of God: Another Note on the Theology of Nominalism," *ibid.* 56 (1963) 59–73; and William J. Courtenay, "Covenant and Causality in Pierre d'Ailly," *Speculum* 46 (1971) 94–119.

D'Ailly's disciple and successor, Jean Gerson, has received equal attention, but more from the standpoint of his mysticism and conciliar theory. A new edition of his work is now available through the editing work of Palémon Glorieux, *Jean Gerson: Oeuvres complètes* (Paris, 1960 ff.). The most significant recent work to appear on Gerson is Steven Ozment, *Homo spiritualis: A Comparative Study of the Anthropology of Johannes Tauler, Jean Gerson and Martin Luther (1509–1516) in the Context of Their Theological Thought* (Leiden, 1969).

On the side of German theology, Henry of Langenstein has commanded the interest of scholars from several countries. Divine causality in relation to the concept of nature has been discussed by Franco Alessio, "Causalità naturale e causalità divina nel 'De habitudine causarum' di Enrico di Langenstein," in *La filosofia della natura nel medioevo* (Atti del terzo congresso internazionale di filosofia mediovale; Milan, 1966). Henry's Christology has been a subject of study for the Franciscan J. Lang, *Die Christologie bei Heinrich von Langenstein* (Freiburg, 1966). Nicholas Steneck is presently engaged on a study of Langenstein on sense knowledge and the internal senses. A contemporary of Langenstein, Henry Totting of Oyta, has recently attracted the attention of one of the major scholars in fourteenth-century studies, A. Lang, "Das Verhältnis von Schrift, Tradition und kirchlichem Lehramt nach Heinrich Totting von Oyta," *Scholastik* 40 (1965) 214–34. Finally, the beginnings for a study of the fifteenth-century theologian Nicholas of Dinklesbühl have been charted by Alois Madre, *Nikolaus von Dinkelsbühl. Leben und Schriften: Ein Beitrag zur theologischen Literaturgeschichte* (Münster, 1965).

The late fourteenth century is no less an area for the publication of important texts. The two prize additions to the working medieval library in this area are Pierre d'Ailly, *Quaestiones super libros sententiarum cum quibusdam in fine adjunctis* (Strassburg, 1490; reprinted Frankfurt, 1968), and Marsilius von Inghen, *Questiones super quattuor libros sententiarum* (Strassburg, 1501; reprinted Frankfurt, 1966).

NOMINALISM AND THE REFORMATION

One of the most important areas of Reformation studies today is the relation of Reformation thought to the intellectual movements of the late Middle Ages. Because of that tie, the recent literature in this last area of late medieval thought has been more frequently surveyed. It is necessary therefore to indicate only the most important studies and to direct the reader to these other bibliographical essays.

The single most important contribution to this topic is Heiko Oberman, *The Harvest of Medieval Theology: Gabriel Biel and Late Medieval Nominalism* (Cambridge, Mass., 1963), which emphasizes the Catholicity of Biel. The series edited by Oberman, *Studies in Medieval and Reformation Thought*, has been especially dedicated to examining connections between the late Middle Ages and Reformation. In addition to those works already mentioned, such as Ozment, are: Jane Dempsey Douglass, *Justification in Late Medieval Preaching: A Study of John Geiler of Keisersberg* (Leiden, 1966), and David C. Steinmetz, *Misericordia Dei: The Theology of Johannes von Staupitz in Its Late Medieval Setting* (Leiden, 1968).

There have been many articles surveying past scholarship and assessing present trends in the understanding of medieval thought on the eve of the Reformation. Ludger Meier, who has devoted much effort to an examination of Scotism and Ockhamism at Erfurt, has covered one aspect of this question in his "Research That Has Been Made and Is Yet to Be Made on the Ockhamism of Martin Luther at Erfurt," *Archivum Franciscanum historicum* 43 (1950) 56–67. In THEOLOGICAL STUDIES 29 (1968) 549–73, Lewis Spitz included a section on Luther's relation to scholasticism and humanism in which he examined the literature on Luther's relation to nominalism. A thorough examination of this topic now appears in Bengt Hägglund, *The Background of Luther's Doctrine of Justification in Late Medieval Theology* (Philadelphia, 1971).[13]

In light of the breadth of research presently being done in the area of

---

[13] It is interesting to compare this study with Hägglund's earlier work: *Theologie und Philosophie bei Luther und in der occamistischen Tradition: Luthers Stellung zur Theologie von der doppelten Wahrheit* (Lund); "Luther et l'occamisme," *Positions luthériennes* 3 (1955) 213–23.

734

late medieval studies, it would be presumptuous to select out, for purposes of summary, one or two major themes, or to predict the course of future research. The more extensive availability of the sources, however, allows one to believe that we have been looking at only the first essays in what will soon become an even more rapidly changing field.

University of Wisconsin, Madison

XIII

LATE MEDIEVAL NOMINALISM REVISITED: 1972-1982

New intellectual currents that are characterized, whether justly or not, as radical, have always been more attractive to historians than their traditional, less colorful alternatives. So it is that late medieval nominalism continues to be a lively research area, while fourteenth-century realism is largely ignored as an idea whose time was then passed. Since 1972 [1] a number of studies have appeared that refine our understanding of nominalism and alter our approach to the intellectual currents associated with it in late medieval thought. The contributions that will have the most lasting effect in this area of study are the new critical editions that have made the sources of fourteenth-century thought far more accessible. The majority of the writings of William of Ockham have now been edited, the most important for our understanding of his nominalism being his *Sentences* commentary, especially Book I (the *Ordinatio*), and the *Summa logicae*.[2] The high quality of these editions has been widely recognized and has set the standard and model for recent text editing in medieval philosophy. Equally important and carefully edited is the new edition of the *Sentences* commentary of Gregory of Rimini, the key work for understanding the reception of Ockham at Paris and the development of nominalism as well as Augustinianism on the Continent.[3] In addition, individual questions and treatises from Richard Fitzralph, Walter Chatton, Adam Wodeham, Thomas Bradwardine, Richard Kilvington, Roger Swyneshead, John Buridan, and others have been edited.[4] In short, far more sources

---

[1] For the earlier literature see W. J. Courtenay, "Nominalism and Late Medieval Thought: A Bibliographical Essay," *Theological Studies*, 33 (1972), 716-734; and a longer study also composed in 1972: "Nominalism and Late Medieval Religion," in *The Pursuit of Holiness*, eds. C. Trinkaus and H. A. Oberman (Leiden, 1974), 26-59.

[2] William of Ockham, *Scriptum in librum primum sententiarum ordinatio*, eds. G. Gál, S. Brown, G. Etzkorn, and F. Kelley. *Opera theologica*, Vols. I-IV (St. Bonaventure, N.Y., 1967-79); *Summa logicae*, eds. Ph. Boehner, G. Gál, and S. Brown. *Opera philosophica*, Vol. I (St. Bonaventure, N.Y., 1974).

[3] Gregory of Rimini, *Lectura super primum et secundum sententiarum*, ed. D. Trapp (Berlin, 1979ff.). The volumes, edited in Tübingen, are appearing in the series Spätmittelalter und Reformation: Texte und Untersuchungen under the direction of H. A. Oberman.

[4] The *Quaestio biblica* of Richard Fitzralph on future contingents has been edited by J.-F. Genest in his thesis, "Le *De futuris contingentibus* de Thomas Bradwardine," Mémoire pour le Diplôme de l'Ecole pratique des hautes études (5e section), (Paris, 1975), 137-188, along with similar texts from Adam Junior and John Stuklee. For Chatton: L. Cova, "La quarta questione del prologo del 'commento alle sentenze' di Walter Catton," *Rivista critica di storia della filosofia*, 30 (1975), 303-330. For Wodeham: G. Gál, "Adam of Wodeham's Question in the 'complexe significabile' as the Immediate Object of Scientific Knowledge," *Franciscan Studies*, 37 (1977), 66-102; K. Tachau, "Adam of Wodeham on First and Second Intentions," *Cahiers de l'Institut du moyen-âge grec et latin*, 35 (1980), 29-55. Bradwardine's treatise mentioned above is more accessible in J.-F. Genest, "Le 'De futuris con-

for determining the thought and interrelation of fourteenth-century authors are now available, and those texts, in turn, have already had an effect on the meaning and influence of nominalism in the intellectual life of that period.

Much of the recent discussion on the meaning of nominalism has centered on a comparison of the logic of Peter Abelard and William of Ockham. More than a generation ago Paul Vignaux took that approach in his seminal article on nominalism.[5] In his book in 1969 and in a 1971 paper, published in 1974, Jean Jolivet returned to that theme.[6] Abelard and Ockham were both nominalists primarily in the sense that they espoused non-realism. Making use of the research on thirteenth-century Modist logic that has been done in the last few decades, Jolivet was able to demonstrate the radically different intellectual contexts in which Abelard and Ockham lived and wrote and, from that, the two different approaches to the relations of thought, language, and things. Both placed their primary emphasis on individual things and considered universal concepts to be derived from and in some sense descriptive of individuals. The world of Abelard, however, was still a world in which logic was an integral part of grammar and rhetoric, and Abelard understood the problem of the universal as much in a grammatical way as from the standpoint of dialectic. Ockham's nominalism was worked out against the necessitarianism of Greco-Arabian metaphysics as well as against the linguistic entities of the speculative grammarians. For Abelard the process of signification creates the idea; for Ockham the idea signifies.

Building upon the remarks of Jolivet, Paul Vignaux returned to the question of Abelard's nominalism in two articles in 1975 and 1977.[7] The first updated some aspects of his 1930 article and raised some questions that he felt should be addressed by current research. Vignaux modified his earlier assessment of Abelard by recognizing, as did Gandillac and Jolivet, a stronger current of Platonism alongside his nominalism. Vignaux adopted

---

tingentibus' de Thomas Bradwardine,'' *Recherches Augustiniennes*, **14** (1979), 249-336. For Kilvington: F. Bottin, ''L'*opinio de insolubilibus* di Richard Kilmyngton,'' *Rivista critica di storia della filosofia*, **28** (1973), 408-421, and the critical edition and English translation of Kilvington's *Sophismata*,edited by Norman Kretzmann,is soon to appear. For Swyneshead: P. V. Spade, ''Roger Swyneshed's *Obligationes*: Edition and Comments,'' *Archives d'histoire doctrinale et littéraire du moyen âge*, **44** (1977), 243-285; ''Roger Swyneshed's Insolubilia: Edition and Comments,'' *Archives d'histoire doctrinale et littéraire du moyen âge*, **46** (1979), 177-220. For Buridan, *Sophismata*, ed. T. K. Scott. Grammatica speculativa, Vol. I (Stuttgart, 1977), and additional texts in *The Logic of John Buridan*, ed. J. Pinborg (Copenhagen, 1976).

[5] P. Vignaux, ''Nominalisme,'' *Dictionnaire de théologie catholique*, 11/1 (Paris, 1930), cols. 717-84; *Nominalisme au XIV⁰ siècle* (Montreal, 1948).

[6] J. Jolivet, *Arts du langage et théologie chez Abailard*, Etudes de philosophie médiévale, Vol. 58 (Paris, 1969); ''Comparaison des théories du langage chez Abélard et chez les nominalistes du XIVe siècle,'' in *Peter Abelard*. Proceedings of the International Conference, Louvain, May, 1971, ed. E. M. Buytaert, *Mediaevalia Lovaniensia*, I/2 (Louvain, 1974), 163-178.

[7] P. Vignaux, ''Note sur le nominalisme d'Abélard,'' in *Pierre Abélard—Pierre le Vénérable* (Paris, 1975), pp. 523-529; ''La problématique du nominalisme médiéval peut-elle éclairer des problèmes philosophiques actuels?'' *Revue philosophique de Louvain*, 75 (1977), 293-331.

Jolivet's more neutral and more encompassing term "non-realism" as well as Jolivet's recognition of the different intellectual worlds in which Abelard and Ockham lived. Vignaux directed future scholarly attention toward the problem of signification and the crucial relation or contrast between Ockham's and Rimini's epistemologies, especially on the object of knowledge. These views were further elaborated in the second article, which set forth a new model of medieval nominalism based on "non-realism," language analysis, empiricism, and the use of the absolute/ordained distinction concerning the power of God.

Taking Jolivet's work into consideration, Martin Tweedale carefully analyzed from his own perspective the nominalism of Abelard and Ockham.[8] Both shared the nominalist view "that only things which can be common to many so as to be predicable of many are signs" (p.8), speaking here of common nouns. Moreover, both understood logic as the study of signs, principally verbal signs. But Tweedale felt that Ockham went beyond Abelard in two ways: first, in Ockham's method of reducing or converting troublesome propositions into multiple equivalent propositions containing "only nouns that denoted ordinary genuine things like concrete substances and observable qualities" (p.9); second, in his belief that the object of knowledge was the conclusion of the mental proposition, that "the 'objects' and 'subjects' of scientific knowledge are signs" (p.9) and are only indirectly about things that the signs signify. Neither Abelard nor Ockham espoused any subjectivism that what we know is determined by how we conceive things. Things exist independently of the way we conceive them.

Tweedale's book has come in for praise and criticism, the latter being directed mostly at his interpretation of Abelard's *status* and his reluctance to go beyond describing what Abelard's position on universals was *not*. In the course of his review of Tweedale's book, Paul Spade put forth one of the most useful suggestions to date, distinguishing two different notions of universality.[9] The first, which he terms Aristotelian, can be defined as "being predicable of many," while the second, which he calls "Boethian," can be defined as "being common to many". According to the first definition, "a nominalist is one who says that only linguistic terms are predicable of many," and both Abelard and Ockham would subscribe to this type of nominalism. According to the second definition, "a nominalist is one who says that nothing is common to many in the way Boethius describes," namely common to many as a whole, simultaneously, and in such a way that it enters into the very structure of the things to which it is common. By this second definition Ockham was a nominalist, while Abelard was a realist.

It was largely on the grounds of Ockham's rejection of "common natures" inherent in things of the same genus and species, and his corresponding view that abstract nouns (such as "whiteness" or "humanity") and the propositions that contain them are only linguistic shorthand for the composite of individual qualities and the individual propositions that contain them ('A' is white, 'B' is white, etc.) that has led most historians of medieval

[8] M. M. Tweedale, *Abailard on Universals* (Amsterdam, 1976).

[9] P. V. Spade's review of Tweedale's *Abailard on Universals*, in *Noûs*, 14 (1980), 479-483.

philosophy, most recently Armand Maurer,[10] to continue to label Ockham a nominalist. Both epistemologically (how we come to know or form a universal concept) and ontologically (the degree or type of reality possessed by a universal concept) Ockham was a nominalist. On the other hand, Ockham did believe that things of the same species were, in reality, similar, although he rejected as awkward and misleading the notion that they "shared" a particular quality or held it "in common". The perception that the quality "white" in 'A' is similar to the quality "white" in 'B' for purposes of classification was not, for Ockham, a figment of our imagination. Propositions containing universal terms are legitimate inferences based on our experience with individual things in external reality. We are not locked into our individual minds in such a way that we cannot know external reality or discuss that reality meaningfully with others. The long-standing realization, reaffirmed by Tweedale and Stephen Brown, has led a number of scholars to discard the label nominalism in application to Ockham, whom they prefer to label a realistic conceptualist.[11]

Whatever labels scholars choose to employ, there is general agreement in understanding Ockham's actual views. The more serious difficulties, as Paul Vignaux noted, lie with the role Ockham's nominalism played in succeeding generations, particularly Ockham's understanding of the object of knowledge and the meaning of propositions as these affected the development of the solution known as the *complexe significabile* and the role of Gregory of Rimini in that development. For Ockham, the object of knowledge was the proposition or, more precisely, the conclusion of a demonstration. For Walter Chatton, the object of knowledge was the thing itself to which the proposition referred. For Gregory of Rimini the object of knowledge was the entire significate of the proposition, what was called the *complexe significabile*. Beginning with Hubert Elie's history of the origin, development, and influence of the *complexe significabile* and Mario Dal Pra's and E. A. Moody's modifications on the pre-Gregorian phase of discussion, the issue was addressed by Ruprecht Paqué (1970), Norman Kretzmann (1970), and Fritz Hoffmann (1971).[12] Within the last decade or more two major discov-

[10] A. Maurer, "Some Aspects of Fourteenth-Century Philosophy," *Mediaevalia et Humanistica*, Ser. 2, 7 (1976), 175-188.

[11] S. F. Brown, "A Modern Prologue to Ockham's Natural Philosophy," in *Sprache und Erkenntnis im Mittelalter*, Akten des VI. internationalen Kongresses für mittelalterliche Philosophie der Société internationale pour l'étude de la philosophie médiévale, Miscellanea Mediaevalia, 13/1 (Berlin, 1981), 107-129, which is the clearest statement to date of Ockham's nominalism. For earlier discussions see Ph. Boehner, "The Realistic Conceptualism of William Ockham," in *Collected Articles on Ockham*, ed. E. M. Buytaert, Franciscan Institute Publications, Phil. ser. 12 (St. Bonaventure, N.Y., 1958), 156-174; G. Leff, *William of Ockham* (Manchester, 1975).

[12] H. Elie, *Le complexe significabile* (Paris, 1936); M. Dal Pra, "Linguaggio e conoscenza assertiva nel pensiero di Roberto Holkot," *Rivista critica di storia della filosofia*, 11 (1956), 15-40; "La teoria del 'significato totale' delle proposizione nel pensiero di Gregorio da Rimini," *ibid.*, 287-311; E. A. Moody, "A Quodlibetal Question of Robert Holkot, O.P. on the Problem of the Objects of Knowledge and of Belief," *Speculum*, 39 (1964), 53-74; R. Paqué, *Das Pariser Nominalistenstatut* (Berlin, 1970); N. Kretzmann, "Medieval Logicians on the Meaning of the *Propositio*," *The Journal of Philosophy*, 67 (1970), 767-787; F. Hoffmann, "Der Satz als

eries have altered the history of that idea. The first was Heinrich Schepers' demonstration (1970-72) that William Crathorn already in 1330 at Oxford put forward the theory that the object of knowledge was the total significate of the proposition.[13] Crathorn's elaboration of this idea revealed it to be essentially the position that Rimini later adopted at Paris under the phrase *significatum totale conclusionis*. The second discovery came in 1977 with the edited text of one of the questions of Adam Wodeham's *Lectura secunda* containing the idea of "the total significate of the conclusion" and the arguments that later appeared in Rimini, who borrowed them from that source.[14] Gabriel Nuchelmans' (1973) and Willigis Eckermann's (1978) historical surveys of the problem took Schepers' discovery into consideration, leading Eckermann to speculate that Rimini may have read Crathorn, or at least Holcot.[15] The Wodeham text edited by Gedeon Gál solved the problem of Rimini's source. Unfortunately, the most recent survey of the question by Amandio Coxito (1981) is untouched by the discoveries of Schepers and Gál.[16]

Volker Wendland (1981) has rewritten the history of the question on the basis of Schepers' *and* Gál's discoveries, although part of the chronology he gives may have to be revised.[17] At present it is uncertain who should be credited with the creation of the idea of the *complexe significabile*. Wendland has assumed Crathorn, since he was writing in 1330 and the *Lectura secunda* of Wodeham was compiled after his Oxford lectures (1330-32, or 1331-33). But the section of the *Lectura secunda* that discusses the *complexe significabile* was taken from Wodeham's London lectures, which certainly preceded Book III of his Oxford lectures and may well have preceded the entire Oxford lectures (see my *Adam Wodeham*, 126-27). If the latter is true, then Wodeham is the originator of the idea sometime shortly before 1330. At the moment the case points in the direction of Adam Wodeham.

There are several ramifications to Gál's discovery. First, Wodeham was a far more independent, critical, and creative thinker than has previously

Zeichen der theologischen Aussage bei Holcot, Crathorn, und Gregor von Rimini," in *Der Begriff der Repräsentatio im Mittelalter, Miscellanea Mediaevalia*, 8 (Berlin, 1971), 296-313. For important contributions to the broader discussion, see H. Enders, *Sprachlogische Traktate des Mittelalters und der Semantikbegriff*, Veroffentlichungen des Grabmann-Institutes, 20 (Munich, 1975) and F. Bottin, *Le antinomie semantiche nella logica medievale* (Padua, 1976).

[13] H. Schepers, "Holkot contra dicta Crathorn," *Philosophisches Jahrbuch*, 77 (1970), 320-354; 79 (1972), 106-136.

[14] G. Gál, "Adam of Wodeham's Question on the 'complexe significabile' as the Immediate Object of Scientific Knowledge," *Franciscan Studies*, 37 (1977), 66-102.

[15] G. Nuchelmans, *Theories of the Proposition* (Amsterdam, 1973), esp. 177-242; W. Eckermann, *Wort und Wirklichkeit. Das Sprachverständnis in der Theologie Gregors von Rimini und sein Weiterwirken in der Augustinerschule* (Wurzburg, 1978).

[16] A. A. Coxito, *Logica, semantica e conhecimento na escolastica peninsular pre-renascentista* (Coimbra, 1981).

[17] V. Wendland, "Die Wissenschaftslehre Gregors von Rimini in der Diskussion," in *Gregor von Rimini. Werk und Wirkung bis zur Reformation*, ed. H. A. Oberman, Spätmittelalter und Reformation, Texte und Untersuchungen, 20 (Berlin, 1981), 241-300.

164

been thought. Second, the idea of the *complexe significabile* was probably not propounded in anti-Ockham circles but was rather the achievement of someone who was personally and intellectually close to Ockham yet willing to reject or modify certain ideas, just as Ockham himself made changes in his own thought through the questions and critique of Burley and Chatton.[18] Third, on this issue one finds Wodeham, Crathorn, and Rimini over against Ockham and Holcot, thus raising some serious questions about what Ockhamism meant in the two decades after Ockham left England for Avignon, Italy, and Munich.

A number of recent studies have explored the relationship between nominalism and late medieval theology, political thought, economic theory, science, and literature, which require separate treatment elsewhere.[19] Perhaps the most significant feature of present research for future work is the growing realization of the independence of fourteenth-century thinkers and the difficulty of speaking about school traditions, even of Ockhamists and nominalists, between 1320 and 1400.[20] The same constellation of ideas and values, perceptions and approaches, can only rarely be found in any two masters. Fourteenth-century logicians, natural philosophers, and theologians must be looked at individually, not as members of schools of thought. This means that for the moment at least, the nominalism of the fourteenth century, if we are to really understand it, must be studied nominalistically.

University of Wisconsin.

Reprinted by permission of the Journal of the History of Ideas *from vol. 44, no. 1 (Jan.-March 1983), pp. 159-164.*

[18] S. F. Brown, "Walter Burley's Treatise *De suppositionibus* and its influence on William of Ockham," *Franciscan Studies*, **32** (1972), 15-64; G. Gál, "Gualteri de Chatton et Guillelmi de Ockham controversia de natura conceptus universalis," *Franciscan Studies*, **27** (1967), 191-212.

[19] Among the many important studies in these areas are B. Hamm, *Promissio, Pactum, Ordinatio. Freiheit und Selbstbindung Gottes in der scholastischen Gnadenlehre* (Tübingen, 1977); H. A. Oberman, *Werden und Wertung der Reformation* (Tübingen, 1977); J. E. Murdoch and E. D. Sylla, eds., *The Cultural Context of Medieval Learning*; the other contributions in *Gregor von Rimini. Werk und Wirkung bis zur Reformation* (Berlin, 1981); A. Maurer, "The Unity of a Science: St. Thomas and the Nominalists," in *St. Thomas Aquinas, 1274-1974. Commemorative Studies* (Toronto, 1974), II, 269-291.

[20] W. J. Courtenay, "John of Mirecourt and Gregory of Rimini on Whether God Can Undo the Past," *Recherches de Théologie ancienne et médiéval*, **39** (1972), 224-256; **40** (1973), 147-174; *Adam Wodeham* (Leiden, 1978); and especially K. Tachau, "The Problem of the *species in medio* at Oxford in the Generation after Ockham," *Mediaeval Studies*, **44** (1982), 394-443.

INDEX